D0218340

Annual Editions: The Family,
42e

Patricia Hrusa Williams

http://create.mheducation.com

ISBN-10: 1259409376   ISBN-13: 9781259409370

Contents

Preface

In publishing ANNUAL EDITIONS we recognize the enormous role played by the magazines, newspapers, and journals of the public press in providing current, first-rate educational information in a broad spectrum of interest areas. Many of these articles are appropriate for students, researchers, and professionals seeking accurate, current material to help bridge the gap between principles and theories and the real world. These articles, however, become more useful for study when those of lasting value are carefully collected, organized, indexed, and reproduced in a low-cost format, which provides easy and permanent access when the material is needed. That is the role played by ANNUAL EDITIONS.

The purpose of *Annual Editions: The Family,* 42/e is to bring to the reader the latest thoughts and trends in our understanding of the family. Articles consider current concerns, problems, potential solutions, and ways families remain resilient in the face of adversity. The volume also presents alternative views on family relationships, processes, patterns, and structures. The intent of this anthology is to explore family relationships and to reflect the family's evolving function and importance. The articles in this volume are taken from professional journals as well as other professionally oriented publications and popular lay publications aimed at both special populations and a general readership. The selections are carefully reviewed for their currency and accuracy.

In the current edition, a number of new articles have been added to reflect reviewers' comments on the previous edition. As the reader, you will note the tremendous range in tone and focus of these articles, from first-person accounts to reports of scientific discoveries as well as philosophical and theoretical writings. Some are more practical and applications-oriented, while others are more conceptual and research-oriented. Together they highlight the multidisciplinary nature of the study of the family and the myriad of influences that shape the family as a social structure and unit of socialization.

This anthology is organized to address many of the important aspects of family and family relationships. The first unit takes an overview perspective and looks at varied viewpoints on the family. The second unit examines the beginnings of relationships as individuals go through the process of exploring and establishing connections. The third unit examines family communication, relationships, and interactions in various types of relationships including marital, parent-child, sibling, and intergenerational relationships. The fourth unit is concerned with crises and ways in which these can act as challenges and opportunities for families and their members. Finally, the fifth unit takes an affirming tone as it looks at family strengths and rituals, ways of empowering families, and emerging trends within families and their formation.

Annual Editions: The Family, 42/e is intended to be used as a supplemental text for lower-level, introductory marriage, family, or sociology of the family classes, particularly when they tie the content of the readings to essential information on marriages and families, however they are defined. As a supplement, this book can also be used to update or emphasize certain aspects of standard marriage and family textbooks. Because of the provocative nature of many of the essays in this anthology, it works well as a basis for class discussion, debate, and critical thinking exercises about various aspects of marriages and family relationships. This edition of *Annual Editions: The Family* contains websites noted after each article that can be used to further explore topics addressed in the readings.

Editor

Patricia Hrusa Williams is an Associate Professor in the Department of Early Childhood and Elementary Education at the University of Maine at Farmington. She received her BA in Health & Society and Psychology from the University of Rochester. Her PhD is in Applied Child Development from Tufts University. Dr. Williams' primary areas of interest are family support programs, parental involvement in early childhood education, infant-toddler development, service learning, and the development of writing and critical thinking skills in college students. She has authored, co-authored, or edited over 15 published articles in books, academic journals, and the popular press. Dr. Williams lives with her husband and three children in the mountains of western Maine.

Academic Advisory Committee

We would like to thank everyone involved in the development of this volume. Our appreciation goes to those who provided comments on the previous edition as well as those who suggested articles to consider for inclusion in this edition.

Unit 1

UNIT

Prepared by: Patricia Hrusa Williams, *University of Maine at Farmington*

Evolving Perspectives on the Family

Our image of what family is and what it should be is a powerful combination of personal experience, family forms we encounter or observe, and attitudes we hold. Once formed, this image informs decision making and interpersonal interactions throughout our lives with far-reaching effects. On an intimate level, it influences individual and family development as well as the relationships we create and maintain, both inside and outside the family. On a broader level, it affects legislation, social policy, and programmatic supports developed and offered to couples, parents, and families. In many ways, the images we build and hold can be positive. They can act to clarify our thinking and facilitate interaction with like-minded individuals. They can also be negative, narrowing our thinking and limiting our ability to appreciate and see the value of how others carry out family functions. Interaction with others can also be impeded because of contrasting views.

This unit is intended to meet several goals in exploring the evolving family including: (1) to sensitize the reader to sources of beliefs about the "shoulds" of the family—what the family should be and the ways in which family roles and functions should be carried out, (2) to show how different views of the family can influence attitudes toward community responsibility and family policy, and (3) to show how changes in society are altering family characteristics, structures, relationships, and functions. Among the issues to be considered in this unit include how historical, demographic, social, and philosophical changes are influencing families, marriage, relationships, and the nature of family life in the U.S. and abroad.

Prepared by: Patricia Hrusa Williams,
University of Maine at Farmington

Article

The Changing Face of the American Family

TIM STANLEY

Learning Outcomes

After reading this article, you will be able to:

- Explain the meaning and origins of the term "nuclear family."

- Describe shifts in family structure from 1900 to the present.

- Recognize differences in the ways the media have portrayed families from 1950 to the present.

On September 20th, 1984 a new sitcom aired on NBC. *The Cosby Show* starred Bill Cosby as Heathcliff 'Cliff' Huxtable, a middle-class, black obstetrician living with his wife and five children in Brooklyn, New York. It kicked off with a situation that millions of parents could identify with: Cliff's son, Theo, had come home with a report card covered in Ds. Theo's mother was deeply upset and Cliff was furious. But Theo said that his bad grades didn't bother him because he didn't want to go to college. His goal was to grow up to be like 'regular people' and, if Cliff loves his son, won't he accept him for what he is? The audience applauded. This was what TV had been teaching them for over a decade, that love and understanding were more important than competition and success. But, to their shock, Cosby's character didn't agree. 'Theo,' he said, 'that is the dumbest thing I ever heard! No wonder you get Ds in everything! . . . I'm telling you, you are going to try as hard as you can. And you're going to do it because I said so. I am your father. I brought you into this world, and I will take you out!' The audience's laughter was nervous at first, but by the end of the scene they were clapping wildly. Bill Cosby had just turned the liberal logic of TV Land on its head. 'Father knows best' parenting was back.

This scene is discussed in the PBS documentary *America in Primetime,* shortly to be shown by the BBC.

The programme makes the point that because the Cosbys are African-Americans, we might presume that the politics of the show are liberal—sitcoms in the 1970s had tended to use black characters to explore poverty and racism. Yet Cliff Huxtable's old fashioned parenting had much more in common with the optimistic conservatism of the 1980s presidency of Republican Ronald Reagan. The Huxtables were wealthy, professional, churchgoers, dominated by a stern father. Alas, among black families their traditional structure increasingly made them the exception rather than the rule. In the America of the 1980s divorce and illegitimacy were rising fast. By 1992, when the show ended, 68 per cent of African-American babies were born out of wedlock. The last episode of *Cosby* coincided with riots in Los Angeles, the product of economic segregation and black fury at a brutal police force. The show might have started out as a healthy antidote to touchy-feely liberalism, but it ended as escapist fantasy.

The Cosby Show's huge viewing figures—among both blacks and whites—tell a confusing story. On the one hand divorce and illegitimacy were changing the character of the American family for good. Un-wed co-habitation was more likely; partners were more inclined to abandon an unhappy relationship; sex outside marriage was common. On the other hand Americans still held heterosexual marriage in high regard and wanted to watch shows that affirmed it. The big TV hits of the 1980s were all centred around traditional families— *Mr Belvedere, Who's The Boss?, Growing Pains.* Ronald Reagan's favourite show was *Family Ties,* which starred Michael J. Fox as a teenager who rebelled against his liberal parents by campaigning for Ronald Reagan.

The answer to this paradox lay in the enduring appeal of the nuclear family. America's nuclear unit wasn't around very long. It was forged by the unique economic and political circumstances of the 1950s, was undermined by social revolution in the 1960s and was revived as an ideal in the 1970s by a conservative movement with a deceptively rosy view of the past. But, while the nuclear family was only representative of how a number of people lived for a few years, its myth has hardened into an ideology. For many Americans it remains synonymous with the hallowed promise of the American dream.

Sitcom Suburbia

In 1957 CBS premiered a TV show called *Leave it to Beaver.* It starred Jerry Mathers as Theodore 'The Beaver' Cleaver, an inquisitive boy who lived with his parents June and Ward in a leafy suburb. The plot of every episode was the same: Beaver got in trouble, his parents reprimanded him and our hero would learn something about the realities of life.

In one storyline Beaver met the son of divorced parents and was jealous of all the presents he got from his estranged dad. But he quickly discovered that divorce also leads to insecurity and depression, so the episode ended with Beaver begging his parents never to part. Divorce wasn't the only model of social dysfunction that the show explored: spinsters like prim Aunt Martha were sexless harpies, while bachelors, like Andy the alcoholic handyman, were layabout bums. It was a world of conservative certainty, held together by a terror of nonconformity.

Today *Leave it to Beaver* is shorthand for the calm and luxury of American life before the storm of the 1960s. In fact the world that it depicted was a historical aberration; before 1950 things had been very different. In 1900 the vast majority of women went out to work and the US had the highest divorce rate in the world. Roughly one in ten children grew up in a single-parent household, hundreds of thousands of offspring were abandoned due to shortages of money and families were plagued with disease and death. Between 35 and 40 per cent of children lost a parent or a sibling before their 20s.

It wasn't until the 1950s that life began to get sweeter and more stable for the average American. The decade was characterised by a rising birth rate, a stable divorce rate and a declining age of marriage. In 1950 most married women walked down the aisle aged just 20. Only 16 per cent of them got a job outside the home and a majority of brides were pregnant within seven months of their wedding. They didn't stop at one child: from 1940 to 1960 the number of families with three children doubled and the number of families having a fourth child quadrupled.

Contemporary anthropologists dubbed this the 'nuclear family'. They meant nuclear as in a unit built around the nucleus of the father and mother, but the name also resonates with the politics of the Cold War. The family was on the front line of an existential conflict between communism and capitalism. On the communist side, the propagandists said, were collectivism, atheism and poverty. On the capitalist side was self-reliance, freedom of religion and a degree of material comfort unparalleled in US history. Science was eradicating disease, salaries were rising, household goods were alleviating drudgery and the nuclear family had a friend in big business.

The advertising agencies tried to create the model of the perfect housewife. A famous article in *Housekeeping Monthly* of May 13th, 1955 explained what perfection entailed:

> *Your goal: To try and make sure your home is a place of peace, order, and tranquility where your husband can renew himself in body and spirit. . . . Make him comfortable. Have him lean back in a comfortable chair or have him lie down in the bedroom. . . . Arrange his pillow and offer to take off his shoes. Speak in a low, soothing and pleasant voice. . . . Remember, he is the master of the house and as such will always exercise his will with fairness and truthfulness. You have no right to question him. A good wife always knows her place.*

Having popularised the ideal of a 'good wife', the advertisers recommended products that would put perfection within her reach. 'Christmas Morning, She'll Be Happier With a Hoover!' claimed one ad, which featured a housewife excitedly examining her new vacuum cleaner. Spending on advertising rose from $6 billion in 1950 to over $13 billion in 1963.

The efforts of advertising's Mad Men were central to the 1950s boom. Robert Sarnoff, president of the National Broadcasting Company, said in 1956: 'The reason we have such a high standard of living is because advertising has created an American frame of mind that makes people want more things, better things, and newer things.' He was probably right. Private debt doubled during the 1950s, driving up profit and productivity and returning much of it to the male wage earner. The economy grew by roughly 37 per cent, with low rates of inflation and unemployment. By 1960 the average family had 30 per cent more purchasing power than it had had in 1950. The nuclear unit was the engine of America's growth and the main beneficiary of its economic greatness.

The Sixties Swing Out of Control

But was everyone really as happy as the ads implied? In 1963 a book hit the shelves that claimed to expose all the oppression and misery that lay behind *Leave it to Beaver*'s white picket fences. Its author, Betty Friedan, described herself as a housewife and mother from the New York suburbs. In 1957 Friedan had been asked to conduct a survey of former Smith College classmates. The results depressed her. Girls who had studied and excelled at the arts and sciences were expected to surrender their minds and personalities to their roles as wives: 89 per cent of the Smith alumni who answered her survey were now homemakers. Intellectually repressed and lacking anyway to express themselves beyond cooking or sex, the housewife of the 1960s was suffocated by what Friedan called the feminine mystique. 'Each suburban wife struggles with it alone' she wrote. 'As she made the beds, shopped for groceries, matched slipcover material, ate peanut butter sandwiches with her children, chauffeured Cub Scouts and Brownies, lay beside her husband at night—she was afraid to ask even of herself the silent question—"Is this all?" '

The Feminine Mystique stayed on *The New York Times* bestseller list for six weeks and laid the groundwork for a feminist revolution that would redefine the nuclear unit forever. Friedan wanted women to take control of their lives and the shortcuts to liberation were contraception and employment. But the book wasn't quite the impartial account that its author claimed. Although she was technically a homemaker, Friedan was not an apolitical housewife who spent her evenings arranging her husband's pillow. She was active in socialist politics and had worked as a journalist for the United Electrical Workers union for a number of years after her marriage. Friedan probably hid all these details because she wanted to divorce feminism from radicalism and so make it more palatable to the average woman. More troublingly, she exaggerated the degree to which the women of Smith College were the passive victims of patriarchy. In fact most of the housewives who answered her survey said they were the happiest they had ever been—a majority expressed no desire to return to the world of work. But they did not buy the advertisers' myth of suburban fulfilment and many said that they felt frustrated that they could not use their intellect in more demanding ways. Instead they were channelling those energies into voluntary work and party political activism. Contemporary women were already finding ways to overcome the feminine mystique, while retaining their identities as wives and mothers.

Although Friedan and the women's liberation movement sometimes imagined that they masterminded the 1960s cultural revolution their role was actually to politicise social changes that were already happening. Just as science helped to forge the nuclear family, with better nutrition and disease control, so it created the conditions for its destruction. In 1960 the US Food and Drug Administration officially licensed the sale of the oral contraceptive known as the Pill. By 1962 an estimated 1,187,000 women were using it. Policy makers thought the Pill would strengthen the nuclear family by increasing disposable income via reduced pregnancies. What it did in practice was to weaken the links between sexual pleasure, childbirth and marriage. Sex before and outside marriage increased, while women who had married became more likely to seek work or stay in it.

The effects of such subtle changes in sexual practice were startling. Between 1960 and 1980 the divorce rate almost doubled. In 1962 only half of all respondents disagreed with a statement suggesting that parents who don't get along should stay together for the children; by 1977 over 80 per cent disagreed. In the early 1960s roughly half of women told pollsters that they had engaged in premarital sex. By the late 1980s the figure was five out of six. In the early 1960s approximately three quarters of Americans said premarital sex was wrong. By the 1980s that view was held by only one third of the nation. The most obvious legacy of shifting attitudes was the rocketing rate of births out of wedlock. In 1960 only five per cent of births were attributed to single mothers. By 1980 the figure was 18 per cent and by 1990 it was 28 per cent.

Both Left and Right were worried that America was coming apart. Although the 1960s were dominated by the struggles over Vietnam and Civil Rights, an equally big policy challenge was how to save the nuclear family unit. The Left concluded that the answer was greater government support. In 1965 the liberal sociologist Daniel Patrick Moynihan published *The Negro Family: The Case For National Action*. A study of poverty in the African-American ghetto, the so-called *Moynihan Report* argued that the underlying cause of inequality between black and white was not economics or race but family structure. Moynihan believed that the growing incidence of single motherhood was raising a generation of African-American males who lacked a model of self-reliance, discipline and authority. He advised Democratic President Lyndon Johnson that the solution was job training and education programmes that would empower black fathers to raise their family on a single salary. The welfare state would have to grow.

Johnson declared a 'War on Poverty' that created a plethora of entitlements to individuals. The use of government subsidies to buy meals (which had been around since the 1930s) increased dramatically under both Democrat and Republican administrations: the number of individuals using food stamps jumped from 500,000 in 1965 to 10 million in 1971. The overall effect was a fall in the proportion of Americans living in poverty from 19 per cent in 1964 to 11.1 per cent in 1973. But government generosity did nothing to stop the decline of the nuclear unit. Conservatives argued that it actually undermined the family by subsidising absentee fathers, educational underachievement, crime, drugs and a new, somewhat racialised, form of segregation between those in work and those on the dole. Moynihan's ambition to rescue the black family failed. While the median black family income rose 53 per cent in the 1960s, the rate of single parenthood also increased by over 50 per cent. Conservatives began to argue that the welfare state was not the solution but part of the problem. They claimed that the real goal of liberals like Friedan and Johnson was to create a world in which the nuclear family no longer existed.

Lost Age of Innocence

In 1976 America went to the polls to elect a new president. Its choice was Jimmy Carter, a former peanut farmer and one-term governor of Georgia. With his photogenic family and foursquare humility, the Baptist Carter felt like a throwback to the *Leave it to Beaver* spirit. In the mid-1970s America was experiencing a wave of nostalgia for the 1950s; movies like *Grease* and *American Graffiti* celebrated a lost age of innocence and certainty. Carter said that if he won the election he would hold a White House 'Conference on the Family' to discuss the best way of reviving some of those old values. It was exactly the kind of consensus-building, moral politics that Carter loved.

But after Carter's inauguration the White House announced a name change. The Conference on the Family would become the Conference on Families, reflecting the growing diversity of American family structures. Presidential aides pointed out that roughly a third of families no longer adhered to what they described as the 'nostalgic family'—their rather patronising term for the nuclear unit. One person who welcomed the rebranding was delegate Betty Friedan. In her 1981 book *The Second Stage* she wrote that she was pleased the conference recognised the most important shift in American life that had occurred in the last 20 years: 'women now work'. Indeed they did. In 1950 the proportion of married women under 45 who worked was just 26 per cent; by 1985 it would hit 67 per cent. The growing expectation—and need—for women to enter the labour market had a dramatic impact upon gender roles, child-rearing and patterns of cohabitation. Life for the Seventies woman was more independent and more complex.

Friedan hoped that the conference would continue the work of the Johnson administration in expanding government aid to individuals struggling to get by in the new social order. Recession made the task all the more important: 'With men being laid off in both blue-collar and white-collar jobs, with inflation showing no let-up, women's opportunity needed [legal] underpinning to insure the survival of the family.'

Friedan's manifesto was something that many European nations would enthusiastically embrace in the 1980s: accept that the family is no longer nuclear and build the welfare and employment opportunities necessary to strengthen its new incarnation. But this wasn't Europe and many Americans responded to social change with either resistance or denial. When the conference was finally held in 1980 it was dominated by polarising minorities of feminists and social conservatives.

America was undergoing a religious revival and the cultural Right was evolving into a well-oiled political machine. Its delegates to the Conference on Families believed that women's best hope of 'liberation' was found in marriage, where their compassionate instinct for motherhood formed a perfect union with their husbands' authority. To the feminists at the conference such views were the last gasp of an old, patriarchal order that was out of step with the unstoppable march of progress. Boasting superior numbers of delegates, the feminists were able to push through platforms endorsing abortion on demand and gay rights. Their success gave them the illusion of political momentum.

But the press and the public were rather more interested in the rhetoric of the conservative delegates, who staged a colourful walkout. Outside the conference, the anti-feminist activist Connie Marshner told the media that 'families consist of people related by heterosexual marriage, blood and adoption. Families are not religious cults, families are not Manson families, families are not heterosexual or homosexual liaisons outside of marriage.' Marshner's simple language articulated the feelings of millions of Americans that the sexual revolution was not just replacing the nuclear unit with something more complex—it was destroying the very concept of family itself.

Recognising that this view was gaining currency Carter tried to charm several televangelists at a White House breakfast in January 1980. The meeting was a disaster. When it was over, the preacher Tim LaHaye prayed 'God we have got to get this man out of the White House and get someone in here who will be aggressive about bringing back traditional moral values'. The religious Right decided that its best shot was Republican Ronald Reagan. When Reagan beat Carter by a landslide in November 1980 he captured two thirds of the white evangelical vote. Politics for the next 30 years would be dominated by the conservatism of Marshner, not the progressive ambitions of Friedan.

The Paradox of the American Family

Since the 1980s the American family has continued its inexorable evolution towards greater diversity and complexity. Yet America's popular culture, just like *The Cosby Show*, continues to celebrate a 1950s' vision of 'living right, living free'.

It is tempting to accuse conservatives of promoting paradoxical politics that are out of step with the modern world. In 2012 an estimated 19 per cent of gay people are raising a child in the US, yet every referendum on gay marriage has resulted in its ban. States like Texas offer abstinence promotions in place of sex education, yet people who take a chastity pledge are statistically more likely to get pregnant outside marriage than those who do not. And despite feminism's supposed grip upon the American imagination, voters are more anti-abortion than at any point since the 1980s. Against the European trend toward social liberalism the United States looks even more conservative today than it was when Bill Cosby first told his son to quit griping and start revising.

But the nuclear family endures as an ideal for good reason. For many middle-class whites the 1950s really were the Golden Age. At home families were large and stable and often kept by a single, generous wage. America was the workshop of the world, producing a flood of consumer goods that improved the lives of millions. Abroad the USA established itself as a model of the good life. The American Dream—meritocratic and capable of reaping great rewards—set an international standard for democratic capitalism. Never again would Americans tell pollsters that they were as content in their own lives or as confident about their country's direction. It was an age of innocence and sometimes that innocence blinded people to the realities of patriarchy and racism. But it will remain the yardstick by which Americans judge their country for a very long time.

Further Reading

David Allyn, *Make Love, Not War. The Sexual Revolution: An Unfettered History* (Little, Brown, 2000).

Mary Dalton and Laura Linder (eds.), *The Sitcom Reader: America Viewed and Skewed* (SUNY Press, 2005).

Daniel Horowitz, *Betty Friedan and the Making of The Feminine Mystique: The American Left, The Cold War, and Modern Feminism* (University of Massachusetts Press, 1998).

Dominic Sandbrook, *Mad as Hell: The Crisis of the 1970s and the Rise of the Populist Right* (Knopf, 2011).

Critical Thinking

1. Explain what the term "nuclear family" means and its origins.

2. There has been much debate about what kind of family structure is best for U.S. families. What structure do you view as most adaptive and why?

3. How have social, political, economic, and religious forces and scientific changes affected the structure, functioning, and expectations we have for families in the United States?

4. Do you feel that the media have portrayed the American family fairly and honestly? Why or why not?

5. How should we define what a family is in the United States today?

Create Central

www.mhhe.com/createcentral

Internet References

World Family Map
http://worldfamilymap.org/2013

Australian Institute of Family Studies
www.aifs.gov.au

Feminist Perspectives on Reproduction and the Family
http://plato.stanford.edu/entries/feminism-family
Kearl's Guide to the Sociology of the Family
www.trinity.edu/MKEARL/family.html

TIM STANLEY is associate fellow of the Rothermere American Institute, Oxford University. His documentary *Sitcom USA* will be broadcast on BBC2 on October 27th 2012 at 9 pm.

Article　　　　Prepared by: Patricia Hrusa Williams, *University of Maine at Farmington*

Five Reasons We Can't Handle Marriage Anymore

Anthony D'Ambrosio

Learning Outcomes

After reading this article, you will be able to:

- Identify factors which contribute to marital stability and longevity.

- Analyze how changes in modern society may serve to promote marital dissolution.

- Suggest ways to strengthen relationships in a time of great technological and social change.

Marriages today just don't work. The million dollar question? Why not? It's a pretty simple concept—fall in love and share your life together. Our great grandparents did it, our grandparents followed suit, and for many of us, our parents did it as well. Why the hell can't we?

Many of you will ask what gives me the right to share my advice or opinions. I've been divorced myself. But I'm only one of the many people today that have failed at marriage. And while some of us have gone through a divorce, others stay in their relationships, miserably, and live completely phony lives. These same people, though, are quick to point the finger and judge others for speaking up.

I've spent the better part of the last three years trying to understand the dating scene again. Back when I met my ex-wife in 2004, things were just so different. Social media had yet to explode. I had this desire to ask her about her day simply because I didn't know. Texting was just starting to make its way into mainstream society, so if I wanted to speak to her, I had to call her. If I wanted to see her, I had to drive to her house and knock on her door. Everything required an action on my part, or hers. Today, things are different though.

To my ex-wife: I wish I would have held you tighter.

Looking back nearly 11 years, I began to wonder how different things were for the older generations. More importantly, I wonder how different they will be for my children.

Our generation isn't equipped to handle marriages—and here's why:

1) Sex Becomes Almost Non-Existent

I don't know about you, but I am an extremely sexual person. Not only do I believe it's an important aspect of a relationship, I believe it's the most important. Beyond being pleasurable, sex connects two individuals. There's a reason why it's referred to as making love. There's just something about touching someone, kissing someone, feeling someone that should make your hair stand up.

I'm baffled by couples who neglect having sex, especially younger ones. We all desire physical connection, so how does cutting that off lead you to believe your marriage will be successful? It's like telling someone you'll take them out to a restaurant but they can't order food.

Instead, we have sex once every couple of weeks, or when it's time to get pregnant. It becomes this chore. You no longer look at your partner wanting to rip their clothes off, but rather instead, dread the thought. That's not crazy to you?

It's not just boredom that stops sex from happening. Everywhere you look, there's pictures of men and women we know half naked—some look better than your husband or wife. So it becomes desirable. It's in your face every single day and changes your mindset. It's no wonder why insecurities loom so largely these days. You have to be perfect to keep someone attracted to you. Meanwhile, what your lover should really be attracted to is your heart. Maybe if you felt that connection beyond a physical level, would you realize a sexual attraction you've never felt before.

2) Finances Cripple Us

Years ago, it didn't cost upward of $200,000 for an education. It also didn't cost $300,000-plus for a home. The cost of living was very different than what it is now. You'd be naive to believe this stress doesn't cause strain on marriages today.

You need to find a job to pay for student loans, a mortgage, utilities, living expenses, and a baby. Problem is, it's extremely difficult to find a job that can provide an income that will help you live comfortably while paying all of these bills—especially not in your mid-20s.

This strain causes separation between us. It halts us from being able to live life. We're too busy paying bills to enjoy our youth. Forget going to dinner, you have to pay the mortgage. You'll have to skip out on an anniversary gift this year because those student loans are due at the end of the month. Vacations? Not happening. We're trying to live the way our grandparents and parents did in a world that has put more debt on our plate than ever before. It's possible, but it puts us in an awful position.

Part of life is being able to live. Not having the finances to do so takes away yet another important aspect of our relationships. It keeps us inside, forced to see the life everyone else is living.

3) We're More Connected than Ever Before, but Completely Disconnected at the Same Time

Let's face it, the last time you "spoke" to the person you love, you didn't even hear their voice. You could be at work, the gym, maybe with the kids at soccer. You may even be in the same room. You told your wife you made dinner reservations . . . through a text message. Your husband had flowers delivered to your job . . . through an app on his phone. You both searched for furnishings for your new home . . . on Pinterest. There's no physical connection attached to anything anymore.

We've developed relationships with things, not each other. Ninety-five percent of the personal conversations you have on a daily basis occur through some type of technology. We've removed human emotion from our relationships, and we've replaced it with colorful bubbles.

Somehow, we've learned to get offended by text on a screen, accusing others of being "angry" or "sad" when, in fact, we have no idea what they are feeling. We argue about this—at length. We've forgotten how to communicate yet expect healthy marriages. How is it possible to grow and mature together if we barely speak?

Years ago, my grandmother wouldn't hear from my grandfather all day; he was working down at the piers in Brooklyn.

But today, if someone doesn't text you back within 30 minutes, they're suddenly cheating on you.

You want to know why your grandmother and grandfather just celebrated their 60th wedding anniversary? Because they weren't scrolling through Instagram worrying about what John ate for dinner. They weren't on Facebook criticizing others. They weren't on vacation sending Snapchats to their friends. No. They were too preoccupied loving and respecting one another. They were talking to each other at dinner, walking with each other holding hands instead of their phones. They weren't distracted by everything around them. They had dreams and chased them together.

4) Our Desire for Attention Outweighs Our Desire to be Loved

Even years ago, people would clamor over celebrities. When I think back, I can imagine young women wanting to be like Marilyn Monroe. She was beautiful, all over magazines, could have any man she wanted and, in fact, did.

But she was a celebrity. And in order to be a successful one, she had to keep all eyes on her. Same holds true for celebrities today. They have to stay in the spotlight or their fame runs out, and they get replaced by the next best thing.

Social media, however, has given everyone an opportunity to be famous. Attention you couldn't dream of getting unless you were a celebrity is now a selfie away. Post a picture, and thousands of strangers will like it. Wear less clothing, and guess what? More likes.

It's more than that though. What about the life you live? I see pictures of people decked out in designer clothes, posted up in some club with fancy drinks—people that I know are dead broke. But they portray themselves as successful because, well, they can. And they get this gratification from people who like and comment on their statuses or pictures.

If you want to love someone, stop seeking attention from everyone because you'll never be satisfied with the attention from one person.

Same holds true for love. Love is supposed to be sacred. You can't love someone when you're preoccupied with worrying about what others think of you. Whether it be posting pictures on social media, buying homes to compete with others, or going on lavish vacations—none of it matters.

5) Social Media Just Invited a Few Thousand People into Bed with You

We've thrown privacy out the window these days. Nothing is sacred anymore, in fact, it's splattered all over the web for the world to see. Everywhere we go, everything we do—made public. Instead of enjoying the moment, we get lost in cyberspace, trying to figure out the best status update, or the perfect filter. Something as simple as enjoying breakfast has become a photo shoot. Vacations are no longer a time to relax, but more a time to post vigorously. You can't just sit back and soak it all in.

There's absolutely nothing wrong with sharing moments of your life. I do it myself. But where do we draw the line? When does it become too much?

We've invited strangers into our homes and brought them on dates with us. We've shown them our wardrobe, drove with them in our cars, and we even showed them our bathing suits. Might as well pack them a suitcase, too.

The worst part about all this? It's only going to get worse.

Immediately, people will assume that my failed marriage is why I am expressing these emotions; that's not the case. It's what I see around me every single day that inspired me to write this article.

Marriage is sacred. It is the most beautiful sacrament and has tremendous promise for those fortunate enough to experience it. Divorced or not, I am a believer in true love and building a beautiful life with someone. In fact, it's been my dream since I was young.

I hope you never experience the demise of your love. It's painful, and life changing; something nobody should ever feel. I do fear, however, that the world we live in today has put roadblocks in the way of getting there and living a happy life with someone. Some things are in our control, and unfortunately, others are not.

People can agree or disagree. I'm perfectly okay with that.

Critical Thinking

1. The author states in the very beginning of the article "Marriages today just don't work." Do you agree or disagree with him? Why?

2. The article considers five stresses and strains which the author feels contribute to the failure of modern marriages. Evaluate each, considering their role in developing, maintaining, and dissolving relationships in the modern world.

3. Where do you feel marriage is going as a social institution? What are roadblocks to lifelong love and commitment with another person and how might they be overcome?

Internet References

National Healthy Marriage Resource Center
http://www.healthymarriageinfo.org/index.aspx
Psychology Today: Divorce
https://www.psychologytoday.com/basics/divorce
Two of Us
http://www.twoofus.org

ANTHONY D'AMBROSIO, 29, of Wall has built a large following after the success of his relationship columns that regularly appear on these pages. Today, he discusses why marriages just don't work for people of his generation. D'Ambrosio is now divorced after getting married in 2012.

Article   Prepared by: Patricia Hrusa Williams, *University of Maine at Farmington*

Family Matters

What's the most important factor blocking social mobility? Single parents, suggests a new study.

W. BRADFORD WILCOX

Learning Outcomes

After reading this article, you will be able to:

- Identify community and family factors associated with social mobility in the United States.

- Describe how single parenthood may be linked with other factors that limit children's later economic outcomes.

Next week, in his State of the Union address, President Obama is expected to return to a theme he and many progressives have been hitting hard in recent months: namely, that the American Dream is in trouble and that growing economic inequality is largely to blame. In a speech to the Center for American Progress last month, Obama said: "The combined trends of increased inequality and decreasing mobility pose a fundamental threat to the American Dream." Likewise, [The] *New York Times* columnist Paul Krugman recently wrote that the nation "claims to reward the best and brightest regardless of family background" but in practice shuts out "children of the middle and working classes."

Progressives like Obama and Krugman are clearly right to argue that the American Dream is in trouble. Today, poor children have a limited shot at moving up the economic ladder into the middle or upper class. One study found that the nation leaves 70 percent of poor children below the middle class as adults. Equally telling, poor children growing up in countries like Canada and Denmark have a greater chance of moving up the economic ladder than do poor children from the United States. As Obama noted, these trends call into question the "American story" that our nation is exceptionally successful in delivering equal opportunity to its citizens.

But the more difficult question is: Why? What are the factors preventing poor children from getting ahead? An important new Harvard study that looks at the best community data on mobility in America—released this past weekend—suggests a cause progressives may find discomforting, especially if they are interested in reviving the American Dream for the 21st century.

The study, "Where is the Land of Opportunity?: The Geography of Intergenerational Mobility in the United States," authored by Harvard economist Raj Chetty and colleagues from Harvard and Berkeley, explores the community characteristics most likely to predict mobility for lower-income children. The study specifically focuses on two outcomes: absolute mobility for lower-income children—that is, how far up the income ladder they move as adults; and relative mobility—that is, how far apart children who grew up rich and poor in the same community end up on the economic ladder as adults. When it comes to these measures of upward mobility in America, the new Harvard study asks: Which "factors are the strongest predictors of upward mobility in multiple variable regressions"?

1) Family structure. Of all the factors most predictive of economic mobility in America, one factor clearly stands out in their study: family structure. By their reckoning, when it comes to mobility, "the strongest and most robust predictor is the fraction of children with single parents." They find that children raised in communities with high percentages of single mothers are significantly less likely to experience absolute and relative mobility. Moreover, "[c]hildren of married parents also have higher rates of upward mobility if they live in communities with fewer single parents." In other words, as Figure 1 indicates, it looks like a married village is more likely to raise the economic prospects of a poor child.

What makes this finding particularly significant is that this is the first major study showing that rates of single parenthood

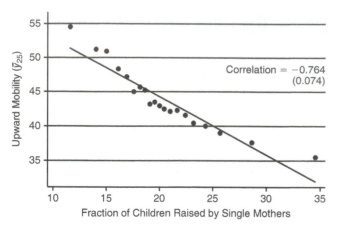

Figure 1   Upward Mobility by Share of Single Mothers in a Community   A. Upward Mobility vs. Fraction Single Mothers in CZ

Source: Chetty et al. 2014

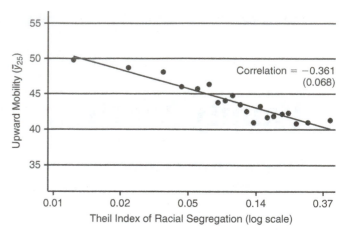

Figure 2   Upward Mobility by Racial Segregation in a Community   A. Upward Mobility vs. Theil Index of Racial Segregation

Source: Chetty et al. 2014

at the community level are linked to children's economic opportunities over the course of their lives. A lot of research—including new research from the Brookings Institution—has shown us that kids are more likely to climb the income ladder when they are raised by two, married parents. But this is the first study to show that lower-income kids from both single- and married-parent families are more likely to succeed if they hail from a community with lots of two-parent families.

2) Racial and economic segregation. According to this new study, economic and racial segregation are also important characteristics of communities that do not foster economic mobility. Children growing up in communities that are racially segregated, or cluster lots of poor kids together, do not have a great shot at the American Dream. In fact, in their study, racial segregation is one of only two key factors—the other is family structure—that is consistently associated with both absolute and relative mobility in America. Figure 2 illustrates the bivariate association between racial segregation and economic mobility.

3) School quality. Another powerful predictor of absolute mobility for lower-income children is the quality of schools in their communities. Chetty et al. measure this in the study by looking at high-school dropout rates. Their takeaway: Poor kids are more likely to make it in America when they have access to schools that do a good job of educating them.

4) Social capital. In a finding that is bound to warm the heart of their colleague, Harvard political scientist Robert Putnam, Chetty and his team find that communities with more social capital enjoy significantly higher levels of absolute mobility for poor children. That is, communities across America that have high levels of religiosity, civic engagement, and voter involvement are more likely to lift the fortunes of their poorest members.

5) Income inequality. Finally, consistent with the diagnosis of Messrs. Obama and Krugman, Chetty and his team note that income inequality within communities is correlated with lower levels of mobility. However, its predictive power—measured in their study by a Gini coefficient—is comparatively weak: According to their results, in statistical models with all of the five factors they designated as most important, economic inequality was *not* a statistically significant predictor of absolute or relative mobility.

Chetty, who recently won the John Bates Clark Medal for his achievements as an economist under the age of 40, has been careful to stress that this research cannot prove causation—that removing or adding these factors will cause mobility in America. The study also acknowledges that many of these key factors are correlated with one another, such as income inequality and the share of single mothers in a community. This means that economic inequality may degrade the two-parent family *or* that increases in single parenthood may increase economic inequality. But what does seem clear from this study of the "land[s] of opportunity" in America is that communities characterized by a thriving middle class, racial and economic integration, better schools, a vibrant civil society, and, especially, strong two-parent families are more likely to foster the kind of equality of opportunity that has recently drawn the attention of Democrats and Republicans alike.

Throughout his presidency, Barack Obama has stressed his commitment to data-driven decision-making, not ideology. Similarly, progressives like Krugman have stressed their scientific bona fides, as against the "anti-science" right. If progressives like the president and the Nobel laureate are serious about reviving the fortunes of the American Dream in the 21st century in light of the data, this new study suggests they will need to take pages from *both* left and right playbooks on matters ranging from zoning to education reform. More fundamentally, these new data indicate that any effort to revive opportunity in America must run through two arenas where government has only limited power—civil society and the American family. This is a tall order, to be sure, but unless President Obama, and progressives more generally, can enlist a range of political, civic, business, and cultural leaders—not to mention parents—in this undertaking, this new study suggests they will not succeed in achieving one of their most cherished goals: reviving America as a "land of opportunity."

Critical Thinking

1. How do you think growing up in a community with many single-parent families influences children's development, experiences, and future aspirations?
2. Why can't we say single parenthood causes children to remain mired in the cycle of poverty and unable to achieve social mobility?
3. What types of interventions and supports are needed to assist the children of single-parent families and those who reside in communities where single parents predominate?

Create Central

www.mhhe.com/createcentral

Internet References

Child Trends
http://www.childtrends.org

Fragile Families and Child Wellbeing Study, Princeton and Columbia Universities
http://www.fragilefamilies.princeton.edu

World Family Map
http://worldfamilymap.org/2014/about

W. BRADFORD WILCOX is director of the National Marriage Project and a visiting scholar at the American Enterprise Institute. Follow him on Twitter.

Article   Prepared by: Patricia Hrusa Williams, *University of Maine at Farmington*

Bridging Cultural Divides: The Role and Impact of Binational Families

SAMANTHA N.N. CROSS AND MARY C. GILLY

Learning Outcomes

After reading this article, you will be able to:

- Define the term "binational family."

- Explain trends and changes in the demographic composition of U.S. families.

- Understand how immigration, culture, and intermarriage influences family decision making.

The press has given considerable attention recently to what unites diverse groups within or between countries—groups separated by culture, ideology, race, religion, or economic status. Much of this talk has stemmed from the unique background of President Barack Obama (the product of a binational relationship), often presented as the rare candidate who could bridge barriers of race, culture, ideology, and party. However, the discourse is primarily at a macro level. In politics, as in marketing, it is often overlooked that for barriers to truly be breached, change and exchange also must occur at more micro levels. This essay argues that binational families (with partners from different countries) provide an important micro-setting for appreciating marketplace diversity and inclusion and the bridging of cultural divides.

> **Mélange, hotch-potch, a bit of this and a bit of that is how newness enters the world.**
>
> —Rushdie (1990)

Brown (1979) contends that two important changes have happened, at both micro and macro levels, that require a major reorientation in researchers' thinking: the change in the composition and structure of the American family and market globalization. Andreasen (1990, p. 848) also notes that accelerating rates of immigration have a considerable effect on the level of "intranational and international cultural interpenetration." He argues that it is the responsibility of consumer researchers to describe and explain both the nature of cultural interpenetration and the consequences for both the immigrant and the penetrated cultural groups (Andreasen 1990). This is important for both advancement of knowledge and societal benefit.

The foreign-born population in countries worldwide has increased; for example, the United States saw an increase of 85% between 1990 and 2009, from 19.8 million to 36.7 million (U.S. Census Bureau 2010). Similarly, in the United Kingdom, the foreign-born population almost doubled between 1993 and 2011, from 3.8 million to approximately 7.0 million (Rienzo and Vargas-Silva 2012). This growth in the number of immigrants inevitably has an impact on the growth of intermarriages (Bean and Stevens 2003). Yet marketing research studies that examine this notion of cultural interpenetration, though growing, remain limited. More work is needed to explore the nature and consequences of cultural interpenetration, within both the family and society.

In this essay, the driving questions are as follows: What is the role of the binational family and what are the implications for marketplace diversity, inclusion, and creativity? We begin with a brief overview of studies in family decision making and cultural interpenetration. This is followed by a discussion of the role of the binational family as a familial and societal force. We end with implications for marketing, public policy, and society.

Studies in Family Decision Making

Over the past 50 years, research in household decision making has predominantly focused on gender roles in the purchase or consumption of a particular product or service. The emphasis has been on which partner has the most influence, the factors contributing to the differing levels of influence, and how that influence has changed over time (e.g., Belch and Willis 2002; Blood and Wolfe 1960; Commuri and Gentry 2005; Davis and Rigaux 1974; Ford, LaTour, and Henthorne 1995; Qualls 1987; Spiro 1983; Wolfe 1959).

Several theories have evolved to explain the bases of power and influence in the home. Blood and Wolfe's (1960) resource theory proposes that as women became more educated and contributed more income, decision-making processes became more egalitarian. Raven, Centers, and Rodrigues (1975) later applied social power theory, developed by French and Raven (1959), to the family decision-making process. Qualls (1987) concludes that family decision making should be viewed as a network of household relationships rather than as a series of static independent actions. Webster (2000) notes that the particular cultural characteristics of the society determine individual behavior and the type of decision making prevalent in households.

Nevertheless, Commuri and Gentry (2000) insist that the definition of the family must be enlarged, with more studies examining family composition, nontraditional family structures, and cross-cultural comparisons. They note a tendency to emphasize family member characteristics and the effect on relative household influence rather than the characteristics and identity of the household itself. Epp and Price (2008) offer insights into family identity and consumption practices and consider nontraditional family forms, including divorced couples and their children. However, they do not consider binational families, in which members face challenges from the outset with defining and reconciling their disparate identities (Cross and Gilly 2012).

We also argue that it is important to understand how the family functions as a unit or group. While an important foundational knowledge has been developed, the family decision-making literature to date and the critiques of it (Commuri and Gentry 2000; Olsen and Cromwell 1975) have taken a predominantly inward focus. The emphasis has been on the internal impact of influence strategies, decision processes, and identity on household purchase choices. Yet given the importance of the family as a key social and consumption unit (Davis 1970), researchers also must appreciate the wider role of evolving nontraditional family units within diverse societies. We address this gap by examining the role and influence of the binational family.

In addition, in studies of the family or household, researchers draw parallels between the family and other social or structured groups. The family is often described as an institution (Laslett 1973): a collective entity with members who participate and contribute within and outside its social structure or system. Researchers discuss issues of household production, family dynamics, decision-making roles, responsibilities and tasks, housework, conflict, management of domestic labor, expertise, resource allocation, and influence strategies (Commuri and Gentry 2000, 2005). Researchers tend to view spousal relations as partnerships and the family as a unit whose members engage in family planning. The family as an entity also goes through different stages, described as the family life cycle (Gilly and Enis 1982; Murphy and Staples 1979; Wagner and Hanna 1983). These parallels allow additional analogies between the inclusive role of binational families and diversity inclusion in other settings.

Studies in Cultural Interpenetration

While the family decision-making literature has considered culture (Davis and Rigaux 1974; Ford, LaTour, and Henthorne 1995; Green et al. 1983; Wallendorf and Reilly 1983; Webster 1994, 2000), it mainly makes comparisons of culturally homogeneous households in one country with culturally homogeneous households in another country. This research indicates that culture affects family decision-making styles, but it offers little insight into cultural differences *within* families (Cross 2007). Research on immigrants bringing their own culture to another country is also fairly common in consumer behavior, marketing, anthropology, and sociology research. However, this cultural interpenetration research focuses on the individual and/or group experience rather than the experience of two cultures within one household.

Stewart (1999, pp. 40–41) argues that anthropology researchers' increased interest in cultural interpenetration has resulted in critiques of earlier views of " 'culture' that cast it as too stable, bounded, and homogeneous to be useful in a world characterized by migrations (voluntary or forced), cheap travel, international marketing, and telecommunications." He suggests that cultural interpenetration and borrowing are now viewed as "part of the very nature of cultures" because of their porousness. Although the studies he cites involve subgroups navigating the majority culture (e.g., Anglo-Indians in Madras), his conclusion that syncretism (mixing of different beliefs) is not eliminated as assimilation occurs suggests that cultural mixing occurs at the binational household level. Craig and Douglas (2006) go further to advocate that cultural mixing enriches both cultures. Thus, we infer that families also benefit from cultural mixing.

Appadurai (1990) identifies five global "flows" that affect cultural interpenetration. One, ethnoscapes, is relevant here. He argues that the flow of people (including immigrants, students, and tourists) helps transmit cultural content. Several empirical studies of immigrant groups support this idea. For example, Peñaloza and Gilly (1999) find that Mexican immigrants' consumption behavior is affected by living in the United States and that the marketers serving them alter product offerings and ways of doing business.

Immigrants must adopt products and practices in their country of residence, but research indicates that they are not wholly assimilated and keep some of their own cultural traditions, adopt some traditions of the host culture, and combine cultures in creative ways (Oswald 1999). While studies of immigrants reveal that most intend to return to their native country (Oswald 1999; Peñaloza 1994), intermarriage makes such a return much less likely. Thus, while immigrants in binational relationships may share some attributes with other immigrants, if they live in their partner's country, they are expected to establish deeper roots within that culture.

The Role of Binational Families

In this essay, the term "binational family" refers to a family with partners born and raised in different countries of origin. Several other terms are also prevalent in the literature (e.g., "bicultural," "biethnic," "interethnic"). "Bicultural" often refers to a person's ability to comfortably navigate life in two different cultures and implies familiarity with the language and customs in two different cultural contexts (e.g., Lau-Gesk 2003; Luna, Ringberg, and Peracchio 2008). In a binational family, at least one of the partners is an immigrant to the country of residence and is considered bicultural. Similarly, "biethnic" or "interethnic" specifically refer to familiarity within, or a combination of, two different ethnic groups (i.e., a crossing of ethnic lines), even for participants born and reared in the same country (Alba and Nee 2003; Freeman 1955). Binational families may also be biethnic or biracial, which refers to the crossing of racial boundaries. We focus on the dynamics within the binational family—dynamics that often encompass the nuances of other mixed families, whether bicultural, biethnic, or biracial.

As a unit comprising family members with ties both within and outside their country of residence, the binational family, and the individual partners within the family, play an intermediary role. They provide a conjugal and communal link between different cultural norms and perspectives. Through that link, each partner also gains access and exposure to the history, traditions, social norms, and consumption experiences of the country from which his or her partner originated. When the family resides in the native country of one of the spouses, this connection is particularly important for the immigrant spouse trying to navigate

the vagaries of an unfamiliar host culture. Meng and Gregory (2005) argue that the immigrant spouse gains an economic labor advantage through intermarriage—an "intermarriage premium." Cross and Gilly (2012) also posit that the native spouse functions as a cultural intermediary and navigator for the immigrant spouse. Although Wamwara-Mbugua (2007) did not study binationals, she finds that Kenyan immigrant couples delegated initial decision making to the spouse who had been in the United States longer, even when it conflicted with traditional Kenyan gender roles. Lauth Bacas (2002) notes that cross-border marriage partners perform the role of gatekeeper to each cultural context. This gatekeeping role moves beyond that of the "kinkeeper"—the role ascribed to the individual family member responsible for maintaining kinship ties (Leach and Brathwaite 1996; Rosenthal 1985). Although not explored in this essay, the kin-keeping role in binational families should be inherently more complex, given the cross-cultural dynamics.

However, the influence goes beyond the household. The binational family unit is often viewed as atypical or novel, inciting curiosity and drawing attention from the wider community in which the family resides. This, and other nontraditional family structures, may initially exacerbate cultural and societal divides, leading to negative consequences such as prejudice, stigmatization, and even threat. Yet we argue that, over time, the increased presence of binational and other culturally heterogeneous families eventually provides a starting point for greater tolerance and appreciation of voluntarily formed diverse unions. These families allow people with disparate backgrounds to meet and exchange perspectives. This cultural exchange provides opportunities for growth in knowledge and understanding, to enhance the range of experiences, and to create new customs and novel consumption relationships.

The Binational Family as Bridge, Broker, and Boundary Spanner

The exposure gained through the marriage of people with differing cultural backgrounds affects the entire unit—the partners, children, and members of family and social networks, as well as the surrounding community. In the management innovation literature, several terms have been used to describe people who provide a link between different individuals, groups, and experiences.

Wasserman and Faust (1994, p. 114) describe one of these terms, "bridge," as a "critical tie" and note that "the removal of a bridge leaves more [disparate] components than when the bridge is included." Lin (1999) highlights the importance and usefulness of accessing and extending bridges in networks to obtain missing resources and facilitate information and influence flows. Another metaphor is that of a "broker." Hargadon and Sutton (1997, p. 716) note that the product design firm IDEO acts as a technology broker by introducing unknown solutions and creating new products "that are original combinations of existing knowledge from disparate industries." The authors also distinguish the firm acting as technology broker and the engineers within IDEO, who themselves act as "individual technology brokers." Williams (2002) uses the term "boundary spanner" to describe people who manage across divides. He believes that more focus is needed on the nature and behavior of these boundary spanners, also described as "diversity seekers" (Brumbaugh and Grier 2013), constructs that should be explored within different institutional and contextual situations.

These terms ("bridge," "broker," "boundary spanner," and "diversity seeker") refer to the person who is able to link otherwise disconnected groups. Individual members of binational families *do* play key parts in maintaining harmonious and continuous links between family members in the different cultures. However, we argue that *both* the binational family unit and its members play a similar structural and symbolic role in binding disparate families, networks, cultures, and communities. In the binational family structure, the union itself, not just a single person, functions as "a bridge between cultures," allowing cultural exchange between the partners, who are themselves cultural bridges (Lauth Bacas 2002). This unconventional union of culturally dissimilar partners unifies the two cultures and support structures of the partners in different countries. Prior existence of this link is slim to unlikely, given the geographical, cultural, and other boundaries between the partners. Thus, in the early stages of the household, this central position is unifying. As time passes and the partnership and families evolve, the link persists, even if the binational household dissolves. This is a bridge that binds and is practically irrevocable, particularly when children result. Thus, the impact of the binational union is pervasive and inclusive as social and family networks become interconnected.

The Binational Family as a Venue for Creative Consumption

Foner (1997, p. 961) notes that first-generation immigrants who relocate from one county to another "fuse . . . the old and the new to create a new kind of family life." Foner, a sociologist, points out that for these immigrants, the family is a place where "creative culture-building takes place." In the linguisitics literature, Baron and Cara (2003, pp. 6–7) describe a similar process as the "creative response" of people encountering one another and new situations. They refer to this as a creolization process that can occur whenever members of different cultures meet in "expressive interaction . . . [allowing] us to see cultural

encounters as a process of continuous creative exchange." This process is often central to the maintenance and evolution of society.

As a unit in which cultural encounters occur daily, the binational family can also be viewed as a unique setting for creative culture building. It can even be argued that this creative process is vital to the maintenance of harmonious relations within the household and the very longevity of the family unit. Ultimately, the binational family lies at the intersection of the cultures of the two spouses. At this intersection, cross-cultural interactions, unique blending processes, and creative consumption experiences thrive. This cross-fertilization process between the different cultures occurs through conflict and compromise and through simultaneous fusion and diffusion. It eventually leads to a merging of meaning systems, to create new variations that transcend the individual preferences of the spouses. As a deviation from the traditional family structure, in this kind of family, deviation from norms and "inventive combination" (Hargadon and Sutton 1997) most likely occur. This process inevitably extends beyond the binational family unit and has an impact on the diversity of marketplace offerings, societal tolerance for difference, and the cultural flexibility of the surrounding communities.

Implications for Marketing and Public Policy

Binational families are a growing and inevitable phenomenon. This familial structure accommodates diversity and shapes the preferences, choices, experiences, and perspectives of the family members and those whom they encounter. We advocate that the existence of these families offers several societal and public policy implications.

Research suggests that for immigrant spouses, social and economic adaptation is enhanced when immigrants and natives intermarry (Cross and Gilly 2012; Meng and Gregory 2005). This enhanced participation and contribution strengthens the family and the immigrant partner's commitment to and identification with the new home country, which leads to greater engagement in prosocial behaviors. Immigrants who intermarry are also less likely to segregate in immigrant enclaves. Their inclusion in the wider, dominant community has a positive influence on public perception of immigrants, providing an alternate community perspective to national political sensationalism about immigration. Binational families also include same-sex couples. Yet in countries in which same-sex unions are not legally recognized, exclusionary immigration policies continue to be a threat that policy makers must acknowledge.

In communities in which binational and immigrant families co-reside with native families, immigrant spouses may seek marketplace offerings from their home countries. The acquisition of less accessible, preferred items is influenced by and affects export/import laws and customs restrictions. When natives and immigrants intermarry, members of their social networks are also exposed to these items. Norms slowly change about the acceptability and co-consumption of initially novel products with more familiar items. Vendors in these communities can capitalize on increased opportunities to meet changing marketplace expectations with creative product combinations and service experiences. Both partners in binational families also tend to take an active role in food shopping, to meet their differing cultural preferences (Cross and Gilly 2012). This has implications for grocery store vendors, who typically focus their marketing efforts on females and mono-national families, rather than on both genders and culturally mixed families.

Members of binational families, particularly the children, acquire a level of intercultural competence (Demangeot et al. 2013) and flexibility through the ongoing cross-cultural interactions within the home. They thus provide a potential recruitment pool for public and private employers seeking employees to participate in cross-cultural teams, who can lead an increasingly diverse workforce and serve a multicultural domestic and global population.

Conjugal tolerance eventually leads to societal tolerance. The insights gained from studying the processes and interactions within binational families move beyond prior notions of the "melting pot" or "salad bowl" concepts of assimilation, toward more fluid alternatives for harmonious cross-cultural coexistence and the resolution of intercultural conflict. In the United States, policies on individual self-classification on the census and elsewhere have changed. As the presence of binational families expands, so too will other perceptions of normalcy (Baker 2006) evolve, leading to a more dynamic, innovative, inclusive marketplace and global society.

References

Alba, Richard and Victor Nee (2003), *Remaking the American Mainstream.* Cambridge, MA: Harvard University Press.

Andreasen, Alan R. (1990), "Cultural Interpenetration: A Critical Consumer Research Issue for the 1990s," in *Advances in Consumer Research*, Vol. 17, Marvin E. Goldberg, Gerald Gorn, and Richard W. Pollay, eds. Provo, UT: Association for Consumer Research, 847–49.

Appadurai, Arjun (1990), "Disjuncture and Difference in the Global Cultural Economy," in *Media and Cultural Studies*, Meenakshi Gigi Durham and Douglas M. Kellner, eds. Malden, MA: Blackwell.

Baker, Stacy M. (2006), "Consumer Normalcy: Understanding the Value of Shopping Through Narratives of Consumers with Visual Impairments," *Journal of Retailing*, 82 (1), 37–50.

Baron, Robert and Ana C. Cara (2003), "Introduction: Creolization and Folklore—Cultural Creativity in Process," *Journal of American Folklore*, 116 (459), 4–8.

Bean, Frank D. and Gillian Stevens (2003), *America's Newcomers and the Dynamics of Diversity*. New York: Russell Sage Foundation.

Belch, Michael A. and Laura A. Willis (2002), "Family Decision at the Turn of the Century: Has the Changing Structure of Households Impacted the Family Decision-Making Process?" *Journal of Consumer Behaviour*, 2 (2), 111–24.

Blood, Robert O. and Donald Wolfe (1960), *Husbands and Wives.* New York: The Free Press.

Brown, Wilson (1979), "The Family and Consumer Decision Making: A Cultural View," *Journal of the Academy of Marketing Science*, 7 (4), 335–45.

Brumbaugh, Anne M. and Sonya A. Grier (2013), "Agents of Change: A Scale to Identify Diversity Seekers," *Journal of Public Policy & Marketing*, 32 (Special Issue), 144–55.

Commuri, Suraj and James W. Gentry (2000), "Opportunities for Family Research in Marketing," *Academy of Marketing Science Review*, 8 (accessed October 15, 2012), [available at http://www.amsreview.org/articles/commuri08-2000.pdf].

——— and ——— (2005), "Resource Allocation in Households with Women as Chief Wage Earners," *Journal of Consumer Research*, 32 (September), 185–95.

Craig, C. Samuel and Susan P. Douglas (2006), "Beyond National Culture: Implications of Cultural Dynamics for Consumer Research," *International Marketing Review*, 23 (3), 322–42.

Cross, Samantha N.N. (2007), "For Better or for Worse: The Intersection of Cultures in Binational Homes," in *Advances in Consumer Research*, Vol. 35, A.Y. Lee and D. Soman, eds. Duluth, MN: Association for Consumer Research, 162–65.

——— and Mary C. Gilly (2012), "Cultural Competence, Cultural Capital and Cultural Compensatory Mechanisms in Binational Households," working paper, Iowa State University.

Davis, Harry L. (1970), "Dimensions of Marital Roles in Consumer Decision Making," *Journal of Marketing Research*, 7 (May), 168–77.

——— and Benny P. Rigaux (1974), "Perception of Marital Roles in Decision Processes," *Journal of Consumer Research*, 1 (1), 51–62.

Demangeot, Catherine, Natalie Ross Adkins, Rene Dentiste Mueller, Geraldine Rosa Henderson, Nakeisha S. Ferguson, James M. Mandiberg, et al. (2013), "Toward Intercultural Competency in Multicultural Marketplaces," *Journal of Public Policy & Marketing*, 32 (Special Issue), 156–64.

Epp, Amber M. and Linda L. Price (2008), "Family Identity: A Framework of Identity Interplay in Consumption Practices," *Journal of Consumer Research*, 35 (June), 50–70.

Foner, Nancy (1997), "The Immigrant Family: Cultural Legacies and Cultural Changes," *International Migration Review*, 31 (4, Special Issue: Immigrant Adaptation and Native-Born Responses in the Making of Americans), 961–74.

Ford, John B., Michael S. LaTour, and Tony L. Henthorne (1995), "Perception of Marital Roles in Purchase Decision Processes: A Cross-Cultural Study," *Journal of the Academy of Marketing Science*, 23 (2), 120–31.

Freeman, Linton (1955), "Homogamy in Interethnic Mate Selection," *Sociology and Social Research*, 39, 369–77.

French, John R.P., Jr., and Bertram Raven (1959), "The Bases of Social Power," in *Studies in Social Power*, Dorwin Cartwright, ed. Ann Arbor, MI: Research Center for Group Dynamics, Institute for Social Research, University of Michigan, 150–67.

Gilly, Mary C. and Ben M. Enis (1982), "Recycling the Family Life Cycle: A Proposal for Redefinition," *Advances in Consumer Research*, Vol. 9, Andrew Mitchell, ed. Ann Arbor: Association for Consumer Research, 271–76.

Green, Robert T., Jean-Paul Leonardi, Jena-Louis Chandon, Isabella C.M. Cunningham, Bronis Verhage, and Alain Strazzieri (1983), "Societal Development and Family Purchasing Roles: A Cross-National Study," *Journal of Consumer Research*, 9 (March), 436–42.

Hargadon, Andrew and Robert I. Sutton (1997), "Technology Brokering and Innovation in a Product Development Firm," *Administrative Science Quarterly*, 42 (4), 716–49.

Laslett, Barbara (1973), "The Family as a Public and Private Institution: An Historical Perspective," *Journal of Marriage and the Family*, 35 (3, Special Section: New Social History of the Family), 480–92.

Lau-Gesk, Loraine G. (2003), "Activating Culture Through Persuasion Appeals: An Examination of the Bicultural Consumer," *Journal of Consumer Psychology*, 13 (3), 301–315.

Lauth Bacas, Jutta (2002), "Cross-Border Marriages and the Formation of Transnational Families: A Case Study of Greek–German Couples in Athens," Transnational Communities Programme Working Paper Series (accessed October 15, 2012), [available at www.transcomm.ox.ac.uk/working%20papers/WPTC-02-10%20Bacas.pdf].

Leach, Margaret S. and Dawn O. Brathwaite (1996), "A Binding Tie: Supportive Communication of Family Kinkeepers," *Journal of Applied Communication Research*, 24 (3), 200–216.

Lin, Nan (1999), "Building a Network Theory of Social Capital," *Connections*, 22 (1), 28–51.

Luna, David, Torsten Ringberg, and Laura A. Peracchio (2008), "One Individual, Two Identities: Frame Switching Among Biculturals," *Journal of Consumer Research*, 35 (2), 279–93.

Meng, Xin and Robert G. Gregory (2005), "Intermarriage and the Economic Assimilation of Immigrants," *Journal of Labor Economics*, 23 (1), 135–75.

Murphy, Patrick E. and William A. Staples (1979), "A Modernized Family Life Cycle," *Journal of Consumer Research*, 6 (1), 12–22.

Olson, David H. and Ronald E. Cromwell (1975), "Methodological Issues in Family Power," in *Power in Families*, Ronald E. Cromwell and David H. Olson, eds. New York: Sage Publications, 131–50.

Oswald, Laura R. (1999), "Culture Swapping: Consumption and the Ethnogenesis of Middle-Class Haitian Immigrants," *Journal of Consumer Research*, 25 (March), 303–318.

Peñaloza, Lisa N. (1994), "Atravesando Fronteras/Border Crossings: A Critical Ethnographic Exploration of the Consumer Acculturation of Mexican Immigrants," *Journal of Consumer Research*, 21 (June), 32–54.

——— and Mary C. Gilly (1999), "Marketer Acculturation: The Changer and the Changed," *Journal of Marketing*, 63 (July), 84–104.

Qualls, William J. (1987), "Household Decision Behavior: The Impact of Husbands' and Wives' Sex Role Orientation," *Journal of Consumer Research*, 14 (2), 264–79.

Raven, Bertram H., Richard Centers, and Aroldo Rodrigues (1975), "The Bases of Conjugal Power," in *Power in Families*, Ronald E. Cromwell and David H. Olson, eds. New York: Sage Publications, 217–32.

Rienzo, Cinzia and Carlos Vargas-Silva (2012), "Migrants in the UK: An Overview," *The Migration Observatory*, (May 15), (accessed June 30, 2012), [available at http://migrationobservatory.ox.ac.uk/briefings/migrants-uk-overview].

Rosenthal, Carolyn J. (1985), "Kinkeeping in the Familial Division of Labor," *Journal of Marriage and Family*, 47 (4), 965–74.

Rushdie, Salman (1990), *In Good Faith*. London: Granta.

Spiro, Rosann L. (1983), "Persuasion in Family Decision-Making," *Journal of Consumer Research*, 9 (4), 393–402.

Stewart, Charles (1999), "Syncretism and Its Synonyms: Reflections on Cultural Mixture," *Diacritics*, 29 (Autumn), 40–62.

U.S. Census Bureau (2010), "2010 Census Data," [available at http://www.census.gov/2010census/data].

Wagner, Janet and Sherman Hanna (1983), "The Effectiveness of Family Life Cycle Variables in Consumer Expenditure Research," *Journal of Consumer Research*, 10 (3), 281–91.

Wallendorf, Melanie and Michael D. Reilly (1983), "Ethnic Migration, Assimilation, and Consumption," *Journal of Consumer Research*, 10 (3), 292–302.

Wamwara-Mbugua, L. Wakiuru (2007), "An Investigation of Household Decision Making Among Immigrants," in *Advances in Consumer Research*, Vol. 34, Gavan Fitzsimons and Vicki Morwitz, eds. Valdosta, GA: Association for Consumer Research, 180–86.

Wasserman, Stanley and Katherine Faust (1994), *Social Network Analysis*. Cambridge, UK: Cambridge University Press.

Webster, Cynthia (1994), "Effects of Hispanic Ethnic Identification on Marital Roles in the Purchase Decision-Process," *Journal of Consumer Research*, 21 (2), 319–31.

——— (2000), "Is Spousal Decision Making a Culturally Situated Phenomenon?" *Psychology & Marketing*, 17 (12), 1035–58.

Williams, Paul (2002), "The Competent Boundary Spanner," *Public Administration*, 80 (1), 103–124.

Wolfe, Donald M. (1959), "Power and Authority in the Family," in *Studies in Social Power*, Dorwin Cartwright, ed. Ann Arbor, MI: Research Center for Group Dynamics, Institute for Social Research, University of Michigan, 99–117.

Critical Thinking

1. Why do you think the authors have chosen to use the term "binational family" instead of referring to these families using some other terms mentioned in the article such as bicultural, biethnic, or interethnic?

2. How do you think being a binational family influences family dynamics and interactions between couples and family members?

3. What are special considerations and things to keep in mind when working with binational families?

Create Central

www.mhhe.com/createcentral

Internet References

Family and Culture
http://familyandculture.com/index.html

World Fact Book
https://www.cia.gov/library/publications/the-world-factbook

World Family Map
http://worldfamilymap.org/2014/about

SAMANTHA N.N. CROSS is Assistant Professor of Marketing, College of Business, Iowa State University. MARY C. GILLY is Professor of Marketing, Paul Merage School of Business, University of California, Irvine. Financial support to the first author through the Ray Watson Doctoral Fellowship at the University of California, Irvine; the Academy of Marketing Science Jane K. Fenyo Best Paper Award for Student Research; and the ACR/Sheth Foundation Dissertation Grant is gratefully acknowledged.

Article

Prepared by: Patricia Hrusa Williams,
University of Maine at Farmington

Matches Made on Earth
Why Family Values Are Human Values

NANCIE L. GONZALEZ

Learning Outcomes

After reading this article, you will be able to:

- Recognize the social construction of "family values" in families and society.

- Identify the impact of religion in how family values are constructed.

- Illustrate the diversity of family values.

The term "family values," the importance of which fundamentalist Christians have been preaching for decades, continues to permeate religious and political printed matter and discussions in the United States today. The conservatives' concept of family values is generally characterized by abstinence from sex until marriage, which is then entered into with a like-minded individual of the opposite sex and is thereafter permanent and free from adultery. It is also expected that children will ensue, either through birth or adoption. In line with these prescriptions, proponents of traditional family values foment prejudice and activism against divorce, abortion, homosexuality, single-parent families, and even the choice not to have children. The fact that their efforts have become more intensive and intrusive lately can be explained, I believe, by the increasingly tolerant and diverse sexual, racial, and religious views and behavior of the American public at large.

The problem isn't that some people espouse conservative ideals of family, but that they promulgate them as the only way to live, looking down upon and often demonizing those with other values. Indeed, the family values crowd often refers to any who oppose its agenda as having no values at all. They support their ideals as based upon divine "truth" by quoting the Bible and rejecting scientific evidence that supports a different set of explanations for the existence and history of humankind. They repeatedly argue that more general social acceptance of other ways to live will endanger their own. This fear has inspired efforts for decades to influence our school boards and our local, state, and national governments to change text books, curricula, and the law to reflect socially conservative views. When these fail, parents turn to private schools or home schooling, and later enroll their offspring in one of the several conservative Christian colleges whose faculties and administrative personnel are vetted to make sure their values are religiously and politically "correct." The fact that some of these schools are admittedly training their graduates to seek public office or employment in state and national venues is further evidence of their intolerance, and their misunderstanding of the nature of society and culture.

Most of the idealistic family values held by conservative Christians today are not now nor have they ever been characteristic of the world at large. Statistics, as well as more informal evidence suggest that the so-called nontraditional behaviors they condemn are now common throughout the United States and much of the industrialized world, often despite laws forbidding them. Furthermore, such behaviors have existed in many parts of the world for centuries. The problem I see for humanists is to convince much of the conservative American public that these prejudices and fears are unwarranted on at least two grounds: 1) family values are the products of human sociocultural conditions, and cannot be attributed to either divine or biological imperatives, and 2) pluralism in marriage and family values should be expected in any large twenty-first century society as a result of technological advances that have made globalization both possible and perhaps inevitable.

If neither a deity nor our genes are wholly determinative, we must ask our conservative counterparts: what accounts for the vast panorama of intimate human bonding practices, either in the past, or today?

It may be useful to consider what social and biological scientists have concluded about the origin and nature of marriage and the family. All animals must struggle for self and species survival, which demands food, defense, reproduction, and care of newborns until they can care for themselves. Both genetics and learning are involved for all species, but only humans have created *social institutions* to help themselves in these endeavors. By social, I mean any kind of bonding with other humans to share in the food quest; to ward off environmental and other dangers; to reproduce, nurture, and educate the young; and to provide physical and psychological well-being for themselves, their children, and their neighbors. The specific characteristics of these institutions vary with the society; trial and error must have occurred over time, and some societies failed to persist. But those institutions that worked well became customary, "traditional," and thus value-laden. Children would be taught by example and by experience. But traditions change as cultural evolution occurs and as societies grow, develop new technologies, and increasingly influence each other. The young and the most pragmatically minded are likely to change with the times, yet there are always some who cling to the older ways—not that this is, in itself, dysfunctional, for the "old ways" still serve some purposes, and sometimes are reinstated or reinterpreted by succeeding generations.

Although marriage and the family have existed in all human societies and form the primary roots of all the particulars of family values everywhere, different societies have constructed their own definitions of incest; permissible marriage partners; appropriate sexual behavior before, during, and after marriage; "normal" and alternate sexual orientations; ideal post-marital residence; and composition of the ideal family and household, including what to do if too many children "appear," or if conception occurs at an inconvenient time. For example, marriages that we likely consider incestuous but others don't include marriage between first cousins, especially patrilateral parallel cousin marriage (where the children of two brothers marry) seen in some parts of the Middle East and Africa. Among some Bedouin cultures, there was even a stated preference for such a marriage. Similarly, cross-cousin marriage is widespread in many "tribal" societies, including the Yanomamo in South America.

Different societies have constructed their own definitions of incest appropriate sexual behavior, "normal" and alternate sexual orientations, and ideal post-marital residence.

Formal bonding or marriage rituals probably developed in very early human societies, since it was important then as now to confer legitimacy of the children in relation to membership in whatever social unit was pertinent (tribe, clan, patrilineage, matrilineage, nation-state, religious group, and so forth). Formal marriage also establishes rights of inheritance of property, as well as social position. In many societies, including our own, women, and to a lesser extent, men, are treated like adolescents until they marry.

Neither religious nor biological explanations for conservative family values take into account the fact that even the notion of two sexes is not, and probably never has been, biologically correct. We have no way to know whether prehistoric societies recognized inborn sexual variations, what the frequency of such variations might have been, or whether "different" newborns would even have been allowed to live. However, colonial travelers to America noted that some native cultures recognized the existence of some among them whose bodies, psyches, or both weren't comfortable living in either of the two primary gender roles of male or female. They called these people "two spirits" and provided a socially acceptable niche for them.

Homosexuality of different types has been documented throughout Western civilization since at least the ancient Greeks. However, only in the current century has the recognition developed in Western societies that sexual orientation is not merely a matter of differences in genitalia, and that it isn't a mere matter of choice. The growing acceptance of the idea that sexuality and sexual identity should not alter one's basic humanity and civil rights has led to changes in the laws in many countries, including the decriminalization of certain sex practices and the legalization of same-sex marriage. At the time of this writing, five U.S. states as well as the District of Columbia now allow gay and lesbian couples to marry, and in three more states same-sex marriages are recognized but not performed legally. Nine other states recognize certain legal rights of same-sex couples through civil unions, domestic partnerships, or reciprocal beneficiary laws. Still, these arrangements are only gradually becoming acceptable to the general public, and since same-sex marriage hasn't been documented as legal in any society in history, we shouldn't be surprised that it is and will remain controversial for some time. Nevertheless, it should now be added to the evidence we have for different kinds of marriage and family institutions.

Studies of pre-agricultural and pre-industrial societies, as well as continuing historical research over the past century have documented such a variety of marriage customs and rules that a God hypothesis would almost have to suggest an anthropological deity who understood that no single practice should be imposed upon all. However, the following discussion focuses not on the supernatural, but the natural ways in which human pair bonding and family formation have occurred. These include *monogamy* as the permanent or lifetime union of two persons, usually, but not always, of opposite sex. This was probably the most common marriage form for Paleolithic foragers, as was the nuclear family. However, that small unit had affinal relatives (we call them in-laws), some of whom lived together in what anthropologists call a band. As the noted nineteenth-century anthropologist Edward B. Tylor suggested, early societies had to "marry out or die out." Institutions promoting reproduction and care of the young were crucial to social survival.

Polygamy is often confused with *polygyny—the* union of one man with several wives—but polygamy also includes *polyandry—one* woman with several husbands. All of these forms, especially polygyny, were more typical of larger, more advanced societies based upon pastoralism, agriculture, or both. The advantages were to enlarge the family unit by drawing in more nubile and fertile women, while at the same time providing care for those who might no longer have been able to bear children. If the sex ratio, for whatever reason, was unbalanced, as it was among early converts to the Church of the Latter Day Saints, polygyny also was a way for new single young women to be immediately drawn in to an existing family. The custom was formally abolished by the Mormons in the early part of the twentieth century, but the family values created more than one hundred years earlier have held on for some.

Polyandry has been fairly rare, practiced primarily in the Himalayan regions of Nepal, Tibet, India, and Bhutan. It has also occurred in the Canadian Arctic, Nigeria, and Sri Lanka, and is known to have been present in some pre-contact Polynesian societies, though probably only among higher caste women. Some forms of polyandry appear to be associated with a perceived need to retain aristocratic titles or agricultural lands within kin groups, and/or because of the frequent absence, for long periods, of a man from the household. In Tibet the practice is particularly popular among the priestly Skye class but also among poor small farmers who can ill afford to divide their small holdings. As to the latter variety, as some males return to the household, others leave for a long time, so that there is usually one husband present. Fraternal polyandry occurs when multiple brothers share a common wife. This occurs in the pastoral Toda community in Southern India. Similarly, among the Tibetan Nyinba, anthropologist Nancy Levine described the strong bond between brothers as essential in creating a strong sense of family unity and keeping land holdings intact, thus preserving socioeconomic standing.

Group marriage involving multiple members of both sexes has sometimes been averred to have existed; however, there appears to be no reputable description of it in the anthropological or historical literature. In recent years a movement has arisen that produces something very similar to the idea of group marriage; the term *polyamory* has been offered to describe plural simultaneous attachments between and among people, including lesbian, gay, bisexual, and transgendered individuals (LGBTs). From the perspective of this writing, this may or may not be new under the sun, but it doesn't (yet?) constitute marriage.

Serial monogamy is perhaps the most common type of marriage known in much of the world today. Individuals in such unions may have only one spouse but, shedding that one, they may contract any number later—again, usually only one at a time, except in those societies that still accept and approve polygyny. Serial monogamy depends on the existence of easy

divorce laws or more informal practices, such as what is generally called "living together." *Domestic partnerships* by law may or may not be considered marriages. In the United States persons of both the same and opposite sex have for some time entered into such unions, but those of opposite sex partners have generally received greater social acceptance, even without the legal protections, status, or financial benefits society offers to married couples.

Why do some people choose not to abide by the marriage rules of their own society? Obviously, reasons vary. Some think a trial marriage to be a good idea; others simply don't care about rules of any kind. A few may be prohibited from marrying because one or the other is already bound by a previous, legitimate union which can't be formally dissolved. And while others have simply adopted a more individualized lifestyle, some are still convinced of the values of marriage in a previous age (as in polygyny). In short, the choice of whether and whom to marry has increasingly been seen as a personal, individual decision, and it is no longer important to the functioning of the modern industrial state that all persons marry, unless they wish the state to adjudicate property or child custody rights.

Co-residence of the partners and the creation of a household are usually, but not always, typical in any kind of marriage. Yet households vary enormously in both size and composition, and usually, but not always, include some kind of family. In societies in which men must find work through short or long term emigration, *consanguineal households* have arisen that contain no married pair. Such a household is most often headed by an elderly woman, together with some of her sons and daughters and their children. The marital partners of these co-residential adults live elsewhere—often with their own mothers. The United States today is also seeing an increase in extended families moving in together due to economic constraints, as well as "single" parents who live with a partner.

A study by the Pew Research Center released in November, titled, "The Decline of Marriage and Rise of New Families," revealed changing attitudes about what constitutes a family. Among survey respondents, 86 percent said a single parent and child constitute a family; 80 percent considered an unmarried couple living together with a child a family; and 63 percent said a gay or lesbian couple raising a child is a family.

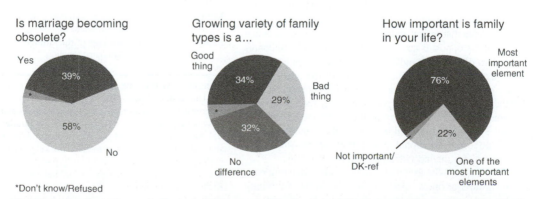

Is marriage becoming obsolete?
Yes 39%
No 58%
*
*Don't know/Refused

Growing variety of family types is a...
Good thing 34%
Bad thing 29%
No difference 32%
*

How important is family in your life?
Most important element 76%
One of the most important elements 22%
Not important/ DK-ref

Data from the Pew Research Center's 2010 survey, "The Decline of Marriage and Rise of New Families"

Obviously, the "traditional family" so highly valued by the religious right can't be considered as the typical American household today. Instead, the term "family" has taken on a much broader meaning to incorporate various combinations of persons of different genders, sexual orientations, and familial or non-familial relationships living together, as in the refrigerator magnet that proclaims, "Friends Are the Family You Choose for Yourself."

We still, and always will, value the need to bond with others. Kinship remains one major way to do so, but social and geographical mobility have lessened its role as the most important tie that binds. Today it may be similar age groups, vocations, or philosophical views on the nature of the universe or of the hereafter that form the basis of relationships. People will continue to find or invent ways to get together, live together, and share what is important in life with others.

D oes this mean that marriage and the family as we know it will likely disappear in the near future as Focus on the Family fears? Does the fact that many young people of various genders and sexual identities choose not to marry or stay married, nor to form traditional households augur the demise, or even the diminution in value of these institutions in our society? Should the legal sanctioning of same-sex marriage in any way affect the dignity of opposite-sex couples joined by similar ceremonies? I think not. Society has, for the most part, already accepted the newer bonding patterns described above—at least for persons of opposite sex.

Taking away any social stigma, LGBT couples will likely experience the same joys and struggles in marriage as straight couples do, thus proving that sexual orientation is irrelevant when it comes to pair-bonding. Although the ethnographic and historical evidence doesn't confirm that true marriages were ever legally sanctioned between persons thought to be of the same sex, present-day reminiscences and folklore suggest that love, sex, and companionship were known and accepted among them, and that untold numbers of people have lived in happy unions with persons perceived to be of the same sex for perhaps hundreds of years.

F inally, what about love and companionship? It is only in modern Western society that these have become the very most important components of marriage. There is no evidence that these occur only between spouses of opposing sex or gender. The idea that sexual activity is only appropriate between members of the opposite sex is a product of our cultural conditioning, born of the thousands of years when it was important to keep people focused on finding a mate of the opposite sex to ensure continued reproduction. The need for population control, rather than survival of the species or of any specific society, makes this value irrelevant today, as it does for the idea that all marriages should produce children. Also, the extended family of yore is no longer functional in industrial society—today one does indeed marry the individual, not the whole family.

Sex is no longer seen as a major reward for contracting marriage, regardless of one's sexual orientation. Tests of virginity

have disappeared as premarital sex with more than one partner has become more common and seems to be a largely irrelevant factor for many marriages, including the first. Yet, the fact that homosexual and lesbian partners engage in sexual activities without marriage is always seen as a disgrace, even for many of them who may share the traditional religious notion that unmarried sex is a sin.

As we continue to consider the nature and causes of the diversity of family values in the post-industrial, individualistic, global society in which we now live, I hope that the single set of specific rules of behavior promulgated by Focus on the Family and other such organizations comes to be seen as outmoded, even by the so-called moral majority. As the U.S. Constitution has always insisted, all citizens should have equal rights, so for those who find the "old ways" to their taste, we should wish them well, but plead with them not to damage the lives of those who choose to live or even to think differently, nor to forget that our nation was founded by outsiders and has continually accepted those from other cultures, and that we have, in fact, valued and profited by our diversity.

Critical Thinking

1. What are some of your family values? Where do your family values come from?

2. Do you feel that family values are a naturally occurring phenomenon or are they learned from society and culture?

3. After reading this article, are there some family values from your family of origin that differ now that you are in college?

4. What do you think about the author's question about "marriage and the family as we know it" disappearing?

Create Central

www.mhhe.com/createcentral

Internet References

World Family Map
http://worldfamilymap.org/2013
Australian Institute of Family Studies
www.aifs.gov.au
Feminist Perspectives on Reproduction and the Family
http://plato.stanford.edu/entries/feminism-family
Kearl's Guide to the Sociology of the Family
www.trinity.edu/MKEARL/family.html

NANCIE L. GONZALEZ is Professor Emeritus of Anthropology at the University of Maryland. She has conducted ethnographic and ethnohistorical research on marriage and family patterns in a number of societies, including the American Southwest, the Caribbean, Central America, China, and the West Bank and has published widely since the 1960s. She is presently working on a memoir dealing with changes in marriage and family patterns as revealed in letters and diaries from five generations of her own family. She lives in Richmond, Virginia.

Gonzalez, Nancie L. From *The Humanist*, January/February 2011, pp. 14–17. Copyright © 2011 by Nancie L. Gonzalez. Reprinted by permission of the author.

Unit 2

UNIT

Prepared by: Patricia Hrusa Williams, *University of Maine at Farmington*

Exploring and Establishing Relationships

By and large, we are social animals, and as such, we seek out meaningful connections with other humans. John Bowlby, Mary Ainsworth, and others have proposed that this drive toward deep connections is biologically based and is at the core of what it means to be human. However it plays out in childhood and adulthood, the need for connection, to love and be loved, is a powerful force moving us to establish and maintain close relationships. As we explore various possibilities, we engage in the complex business of relationship building. In doing this, many processes occur simultaneously. Messages are sent and received; differences are negotiated; assumptions and expectations are or are not met. The ultimate goals are closeness and continuity. How we feel about others and what we see as essential to these relationships play important roles as we work to establish and maintain these connections.

In this unit, we look at factors that underlie the establishment and beginning stages of relationships. Among the topics to be covered in this unit are explorations of factors that influence how and why connections are built. Factors explored include biology, emotions, physical attraction, sex, personality, and the context in which relationships are established and developed. Changing views and practices in sex education, mating, relationships, marriage, commitment, family formation, procreation, and early family development are explored. Together, the unit tries to investigate and understand the evolution of intimate and family relationships in our ever-changing society.

Article   Prepared by: Patricia Hrusa Williams, *University of Maine at Farmington*

What Schools Should Teach Kids About Sex

In America, the subject is often limited to "a smattering of information about [humans'] reproductive organs and a set of stern warnings about putting them to use."

Jessica Lahey

Learning Outcomes

After reading this article, you will be able to:

- Understand the role of the federal government, states, local entities, and public schools in sex education.

- Identify the differences between the three basic forms of sex education offered in the United States: comprehensive, abstinence-based, and abstinence-only.

- Explain the reasons why sex education is such a controversial topic in the United States.

"There is probably no subject that has posed greater headaches to teachers than sex education," writes NYU history and education professor Jonathan Zimmerman in his new book, *Too Hot to Handle: A Global History of Sex Education.* And no other topic illustrates the complexity and emotion that lies at the heart of the debates about parental, local, and federal control over education.

While every state offers some form of sex education, the substance and style of the given curriculum can range from comprehensive to significantly circumscribed, largely depending on local politics and beliefs. In many of America's school districts, sex education looks a lot like the current "global norm," which is described by Zimmerman in his book as, "a smattering of information about their reproductive organs and a set of stern warnings about putting them to use."

The question of who should be teaching sex education, and what form that instruction should take, is increasingly problematic in this diverse and often ideologically divided nation. There's little agreement on what should be included in sex education courses, let alone how, and at what ages it should be taught. The author Alice Dreger, writing for the *Pacific Standard,* pointed out that 44 percent of Americans mistakenly believe sex education is already covered by the Common Core standard. So, she asks, "Why Isn't Sex Education a Part of the Common Core?" On the other hand, sex-advice columnist and author Dan Savage suggests that if the country can't offer effective sex education, maybe it should be looking to families, the Internet, or even independent sex instructors such as Dr. Karen Rayne of Unhushed, or Amy Lang of Birds + Bees + Kids.

Whatever the issue, American adolescents need comprehensive sex education, well, because American adolescents have sex. According to the CDC, almost half—47 percent—of all U.S. high school students have had sexual intercourse, 34 percent of them during the previous three months. And 41 percent of those kids admit they did not use a condom the last time they had sex even though such contraception is highly effective against pregnancy and the spread of sexually transmitted infections such as HIV. That statistic might help explain why the U.S. has the highest teen pregnancy rate in the developed world and why America's adolescents account for nearly half of the 19 million new cases of STIs each year—even though, as the CDC indicates, teens represent only a fourth of the nation's sexually active people.

It appears that America isn't alone in neglecting the sexual education of its teens. That's evidenced by findings from the

U.K.'s third national Survey of Sexual Attitudes and Lifestyles, which was conducted among 4,000 adolescents and young adults and released today by the country's Medical Research Council. The report reveals that in Britain, teens learn about sex from (in descending order of popularity) school, friends, the media, the Internet, and pornography. Despite access to these types of "information," approximately seven in 10 adolescents felt that they should have known more about sex before their first experience having intercourse. Specifically, they wished they knew more about contraception, how to reduce the health risks of sexual behavior, and "how to make sex more satisfying."

Meanwhile, the list of the most recently asked questions on Scarleteen.com, one of the most popular sex-education sites on the Internet, shows that these are the concerns of the 1 billion users (54 percent of whom are from the U.S.) who apparently visited the site since its launch in 2006:

> (Scarleteen's slogan? "Sex education for the real world: Inclusive, comprehensive and smart sexuality information and help for teens and 20s.")

The sex topics British teens want to know more about, and answers to the questions Scarleteen and Savage receive weekly, are inconsistently taught in U.S. schools—probably due to uneven requirements and the decentralization of policymaking. Because virtually every aspect of education, let alone that involving sex, does not fall under the control of the federal government, state, and more often local, entities decide what goes in—and what stays out—of the classroom. While every state engages in some form of sex education for public school children, only 13 of them have laws requiring that, if such a curriculum is offered, it must be medically accurate and based on scientific evidence. Meanwhile, just 18 states and the District of Columbia require that schools "provide instruction on contraception." While 26 states and the D.C. teach about healthy sexuality and decision-making, 19 states require that school-based sex education emphasize the importance of abstinence until marriage. Many of these standards, moreover, are open to interpretation.

Sex education takes three basic forms in the U.S.: comprehensive, abstinence-based, and abstinence-only. The comprehensive approach, according to the Sexuality Education and Information Council of the United States, provides "age- and developmentally appropriate sexual health information" that is medically accurate, informed by scientific evidence, and sensitive to the needs of all young people. Topics covered by such a curriculum include "human development, abstinence, contraception, disease and pregnancy prevention, as well as skill development for healthy relationships and decision-making."

Abstinence-based sex education, on the other hand, specifically promotes abstinence while providing some or all of the elements of the comprehensive approach; abstinence-only models, of course, teach only abstinence until marriage. Abstinence-only curricula don't provide any information on contraception beyond its failure rates.

Comprehensive programs are slowly gaining ground in the U.S. Still, abstinence-only programs have been well-funded over the years, beginning with the Reagan Administration and the federal block grant for maternal and child health services under Title V of the Social Security Act—despite evidence that these programs are ineffective when it comes to better sexual health. According to multiple peer-reviewed studies, abstinence-only programs do not delay the average age of the first time a person has sexual intercourse, nor do they prevent the spread of STIs or reduce the number of sexual partners someone has during adolescence. The peer-reviewed *Journal of Adolescent Health* came out against abstinence-only education in a 2006 position paper, stating that while abstinence is a healthy choice for teens, "Providing 'abstinence only' or 'abstinence until marriage' messages as a sole option for teenagers is flawed from scientific and medical ethics viewpoints."

Many advocates and experts agree. As Savage, a longtime critic of abstinence-only education, recently told me in a phone interview, he supports having sex education in schools but believes "[the country] should stop pretending what passes for sex education is sex education." Savage has been commentator and sex advice columnist since 1991, both in his Savage Love column and his extremely popular "Savage Love" podcast. He's thus familiar with the full range of questions Americans have about sex. Savage agrees that the topics most school programs cover, such as reproductive biology, are important [but] emphasized that curricula often ignore topics such as consent, pleasure, and effective communication about sex.

So I asked Savage to elaborate on what a comprehensive sex-education curriculum should cover:

> We should be teaching the real things that can trip people up, things that can ruin people's lives or traumatize them, like what is and isn't consent, and what is and isn't on the menu, and what are you or are you not comfortable with, and how do you advocate for yourself, and how do you draw someone out and solicit their active consent so that you don't accidentally traumatize someone? We need to talk about sex for pleasure, which is 99.99 percent of the sex that people have, and that's 99.99 percent of what's not covered in even what liberals and progressives would look at and say, "Oh, look at that good sex ed!"

Savage claims that despite the nation's outward appearance of progress on matters such as marriage and gender equality, "Sex education has gone backward. When it comes to our children, there is more information and more truthfulness out there about sex, sexuality, gender identity, everything, than there has ever been. Social conservatives know they can't undo the sexual revolution, or unmake gay people, or roll back women's empowerment—but they have it in their heads that they can reverse engineer the future by raising today's children in ignorance."

To illustrate the consequences of such ignorance, Savage analogized the state of sex education today to a driver's education class that focuses exclusively on the mechanics of the internal combustion engine, with no mention of brakes, steering, red lights, and stop signs. "That's sex ed in America. We hand kids the keys to the car, and when they drive straight into walls, we say, 'See? See? If we'd only kept them a little more ignorant, this wouldn't be happening!'"

But for Zimmerman, conservatives aren't the only culprits responsible for the country's failure to progress on sex education: "Dan is right to be sanguine about any kind of real substantial change, but it's actually because of our country's diversity. The more diverse the world becomes, and the more it globalizes, the faster people and ideas move across borders, the more difficult [agreeing how to teach] sex ed becomes."

Even proponents of progressive, comprehensive sex education disagree about what phenomena are hindering its development. While some advocates may like the idea of a comprehensive national standard for the subject, such as Alice Dreger's vision of sex education as a Common Core standard, Zimmerman believes allowing schools to experiment with content or format would be key to promoting innovation.

The United States might be one of the places where we will see a little bit more variation and experimentation, and that's because we *don't* have a national system. There are compelling reasons to think about national standards and national curriculum, but where sex ed is concerned, you have to think about some of the downsides of that, too, which is how it might inhibit experimentation and variation.

That experimentation and variation flourishes in independent sex-education classes around the country, such as those that Rayne teaches at the Austin-based Unhushed. Rayne, an author, sex educator, and the chair of the National Sex Ed Conference, is doggedly optimistic in her predictions about the future of sex education in America, largely because she knows firsthand about the demand for progressive,

comprehensive curricula. "I do think we've come a long way," she said in a phone interview. "I've seen a lot of change that's happened since I started in sex education [in 2007]. People are much more open to it. The laws are improving—I would not say that they are great—but they are improving. The Texas Freedom Network does really good research on sex education in Texas and its findings show a clear trajectory toward openness, honesty, and fact-based information, so I do see that happening here and also nationally."

Zimmerman doubts a comprehensive national sex ed curriculum will ever happen. To him, the U.S. is simply too diverse for one solution to fit all. As he concludes in *Too Hot to Handle*, sex education serves as "a mirror, reflecting all the flux and diversity—and the confusion and instability—of sex and youth in our globalized world." No matter how rapidly sex education evolves, he believes, it will always be playing catch-up—to the media, to the Internet, and to everything adolescents talk about when adults are not around.

Critical Thinking

1. Why is sex education such a controversial topic in the United States?

2. What do you think should be the basic components of a sex education program which is offered in public schools in the United States?

3. Sex education has moved from the classroom to the web. Review at least one site listed here (Go Ask Alice, Scarleteen, Unhushed). Identify strengths and weaknesses of web-based sex education resources.

Internet References

Go Ask Alice!
   http://www.goaskalice.columbia.edu
AVERTing HIV and AIDS: Sex Education That Works
   http://www.avert.org/sex-education-works.htm
Scarleteen
   http://www.scarleteen.com
State Policies on Sex Education in Schools
   http://www.ncsl.org/research/health/state-policies-on-sex-education-in-schools.aspx
Unhushed
   http://www.unhushed.net

Article   Prepared by: Patricia Hrusa Williams, *University of Maine at Farmington*

Sex and the Class of 2020: How Will Hookups Change?

CONOR FRIEDERSDORF

Learning Outcomes

After reading this article, you will be able to:

- Understand the legal definition of affirmative consent.

- Analyze how affirmative consent law may impact the sexual behavior of college students.

- Recognize gender differences and stereotypes regarding consent, date rape, and sexual behavior.

As California's colleges and universities adjust to a new state law mandating a standard of "affirmative consent" in sexual assault and rape cases—as well as campus judicial proceedings with a "preponderance of the evidence" standard of guilt—observers are trying to anticipate how these policy changes will affect the lived culture of sexual acts among students, most in their late teens or early 20s. The law's effect on campus culture will determine whether it advances the ends sought by supporters, who hope to reduce the incidence of sex crimes. Yet there is broad disagreement about whether and how sexual culture will adapt to the new regime. Even those who agree that the law is good or bad disagree about its likely effects.

What follows are some of the wildly divergent forecasts, some hopeful, others cautionary. Taken together, they illuminate different notions of human nature, the reach of public policy, and what life on California's many college campuses is actually like. The scenarios that they anticipate are not always mutually exclusive.

It Will Be Harder to Get Away with Rape

In the 2008 essay collection *Yes Means Yes!: Visions of Female Sexual Power and a World Without Rape*, contributor Jill Filipovic captured something very much like what supporters of California law hope sex on campus will look like in the near future.

"Plenty of men are able to grasp the idea that sex should be entered into joyfully and enthusiastically by both partners, and that an absence of 'no' isn't enough—'yes' should be the baseline requirement," she wrote. "And women are not empty vessels to be fucked or not fucked; we're sexual actors who should absolutely have the ability to say yes when we want it, just like men, and should feel safe saying no—even if we've been drinking, even if we've slept with you before, even if we're wearing tight jeans, even if we're naked in bed with you. Anti-rape activists further understand that men need to feel empowered to say no also. If women have the ability to fully and freely say yes, and if we establish a model of enthusiastic consent instead of just 'no means no,' it would be a lot harder for men to get away with rape. It would be a lot harder to argue that there's a 'gray area.' It would be a lot harder to push the idea that 'date rape' is less serious than 'real' rape, that women who are assaulted by acquaintances were probably teases, that what is now called 'date rape' used to just be called seduction."

Sex Will Be Hotter and More Enjoyable

There is a long history, Ann Friedman writes in *New York*, of young women having sex "that's consensual but not really much fun," and as long a history "of their male partners walking home the next morning thinking, 'Nailed it.'" She believes that "these droves of sexually dissatisfied young women will be unwitting beneficiaries" of California's new law, because "confirming consent leads to much hotter sex." She doesn't anticipate that the law will thwart rapists, "who clearly don't care about consent, be it verbal or nonverbal." But she believes that "most young men . . . *are* worried about inadvertently doing something in bed that their partner doesn't welcome" and "actively thinking about whether their partner is enjoying herself." As a result, they'll now find life "easier for both them and the women they sleep with," because the law "creates a compelling reason for both parties to speak up and talk about what they like. In essence, the new law forces universities—and the rest of us—to acknowledge that *women like sex*. Especially sex with a partner who wants to talk about what turns them on."

Sex Will Be Scary and Anxiety-Inducing

If implemented as intended, California's affirmative-consent law will intrude on "the most private and intimate of adult acts," Ezra Klein posits. It will settle "like a cold winter on college campuses, throwing everyday sexual practice into doubt," creating "a haze of fear and confusion over what counts as consent" and causing men "to feel a cold spike of fear when they begin a sexual encounter." Meanwhile, "colleges will fill with cases in which campus boards convict young men (and, occasionally, young women) . . . for genuinely ambiguous situations" in cases that "feel genuinely unclear and maybe even unfair." Klein is a supporter of the law. His followup article on the *culture* of affirmative consent is worth your while.

Hookup Culture Will Wither under Neo-Victorianism

Heather MacDonald describes affirmative-consent laws and the activist movement that produced them as "a bizarre hybrid of liberationist and traditionalist values" that "carefully preserves the prerogative of no-strings-attached sex" but adds "legalistic caveats that allow females to revert at will to a stance of offended virtue." She regards the "assumption of transparent contractual intention" to be "laughably out of touch with reality," and believes it implicitly treats women as "so helpless and passive that they should not even be assumed to have the strength or capacity to say 'no'" to stop unwanted sexual encounters, ushering in "a neo-Victorian ethos which makes the male the sole guardian of female safety."

Judging that the policies ushered in by this neo-Victorian ethos misunderstand sex and will take the fun out of it, she tells her fellow conservatives, "What's not to like? Leave laments about the inhibition of campus sex to *Reason* magazine." As she sees it, "If one-sided litigation risk results in boys taking a vow of celibacy until graduation, there is simply no loss whatsoever to society and only gain to individual character. Such efforts at self-control were made before, and can be made again."

Another conservative, Conn Carroll, reaches a closely related conclusion. "If you are in a committed relationship there is very little chance each new amorous encounter with your partner will result in hard feelings either way," he declares. "But if you are constantly switching partners, each new pairing is a roll of the dice. You have no idea how each woman will react the next morning. If you sleep around there are simply way more opportunities for things to blow up in your face."

Misogyny on Campus Will Increase

Like supporters of affirmative-consent laws, Ross Douthat of *The New York Times* doesn't anticipate that disciplinary cases springing from them will be particularly common, at least not enough to affect the behavior of the average student. "It seems very unlikely that any campus policy is suddenly going to make assault allegations commonplace, in a way that would have them intruding frequently into the social life of the typical college-going male," he writes. "Instead, 'yes means yes' will create a kind of black swan situation, where only *every once in a while* a man gets expelled for rape under highly ambiguous circumstances. And because the injustices or possible injustices will be rare, that 'every once in while' will not actually have much of a deterrent effect on men confronted with an opportunity for a drunken hook-up, in the same way that other very occasional disastrous consequences of binge drinking (e.g., death) seem remote to young men (or young women) who head out to get hammered on a typical Saturday night."

But he isn't arguing that there will be no significant cultural impact. Rather, he believes college males will react sort of like cable news viewers who develop persecution complexes:

It will be a distant-seeming outrage that mostly feeds a sense of grievance and persecution among the men who might (but mostly won't) suffer unjust treatment at the university's hands. Which means that rather than being a spur to some sort of reborn chivalry or new-model code of male decency, it will mostly encourage the kind of toxic persecution fantasies that already circulate in the more misogynistic reaches of male culture. See, *the feminazis really are out to get us,* the argument will go, and in bro lore the stories of men railroaded off campus won't be seen as cautionary tales; they'll be seen as war stories, martyrologies (in which even actual, clear-as-day predators are given the benefit of the doubt), the latest battle in the endless struggle between the *Animal House* gang and Dean Wormer . . . reincarnated now, in our more egalitarian feminist era, as a castrating Nurse Ratched.

The new standard of consent, in this scenario, will be neither reasonable enough to be embraced as a model nor consistently punitive enough to scare men away from drunken wooing. Instead, it will have a randomness, an arbitrariness, and an occasional absurdity that will encourage a mix of resentment and resistance. As such, it will lock in an aspect of contemporary sexual culture that social conservatives probably don't talk enough about: The kind of toxic misogyny that feminists rightly call out and critique, but that also exists in a kind of twisted symbiosis with certain aspects of feminist ideology–answering overzealous political correctness with reactionary transgressiveness, bureaucratic pieties with deliberate blasphemy, ideologies of gender with performative machismo.

Sexual Harassment Will Change

Hanna Rosin's *Atlantic* cover story on sexting among teens includes a passage about what prompts one young person to send a naked photo to another at one high school: "Boys and girls were equally likely to have sent a sext, but girls were much more likely to have been asked to—68 percent had been," she wrote. "Plenty of girls just laugh off the requests. When a boy asked Olivia, who graduated last year from Louisa County High, 'What are you wearing?,' she told me she wrote back, 'Stinky track shorts and my Virginity Rocks T-shirt.' A boy asked another student for a picture, so she sent him a smiling selfie. 'I didn't mean your face,' he wrote back, so she sent him one of her foot. But boys can be persistent—like, 20-or-30-texts-in-a-row persistent. 'If we were in a dark room, what would we do?' 'I won't show it to anyone else.' 'You're only sending it to me.' 'I'll delete it right after.'"

Today's male high-schooler pestering a classmates with 30 texts in a row asking to see her boobs is tomorrow's drunk freshman at a UC-Santa Barbara house party. It is conceivable that he will be acculturated into seeking affirmative-consent—and that he will seek it by asking for intercourse or a blow job *again and again and again.* At what point is he guilty of sexually harassing one or more of his new classmates? I suspect that's an issue campuses will face more frequently as consent-seeking becomes both affirmatively encouraged and more explicit than before. The spirit of the standard would of course preclude pestering one's way to "yes." But we're talking about regime created precisely to address the behavior of young men who'll adhere to the letter of the law or social norm *at most.* A new standard won't extinguish their impulse to push the limits as far as they can while avoiding punishable acts. Pestering may be their adaptation. And somewhere, sorority girls will arrive at a frat party where, upon entering (if not as a condition) they'll confront men pressuring them to preemptively consent. "This bracelet means you're good to hook up–and it comes with a free shot!"

Will that be tolerated?

Women Will Face Charges More Often Than Expected

Some opponents of California's law have argued that predatory men will "game" the new system by responding to an accusation of sexual assault with a countercharge of their own. Consider a case arising from drunken sex that one party regrets the next day. A college male is informed that charges are being brought against him. "She couldn't give consent? Neither could I. In fact, I felt uncomfortable too—she came to my room, neither asked for nor got a yes, and I was way more drunk." Such a case could present thorny issues for a campus tribunal.

But I'm imagining a different scenario, in which the affirmative-consent regime coincides with a noticeable increase in *earnest* complaints by men against women. It isn't that I foresee a monumental shift. At the same time, if campus norms about consensual sex change significantly and rapidly, just as traditional taboos against women initiating sex are waning and explicit efforts are made to diminish taboos against reporting sexual assaults, is it possible that a population acculturated to expect men always want sex will make and be called on more misjudgments?

Consider the following passage from the fascinating *New York Times Magazine* article on Wellesley, a women's college, and the growing number of trans men attending it:

Kaden Mohamed said he felt downright objectified when he returned from summer break last year, after five months of testosterone had lowered his voice, defined his arm muscles and reshaped his torso. It was attention that he had never experienced before he transitioned. But as his body changed, students he didn't even know would run their hands over his biceps. Once at the school pub, an intoxicated Wellesley woman even grabbed his crotch and that of another trans man.

"It's this very bizarre reversal of what happens in the real world," Kaden said. "In the real world, it's women who get fetishized, catcalled, sexually harassed, grabbed. At Wellesley, it's trans men who do. If I were to go up to someone I just met and touch her body, I'd get grief from the entire Wellesley community, because they'd say it's assault—and it is. But for some reason, when it's done to trans men here, it doesn't get read the same way. It's like a free pass, that suddenly it's O.K. to talk about or touch someone's body as long as they're not a woman."

How would a disciplinary panel at Wellesley react to a trans man charging a woman with sexual assault? How would UC-San Diego's student body react to a straight male bringing charges against a straight female for giving him a blow job when he was very drunk that he regretted the next day—or two weeks later upon realizing that he contracted an STD from the encounter? My guess is that, 10 years hence, such cases will be far from common, but still far more common than they currently are.

Sexual Assault Will Become a Sometimes Less Serious Charge

That isn't to say that *all* sexual assaults would be treated less seriously in this scenario. Some sex crimes will always strike people as maximally abhorrent and awful. But if a person can technically run afoul of sexual-assault rules by, say, misreading the vibe on a first date, leaning over during the movie, and initiating an unwanted kiss, there will be scenarios on the margin—perhaps not that one exactly, but you get the idea—where observers agree affirmative consent was violated *and* that some sanction is warranted, but nevertheless feel the incident is different in degree or kind than their bygone notion of what the crime "sexual assault" is.

There are two spins to put on this. On one hand, perhaps it is salutary to maintain undiminished taboos around *all* rape and sexual assault, preserving clarity about its awfulness, avoiding ignorant tropes like the canard that date rape isn't "as bad" as stranger rape, and conferring maximal opprobrium on those who act sexually without consent. Or perhaps a spectrum of opprobrium would be salutary, as in cases where the victim regards himself or herself as having been wronged, but eschews taking any action because he or she doesn't believe it was sexual assault, or want to be subjected to—or subject someone else to—a sexual-assault case. In some ways, this is similar to the tension between wanting racism to carry a powerful taboo and seeing situations where that very taboo makes it harder to call out and remedy conduct that is mildly racially offensive.

* * *

Though some of the foregoing scenarios are of my own creation, I don't have any idea how affirmative-consent laws will actually play out on California's college campuses, how variable the effect will be on different college campuses, or whether the overall change in sexual culture will be salutary, negative, or negligible. By temperament, I tend to worry about unintended consequences more than most, but the legislature

has spoken and early results will be in soon enough. I hope to report on campuses and find out how they're working.

It is nevertheless worth thinking through scenarios like the ones above, for the law is very likely to have a mishmash of positive and negative consequences coexisting with one another—and perhaps anticipating potential pitfalls as well as opportunities for worthwhile change can help college students and administrators to steer things in a slightly better direction than they'd float on their own.

With that in mind, I hope current college students (or recent grads) who've made it through the musings of out-of-touch oldsters like me will reflect on their observations and experiences, and then send e-mail articulating how *they* think affirmative-consent laws will play out (or have played out) on campus. What are commentators who haven't themselves been college students for years or decades missing, or misunderstanding, about sexual culture on campus today or how it will change? Insightful e-mail sent to conor@theatlantic.com will published as reader letters.

Critical Thinking

1. What are the requirements of California's affirmative consent law?

2. If this law were enacted in your state and on your campus how might it change your sexual behavior and that of your fellow students? Do you think there would be gender differences in reactions and responses to the law? If so, how might the behavior of male versus female college students be differentially impacted?

3. How effective do you think the law will be in preventing sexual assault among college students? What else might be needed besides the legislation to decrease rates of date rape and sexual violence on college campuses?

Internet References

American College Health Association: Campus and Sexual Violence
http://www.acha.org/Topics/violence.cfm

California's Affirmative Consent Law
https://leginfo.legislature.ca.gov/faces/billNavClient.xhtml?bill_id=201320140SB967

National Sexual Violence Resource Center: Campus Sexual Violence Resource List
http://www.nsvrc.org/saam/campus-resource-list

Article   Prepared by: Patricia Hrusa Williams, *University of Maine at Farmington*

Sex Doesn't Have to Make Sense

It's not entirely, or even mostly, about the evolution of the species.

AGUSTÍN FUENTES

Learning Outcomes

After reading this article, you will be able to:

- Identify ways evolution influences sexual attraction and behavior.

- Understand multiple reasons humans engage in sexual behavior and select partners besides those related to biology or procreation.

We're often told that how or why we have sex is the result of an evolved strategy. Such assertions seek to inform us of the real reason why we have sex the way we do—and most people equate "evolved" with "natural." This is a problem, because sex does not serve only one purpose, and there is no one "right" way to have sex.

Don't get me wrong: Our bodies and behavior are shaped by our evolutionary histories, and evolutionary processes do influence why and how we have sex. Sex evolved millions of years ago and has worked out pretty well for many organisms on the planet. But sex is complicated, very complicated, even for the simplest of worms. So why should it be any easier to understand in humans?

Unfortunately, instead of embracing the complexity of sex, many recent "evolutionary" hypotheses get too specific about *attraction* and sex. One tells us that men naturally find women with tattoos more sexually attractive because they are sending signals of heightened receptivity. Another that men naturally prefer a specific waist-to-hip ratio (the "hourglass" figure) in their female sex partners because it signals better reproductive qualities. There is even one that tells us that women prefer men with the most symmetrical faces because they have "better genes" and that these men give off a scent that indicates

the quality of their symmetry and really turns on women at the peak of their fertility cycle.

All of these hypotheses make two assumptions:

1. People really have sex because sex is "for" reproduction.
2. Sexual attraction is primarily driven by evolved tendencies.

These assumptions imply that if one is not a heterosexual, has no interest in sex, does not behave like the hypotheses predict, or is primarily interested in sexual activity that does not involve the possibility of a sperm and egg meeting up, he or she is doing something out of the evolutionary norm, and maybe even "unnatural." They also underplay the enormous complexity in human social lives and individual experience and represent a serious misunderstanding of how evolution works, what sex is, and why humans have it.

Behavioral and physiological processes (like attraction and sexual activity) are not "evolved *for*" a purpose, they are "evolved *as*" part of a system. Our hands did not evolve *for* the fine-tuned motor skills we have. They evolved increasingly better capacities at fine-tuned motor skills *as part of* our changing bodies, brains, and ecologies over time—as part of a system. Human hands are perfectly designed to play online games and to text and tweet, but they did not "evolve" for any of those things. Hands also help build, cook, massage, tie knots, send signals, play the piano—our anatomy and behavior are shaped by evolutionary history, but that history does not necessarily predetermine how we use them. Sex can involve genital-genital contact and even the exchange of fluids, and possibly end up in reproduction, but sexual *activity* is not limited to, or always driven by, those aspects.

In fact, all evolutionary processes need to do is ensure that individuals within a species want to, at least occasionally, have sex with each other and that some of that sex results in reproduction. Of course, given the way natural selection and other processes of evolution work, some behavioral and physiological processes will be favored over time and become more common in subsequent populations. This "favoring" might occur through being particularly attractive to sexual partners or it might be related to improved abilities to get food, avoid predators, and/or cooperate better or fight more effectively with other members of the species. The reasons for why and how we have sex are not always, or even necessarily, tied to making babies or even to the evolutionary quality of reproductive partners.

Sex in many species (humans, primates, whales, and dolphins, for example) can be as much about building bonds and friendships, and negotiating conflicts and providing social support, as it is about reproduction. In humans it's even more social and more frequent than in other animals. Most human sex, including heterosexual genital-genital contact, does not result in reproduction—in fact, much of it occurs outside any possibility of reproduction.

Sure, there might be benefits to having sex with a partner who has a specific physical or genetic characteristic, but it also might be really fun and/or socially beneficial to have sex with someone who does not. In most cases, the specific details of each bout of sexual activity do not matter in the bigger evolutionary picture. In a strict biological evolutionary context all that matters is whether or not you and/or your close relatives get copies of your genetic material into the next generation. The "how" is not so important.

The point is that in complex social animals (and humans are amongst the most social and the most complex) no single evolutionary explanation is going to come close to providing an encompassing explanation for why they do what they do, or feel what they feel.

As such, how can we get a better handle on why we have sex (or not) the way we do? Sex and sexuality in humans, across the lifespan, is messy and changes depending on a multitude of variables. Looking for one or even two core explanations of why you feel and act the way you do will leave you with a very incomplete answer. For example, being attracted to someone does not necessarily create a desire to have sex with them. Alternately, being attracted to someone is not always the first reason, or even a necessary reason, for people to have sex. Also, humans can have a huge range of sexual desires, urges, and feelings on which they may or may not act. Evolutionary history tells us a lot about the general parameters of sexual

activity; a bit about why sex feels the way it does; and maybe even a little about why we get turned on (or off) by something. But thinking simply in a model that relates sex to the likelihood of reproduction tells us very little about how individuals experience feelings, desires, and sexuality.

Biological sex is the result of entangled biologies, bodies, minds, experiences, and expectations. Why would we expect any less complexity in how and why we actually engage in sexual activity? Each of our sex lives exists in the context of a particular society with rules and expectations, in a particular cultural history wherein we are told what is correct and incorrect about sex, and in the context of our evolving biology.

Trying to pigeonhole sex into one or two "real" explanations is fruitless and damaging. A better approach is to recognize the multiple influences on our actions, to recognize that there are many fruitful ways to successfully be human, and to try to understand how sex and sexuality emerge and play out for individuals, in societies, and across our species.

Evolutionary hypotheses, societal expectations, and personal experience all matter in explaining why we do what we do. Choosing one as more important than the others is not going to make sex any less complex, or easier to deal with. As the science writer Carl Zimmer tells us about the vinegar worm, even "in the simplest animal imaginable, sex can be wonderfully difficult to decipher."

Critical Thinking

1. How does biology and evolution influence attraction and sex?

2. What are some assumptions we have about how we choose our sexual partners and have sex with them?

3. The author states that "Biological sex is the result of entangled biologies, bodies, minds, experiences, and expectations." What does he mean by this? Are we always logical in our choices of partners and why we have sex? Why/why not?

Internet References

PBS (WGBH, Boston): Evolution and Sex
http://www.pbs.org/wgbh/evolution/sex
The Kinsey Institute
http://www.kinseyinstitute.org
The Society for the Scientific Study of Sexuality
http://www.sexscience.org

Article

Prepared by: Patricia Hrusa Williams,
University of Maine at Farmington

12 Rude Revelations about Sex

ALAIN DE BOTTON

Learning Outcomes

After reading this article, you will be able to:

- Explain the science behind sex, sexual desire, and sexual behavior.

- Examine some of the major themes in the study of sex and intimate relationships.

- Understand sexual terms such as erotic and intimacy.

- Recognize the emotional and physical manifestations of sexual desire and behavior.

We have been led to believe, is as natural as breathing. But in fact, contends British philosopher Alain de Botton, it is "close to rocket science in complexity." It's not only a powerful force, it's often contrary to many other things we care about. Sex inherently sets up conflicts within us. We crave sex with people we don't know or love. It makes us want to do things that seem immoral or degrading, like slapping someone or being tied up. We feel awkard asking the people we love for the sex acts we really want.

There's no denying that sex has its sweaty charms, and in its most exquisite moments dissolves the isolation that embodied life imposes on us. But those moments are rare, the exception rather than the rule, says de Botton, founder of London's School of Life. "Sex is always going to cause us headaches; it's not something we can miraculously grow relaxed about." We suffer privately, feeling "painfully strange about the sex we are either longing to have or struggling to avoid."

If we turn to sex books to help us work out this central experience of our lives, we are typically assured that most problems are mechanical, a matter of method. In his own new book, *How to Think More About Sex*, de Botton makes the case that our difficulties stem more from the multiplicity of things we want out of life, or the accrual of everyday resentments, or the weirdness of the sex drive itself. Here are some of the most basic questions it answers.

Why do most people lie about their true desires?

It is rare to go through life without feeling that we are somehow a bit odd about sex. It is an area in which most of us have a painful impression, in our heart of hearts, that we are quite unusual. Despite being one of the most private activities, sex is nevertheless surrounded by a range of powerfully socially sanctioned ideas that codify how normal people are meant to feel about and deal with the matter. In truth, however, few of us are remotely normal sexually. We are almost all haunted by guilt and neuroses, by phobias and disruptive desires, by indifference and disgust. We are universally deviant—but only in relation to some highly distorted ideals of normality.

Most of what we are sexually remains impossible to communicate with anyone whom we would want to think well of us. Men and women in love instinctively hold back from sharing more than a fraction of their desires out of a fear, usually accurate, of generating intolerable disgust in their partners.

Nothing is erotic that isn't also, with the wrong person, revolting, which is precisely what makes erotic moments so intense: At the precise juncture where disgust could be at its height, we find only welcome and permission. Think of two tongues exploring the deeply private realm of the mouth—that dark, moist cavity that no one but our dentist usually enters. The privileged nature of the union between two people is sealed by an act that, with someone else, would horrify them both.

What unfolds between a couple in the bedroom is an act of mutual reconciliation between two secret sexual selves emerging at last from sinful solitude. Their behavior is starkly at odds with the behavior expected of them by the civilized world. At last, in the semi-darkness a couple can confess to the many wondrous and demented things that having a body drives them to want.

Why is sex more difficult to talk about in this era, not less?

Whatever discomfort we feel around sex is commonly aggravated by the idea that we belong to a liberated age—and ought by now to be finding sex a straightforward and untroubling matter, a little like tennis, something that everyone should have as often as possible to relieve the stresses of modern life.

The narrative of enlightenment and progress skirts an unbudging fact: Sex is not something we can ever expect to feel easily liberated from. It is a fundamentally disruptive and overwhelming force, at odds with the majority of our ambitions and all but incapable of being discreetly integrated within civilized society. Sex is not fundamentally democratic or kind. It refuses to sit neatly on top of love. Tame it though we might try, it tends to wreak havoc across our lives; it leads us to destroy our relationships, threatens our productivity, and compels us to stay up too late in nightclubs talking to people whom we don't like but whose exposed midriffs we wish to touch. Our best hope should be for a respectful accommodation with an anarchic and reckless power.

How is sex a great lie detector?

Involuntary physiological reactions such as the wetness of a vagina and the stiffness of a penis are emotionally so satisfying (which means, simultaneously, so erotic) because they signal a kind of approval that lies utterly beyond rational manipulation. Erections and lubrication simply cannot be effected by willpower and are therefore particularly true and honest indices of interest. In a world in which fake enthusiasms are rife, in which it is often hard to tell whether people really like us or whether they are being kind to us merely out of a sense of duty, the wet vagina and the stiff penis function as unambiguous agents of sincerity.

A kiss is pleasurable because of the sensory receptivity of our lips, but a good deal of our excitement has nothing to do with the physical dimension of the act: It stems from the simple realization that someone else likes us quite a lot.

What is the lure of sex in the back of an airplane?

Most of the people we come in contact with in daily life hardly notice us. Their businesslike indifference can be painful and humiliating for us—hence, the peculiar power of the fantasy that life could be turned upside down and the normal priorities reversed. The eroticism of nurses' uniforms, for example, stems from the gap between the rational control they symbolize and the unbridled sexual passion that can for a while, if only in fantasy, gain the upper hand over it.

Just as uniforms can inspire lust by their evocation of rule-breaking, so can it be exciting to imagine sex in an unobserved corner of the university library, in a restaurant's cloakroom, or in a train car. Our defiant transgression can give us a feeling of power that goes beyond the merely sexual. To have sex in the back of an airplane full of business travelers is to have a go at upending the usual hierarchy of things, introducing desire into an atmosphere in which cold-hearted discipline generally dominates over personal wishes. At 35,000 feet up, just as in an office cubicle, the victory of intimacy seems sweeter and our pleasure increases accordingly. Eroticism is most clearly manifest at the intersection between the formal and the intimate.

Is pornography a betrayal of humanity?

Pornography is often accused of being comfortingly "fake" and therefore unthreatening to the conduct of any sensible existence. But it is deeply contrary to the rest of our plans and inclinations,

rerouting rational priorities. Most pornography is humiliating and vulgar. Nobility has surely been left far behind when an anonymous woman is forced onto a bed, three penises are roughly inserted into her orifices, and the ensuing scene is recorded. Yet this poison is not easy to resist. Thousands of content providers have exploited a design flaw of the male—a mind designed to cope with little more tempting than the occasional sight of a tribeswoman across the savannah. There is nothing robust enough in our psyche to compensate for developments in technology. Pornography, like alcohol and drugs, reduces our capacity to tolerate ambiguous moods of free-floating worry and boredom. Internet pornography assists our escape from ourselves, helping us to destroy our present and our future with depressing ease. Yet it's possible to conceive of a pornography in which sexual desire would be invited to support, rather than undermine, our higher values. It could be touching and playful. It could show people having sex who like one another, or people like those we know from the rest of life rather than aberrations. No longer would we have to choose between being human and being sexual.

Why is "Not tonight, Dear" so destructive?

Logic might suggest that being married or in a long-term relationship must guarantee an end to the anxiety that otherwise dogs attempts by one person to induce another to have sex. But while either kind of union may make sex a constant theoretical option, it will neither legitimate the act nor ease the path toward it. Moreover, against a background of permanent possibility, an unwillingness to have sex may be seen as a far graver violation of the ground rules than a similar impasse in other contexts. Being turned down by someone we have just met in a bar is not so surprising or wounding. Suffering sexual rejection by the person with whom we have pledged to share our life is much odder and more humiliating.

Why is impotence an achievement?

There are few greater sources of shame for a man, or feelings of rejection for his partner. The real problem with impotence is the blow to the self-esteem of both parties.

We are grievously mistaken in our interpretation. Impotence is the strangely troublesome fruit of reason and kindness intruding on the free flow of animal impulses, of our new inclination to wonder what another might be feeling and then to identify with his or her potential objections to our invasive or unsatisfactory demands.

All but the least self-aware among us will sometimes be struck by how distasteful our desire for sex can seem to someone else, how peculiar and physically off-putting our flesh may be, and how unwanted our caresses. An advanced capacity for love and tenderness can ironically render us too sensitive to try to pester anyone else into having sex with us, although now and then we may cross paths with individuals who are not appalled by our longing for urgent and forceful sexual congress, and who see nothing disgusting in even the farthest erotic extremes.

Impotence is at base, then, a symptom of respect, a fear of causing displeasure through the imposition of our own desires or the inability to satisfy our partner's needs—a civilized worry that we will disappoint or upset others. It is an asset that should be valued as evidence of an achievement of the ethical imagination.

What do religions know about sex that we don't?

Only religions still take sex seriously, in the sense of properly respecting its power to turn us away from our priorities. Only religions see it as something potentially dangerous and needing to be guarded against. Perhaps only after killing many hours online at youporn.com can we appreciate that on this one point religions have got it right: Sex and sexual images can overwhelm our higher rational faculties with depressing ease. Religions are often mocked for being prudish, but they wouldn't judge sex to be quite so bad if they didn't also understand that it could be rather wonderful.

Does marriage ruin sex?

A gradual decline in the intensity and frequency of sex between a married couple is an inevitable fact of biological life, and as such, evidence of deep normality—although the sex-therapy industry has focused most of its efforts on assuring us that marriage should be enlivened by constant desire.

Most innocently, the paucity of sex within established relationships has to do with the difficulty of shifting registers between the everyday and the erotic. The qualities demanded of us when we have sex stand in sharp opposition to those we employ in conducting the majority of our other, daily activities. Marriage tends to involve—if not immediately, then within a few years—the running of a household and the raising of children, tasks that often feel akin to the administration of a small business and call on many of the same skills.

Sex, with its contrary emphases on expansiveness, imagination, playfulness, and a loss of control, must by its very nature interrupt this routine of regulation and self-restraint. We avoid sex not because it isn't fun but because its pleasures erode our subsequent capacity to endure the strenuous demands that our domestic arrangements place on us.

Sex also has a way of altering and unbalancing our relationship with our household co-manager. Its initiation requires one partner or the other to become vulnerable by revealing what may feel like humiliating sexual needs. We must shift from debating what sort of household appliance to acquire to making the more challenging request, for example, that our spouse should turn over and take on the attitude of a submissive nurse or put on a pair of boots and start calling us names.

The satisfaction of our needs may force us to ask for things that are, from a distance, open to being judged both ridiculous and contemptible so that we may prefer, in the end, not to

entrust them to someone on whom we must rely for so much else in the course of our ordinary upstanding life. We may in fact find it easier to put on a rubber mask or pretend to be a predatory, incestuous relative with someone we're not also going to have to eat breakfast with for the next three decades.

Why are bread crumbs in the kitchen bad for sex?

The common conception of anger posits red faces, raised voices, and slammed doors, but only too often it just curdles into numbness. We tend to forget we are angry with our partner, and hence become anaesthetized, melancholic, and unable to have sex with him or her because the specific incidents that anger us happen so quickly and so invisibly, in such chaotic settings (at the breakfast table, before the school run) that we can't recognize the offense well enough to mount a coherent protest against it. And we frequently don't articulate our anger, even when we do understand it, because the things that offend us can seem so trivial or odd that they would sound ridiculous if spoken aloud: "I am angry with you because you cut the bread in the wrong way." But once we are involved in a relationship, there is no longer any such thing as a minor detail.

In an average week, each partner may be hit by, and in turn fire, dozens of tiny arrows without even realizing it, with the only surface legacies of these wounds being a near imperceptible cooling between the pair and, crucially, the disinclination of one or both to have sex with the other. Sex is a gift that is not easy to hand over once we are annoyed.

We are unable to rise above the fray and shift the focus from recrimination towards identification of the true sources of hurt and fear. Couples need to appreciate that their hostilities were shaped by the flow of their individual personalities through the distorting emotional canyons of their particular childhoods. We think we already know everything necessary about how to be with another person, without having bothered to learn anything at all. We are unprepared for the effort we must legitimately expend to make even a very decent adult relationship successful.

Why are hotels metaphysically important?

The walls, beds, comfortably upholstered chairs, room service menus, televisions, and tightly wrapped soaps can do more than answer a taste for luxury. Checking into a hotel room for a night is a solution to long-term sexual stagnation: We can see the erotic side of our partner, which is often closely related to the unchanging environment in which we lead our daily lives. We can blame the stable presence of the carpet and the living room chairs at home for our failure to have more sex: The physical backdrop prevents us from evolving. The furniture insists that we can't change—because it never does.

In a hotel room, we may make love joyfully again because we have rediscovered, behind the roles we are forced to play by our domestic circumstances, the sexual identities that first drew us together—an act of aesthetic perception that will have been critically assisted by a pair of terry cloth bathrobes, a complimentary fruit basket, and a view onto an unfamiliar harbor. We can see our lover as if we had never laid eyes on him before.

Why is adultery overrated?

Contrary to all public verdicts on adultery, the lack of any wish whatsoever to stray is irrational and against nature, a heedless disregard for the fleshly reality of our bodies, a denial of the power wielded over our more rational selves by such erotic triggers as high-heeled shoes and crisp shirts, by smooth thighs and muscular calves.

But a spouse who gets angry at having been betrayed is evading a basic, tragic truth: No one can be everything to another person. The real fault lies in the ethos of modern marriage, with its insane ambitions and its insistence that our most pressing needs might be solved with the help of only one other person.

If seeing marriage as the perfect answer to all our hopes for love, sex, and family is naive and misguided, so too is believing that adultery can be an effective antidote to the disappointments of marriage. It is impossible to sleep with someone outside of marriage and not spoil the things we care about inside it. There is no answer to the tensions of marriage.

When a person with whom we have been having an erotic exchange in an Internet chat room suggests a meeting at an airport hotel, we may be tempted to blow up our life for a few hours' pleasure. The defenders of feeling-based marriage venerate emotions for their authenticity only because they avoid looking closely at what actually floats through most people's emotional kaleidoscopes, all the contradictory, sentimental, and hormonal forces that pull us in a hundred often crazed and inconclusive directions.

We could not be fulfilled if we weren't inauthentic some of the time—inauthentic, that is, in relation to such things as our passing desires to throttle our children, poison our spouse, or end our marriage over a dispute about changing a lightbulb. A degree of repression is necessary for both the mental health of our species and the adequate functioning of a decently ordered society. We are chaotic chemical propositions. We should feel grateful for, and protected by, the knowledge that our external circumstances are often out of line with what we feel; it is a sign that we are probably on the right course.

Critical Thinking

1. The author states "few of us are remotely normal sexually." Do you agree or disagree? Why?

2. Describe some practical challenges sexual desires and impulses present in our daily lives.

3. Is sex more physical or emotional? Why?

4. What is a question about sex that has not been addressed in this article?

Create Central

www.mhhe.com/createcentral

Internet References

Go Ask Alice!
www.goaskalice.columbia.edu
The Kinsey Institute for Research in Sex, Gender, and Reproduction
www.kinseyinstitute.org
The Society for the Scientific Study of Sexuality
www.sexscience.org
The Electronic Journal of Human Sexuality
www.ejhs.org/index.htm

ALAIN DE BOTTON is founder of The School of Life, based in London.

Article

Prepared by: Patricia Hrusa Williams,
University of Maine at Farmington

There's No Such Thing as Everlasting Love (According to Science)

EMILY ESFAHANI SMITH

Learning Outcomes

After reading this article, you will be able to:

- Understand differences in theoretical, practical, and scientific definitions of love.

- Explain the science, biochemistry, and physiological components behind love.

In her new book *Love 2.0: How Our Supreme Emotion Affects Everything We Feel, Think, Do, and Become,* the psychologist Barbara Fredrickson offers a radically new conception of love.

Fredrickson, a leading researcher of positive emotions at the University of North Carolina at Chapel Hill, presents scientific evidence to argue that love is not what we think it is. It is not a long-lasting, continually present emotion that sustains a marriage; it is not the yearning and passion that characterizes young love; and it is not the blood-tie of kinship.

Rather, it is what she calls a "micro-moment of positivity resonance." She means that love is a connection, characterized by a flood of positive emotions, which you share with another person—*any* other person—whom you happen to connect with in the course of your day. You can experience these micro-moments with your romantic partner, child, or close friend. But you can also fall in love, however momentarily, with less likely candidates, like a stranger on the street, a colleague at work, or an attendant at a grocery store. Louis Armstrong put it best in "It's a Wonderful World" when he sang, "I see friends shaking hands, sayin' 'how do you do?' / They're really sayin', 'I love you.'"

Fredrickson's unconventional ideas are important to think about at this time of year. With Valentine's Day around the corner, many Americans are facing a grim reality: They are love-starved. Rates of loneliness are on the rise as social supports are disintegrating. In 1985, when the General Social Survey polled Americans on the number of confidants they have in their lives, the most common response was three. In 2004, when the survey was given again, the most common response was zero.

According to the University of Chicago's John Cacioppo, an expert on loneliness, and his co-author William Patrick, "at any given time, roughly 20 percent of individuals—that would be 60 million people in the U.S. alone—feel sufficiently isolated for it to be a major source of unhappiness in their lives." For older Americans, that number is closer to 35 percent. At the same time, rates of depression have been on the rise. In his 2011 book *Flourish,* the psychologist Martin Seligman notes that according to some estimates, depression is 10 times more prevalent now than it was five decades ago. Depression affects about 10 percent of the American population, according to the Centers for Disease Control.

A global poll taken last Valentine's Day showed that most married people—or those with a significant other—list their romantic partner as the greatest source of happiness in their lives. According to the same poll, nearly half of all single people are looking for a romantic partner, saying that finding a special person to love would contribute greatly to their happiness.

But to Fredrickson, these numbers reveal a "worldwide collapse of imagination," as she writes in her book. "Thinking of love purely as romance or commitment that you share with one special person—as it appears most on earth do—surely limits the health and happiness you derive" from love.

"My conception of love," she tells me, "gives hope to people who are single or divorced or widowed this Valentine's Day to find smaller ways to experience love."

You have to physically be with the person to experience the micro-moment. For example, if you and your significant other are not physically together—if you are reading this at work alone in your office—then you two are not in love. You may feel connected or bonded to your partner—you may long to be in his company—but your body is completely loveless.

To understand why, it's important to see how love works biologically. Like all emotions, love has a biochemical and physiological component. But unlike some of the other positive emotions, like joy or happiness, love cannot be kindled individually—it only exists in the physical connection between two people. Specifically, there are three players in the biological love system—mirror neurons, oxytocin, and vagal tone. Each involves connection and each contributes to those micro-moments of positivity resonance that Fredrickson calls love.

When you experience love, your brain mirrors the person's you are connecting with in a special way. Pioneering research by Princeton University's Uri Hasson shows what happens inside the brains of two people who connect in conversation. Because brains are scanned inside of noisy fMRI machines, where carrying on a conversation is nearly impossible, Hasson's team had his subjects mimic a natural conversation in an ingenious way. They recorded a young woman telling a lively, long, and circuitous story about her high school prom. Then, they played the recording for the participants in the study, who were listening to it as their brains were being scanned. Next, the researchers asked each participant to re-create the story so they, the researchers, could determine who was listening well and who was not. Good listeners, the logic goes, would probably be the ones who clicked in a natural conversation with the story-teller.

What they found was remarkable. In some cases, the brain patterns of the listener mirrored those of the storyteller after a short time gap. The listener needed time to process the story after all. In other cases, the brain activity was almost perfectly synchronized; there was no time lag at all between the speaker and the listener. But in some rare cases, if the listener was particularly tuned in to the story—if he was hanging on to every word of the story and really got it—his brain activity actually *anticipated* the story-teller's in some cortical areas.

The mutual understanding and shared emotions, especially in that third category of listener, generated a micro-moment of love, which "is a single act, performed by two brains," as Fredrickson writes in her book.

Oxytocin, the so-called love and cuddle hormone, facilitates these moments of shared intimacy and is part of the mammalian "calm-and-connect" system (as opposed to the more stressful "fight-or-flight" system that closes us off to others). The hormone, which is released in huge quantities during sex, and in lesser amounts during other moments of intimate connection, works by making people feel more trusting and open to connection. This is the hormone of attachment and bonding that spikes during micro-moments of love. Researchers have found, for instance, that when a parent acts affectionately with his or her infant—through micro-moments of love like making eye contact, smiling, hugging, and playing—oxytocin levels in both the parent and the child rise in sync.

The final player is the vagus nerve, which connects your brain to your heart and subtly but sophisticatedly allows you to meaningfully experience love. As Fredrickson explains in her book, "Your vagus nerve stimulates tiny facial muscles that better enable you to make eye contact and synchronize your facial expressions with another person. It even adjusts the miniscule muscles of your middle ear so you can better track her voice against any background noise."

The vagus nerve's potential for love can actually be measured by examining a person's heart rate in association with his breathing rate, what's called "vagal tone." Having a high vagal tone is good: People who have a high "vagal tone" can regulate their biological processes like their glucose levels better; they have more control over their emotions, behavior, and attention; they are socially adept and can kindle more positive connections with others; and, most importantly, they are more loving.

In research from her lab, Fredrickson found that people with high vagal tone report more experiences of love in their days than those with a lower vagal tone.

Historically, vagal tone was considered stable from person to person. You either had a high one or you didn't; you either had a high potential for love or you didn't. Fredrickson's recent research has debunked that notion.

In a 2010 study from her lab, Fredrickson randomly assigned half of her participants to a "love" condition and half to a control condition. In the love condition, participants devoted about one hour of their weeks for several months to the ancient Buddhist practice of loving-kindness meditation. In loving-kindness meditation, you sit in silence for a period of time and cultivate feelings of tenderness, warmth, and compassion for another person by repeating a series of phrases to yourself wishing them love, peace, strength, and general well-being. Ultimately, the practice helps people step outside of themselves and become more aware of other people and their needs, desires, and struggles—something that can be difficult to do in our hyper individualistic culture.

Fredrickson measured the participants' vagal tone before and after the intervention. The results were so powerful that she was invited to present them before the Dalai Lama himself in 2010. Fredrickson and her team found that, contrary to the conventional wisdom, people could significantly increase their vagal tone by self-generating love through loving-kindness meditation. Since vagal tone mediates social connections and bonds, people whose vagal tones increased were suddenly capable of experiencing more micro-moments of love in their days. Beyond that, their growing capacity to love more will translate into health benefits given that high vagal tone is associated with lowered risk of inflammation, cardiovascular disease, diabetes, and stroke.

Fredrickson likes to call love a nutrient. If you are getting enough of the nutrient, then the health benefits of love can dramatically alter your biochemistry in ways that perpetuate more micro-moments of love in your life, and which ultimately contribute to your health, well-being, and longevity.

Fredrickson's ideas about love are not exactly the stuff of romantic comedies. Describing love as a "micro-moment of positivity resonance" seems like a buzz-kill. But if love now seems less glamorous and mysterious than you thought it was, then good. Part of Fredrickson's project is to lower cultural expectations about love—expectations that are so misguidedly high today that they have inflated love into something that it isn't, and into something that no sane person could actually experience.

Jonathan Haidt, another psychologist, calls these unrealistic expectations "the love myth" in his 2006 book *The Happiness Hypothesis*:

> True love is passionate love that never fades; if you are in true love, you should marry that person; if love ends, you should leave that person because it was not true love; and if you can find the right person, you will have true love forever. You might not believe this myth yourself, particularly if you are older than thirty; but many young people in Western nations are raised on it, and it acts as

an ideal that they unconsciously carry with them even if they scoff at it. . . . But if true love is defined as eternal passion, it is biologically impossible.

Love 2.0 is, by contrast, far humbler. Fredrickson tells me, "I love the idea that it lowers the bar of love. If you don't have a Valentine, that doesn't mean that you don't have love. It puts love much more in our reach everyday regardless of our relationship status."

Lonely people who are looking for love are making a mistake if they are sitting around and waiting for love in the form of the "love myth" to take hold of them. If they instead sought out love in little moments of connection that we all experience many times a day, perhaps their loneliness would begin to subside.

Critical Thinking

1. What is your definition of love? What are some similarities and differences between your definition and the ones presented in the article?
2. Explain the love myth.

3. Do you believe that people can be trained to be more loving, as the article implies? Why or why not?
4. What are some advantages and disadvantages of defining love as "micro-moments" of positive feelings and emotions?

Create Central

www.mhhe.com/createcentral

Internet References

Go Ask Alice!
www.goaskalice.columbia.edu

The Kinsey Institute for Research in Sex, Gender, and Reproduction
www.kinseyinstitute.org

The Society for the Scientific Study of Sexuality
www.sexscience.org

The Electronic Journal of Human Sexuality
www.ejhs.org/index.htm

Article   Prepared by: Patricia Hrusa Williams, *University of Maine at Farmington*

Dating As If It Were Driver's Ed

LISA JANDER

Learning Outcomes

After reading this article, you will be able to:

- Recognize risks faced by dating teens.

- Explain why mandating relationship education programs for teens is difficult and controversial.

- Define the components needed for a comprehensive relationship education program for teens and their parents.

"So, what movie do you think I should take Emily to see?" I was sitting in the passenger seat next to my 16-year-old son while he practiced his parallel parking, hoping he would not hit anything. His question made me grip the armrest just a little bit tighter. My head was spinning and my heart was racing trying to block out the image of what "parking" meant for teens when I was in high school. How in the world was I going to prepare him for dating with no manual, instructor, or parental supervision? Just like driving, dating invites a very skewed notion of freedom if not approached with a solid set of guidelines.

Millions of parents watch like deer in the headlights as their kids accelerate into the teen dating years without a map and find themselves in the midst of a crisis: teen sex and pregnancy; couples drinking and doing drugs; dating violence and abuse; plus stress, anxiety, depression, and even suicide. Just sit on the beach during spring break or chaperone a school dance: the boundary lines are blurry at best and fading fast. Teen dating is not what it used to be; our culture and social media have changed the course of teen relationships forever.

Despite every effort to educate teens about the dangers associated with unhealthy choices, statistics indicate that the information may be falling on deaf ears (or maybe an underdeveloped prefrontal cortex). The inconsistent delivery of information on topics such as sex and drugs are proving to be less than effective compared to the cultural pressures that every teen faces. In addition, budget restrictions, limited access to resources, and negative or nonexistent parental influence can become roadblocks to the essential help and guidance teenagers need. Consequently, we have become a reactive society, throwing sandbags against the tide of influence where teens already are in way over their heads.

So, where is the hope for this generation and what are we teaching them about relationships? The reality is that only 22 states and the District of Columbia require sex education in public schools when more than 47 percent of high school students already have had sex, according to a survey by the Centers for Disease Control and Prevention (CDC). Conflicting messages about whether to have protected sex, or none at all, present choices that require a degree of logic and long-term planning that many teens do not possess. Without a proper foundation and ongoing support, teens are left to let their emotions drive them in the heat of the moment, which can result in life-altering consequences. Add social media and mass distribution of smart phones to the equation, and young people are on a collision course with visual imagery that heightens the senses and could make it much easier for them to get into trouble. The signs are there and the culture is paving the way.

With a stream of violent input from the world around them, teen brains also are being rewired and desensitized to the shock of abuse. The CDC provides education on dating violence and abuse through a program called "Dating Matters" in four high-risk communities in the country, and surveys show that 1 in 10 teenagers report experiencing abuse within the past 12 months. Hundreds of localized courses, along with a dozen national organizations, have made huge strides to squash bullying in an effort to minimize dating violence and abuse. Creative programs are introduced in schools during pep assemblies to encourage kindness and respect, as well as raise awareness of physical boundaries.

Dating under the influence also includes the abuse of drugs and alcohol. Thrill-seeking teens are bored with traditional highs and [are] lured into experimentation fueled by concoctions such as "Molly" and "Spice," as well as a new drinking game called NekNominate. Trying to stay ahead of the trend is a full-time job for most parents and educators who simply do not have the time nor information to steer teens away from the latest dangers. Educational programs warn against peer pressure when often the real push is from a "love" influence, which, for the adolescent brain, is much harder to resist.

According to the National Comorbidity Survey-Adolescent Supplement (NCS-A), about 11 percent of adolescents have a depressive disorder by age 18. The World Health Organization states that major depressive disorder is the leading cause of disability among Americans aged 15 to 44. For youth between the ages of 10 and 24, suicide is the third leading cause of death, maintains the National Institute of Mental Health. These troubling statistics have created a flurry of new medication trials, research, and therapies to understand and treat this growing trend. Whether temporary or long term, mild or severe, much of the teen stress in today's world is traced back to relational challenges, which certainly include dating. Teens ending their lives because of a "bad breakup" is becoming more and more common.

So, where does the responsibility for dating safety fall? Is it on the school, parents, community, law, or teen? Perhaps we can learn something from the Driver's Ed program that will help families navigate the teen dating years without a disaster. The evidence shows that very few teens fail Driver's Ed, but millions fail at dating. By looking at the history of driving, we can learn how to help steer teens away from the tragic dating accidents that take them off course.

In the summer of 1886, Karl Benz rolled his pride and joy—a three-wheeled motor car—through the streets of Mannheim, Germany. This "baby" was born seven months earlier, marked by a patent for the design that often is regarded as the "birth certificate of the automobile." Two years later, Benz's wife Bertha and her two sons took a road trip to prove the reliability and practical nature of the vehicle. Bertha traveled a full 112 miles with a maximum speed of 8 miles per hour. There was no seatbelt law, speed limit signs, nor traffic lights. Her daring journey sparked new growth for Benz & Cie. to become the world's largest automobile manufacturer.

In 1902, Ransom Olds opened the door to his large-scale, production line manufacturing of automobiles in Lansing, Mich. Now, vehicle speeds were exceeding 40 miles per hour and people were getting hurt. There was no formal training and drivers were notoriously reckless and unskilled. In the United Kingdom, efforts were made to regulate safety through the Motor Car Act in 1903 by requiring the first mandatory registering of every vehicle. At 17 years old, potential drivers could apply for this newfound freedom—agreeing to travel at a maximum speed of no more than 20 mph.

Over the next nine years, accidents and fatalities spiraled out of control until, finally, in 1913, New Jersey paved the way for mandated education followed by an exam before issuing a license. The timing could not have been more perfect, as Henry Ford significantly expanded the concept of mass production through manufacturing in 1914 and began turning out vehicles that could achieve speeds as high as 65 mph.

The common thread that followed was the undeniable need for the merging of proactive instruction for drivers along with safety measures for automobiles to minimize the ever-growing need for reactive solutions. As the auto industry soared, so did the accident rate. Safety became central to the manufacturing of vehicles backed by laws to improve safety ratings monitored by the Federal Motor Vehicle Safety Standards. There had to be a collective effort on the part of manufacturers, law enforcement, educators, parents, and even new teenage drivers to help them reach their destinations in one piece.

In recent decades, we have seen a surge of safety features developed for cars in an attempt to reduce risk and save the lives of teens who are fueled by dopamine, adrenaline, and an underdeveloped brain, driving a two-ton weapon at speeds of up to 70 mph (or more). Seatbelts, airbags, anti-lock brakes, and shatterproof glass give them far more protection in the event of a collision, but does not eliminate the reality that accidents happen. Every person knows a teenager who has had a close call, or worse.

The good news is that men and women committed to the auto industry work progressively and diligently to invent new security features in a race to get ahead of the tragedies. New laws are passed each year printed in neon yellow on every street corner to slow the speed of driving disasters. Driver's Ed programs are enforced not only to educate, but to give supervised experience to teens so that they have a chance of getting to school and back without getting hit—or hitting something or someone.

Turbo-charged Hormones

So, what is the educational program for teen dating? Parents give teens the thumbs up and a smile and send them off in a pack with turbo-charged hormones to the dark movie theater and hope they do not have an accident. What new safety features have been implemented in the past 50 years to give our teens a better chance at healthy relationships? What proactive laws are in place to protect these young lives from ending up in the junkyard of broken hearts? What can we do as a culture to minimize the risks and enforce education? For teenagers, it seems that "speed dating" is not an event, it is a lifestyle.

The answer may not be as clear as a windshield after a summer rain, but it certainly is becoming more and more obvious.

Social media is not going away and neither is the invention of the teenager. A negative cultural norm is growing more enticing to teenagers, which promotes entitled independence and an Autobahn, boundary-free approach to dating for which there seems to be no exit.

Part of parental responsibility is to provide the opportunity for children to learn which is diverted when smartphones, advertisements, and media are educating our kids without our knowledge. What teens learn about relationships will impact virtually every aspect of their lives: at home, school, work, and in the community and world. Just like a driving accident can min their lives, a dating accident can be just as tragic.

Driver's Education is the government's way of standardizing what all drivers should learn so that young drivers do as little damage to themselves or to others as possible. The state booklet says that parents or guardians are "often the best judge of your teen drivers' progress, skill, and maturity." That is the sugarcoating. Below that it says that "They [meaning the state of Michigan in this case] will notify you by letter if your teen driver is convicted of violating the terms of his or her Graduated Driver License."

To mandate social skills training, dating education, and marriage readiness would evoke a pushback more massive than the 1913 Driver's Ed course law in New Jersey. Nonetheless, how many statistics need to pile up before we gather all of the fantastic efforts of the mighty few that are making a difference and put them into a bill or, at the very least, a required course for parents and teens.

What would the data reveal in 10 years if, today, all eighth-graders and their parents were required to take an eight-week class on "healthy relationships" before the student could attend high school or apply for a driver's license? This course could combine the knowledge of specialists dedicated to their field of expertise in one central location to prepare them to navigate the high school years socially. A certificate of completion, just like a driver's permit, would show that the student had accomplished the work. Insurance companies might even be interested in sponsoring the course—after all, the desire to drive and date shift into gear at right about the same age.

Driver's Ed courses require parents to log 50 hours of supervised drive time with their teen before they are permitted to operate a vehicle alone. Parents do not think twice about monitoring teen driving, but the thought of riding along on a teen date is considered ludicrous. Chaperoning on dates is considered taboo these days, but maybe a contemporary version of this practice should emerge and be supported by parents, schools, and the community. What if parents were required to log 50 hours of community service with their teens prior to their graduation to encourage and foster compassion and kindness in a structured environment?

Teens make up nearly 47 percent of our population but are 100 percent of our future. Teens are not defective; they just are not done yet. There are values, beliefs, morals, habits, and knowledge that still need to be installed. Parents and other healthy adults bridge the gap between teen emotions and mature logic to help them cruise safely into adulthood. We enlist teachers, coaches, pastors, family members, and others to guide and encourage our children. Leaving them to find their own way is like putting them alone in a car blindfolded with no brakes, steering wheel, or GPS. We have the right and the privilege of sliding into that seat beside them and helping them through the obstacle course of relationships. Without our support, they very well could find themselves on a crash course.

Buckle up, parents. It is the law of attraction. Safe teen dating does not happen by accident.

Critical Thinking

1. Why do you feel states have not adopted relationship education programs in the same way they require drivers' education for teens?

2. What do you see as the most important challenges facing teens and their parents when they begin dating?

3. If you were to develop a relationship education program for teens, what would it look like and why? What do you think of the Dating Matters Program mentioned in the article (see http://www.cdc.gov/ViolencePrevention/DatingMatters/index.html)?

Internet References

Dating Matters
  http://www.cdc.gov/ViolencePrevention/DatingMatters/index.html
Go Ask Alice!
  www.goaskalice.columbia.edu
Love is Respect
  www.loveisrespect.org
Two of Us
  http://www.twoofus.org

LISA JANDER who calls herself the Teen Dating Mechanic, is author of *Dater's Ed: Driver's Ed Model for Dating* and the online teen curriculum TeenDatingLicense.com.

Article Prepared by: Patricia Hrusa Williams,
University of Maine at Farmington

The Expectations Trap

Much of the discontent couples encounter today is really culturally inflicted, although we're conditioned to blame our partners for our unhappiness. Yet research points to ways couples can immunize themselves against unseen pressures now pulling them apart.

HARA ESTROFF MARANO

Learning Outcomes

After reading this article, you will be able to:

- Recognize cultural aspects of love and marriage.

- Identify personality characteristics which are important to dating success.

- Describe how culture impacts happiness within relationships.

Six years, ten months, and eight days into their marriage, Sam and Melissa blew apart. Everyone was stunned, most of all the couple themselves. One day she was your basic stressed-out professional woman (and mother of a 3-year-old) carrying the major financial burden of their household. The next day she was a betrayed wife. The affair Sam disclosed detonated a caterwaul of hurt heard by every couple in their circle and her large coterie of friends and family. With speed verging on inevitability, the public knowledge of their private life commandeered the driver's seat of their own destiny. A surge of support for Melissa as the wronged woman swiftly isolated Sam emotionally and precluded deep discussion of the conditions that had long alienated him. Out of respect for the pain that his mere presence now caused, Sam decamped within days. He never moved back in.

It's not clear that the couple could have salvaged the relationship if they had tried. It wasn't just the infidelity. "We had so many background and stylistic differences," says Sam. "It was like we came from two separate cultures. We couldn't take out the garbage without a Geneva Accord." Constant negotiation was necessary, but if there was time, there was also usually too much accumulated irritation for Melissa to tolerate. And then, opening a public window on the relationship seemed to close the door on the possibility of working through the disappointments, the frustrations, the betrayal.

Within weeks, the couple was indeed in discussions—for a divorce. At least they both insisted on mediation, not litigation, and their lawyers complied. A couple of months, and some

time and determination later, they had a settlement. Only now that Sam and Melissa have settled into their mostly separate lives, and their daughter appears to be doing well with abundant care from both her parents, are they catching their respective breaths—two years later.

Americans value marriage more than people do in any other culture, and it holds a central place in our dreams. Over 90 percent of young adults aspire to marriage—although fewer are actually choosing it, many opting instead for cohabitation. But no matter how you count it, Americans have the highest rate of romantic breakup in the world, says Andrew J. Cherlin, professor of sociology and public policy at Johns Hopkins. As with Sam and Melissa, marriages are discarded often before the partners know what hit them.

"By age 35, 10 percent of American women have lived with three or more husbands or domestic partners," Cherlin reports in his recent book, *The Marriage-Go-Round: The State of Marriage and the Family in America Today.* "Children of married parents in America face a higher risk of seeing them break up than children born of unmarried parents in Sweden."

With general affluence has come a plethora of choices, including constant choices about our personal and family life. Even marriage itself is now a choice. "The result is an ongoing self-appraisal of how your personal life is going, like having a continual readout of your emotional heart rate," says Cherlin. You get used to the idea of always making choices to improve your happiness.

The constant appraisal of personal life to improve happiness creates a heightened sensitivity to problems that arise in intimate relationships.

The heightened focus on options "creates a heightened sensitivity to problems that arise in intimate relationships." And negative emotions get priority processing in our brains. "There are so many opportunities to decide that it's unsatisfactory," says Cherlin.

It would be one thing if we were living more satisfied lives than ever. But just gauging by the number of relationships wrecked every year, we're less satisfied, says Cherlin. "We're carrying over into our personal lives the fast pace of decisions and actions we have everywhere else, and that may not be for the best." More than ever, we're paying attention to the most volatile parts of our emotional makeup—the parts that are too reactive to momentary events to give meaning to life.

> **More than ever, we're paying attention to the most volatile parts of our emotional makeup—parts that are too reactive to momentary events to give meaning to life.**

Because our intimate relationships are now almost wholly vehicles for meeting our emotional needs, and with almost all our emotions invested in one relationship, we tend to look upon any unhappiness we experience—whatever the source—as a failure of a partner to satisfy our longings. Disappointment inevitably feels so *personal* we see no other possibility but to hunt for individual psychological reasons—that is, to blame our partners for our own unhappiness.

But much—perhaps most—of the discontent we now encounter in close relationships is culturally inflicted, although we rarely interpret our experience that way. Culture—the pressure to constantly monitor our happiness, the plethora of choices surreptitiously creating an expectation of perfection, the speed of everyday life—always climbs into bed with us. An accumulation of forces has made the cultural climate hostile to long-term relationships today.

Attuned to disappointment and confused about its source, we wind up discarding perfectly good relationships. People work themselves up over "the ordinary problems of marriage, for which, by the way, they usually fail to see their own contributions," says William Doherty, professor of family sciences at the University of Minnesota. "They badger their partners to change, convince themselves nothing will budge, and so work their way out of really good relationships." Doherty believes it's possible to stop the careering disappointment even when people believe a relationship is over.

It's not going to happen by putting the genie back in the bottle. It's not possible to curb the excess of options life now offers. And speed is a fixture of the ongoing technological revolution, no matter how much friction it creates in personal lives. Yet new research points to ways that actually render them irrelevant. We are, after all, the architects of our own passions.

The Purpose of Marriage

Marriage probably evolved as the best way to pool the labor of men and women to enable families to subsist and assure that children survive to independence—and data indicate it still is. But beyond the basics, the purpose of marriage has shifted constantly, says Stephanie Coontz, a historian at Washington's Evergreen State College. It helps to remember that marriage

---

Case Study
Stephen and Christina

Five years into his marriage, not long after the birth of his first son, most of Stephen G.'s interactions with his wife were not pleasant. "I thought the difficulties would pass," he recalls. "My wife, Christina, got fed up faster and wanted me to leave." He was traveling frequently and finances were thin; she'd gone back to school full-time after having worked until the baby was born. "Very few needs were being met for either of us. We were either yelling or in a cold war."

They entered counseling to learn how to co-parent if they indeed separated. "It helped restore our friendship: At least we could talk civilly. That led to deeper communication—we could actually listen to each other without getting defensive. We heard that we were both hurting, both feeling the stress of new parenthood without a support system of either parents or friends. We could talk about the ways we weren't there for each other without feeling attacked. It took a lot longer for the romance to return."

Stephen, now 37, a sales representative for a pharmaceutical company in San Francisco, says it was a time of "growing up. I had to accept that I had new responsibilities. And I had to accept that my partner, now 38, is not ideal in every way although she is ideal in many ways. But her short temper is not enough of a reason to leave the relationship and our two kids. When I wish she'd be different, I have to remind myself of all the ways she is the person I want to be with. It's not something you 'get over.' You accept it."

---

evolved in an atmosphere of scarcity, the conditions that prevailed for almost all of human history. "The earliest purpose of marriage was to make strategic alliances with other people, to turn strangers into relatives," says Coontz. "As society became more differentiated, marriage became a major mechanism for adjusting your position."

It wasn't until the 18th century that anyone thought that love might have anything to do with marriage, but love was held in check by a sense of duty. Even through the 19th century, the belief prevailed that females and males had different natures and couldn't be expected to understand each other well. Only in the 20th century did the idea take hold that men and women should be companions, that they should be passionate, and that both should get sexual and personal fulfillment from marriage.

We're still trying to figure out how to do that—and get the laundry done, too. The hassles of a negotiated and constantly renegotiated relationship—few wish a return to inequality—assure a ready source of stress or disappointment or both.

From We to Me

Our mind-set has further shifted over the past few decades, experts suggest. Today, the minute one partner is faced with dissatisfaction—feeling stressed-out or neglected, having

Case Study
Susan and Tim

Susan Pohlman, now 50, reluctantly accompanied her workaholic husband on a business trip to Italy believing it would be their last together. Back home in Los Angeles were their two teenagers, their luxurious home, their overfurnished lives—and the divorce lawyer she had contacted to end their 18-year marriage.

They were leading such parallel lives that collaboration had turned to competition, with fights over things like who spent more time with the kids and who spent more time working. But knocked off balance by the beauty of the coast near Genoa toward the end of the trip, Tim asked, out of the blue, "What if we lived here?" "The spirit of this odd day overtook me," recalls Susan. At 6 P.M. on the evening before departure, they were shown a beautiful apartment overlooking the water. Despite knowing no Italian, they signed a lease on the spot. Two months later, with their house sold, they moved with their kids to Italy for a year.

"In L.A. we were four people going in four directions. In Italy, we became completely dependent on each other. How to get a phone? How to shop for food? Also, we had no belongings. The simplicity forced us to notice the experiences of life. Often, we had no idea what we were doing. There was lots of laughing at and with each other." Susan says she "became aware of the power of adventure and of doing things together, and how they became a natural bridge to intimacy."

Both Pohlmans found Italy offered "a more appreciative lifestyle." Says Susan: "I realized the American Dream was pulling us apart. We followed the formula of owning, having, pushing each other. You have all this stuff but you're miserable because what you're really craving is interaction." Too, she says, American life is exhausting, and "exhaustion distorts your ability to judge problems."

Now back in the U.S. and living in Arizona, the Pohimans believe they needed to remove themselves from the culture to see its distorting effects. "And we needed to participate in a paradigm shift: 'I'm not perfect, you're not perfect; let's not get hung up on our imperfections.'" But the most powerful element of their move could be reproduced anywhere, she says: "The simplicity was liberating."

---

consumer mind-set is a major portal through which destructive forces gain entry and undermine conjoint life.

"Marriage is for *me*" is the way Austin, Texas, family therapist Pat Love puts it. "It's for meeting *my* needs." It's not about what *I do,* but how it makes me *feel.*

Such beliefs lead to a sense of entitlement: "I deserve better than I'm getting." Doherty sees that as the basic message of almost every advertisement in the consumer culture. You deserve more and we can provide it. You begin to think: This isn't the deal I signed up for. Or you begin to feel that you're putting into this a lot more than you're getting out. "We believe in our inalienable right to the intimate relationships of our choice," says Doherty.

In allowing such free-market values to seep into our private lives, we come to believe that a partner's job is, above all, to provide pleasure. "People do not go into relationships because they want to learn how to negotiate and master difficulties," observes Brown University psychiatrist Scott Haltzman. "They want the other person to provide pleasure." It's partner as service provider. The pleasure bond, unfortunately, is as volatile as the emotions that underlie it and as hollow and fragile as the hedonic sense of happiness.

The Expectations Trap: Perfection, Please

If there's one thing that most explicitly detracts from the enjoyment of relationships today, it's an abundance of choice. Psychologist Barry Schwartz would call it an *excess* of choice—the tyranny of abundance. We see it as a measure of our autonomy and we firmly believe that freedom of choice will lead to fulfillment. Our antennae are always up for better opportunities, finds Schwartz, professor of psychology at Swarthmore College.

Just as only the best pair of jeans will do, so will only the best partner—whatever that is. "People walk starry-eyed looking not into the eyes of their romantic partner but over their romantic partner's shoulder, in case there might be somebody better walking by. This is not the road to successful long-term relationships." It does not stop with marriage. And it undermines commitment by encouraging people to keep their options open.

Like Doherty, Schwartz sees it as a consequence of a consumer society. He also sees it as a self-fulfilling phenomenon. "If you think there might be something better around the next corner, then there will be, because you're not fully committed to the relationship you've got."

It's naïve to expect relationships to feel good every minute. Every relationship has its bumps. How big a bump does it have to be before you do something about it? As Hopkins's Cherlin says, if you're constantly asking yourself whether you should leave, "there may be a day when the answer is yes. In any marriage there may be a day when the answer is yes."

One of the problems with unrestrained choice, explains Schwartz, is that it raises expectations to the breaking point. A sense of multiple alternatives, of unlimited possibility, breeds in us the illusion that perfection exists out there, somewhere, if

---

a partner who isn't overly expressive or who works too hard or doesn't initiate sex very often—then the communal ideal we bring to relationships is jettisoned and an individualistic mentality asserts itself. We revert to a stingier self that has been programmed into us by the consumer culture, which has only become increasingly pervasive, the current recession notwithstanding.

Psychologically, the goal of life becomes *my* happiness. "The minute your needs are not being met then you appropriate the individualistic norm," says Doherty. This accelerating

only we could find it. This one's sense of humor, that one's looks, another one's charisma—we come to imagine that there will be a package in which all these desirable features coexist. We search for perfection because we believe we are entitled to the best—even if perfection is an illusion foisted on us by an abundance of possibilities.

If perfection is what you expect, you will always be disappointed, says Schwartz. We become picky and unhappy. The cruel joke our psychology plays on us, of course, is that we are terrible at knowing what will satisfy us or at knowing how any experience will make us feel.

A sense of multiple alternatives, of unlimited possibility, breeds in us the illusion that the perfect person is out there waiting to be found.

If the search through all possibilities weren't exhausting (and futile) enough, thinking about attractive features of the alternatives not chosen—what economists call opportunity costs—reduces the potential pleasure in whatever choice we finally do make. The more possibilities, the more opportunity costs—and the more we think about them, the more we come to regret any choice. "So, once again," says Schwartz, "a greater variety of choices actually makes us feel worse."

Ultimately, our excess of choice leads to lack of intimacy. "How is anyone going to stack up against this perfect person who's out there somewhere just waiting to be found?" asks Schwartz. "It creates doubt about this person, who seems like a good person, someone I might even be in love with—but who knows what's possible *out* there? Intimacy takes time to develop. You need to have some reason to put in the time. If you're full of doubt at the start, you're not going to put in the time."

Moreover, a focus on one's own preferences can come at the expense of those of others. As Schwartz said in his 2004 book, *The Paradox of Choice: Why More Is Less,* "most people find it extremely challenging to balance the conflicting impulses of freedom of choice on the one hand and loyalty and commitment on the other."

And yet, throughout, we are focused on the partner we want to have, not on the one we want—or need—to be. That may be the worst choice of all.

Disappointment—or Tragedy?

The heightened sensitivity to relationship problems that follows from constantly appraising our happiness encourages couples to turn disappointment into tragedy, Doherty contends.

Inevitably, images of the perfect relationship dancing in our heads collide with our sense of entitlement; "I'm entitled to the best possible marriage." The reality of disappointment becomes intolerable. "It's part of a cultural belief system that says we are entitled to everything we feel we need."

Through the alchemy of desire, wants become needs, and unfulfilled needs become personal tragedies. "A husband who isn't very expressive of his feelings can be a disappointment or a tragedy, depending on whether it's an entitlement," says Doherty. "And that's very much a cultural phenomenon." We take the everyday disappointments of relationships and treat them as intolerable, see them as demeaning—the equivalent of alcoholism, say, or abuse. "People work their way into 'I'm a tragic figure' around the ordinary problems of marriage." Such stories are so widespread, Doherty is no longer inclined to see them as reflecting an individual psychological problem, although that is how he was trained—and how he practiced for many years as an eminent family therapist. "I see it first now as a cultural phenomenon."

First Lady Michelle Obama is no stranger to the disappointment that pervades relationships today. In *Barack and Michelle: Portrait of an American Marriage,* by Christopher Anderson, she confides how she reached a "state of desperation" while working full-time, bringing in the majority of the family income, raising two daughters, and rarely seeing her husband, who was then spending most of his week away from their Chicago home as an Illinois state senator, a job she thought would lead nowhere while it paid little. "She's killing me with this constant criticism," Barack complained. "She just seems so bitter, so angry all the time." She was annoyed that he "seems to think he can just go out there and pursue his dream and leave all the heavy lifting to me."

But then she had an epiphany: She remembered the guy she fell in love with. "I figured out that I was pushing to make Barack be something I wanted him to be for me. I was depending on him to make me happy. Except it didn't have anything to do with him. I needed support. I didn't necessarily need it from Barack."

Certainly, commitment narrows choice. But it is the ability to remember you really do love someone—even though you may not be feeling it at the moment.

Commitment is the ability to sustain an investment, to honor values over momentary feelings. The irony, of course, is that while we want happiness, it isn't a moment-by-moment experience; the deepest, most enduring form of happiness is the result of sustained emotional investments in other people.

Architects of the Heart

One of the most noteworthy findings emerging from relationship research is that desire isn't just something we passively feel when everything's going right; it develops in direct response to what we do. Simply having fun together, for example, is crucial to keeping the sex drive alive.

But in the churn of daily life, we tend to give short shrift to creating positive experiences. Over time, we typically become more oriented to dampening threats and insecurities—to resolving conflict, to eliminating jealousy, to banishing problems. But the brain is wired with both a positive and negative motivational system, and satisfaction and desire demand keeping the brain's positive system well-stoked.

Even for long-term couples, spending time together in novel, interesting, or challenging activities—games, dancing, even conversation—enhances feelings of closeness, passionate love, and satisfaction with the relationship. Couples recapture the excitement of the early days of being in love. Such passion naturally feeds commitment.

From Michelle to Michelangelo

Important as it is to choose the right partner, it's probably more important to *be* the right partner. Most people are focused on changing the wrong person in the relationship; if anyone has to change in a relationship, it's you—although preferably with the help of your partner.

> **Important as it is to choose the right partner, it's probably more important to *be* the right partner. We focus on changing the wrong person.**

Ultimately, "marriage is an inside job," Pat Love told the 2009 Smart Marriages Conference. "It's internal to the person. You have to let it do its work." And its biggest job is helping individuals grow up. "Marriage is about getting over yourself. Happiness is not about focusing on yourself." Happiness is about holding onto your values, deciding who you are and being that person, using your particular talent, and investing in others.

Unfortunately, says Margin family therapist and *PT* blogger Susan Pease Gadoua, not enough people today are willing to do the hard work of becoming a more mature person. "They think they have a lot more choices. And they think life will be easier in another relationship. What they don't realize is that it will be the same relationship—just with a different name."

The question is not how you want your partner to change but what kind of partner and person you want to be. In the best relationships, not only are you thinking about who you want to be, but your partner is willing to help you get there. Psychologist Caryl E. Rusbult calls it the Michelangelo phenomenon. Just as Michelangelo felt the figures he created were already "in" the stones, "slumbering within the actual self is an ideal form," explains Eli Finkel, associate professor of psychology at Northwestern University and frequent Rusbult collaborator. Your partner becomes an ally in sculpting your ideal self, in bringing out the person you dream of becoming, leading you to a deep form of personal growth as well as long-term satisfaction with life and with the relationship.

It takes a partner who supports your dreams, the traits and qualities you want to develop—whether or not you've articulated them clearly or simply expressed vague yearnings. "People come to reflect what their partners see in them and elicit from them," Finkel and Rusbult report in *Current Directions in Psychological Science.*

Case Study
Patty and Rod

Patty Newbold had married "a really great guy," but by the time their 13th anniversary rolled around, she had a long list of things he needed to change to make the marriage work. At 34, she felt depressed, frantic—and guilty, as Rod was fighting a chronic disease. But she had reached a breaking point, "I read my husband my list of unmet needs and suggested a divorce," even though what she really wanted was her marriage back. "I wanted to feel loved again. But it didn't seem possible."

Newbold has had a long time to think about that list. Her husband died the next day, a freak side effect of his medications. "He was gone, but the list remained. Out of perhaps 30 needs, only one was eased by losing him. I was free now to move the drinking glasses next to the sink."

As she read through the list the morning after he died, she realized that "marriage isn't about my needs or his needs or about how well we communicate about our needs. It's about loving and being loved. *Life* is about meeting (or letting go of) my own *needs. Marriage* is about loving another person and receiving love in return. It suddenly became oh so clear that receiving love is something I make happen, not him." And then she was flooded with memories of all the times "I'd been offered love by this wonderful man and rejected it because I was too wrapped up in whatever need I was facing at the time."

Revitalized is "a funny word to describe a relationship in which one party is dead," she reports, "but ours was revitalized. I was completely changed, too." Everything she learned that awful day has gone into a second marriage, now well into its second decade.

Such affirmation promotes trust in the partner and strengthens commitment. And commitment, Rusbult has found, is a key predictor of relationship durability. "It creates positive bias towards each other," says Finkel. "It feels good to achieve our goals. It's deeply satisfying and meaningful." In addition, it immunizes the relationship against potential distractions—all those "perfect" others. Finkel explains, "It motivates the derogation of alternative partners." It creates the perception—the illusion—that even the most attractive alternative partners are unappealing. Attention to them gets turned off—one of the many cognitive gymnastics we engage in to ward off doubts.

Like growth, commitment is an inside job. It's not a simple vow. Partners see each other in ways that enhance their connection and fend off threats. It fosters the perception that the relationship you're in is better than that of others. It breeds the inclination to react constructively—by accommodation—rather than destructively when a partner does something inconsiderate. It even motivates that most difficult of tasks, forgiveness for the ultimate harm of betrayal, Rusbult has shown.

It is a willingness—stemming in part from an understanding that your well-being and your partner's are linked over the long term—to depart from direct self-interest, such as erecting a grudge when you feel hurt.

The Michelangelo phenomenon gives the lie to the soul mate search. You can't find the perfect person; there is no such thing. And even if you think you could, the person he or she is today is, hopefully, not quite the person he or she wants to be 10 years down the road. You and your partner help each other become a more perfect person—perfect, that is, according to your own inner ideals. You are both, with mutual help, constantly evolving.

Critical Thinking

1. Describe some of the influences that culture has on happiness within marriages.
2. In the case study of Stephen and Christina, what do you think were some of the causes of the friction in their relationship?
3. What are some ways that couples can keep their relationships from becoming strained?
4. List some of the expectations that you have or had in a relationship. Did you see any in the reading?
5. Do you think that there is a trend in today's society that marriage should be perfect? Why or why not?

Create Central

www.mhhe.com/createcentral

Internet References

Love Is Respect
www.loveisrespect.org
Relationships Australia
www.relationships.org.au

Article Prepared by: Patricia Hrusa Williams, *University of Maine at Farmington*

The Myth of Wealthy Men and Beautiful Women

JAMES HAMBLIN

Learning Outcomes

After reading this article, you will be able to:

- List characteristics important to romantic attraction and mate selection.
- Explain the concepts of beauty-status exchange and matching.
- Analyze how gender and societal factors influence mate selection.

In one illustrious study of love ("human sexual selection") in 1986, psychologists David Buss and Michael Barnes asked people to rank 76 characteristics: What do you value most in a potential mate?

The winner wasn't beauty, and it wasn't wealth. Number one was "kind and understanding," followed by "exciting personality" and then "intelligent." Men did say they valued appearances more highly than women did, and women said they valued "good earning capacity" more highly than men did—but neither ranked measures of physical attractiveness or socioeconomic status among their top considerations.

People, though, are liars. Experiments that don't rely on self-reporting regularly show that physical attractiveness is exquisitely, at times incomparably, important to both men and women. Status (however you want to measure it: income, formal education, etc.) is often not far behind. In real-life dating studies, which get closer to genuine intentions, physical attractiveness and earning potential strongly predict romantic attraction.

While people tend to prefer people similar to themselves in terms of traits like religiousness or thriftiness, when it comes to beauty and income, more is almost always seen as better. On these "consensually ranked" traits, people seem to aspire to partners who rank more highly than themselves. They don't want a match so much as a jackpot.

The stereotypical example of that is known in sociology as a "beauty-status exchange"—an attractive person marries a wealthy or otherwise powerful person, and both win. It's the classic story of an elderly polymath-billionaire who has sustained damning burns to the face who marries a swimsuit model who can't find Paris on a map but really wants to go there, because it's romantic.

All you need is money or power, the notion goes, and beautiful lovers present themselves to you for the taking.

When Homer Simpson once came into a 500-pound surfeit of sugar, his id instinct was to turn it into fortune and sexual prosperity. "In America," he said, half dreaming after a night spent guarding the mound in his backyard, "first you get the sugar, then you get the power, then you get the women." That's an homage to *Scarface* (in the movie the quote was "money" instead of "sugar"), and it's where both Simpson and Tony Montana went emphatically astray.

University of Notre Dame sociologist Elizabeth McClintock has done exhaustive research on the idea of people exchanging traits. Her work was published last month in *American Sociological Review,* looking at data from 1,507 couples in various stages of relationships, including dating, cohabiting, and married. "Beauty-status exchange accords with the popular conception of romantic partner selection as a competitive market process," McClintock wrote, "a conception widely accepted in both popular culture and academia." She referred specifically to the gendered version, "in which an economically successful man partners with a beautiful 'trophy wife,'" as commonplace.

But McClintock found that outside of ailing tycoons and Donald Trump, in the practical world it basically doesn't exist. Where it does, it doesn't last. The dominant force in mating is *matching.*

What appears to be an exchange of beauty for socioeconomic status is often actually not an exchange, McClintock wrote, but a series of matched virtues. Economically successful women partner with economically successful men, and physically attractive women partner with physically attractive men.

"Sometimes you hear that really nice guys get hot girls," McClintock told me, "[but] I found that really nice guys get really nice girls. [Being nice] is not really buying you any currency in the attractiveness realm. If the guys are hot, too, then sure, they can get a hot girl."

Because people of high socioeconomic status are, on average, rated as more physically attractive than people of lower status, many correlations between one partner's appearance and the other partner's status are spurious and misconstrued.

"Women spend a lot more time trying to look good than men do," McClintock said. "That creates a lot of mess in this data. If you don't take that into account then you actually see there's a lot of these guys who are partnered with women who are better looking than them, which is just because, on average, women are better looking. Men are partnering 'up' in attractiveness. And men earn more than women—we've got that 70-percent wage gap—so women marry 'up' in income. You've got to take these things into account before concluding that women are trading beauty for money."

The study concludes that women aren't really out for men with more wealth than themselves, nor are men looking for women who outshine them in beauty. Rather, hearteningly, people really are looking for . . . compatibility and companionship. Finding those things is driven by matching one's strengths with a partner who's similarly endowed, rather than trying to barter kindness for hotness, humor for conscientiousness, cultural savvy for handyman-ship, or graduate degrees for marketable skills.

At least partly because physically attractive individuals are treated preferentially by the world at large, they enjoy improved school performance, greater occupational success, and higher earnings. So these variables can be hard to isolate.

"It would be very hard to separate out class and attractiveness," McClintock said, "because they're just so fundamentally linked. I can't control for that—but I don't see how anybody could."

Past research has found that both physical attractiveness and education "help a woman achieve upward mobility through marriage (defined as marrying a man of higher occupational status than her father)," McClintock noted in the journal article, "and help her marry a man of high occupational status, in absolute terms." But these studies regularly excluded any evaluation of the men's physical attractiveness, and so didn't address the simple fact that it might just be two attractive people being attracted to one another, probably in attractive clothes in an attractive place, both perpetually well slept. Any "exchange" was an illusion.

McClintock has also found that the pervasive tendency toward rating higher-status people as more attractive seems to perpetuate itself. "Because of that," she said, "there's a bias toward seeing women who are married to high-status men—who are themselves high-status—as being more attractive. It creates this self-affirming circle where we never even stop to ask if we perceive the man as good-looking. We just say she's good-looking, he's high status—and she's good-looking in part because the couple is high-status."

"Assuming that the importance of beauty and status is gendered may cause researchers to overlook men's attractiveness and women's socioeconomic resources," Eli Finkel, a psychologist at Northwestern University, told *New York* magazine, praising McClintock's work. In so doing, scientists misidentify matching as exchange.

"Scientists are humans, too," Finkel claimed, "and we can be inadvertently blinded by beliefs about how the world works. The studies that only looked at men's (but not women's) income and only looked at women's (but not men's) attractiveness were problematic in that way, as was the peer review process that allowed flawed papers like that to be published."

"Controlling for both partners' physical attractiveness may not eliminate the relationship between female beauty and male status," McClintock wrote, "but it should at least reduce this relationship substantially."

Even as its pervasiveness in popular culture is waning, the gendered beauty-status exchange model is harmful in several insidious ways, McClintock said. "It trivializes the importance of women's careers in a social sense: It's telling women that what matters is your looks, and your other accomplishments and qualities don't matter on the partner market. The truth is, people are evaluating women for their looks, and they're evaluating men for their looks. Women are as shallow as men when it comes to appearance, and they should focus on their own accomplishments. If women want an accomplished guy, that's going to come with being accomplished."

So this is just one more place where upward mobility is, it seems, a myth. But in this case, no love is lost. Within the gendered beauty-status exchange model, physical attractiveness "might enable class mobility for women," yes, McClintock wrote, but not without ensuring the women's economic dependency on her husband and anachronistically ignoring her valuation of his physical attractiveness.

"It also sets up this idea of marriage being mercenary," McClintock said, "which doesn't fit with our usual conception that we kind of like our spouse and we want someone that we get along with. It's not just this trade of his money for her beauty, and he's going to dump her as soon as she starts to get some wrinkles around her eyes."

Critical Thinking

1. The article suggests that compatibility is more important than status or physical attractiveness in mate selection. Do you feel this is true? Why/Why not?

2. Why is it so difficult to study the role that status and physical attractiveness have on relationship formation?

3. What factors or characteristics are important to romantic attraction? Mate selection? Are they the same or do they differ?

4. Do men versus women look for different things in relationships? If so, what does each look for?

Internet References

Love is Respect
www.loveisrespect.org

Mating: Psychology Today
https://www.psychologytoday.com/basics/mating

Two of Us
www.twoofus.org

Article   Prepared by: Patricia Hrusa Williams, *University of Maine at Farmington*

Not Wanting Kids Is Entirely Normal

Why the ingrained expectation that women should desire to become parents is unhealthy.

Jessica Valenti

Learning Outcomes

After reading this article, you will be able to:

- Describe what "safe haven" laws are.

- Explain the challenges of motherhood.

- Recognize the negative effects of unintended pregnancies on families and children.

In 2008, Nebraska decriminalized child abandonment. The move was part of a "safe haven" law designed to address increased rates of infanticide in the state. Like other safe haven laws, parents in Nebraska who felt unprepared to care for their babies could drop them off at a designated location without fear of arrest and prosecution. But legislators made a major logistical error: They failed to implement an age limitation for dropped-off children.

Within just weeks of the law passing, parents started dropping off their kids. But here's the rub: None of them were infants. A couple of months in, 36 children had been left in state hospitals and police stations. Twenty-two of the children were over 13 years old. A 51-year-old grandmother dropped off a 12-year-old boy. One father dropped off his entire family—nine children from ages one to 17. Others drove from neighboring states to drop off their children once they heard that they could abandon them without repercussion.

The Nebraska state government, realizing the tremendous mistake it had made, held a special session of the legislature to rewrite the law in order to add an age limitation. Governor Dave Heineman said the change would "put the focus back on the original intent of these laws, which is saving newborn babies and exempting a parent from prosecution for child abandonment. It should also prevent those outside the state from bringing their children to Nebraska in an attempt to secure services."

On November 21, 2008, the last day that the safe haven law was in effect for children of all ages, a mother from Yolo County, California, drove over 1,200 miles to the Kimball County Hospital in Nebraska where she left her 14-year-old son.

What happened in Nebraska raises the question: If there were no consequences, how many of us would give up our kids? After all, child abandonment is nothing new and it's certainly not rare in the United States. Over 400,000 children are in the foster care system waiting to be placed in homes, thousands of parents relinquish their children every year. One woman even sent her adopted child back to his home country with an apology letter pinned like a grocery list to his chest. Whether it's because of hardship or not, many Americans are giving up on parenthood.

In February 2009, someone calling herself Ann logged onto the website Secret Confessions and wrote three sentences: "I am depressed. I hate being a mom. I also hate being a stay at home mom too!" Over three years later, the thread of comments is still going strong with thousands of responses—the site usually garners only 10 or so comments for every "confession." Our anonymous Ann had hit a nerve.

One woman who got pregnant at 42 wrote, "I hate being a mother too. Every day is the same. And to think I won't be free of it until I am like 60 and then my life will be over." Another, identifying herself only as k'smom, said, "I feel so trapped, anxious, and overwhelmed. I love my daughter and she's well taken care of but this is not the path I would have taken given a second chance."

Gianna wrote, "I love my son, but I hate being a mother. It has been a thankless, monotonous, exhausting, irritating and oppressive job. Motherhood feels like a prison sentence. I can't wait until I am paroled when my son turns 18 and hopefully goes far away to college." One D.C.-based mom even said that although she was against abortion before having her son, now she would "run to the abortion clinic" if she got pregnant again.

The responses—largely from women who identify themselves as financially stable—spell out something less explicit than well-worn reasons for parental unhappiness such as poverty and a lack of support. These women simply don't feel that motherhood is all it's cracked up to be, and if given a second chance, they wouldn't do it again.

Some cited the boredom of stay-at-home momism. Many complained of partners who didn't shoulder their share of child care responsibilities. "Like most men, my husband doesn't do much—if anything—for baby care. I have to do and plan for everything," one mother wrote. A few got pregnant accidentally and were pressured by their husbands and boyfriends to carry through with the pregnancy, or knew they never wanted children but felt it was something they "should" do.

The overwhelming sentiment, however, was the feeling of a loss of self, the terrifying reality that their lives had been subsumed into the needs of their child. DS wrote, "I feel like I have completely lost any thing that was me. I never imagined having children and putting myself aside would make me feel this bad." The expectation of total motherhood is bad enough, having to live it out every day is soul crushing. Everything that made us an individual, that made us unique, no longer matters. It's our role as a mother that defines us. Not much has changed.

"The feminine mystique permits, even encourages, women to ignore the question of their identity," wrote Betty Friedan. "The mystique says they can answer the question 'Who am I?' by saying 'Tom's wife . . . Mary's mother.' The truth is—and how long it's been true, I'm not sure, but it was true in my generation and it's true of girls growing up today—an American woman no longer has a private image to tell her who she is, or can be, or wants to be."

At the time she published *The Feminine Mystique,* Friedan argued that the public image of women was largely one of domesticity—"washing machines, cake mixes . . . detergents," all sold through commercials and magazines. Today, American women have more public images of themselves than that of a housewife. We see ourselves depicted in television, ads, movies, and magazines (not to mention relief!) as politicians, business owners, intellectuals, soldiers, and more. But that's what makes the public images of total motherhood so insidious. We see these diverse images of ourselves and believe that the oppressive standard Friedan wrote about is dead, when in fact it has simply shifted. Because no matter how many different kinds of public images women see of themselves, they're still limited. They're still largely white, straight upper-middle-class depictions, and they all still identify women as mothers or non-mothers.

American culture can't accept the reality of a woman who does not want to be a mother. It goes against everything we've been taught to think about women and how desperately they want babies. If we're to believe the media and pop culture, women—even teen girls—are forever desperate for a baby. It's our greatest desire.

The truth is, most women spend the majority of their lives trying *not* to get pregnant. According to the Guttmacher Institute, by the time a woman with two children is in her mid-40s she will have spent only five years trying to become pregnant, being pregnant, and not being at risk for getting pregnant following a birth. But to avoid getting pregnant before or after those two births, she would have had to refrain from sex or use contraception for an average of 25 years. Almost all American women (99 percent), ages 15–44, who have had sexual intercourse use some form of birth control. The second most popular form of birth control after the Pill? Sterilization. And now, more than ever, women are increasingly choosing forms of contraception that are for long-term use. Since 2005, for example, IUD use has increased by a whopping 161 percent. That's a long part of life and a lot of effort to avoid parenthood!

Now, it may be that these statistics simply indicate that modern women are just exerting more control over when and under what circumstances they become mothers. To a large degree that's true. But it doesn't jibe with an even more shocking reality: that half of pregnancies in the United States are unintended. Once you factor in the abortion rate and pregnancies that end in miscarriage, we're left with the rather surprising fact that one-third of babies born in the United States were unplanned. Not so surprising, however, is that the intention to have children definitively impacts how parents feel about their children, and how those children are treated—sometimes with terrifying results.

Jennifer Barber, a population researcher at the University of Michigan, studied more than 3,000 mothers and their close to 6,000 children from a range of socioeconomic backgrounds. Barber and her colleagues asked women who had recently given birth, "Just before you became pregnant, did you want to become pregnant when you did?" Those who answered yes were categorized as "intended"; those who answered no were then asked, "Did you want a baby but not at that time, or did you want none at all?" Depending on their answer, they were classified as "mistimed" or "unwanted." Over 60 percent of the children studied were reported as planned, almost 30 percent were unplanned ("mistimed"), and 10 percent were unequivocally "unwanted."

The results of Barber's research showed that the children who were unintended—both those who were mistimed and those who were unwanted—got fewer parental resources than those children who were intended. Basically, children who were unplanned didn't get as much emotional and cognitive support as children who were planned—as reported both by the researchers and the mothers themselves. Barber's research looked at things like the number of children's books in the home, and how often a parent read to a child or taught them skills like counting or the alphabet for the "cognitive" aspect. For the "emotional" support rating, they developed a scale measuring the "warmth" and "responsiveness" of the mother, how much time the family spent together, and how much time the father spent with the child. Across the board, children who were wanted got more from their parents than children who weren't. Children who were unplanned were also subject to harsher parenting and more punitive measures than a sibling who was intended.

Barber pointed out that this kind of pattern could be due to parental stress and a lack of patience that's "directed explicitly toward an unwanted child," and that a mistimed or unwanted birth could raise stress levels in the parents' interactions with their other children as well. She also says that in addition to benign emotional neglect, parenting unintended children is also associated with infant health problems and mortality, maternal depression, and sometimes child abuse.

[. . .]

When Torry Hansen of Shelbyville, Tennessee, sent her seven-year-old adopted son by himself on a plane back to his home country of Russia with nothing more than a note explaining she didn't want to parent him, she became one of the most reviled women in America. Russian officials were so incensed that they temporarily halted all adoption to the United States. We sometimes expect fathers to shirk their responsibility; but when mothers do it, it shakes the core of what we've been taught to believe about women and maternal instinct.

Anthropologist Sarah Blaffer Hrdy argued in a 2001 Utah lecture, for example, that being female is seen as synonymous with having and nurturing as many children as possible. So when mothers abandon their children, it's seen as unnatural. This simplistic, emotional response to parents—mothers, in particular—who give up their kids is part of the reason Americans have such a difficult time dealing with the issue. As Hrdy says, "No amount of legislation can ensure that mothers will love their babies."

That's why programs like safe haven laws—age limitations or not—will never truly get to the heart of the matter. As Mary Lee Allen, director of the Children's Defense Fund's child welfare and mental health division, has said, "These laws help women to drop their babies off but do nothing to provide support to women and children before this happens."

Unfortunately, discussing the structural issues has never been an American strong suit. Hrdy notes that legislators are too afraid to focus on sensible solutions. "Talking about the source of the problem would require policymakers to discuss sex education and contraception, not to mention abortion, and they view even nonsensical social policies as preferable to the prospect of political suicide."

If policymakers and people who care about children want to reduce the number of abandoned kids, they need to address the systemic issues: poverty, maternity leave, access to resources, and health care. We need to encourage women to demand more help from their partners, if they have them. In a way, that's the easier fix, because we know what we have to do there; the issues have been the same for years. The less-obvious hurdle is that of preparing parents emotionally and putting forward realistic images of parenthood and motherhood. There also needs to be some sort of acknowledgment that not everyone should parent—when parenting is a given, it's not fully considered or thought out, and it gives way too easily to parental ambivalence and unhappiness.

Take Trinity, one of the mothers who commented on the Secret Confessions board about hating parenthood. She wrote, "My pregnancy was totally planned and I thought it was a good idea at the time. Nobody tells you the negatives before you get pregnant—they convince you it's a wonderful idea and you will love it. I think it's a secret shared among parents . . . they're miserable so they want you to be too."

By having more honest conversations about parenting, we can avoid the kind of secret depressions so many mothers seem to be harboring. If what we want is deliberate, thought-out, planned, and expected parenthood—and parenting that is healthy and happy for children—then we have to speak out.

Critical Thinking

1. In Nebraska, why do you think parents were using the "safe haven law" to abandon older children rather than infants, as the law had originally intended?

2. In the article there is a quote by the author which states "American culture can't accept the reality of a woman who does not want to be a mother." Do you agree? Why or why not?

3. What are the challenges of being a mother in modern society? Given these challenges how can we better prepare and support those who become parents by choice or through unintended pregnancies?

Create Central

www.mhhe.com/createcentral

Internet References

Administration for Children and Families: Infant Safe Haven Laws
    https://www.childwelfare.gov/systemwide/laws_policies/statutes/safehaven.cfm

Planned Parenthood
    http://www.plannedparenthood.org

The March of Dimes
    www.marchofdimes.com

Article   Prepared by: Patricia Hrusa Williams, *University of Maine at Farmington*

What Happens to a Woman's Brain When She Becomes a Mother

ADRIENNE LAFRANCE

Learning Outcomes

After reading this article, you will be able to:

- Identity ways the brain changes during pregnancy and the early postpartum period.
- Understand the role of the amygdala and oxytocin for mother-infant bonding.
- Analyze how biology influences caregiving and early parenting behavior.

The artist Sarah Walker once told me that becoming a mother is like discovering the existence of a strange new room in the house where you already live. I always liked Walker's description because it's more precise than the shorthand most people use for life with a newborn: *Everything changes.*

Because a lot of things do change, of course, but for new mothers, some of the starkest differences are also the most intimate ones—the emotional changes. Which, it turns out, are also largely neurological.

Even before a woman gives birth, pregnancy tinkers with the very structure of her brain, several neurologists told me. After centuries of observing behavioral changes in new mothers, scientists are only recently beginning to definitively link the way a woman acts with what's happening in her prefrontal cortex, midbrain, parietal lobes, and elsewhere. Gray matter becomes more concentrated. Activity increases in regions that control empathy, anxiety, and social interaction. On the most basic level, these changes, prompted by a flood of hormones during pregnancy and in the postpartum period, help attract a new mother to her baby. In other words, those maternal feelings of overwhelming love, fierce protectiveness, and constant worry begin with reactions in the brain.

Mapping the maternal brain is also, many scientists believe, the key to understanding why so many new mothers experience serious anxiety and depression. An estimated one in six women suffers from postpartum depression, and many more develop behaviors like compulsively washing hands and obsessively checking whether the baby is breathing.

"This is what we call an aspect of almost the obsessive compulsive behaviors during the very first few months after the baby's arrival," maternal brain researcher Pilyoung Kim told me. "Mothers actually report very high levels of patterns of thinking about things that they cannot control. They're constantly thinking about baby. Is baby healthy? Sick? Full?"

"In new moms, there are changes in many of the brain areas," Kim continued. "Growth in brain regions involved in emotion regulation, empathy-related regions, but also what we call maternal motivation—and I think this region could be largely related to obsessive-compulsive behaviors. In animals and humans during the postpartum period, there's an enormous desire to take care of their own child."

There are several interconnected brain regions that help drive mothering behaviors and mood.

Of particular interest to researchers is the almond-shaped set of neurons known as the amygdala, which helps process memory and drives emotional reactions like fear, anxiety, and aggression. In a normal brain, activity in the amygdala grows in the weeks and months after giving birth. This growth, researchers believe, is correlated with how a new mother behaves—an enhanced amygdala makes her hypersensitive to her baby's needs—while a cocktail of hormones, which find more receptors in a larger amygdala, help create a positive feedback loop to motivate mothering behaviors. Just by staring at her baby, the reward centers of a mother's brain will light up, scientists have found in several studies. This maternal brain circuitry influences the syrupy way a mother speaks to her baby, how attentive she is, even the affection she feels for her baby. It's not surprising, then, that damage to the amygdala is associated with higher levels of depression in mothers.

Amygdala damage in babies could affect the mother-child bond as well. In a 2004 *Journal of Neuroscience* study, infant monkeys who had amygdala lesions were less likely to vocalize their distress, or pick their own mothers over other adults. A newborn's ability to distinguish between his mother and anybody else is linked to the amygdala.

Activity in the amygdala is also associated with a mother's strong feelings about her own baby versus babies in general. In a 2011 study of amygdala response in new mothers, women reported feeling more positive about photos depicting their own smiling babies compared with photos of unfamiliar smiling babies, and their brain activity reflected that discrepancy. Scientists recorded bolder brain response—in the amygdala, thalamus, and elsewhere—among mothers as they looked at photos of their own babies.

Greater amygdala response when viewing their own children was tied to lower maternal anxiety and fewer symptoms of depression, researchers found. In other words, a new mother's brain changes help motivate her to care for her baby but they may also help buffer her own emotional state. From the study:

> Thus, the greater amygdala response to one's own infant face observed in our study likely reflects more positive and pro-social aspects of maternal responsiveness, feelings, and experience. Mothers experiencing higher levels of anxiety and lower mood demonstrated less amygdala response to their own infant and reported more stressful and more negatively valenced parenting attitudes and experiences.

Much of what happens in a new mother's amygdala has to do with the hormones flowing to it. The region has a high concentration of receptors for hormones like oxytocin, which surge during pregnancy.

"We see changes at both the hormonal and brain levels," brain researcher Ruth Feldman told me in an e-mail. "Maternal oxytocin levels—the system responsible for maternal-infant bonding across all mammalian species—dramatically increase during pregnancy and the postpartum [period] and the more mother is involved in childcare, the greater the increase in oxytocin."

Oxytocin also increases as women look at their babies, or hear their babies' coos and cries, or snuggle with their babies. An increase in oxytocin during breastfeeding may help explain why researchers have found that breastfeeding mothers are more sensitive to the sound of their babies' cries than non-breastfeeding mothers. "Breastfeeding mothers show a greater level of [brain] responses to baby's cry compared with formula-feeding mothers in the first month postpartum," Kim said. "It's just really interesting. We don't know if it's the act of breastfeeding or the oxytocin or any other factor."

What scientists do know, Feldman says, is that becoming a parent looks—at least in the brain—a lot like falling in love. Which helps explain how many new parents describe feeling when they meet their newborns. At the brain level, the networks that become especially sensitized are those that involve vigilance and social salience—the amygdala—as well as dopamine networks that incentivize prioritizing the infant. "In our research, we find that periods of social bonding involve change in the same 'affiliative' circuits," Feldman said. "We showed that during the first months of 'falling in love' some similar changes occur between romantic partners." Incidentally, that same circuitry is what makes babies smell so good to their mothers, researchers found in a 2013 study.

The greatest brain changes occur with a mother's first child, though it's not clear whether a mother's brain ever goes back to what it was like before childbirth, several neurologists told me. And yet brain changes aren't limited to new moms.

Men show similar brain changes when they're deeply involved in caregiving. Oxytocin does not seem to drive nurturing behavior in men the way it does in women, Feldman and other researchers found in a study last year. Instead, a man's parental brain is supported by a socio-cognitive network that develops in the brain of both sexes later in life, whereas women appear to have evolved to have a "brain-hormone-behavior constellation" that's automatically primed for mothering. Another way to look at it: the blueprint for mothering behavior exists in the brain even before a woman has children.

Perhaps, then, motherhood really is like secret space in a woman's brain, waiting to be discovered. "Although only mothers experience pregnancy, birth, and lactation, and these provide powerful primers for the expression of maternal care via amygdala sensitization," researchers wrote, "evolution created other pathways for adaptation to the parental role in human fathers, and these alternative pathways come with practice, attunement, and day-by-day caregiving."

In other words, the act of simply caring for one's baby forges new neural pathways—undiscovered rooms in the parental brain.

Critical Thinking

1. What are some concerns and worries women may experience during pregnancy and during the early postpartum period?

2. In what ways does a woman's brain change as a result of pregnancy? What are some of the positive changes which result? Negative ones?

3. Given the dramatic changes women experience, especially after the birth of a first child, what policies and supports are needed to ensure the well-being of new mothers and their babies?

Internet References

The March of Dimes
www.marchofdimes.com

Babycenter: Pregnancy
http://www.babycenter.com/pregnancy

Zero to Three
www.zerotothree.org

Article   Prepared by: Patricia Hrusa Williams, *University of Maine at Farmington*

Sperm Donor, Life Partner

Alana Semuels

Learning Outcomes

After reading this article, you will be able to:

- Identify reasons individuals may choose to develop partnerships only to have children.

- Understand the emotional, legal, and practical strengths and challenges of three-parent families and platonic/non-married parenting partnerships.

Dawn Pieke's relationship imploded just before she reached 40. Pieke had a miscarriage and shortly after, her boyfriend, whom she'd dated for almost a decade, met someone else on a business trip and had an affair. The two broke up and Pieke found herself in a tailspin: She knew she wanted a family, but she also knew her biological clock was ticking, and she wasn't sure, after two separate, decades-long relationships, that she could go through it all again.

A glass of wine in hand, she steeled herself for more dating, signed up for Match.com, and started going on dates in Omaha, Nebraska, where she lives.

"I thought, 'These guys look like jerks . . . I just want a kid, why can't I just have a baby and not worry about if it's *the* guy?'" she told me, in a phone interview. After eight months, she hadn't clicked with anyone.

Pieke, who works in sales, started diligently researching her options, but soon got discouraged. Adoption didn't seem like a good bet: She knew three separate couples trying to adopt, and it was taking forever for them to get approved—a potential single mother would have even more trouble, she figured. Pieke didn't love the idea of going to a sperm bank: She and her twin sister were raised by a single mom and they grew up always wanting to know more about their father. She wanted her child to know both parents, if possible.

"I always thought I would be married and have kids by the time I was 25, but it just didn't turn out that way," she said.

Then one day, she stumbled across something on the Internet that seemed like it might work: A website that connected people who wanted to have kids and raise them together, but without a romantic relationship. She paid a small fee and registered, and right away, a guy in Australia caught her eye. But she didn't contact him. Everyone she knew thought she was crazy to even consider having a child with a stranger.

"My family and friends thought I was nuts, they were like, 'chill out, you'll meet someone,'" she said. "But I thought, 'wow, this could maybe be something.'"

A few months later, Pieke was on the Facebook page of the co-parenting site and she got a message. It was from someone asking if she was looking for a co-parent, and it just happened to be from the very same man she'd seen on the website before, who was living in Australia.

He was gay, and from New York, and shared her beliefs about spirituality—she describes herself as spiritual, but not religious. The two struck up a correspondence. She liked that he was dark-haired, since she is blonde, and figured they might make a good-looking kid, and they agreed on lots of things. Most importantly, they had similar ideas about parenting: They would be gentle and nurturing, with no yelling or spanking, and would not use baby talk, but would instead speak to the child as a "person already full of intelligence," Pieke said.

"It felt like speaking to an old family member," said Fabian Blue, the man she met on the site. He made a documentary about his efforts to find a co-parent, called *The Baby Daddy Project* with the clever tagline, "No Sex, No Marriage, Just the Baby Carriage." Blue would set up his laptop with Pieke on Skype for dinner parties and special events, and the two would talk daily, sharing their hopes and fears for having a family, getting closer and closer to the conclusion that they might just want to make and raise a child together, though without any sort of romantic involvement.

They met in person for the first time in downtown Omaha on Thanksgiving 2011, when he pulled up in a horse-drawn

Cinderella carriage, handed her a bouquet of red roses, and asked, "Will you be my baby mama?" When she said yes, they gave each other high-fives and got into the carriage (you can see footage in this video Blue made about their meeting).

After that, he didn't go back to Australia. Instead, they started experimenting with an at-home insemination kit—basically a cup and a syringe (you can also see somewhat awkward footage of this—G-rated—in Blue's video). Two months and two tries later, Pieke got pregnant. Their daughter, Indigo, was born in October 2012 (yes, there's footage of that, too).

"Women my age hold out for romantic partnerships, if they don't find it, they say, 'well, I guess I'm not going to have kids,'" Pieke told me. "That's where I was when I turned 40, but I said, 'I'm going to make this happen, whether I find a guy or not. I'm not going to wait on guys anymore.'"

It's been decades since Louise Joy Brown, the first "test-tube" baby was born, allowing women to have biological children through in-vitro fertilization, and without a husband. Since then, millions of babies have been born to single women, through both natural conception and in-vitro, who couldn't find the right partner or want to go it on their own. In 2009, 19 percent of births to women aged 35–39 occurred outside of marriage, up from 5 percent in 1970, according to Child Trends, a Washington research group.

But that doesn't mean that women necessarily prefer to do it all themselves: Being a single-parent is financially and emotionally taxing. Studies show that single-parents are more likely to live in poverty, and that mothers earn and learn less, since they have to pay for child care and take more time off from work to care for a child.

That may be why more single women are trying to find a sperm donor who is also involved in a child's life. Sites like Modamily.com, PollenTree.com, and Familybydesign.com serve as places for people to meet potential co-parents: They're kind of like a Match.com for people who want to have kids without having sex.

"This could be a seismic shift in how people view what a family is," said Ivan Fatovic, the founder and CEO of Modamily, which launched in Feburary 2012. Fatovic started the site after talking with some girlfriends in a bar in New York: They were all approaching 40, and hadn't found a mate, and were worried about finding the right partner for them—and father for their children—in a few short years.

"We thought—we can introduce people who share the same vision and values. We're not saying it's better or worse, but we think it's an additional option."

It's not just single women looking for involved parenting partners, either. Increasingly, lesbian couples who want to have children are turning to men they know for genetic material, and are sometimes asking him to share some parenting

responsibilities. It's possible that gay men who use a surrogate to have a child are involving the mother in the child's life too—at least if you believe the premise of the failed 2012 NBC comedy *The New Normal.*

"We are seeing a growing trend of a female, same-sex-couple parenting with the man who provides the genetic material but does not relinquish his rights as a sperm donor," said Diana Adams, a New York lawyer who advises families on issues like these.

To be sure, this new type of family can create a minefield of legal issues. A Florida judge last year allowed the names of three parents on a birth certificate after a sperm donor sued a lesbian couple, who had been his friends, after they asked him to cede parental rights. Last October, California amended its family code to provide that a child can have more than two parents. And the case of Jason Patric, who donated sperm to his ex-girlfriend on the condition he wouldn't be involved in the child's life, and then changed his mind and sued for custody, got widespread media attention in 2012 after Patric started lobbying for more rights for sperm donors.

"Three-parent families will be one of the next major legal issues for the LBGTQ community," Adams said.

Laws vary state-by-state regarding whose name goes on the birth certificate and who is responsible for child support. Generally speaking, in a sperm donor context, if a woman gets pregnant through at-home insemination, the biological father is responsible for child support if there is no donor-insemination contract in place, although the mother might not file for it.

Adams and other lawyers recommend that families decide whether a sperm donor will be a co-parent or just a donor, and sit down with a lawyer to draw up an agreement. If they are planning on co-parenting, there are a few other things they should iron out too: Whether the family is going to share a bank account and retirement accounts, who will cover the financial costs of raising a child, whether the parents want to commit to living in the same city or not. What will happen if one of the parents meets a romantic partner? What if someone gets a career opportunity in another city? What is the division of responsibilities for child care and decision making? What will they do about vaccinations, and medical interventions, and schooling?

Often, just having the conversation is just as important as putting the decisions into a legal document and submitting it to a family court, Adams said.

The legal issues can get even stickier when there are more than two people involved. Fatovic, of Modamily, said he helped a straight couple find a birth mother, because the woman in the couple couldn't have kids and the man wanted his own biological child. All three are involved in parenting. Usually gay couples want the donor or surrogate to cede all parental rights, but sometimes don't draw up any such agreement, Adams said.

New York State even bans paid surrogate pregnancies, part of a response to a 1980s court case in which a surrogate mother refused to give up custody of the baby (the parents who sued to be recognized as legal parents were straight, and eventually won parental rights in court).

Despite the legal issues, more parents can be better for a child's welfare, argues Rachel Hope, author of *Family By Choice: Platonic Partnered Parenting,* published in January. Hope might be one of the first people who tried platonic parenting in recent times—she had a son, who is now 24, with a colleague and best friend. Hope, who is 43, met her second platonic-parenting partner, Paul Wennaro, the creator of the Garden Burger, in Hawaii about 15 years ago. She asked him to be her parenting partner in 2007, and they have a 6-year old daughter, Grace. They all live together in Los Angeles.

But Wennaro is 67, and when Hope decided she wanted another child, he said he wanted to spend his time and energy on Grace. So Hope began an extensive search online, and after three years, found a 58-year-old ER doctor who already has a 13-year-old with a lesbian parenting partner he met on Craigslist. The two clicked, and are starting IVF in January. The three parents are hoping to live together, or at least close to one another, and be a new type of family with their children.

"Throughout history, the model that has worked for humankind was extended family—a village, a tribe," Hope told me. "It's only recently that we've started doing the nuclear family, with one mom and one dad, and it's really a failed experiment."

It's an especially good alternative to single parenthood, Hope said, since single parenting can be so fraught with stresses and challenges.

"The single parents I know are some of the most miserable people I've ever met," she said. "I've met quadriplegics who are happier than the single parents I know."

Of course, there are flaws to be found with this type of parenting. Although there isn't any research about the outcomes of children born into these non-traditional families, W. Bradford Wilcox, the director of the National Marriage Project, said that this type of family could create instability, which studies say is definitely bad for children.

"My concern about platonic parenting is that such an arrangement will not last," he wrote, in an e-mail. "In most cases, one or both of the parties will develop a non-platonic attraction to someone else and move on."

A healthy sexual relationship is what contributes to the emotional and physical bond that keeps many parents together over the long haul, he said. Platonic parents wouldn't have any such relationship.

It's not just the sexual bond: It's that children of platonic parents will miss out on the organic parts of living with a mother and a father who work together to raise them, said Glenn Stanton, director for Family Formation Studies at Focus on the Family.

"Parenting is not a time share," he said. "It's something you've got to own completely and full-time."

If women don't find a man they feel they want to marry and raise children with, he said, they should think about the child's welfare before deciding to have a child. After all, humans often desire a number of things that they sometimes can't have, he added.

It's true that sometimes people marry and have children with the best intentions and then split up, but they raise their children "doing the best they can in spite of the curveball life has thrown them," he said. "The idea of putting yourself intentionally in that situation is a whole other matter."

I asked Stanton whether he thought platonic parents were really any different than two people who marry without a strong romantic bond. You might remember "Marry Him!," an article from *The Atlantic* in 2008, in which single mom Lori Gottlieb caused a firestorm by advising women in their thirties who want children to marry someone without considering passion or an "intense connection."

"My advice is this: Settle!" she wrote. "Marriage isn't a passion-fest; it's more like a partnership formed to run a very small, mundane, and often boring nonprofit business."

Could a platonic-parenting relationship really be that different?, I asked Stanton Yes, Stanton said. Children learn from parents who have committed to sticking together, bumps and all, whether they're perfect life partners or not.

"That's what husbands and wives do, they say, 'I'm going to link up with you, for good and for bad, we're going to make it work.'" he said. "There's something wonderful about that that changes them and makes them better people, and the child learns from that."

But platonic parents commit to a lifetime commitment to raise a child in much the same way, Hope and Pieke argue. Before even trying to get pregnant, the parents nail down plans to make sure the emotional and financial support their child needs will be present from birth. Sometimes more effectively than married couples do, Hope said, since so many marriages end in unhappy divorces with a child torn between two feuding parents.

"We're releasing the expectation that building a family on the shifting sands of a romantic high is a smart thing to do," she said. "This is about building a family on common values, which really makes sense, has staying power, and is what's going to work for the kids."

For women in their thirties and forties, choosing someone to co-parent with can be a smarter decision than trying to find a mate because it takes the pressure off to marry or reproduce with someone you barely know, said Adams.

"A traditional model would have been a woman at 37 scrambling and trying to create a family with a romantic partner who she's known for two months," Adams said. "Wouldn't she be able to create a more stable family bond with her gay best friend of 20 years?"

There are alternatives to platonic parenting: Many single parents find that there are sufficient supports in things like cohousing, where families move into complexes with family dinners, shared living spaces and people in situations like theirs. Teri Hupfer moved into one such complex in the San Francisco area because she had two children, aged 15 months and seven years, and didn't know anyone else with kids.

"I wanted to move somewhere my kids would be able to run around outside and see other kids, but as a lesbian with biracial kids I couldn't see myself in a suburban home," she told me, in an e-mail. Cohousing did the trick. There were lots of families with young children, and they would take turns watching the kids while other parents cooked common meals, worked late, or even went out on dates. Some of the single moms in the complex turned out to be close friends, and their children grew up together too.

When she moved into the complex, 6 of the 32 families were single moms. Now, there are only two, she said, and some are lobbying for no more single mothers, because they are sometimes considered needy, she said. They ask for favors more—help babysitting, or picking up a child from daycare—and can only give back half as much time as couples can.

Dawn Pieke and Fabian Blue feel lucky that their daughter will know both of them, and have both of them involved in her life—they're so happy with their experience that they're trying to write a book about it. They also feel that they've vetted each other more extensively than married couples do. They performed extensive background checks on each other and shared tough moments that they might have tried to hide from a potential romantic partner, like when Pieke called Blue sobbing, nearly incoherent, because her dog died. They did testing to see what their fertility chances would be, and got various medical tests to make sure a potential child wouldn't have any genetic problems. Blue had come close to committing to other potential parenting partners, but something in his gut had told them that the other women weren't the right fit, but Pieke was.

The two felt so comfortable with each other that they didn't even create a co-parenting agreement—when couples get married, they don't sign a co-parenting agreement, Pieke points out. They're just trusting one another to stay involved. It's challenging at times—Pieke needs to stay in Omaha to care for her mother, who has Alzheimer's, and Blue needs to go where he can find a job. He works in high-end hotel management, and is currently based in Alabama. But he flies back frequently, and they're still on the same page about rearing Indigo. They split the costs 50-50.

They're still both looking for romantic partners who will accept their alternative lifestyle. If they don't find them, that's okay too. It's a totally different place than Pieke was in just a few years ago, after her relationship ended and she was left single and afraid that she'd never be able to have a family. She's even glad—in a weird way—about the breakups that led her to where she is now.

"I'm so thankful that everything did happen, because Indigo wouldn't be who she is without her dad," Pieke said. "She's amazing and funny and she's just awesome. Now that she's here, its hard to look back and say I wish this or that would have happened. She's here because of all of that."

Critical Thinking

1. Do you need to be in love and romantically linked to decide to have a child and parent together? Why or why not?

2. What might be some advantages of platonic parenting? Challenges or concerns?

3. What are legal and policy-related issues associated with three-parent families and platonic/non-married parenting partnerships?

Internet References

Path 2 Parenthood, The America Fertility Association
http://www.path2parenthood.org/

Partnered Parenting Magazine
http://www.partneredparenting.com/

Single Mothers by Choice
http://www.singlemothersbychoice.org/

Unit 3

UNIT

Prepared by: Patricia Hrusa Williams, *University of Maine at Farmington*

Family Relationships

And they lived happily ever after. . . . The romantic image conjured up by this well-known final line from fairy tales is not reflective of the reality of family life and relationship maintenance. The belief that somehow love alone should carry us through is pervasive. In reality, maintaining a relationship takes dedication, hard work, and commitment.

We come into relationships, regardless of their nature, with fantasies about how things ought to be. Partners, spouses, parents, children, siblings, and others—all family members, have at least some unrealistic expectations about each other and what their relationships should look and feel like with one another. It is through the negotiation during the course of our lives together that we work through these expectations and hopefully, replace them with other more realistic ones. By recognizing and making their own contributions to the family, members can set and attain realistic family goals. Tolerance, acceptance of differences, and effective communication skills can facilitate this process. Along the way, family members need to learn new skills and develop new habits of relating to each other. This will not be easy, and, try as they may, not everything will be controllable. Patterns of interaction and communication can be hard to change. Factors both inside and outside the family may impede the progress.

Even before we enter a marriage or other committed relationship, attitudes, standards, and beliefs influence our choices. Increasingly, choices include whether we should commit to such a relationship in the first place. From the start of a committed relationship, the expectations both partners have and patterns they have learned during the course of other relationships have an impact. The need to reassess needs, patterns, and negotiate differences is a constant in the development of important relationships.

Adding a child to the family affects the lives of parents in ways that they could previously only imagine. Parenting is a complicated and often confusing process for which most of us have very little training or support. What's the "right" way to rear a child? How does the job of parents change as children grow and have different needs? There are a variety of different philosophies or approaches to parenting, many advocated through the popular media. We also have our own experiences of "being parented" which may influence our goals, choices, and ideals. These factors can all combine to make child rearing more difficult than it might otherwise have been. Other family relationships also evolve, and in our nuclear-family-focused culture, it is possible to forget that family relationships extend beyond those between spouses, parents, and children.

This unit explores marital, parent-child, sibling, and intergenerational relationships within families. Among the topics explored include the characteristics of family communication, successful marriages and same-sex relationships, childrearing philosophies, sibling relationships, and changes in parent-child relationships across the lifespan. A goal is to explore the diversity of structures and contexts in which couples, parents, children, and families develop and evolve.

Article   Prepared by: Patricia Hrusa Williams, *University of Maine at Farmington*

Is Your Relationship Dysfunctional?

Identifying the Markers That Can Get You Back on Track

RANDI GUNTHER

Learning Outcomes

After reading this article, you will be able to:

- Define the term dysfunctional.
- Identify and explain common destructive patterns in relationships.
- Recognize strategies and patterns used in healthy relationships.

All relationships are more or less dysfunctional in different ways and at different times. No perfect relationships exist. In order to stay in a committed relationship, most intimate partners adapt to many disappointments and disillusionments during the time they're together. If there is enough good in the relationship to compensate, they weather those distresses and continue to love each other.

But, if over time, more heartaches than good times happen, the relationship bond weakens. Significantly painful events that occur during that time can be deal breakers. Even initially 90 percent positive relationships can fail after too many broken promises or repeatedly unresolved conflicts. If cumulatively dysfunctional interactions occur, the relationship will not likely survive a major deal breaking situation. Suppressed disillusionments weaken that foundation and make relationship more likely to fail.

Many couples push relationship distresses under the rug without resolution and find much later that they are unable to recover from these festering sorrows. Identifying and exploring these typical relationship damagers might have helped. Had the partners recognized them as they were occurring, they might have had a different perspective and learned some new ways to cope before it was too late. By understanding what their dysfunctional patterns are, couples can strive to overcome them.

I have never seen a long-term relationship that didn't exhibit its own unique self-destructive behaviors. Each couple also has its own way of dealing with them, from ignoring their presence to constantly trying to eradicate them. Successful couples learn, over time, to do whatever they can to diminish these damaging effects. To stay committed to each other, they focus more on the things they love about each other and to minimize troublesome situations.

The following 10 common dysfunctional behaviors should seem familiar to you. They are representations of negative patterns that most couples experience. You may have your own that are not listed here, but identifying and recognizing these ten will give you the heads up for others you may share and help you stop them from damaging your commitment to each other.

Assignment of Blame

"There's been a malfunction. Who's to blame?" This immediate response to a conflict predicts significant hopelessness for resolution. Blame, guilt, defensiveness, counter-accusations, and excuses will certainly follow. By the time either partner finally agrees or doesn't agree as to who is the accountable culprit, the relationship has taken a hit. "Something's gone wrong. What can we learn about what happened, how can we prevent it from happening again, and how can we heal each other," works much better. It requires that both partners are willing to look at their own accountability and reactions. Blame never results in a good outcome.

No one feels good when their partners are disappointed, disillusioned, or blaming of them. People can get in terrible, repetitive arguments that go in circles for long periods of time, careening between blame and defensiveness. If accusations of blame were not thrown around in the beginning, and replaced with mutual and willing accountability, most partners would be more open to a more effective resolution.

Threats of Exile or Abandonment

"I'm out of here." "Get out and stay away from me." Both these phrases are often expressed when the partners in an intimate relationship are exasperated, frustrated, hurt, and angry at each other. Blame activates fears of loss and feelings of worthlessness in the recipient, not good experiences for lovers to engender for any reason.

Often, these words are only meant in the moment and are usually retracted later. Even when the negative feelings subside, the wounds often remain and accumulate. If they aren't taken seriously, they mean nothing. If they are, they may be the tip of an iceberg of dwindling commitment, especially if they are repeated in subsequent conflicts.

More men than women fear exile. More women than men fear abandonment. Both are the reciprocals of each other, and neither is ever a healthy way to resolve differences. If you ever use those phrases, make sure you mean them. Someday, your partner may take you seriously.

Dominance/Submission

Who has the ultimate power to make decisions in your relationship when you cannot agree as to a solution that satisfies both of you? If the relationship is a power hierarchy where one partner consistently is on top, the other, more adaptive partner will eventually lose hope and stop fighting as hard in succeeding conflicts. That leaves all the responsibility for the outcome on the shoulders of the top guy, and submission, martyrdom, and resentment in the emotional belly of the other.

In better relationships, the decision of the moment is generously given by either partner to the one who is better at that particular capability at that time. There is no need for either to always have more than fifty percent influence. When both partners see themselves as members of a great, effective team, neither player needs to be right all the time, or automatically get to direct the outcome of any situation. They work for the ultimate best function of the relationship, regardless of who is given the power at the time, and do so with compromise and support.

Grudges

Grudges come from unexplored, unexpressed, or powerless complaints that are not responded to with due consideration. Grudges can start small and seem too insignificant to fight about but, once buried, can fester and grow.

People who harbor grudges usually do so across the board. They often feel victimized by others, bitter about unfair losses, and resentful of actual or exaggerated injustices. When confronted by their partners, they usually will not reveal the depth of their resentment, but act it out in indirect ways or bring up a slew of past affronts in the middle of an argument.

Intimate partners who carry grudges don't ever let go of the past. They feel powerless in the present without using grudges to fortify their position. Underneath, they often see themselves as people who have been repeatedly cheated.

Ownership

Dysfunctional relationships are all about one person's emotional "ownership" of the other. Whatever the owning partner wants or needs, the owned partner must acquiesce for the minimization of anxiety or dissolution of threats to quiet down. There is only one-way concern and empathy, and it is not in the mind and heart of the partner who feels possession.

In functional, mutually supportive relationships, neither partner feels that they own the course of another's life. They know and accept that couples who truly care want each other's dreams to come true. Of course, they would rather be part of those dreams and there is grieving when that cannot be, but they would never ask that their partners become less of who they were meant to be just to stay together. That doesn't mean that they quit easily or run when things are tough. They are open and authentic with each other from the beginning and sad endings are not unexpected.

Interestingly enough, those partners who love without control are rarely left behind. They are rare specimens of what it means to feel true chivalry, the exquisite satisfaction of making sure that someone loved is free to stay or go. When that door is truly open, few partners go through it. They know that they are with someone who is not easy to replace.

Disloyalty

Destructive triangles are often part of dysfunctional relationships. One partner talks to someone outside the relationship about the intimate situations that lie within it without the other partner's knowing or consent. That confidante then knows things about that partner they may have no right to know. He or she, armed with information the other partner does not know is shared, may offer advice that may alter the situation unilaterally.

It is common for friends to gain advice and support from other friends when they are distressed about their relationships, but there is a big difference when doing so means selling out their partners' most intimate and vulnerable feelings and behaviors. It is especially problematic when the unknowing partner is also friends with the confidante. The resulting awkwardness can be significantly uncomfortable and many a time that trusted friend tells the outside partner. Now the concomitant disloyalties multiply, leaving everyone in the triangle wondering who to trust.

Winner or Loser Arguments

When couples argue, they usually stop listening to each other early in that conflict. Within a very short period of time, it would be difficult for either to know or understand what the other is feeling. Great conflict resolution, on the other hand, can only occur when the partners in an intimate relationship stay deeply connected to their own feelings and also those of the other.

It is like a powerfully effective debate. At the blowing of a symbolic whistle, each could play the other's part. They realize that there are two sides to every disagreement and that compromise often requires innovation. That means that both partners are mutually searching for a resolution that holds both of their needs intact as much as possible.

Arguments are very different. Each partner will use whatever means are at hand to push his or her side of the "truth" no matter what the other needs. They may go on for round after round, losing sight of whatever they were arguing about to begin with, because neither is willing to give up his or her point of view or accept defeat. Eventually, all arguments cease. There is usually no clear winner or loser, because the couple now has to figure out how to resume intimate connection and both are either hurting or mad.

Most arguments neither solve a problem nor help either partner feel better about themselves. Assumptions are made on both sides and acted upon as if they were true. There is little inquiry or openness to any reasoning that might upend what is already felt or demanded. The argument ends when one or the other partner is just too tired to go on and retreats. Too many of these unresolved conflicts predict potential relationship failure. Emotional scars form that can make each succeeding negative interaction less likely to result in healing.

Snapshots Versus Moving Pictures

More men live in the moment and capture that moment with an emotional or mental snapshot. Though they seem to enjoy thinking about the past and future in battle, business, or sports, they strongly avoid doing so in their intimate relationships.

More women, on the other hand, are weavers of time. In their intimate relationships, they want to remember the past and anticipate the future, concerned about not repeating repetitive negative patterns and making a better future by doing so. They are content with snapshots of memories that bring back nostalgic feelings to enrich the moment, but need to make them relevant to what comes next.

Obviously, both genders are capable of using the past as the best source of learning, and the future as the most reliable place to plan for, but do that in different areas. To achieve a better compromise, they must enter each other's important realities and share that experience. There is no way to keep the past from being repeated in the future without that kind of teamwork.

Boundary Violations

Boundaries are the way people keep their internal vulnerabilities, concerns, and insecurities safe. The way we were raised as children plays a significant part in how easily we give up our rights to those decisions. Parents who consistently violate boundaries teach their children that they have no right to privacy in any situation.

In dysfunctional relationships, one or both partners often feel little conflict about entering the other's private world without permission. They believe that what is their partner's is also theirs, without question or concern. That can apply to material things, thoughts, feelings, plans, or desires. "What's mine is mine, and what's yours is mine," is their appropriate justification. And, in addition, once any of those "possessions" are usurped, they can be used in any way the partner now in possession wishes.

The other end of sorrowful dysfunction is when a partner doesn't know his or her boundary rights and gives up what is their right without question or argument. That means acquiescing to any demand the other partner wants, whether it is good for them or not.

Partners who violate boundaries may do so, not so much out of maliciousness, but out of the fear that their partners are keeping things from them that would affect their lives if they knew. Those who allow their boundaries to be violated may be seeking intimate blending without thought of consequences.

Early in romantic relationships, people often throw away the need for privacy and open their boundaries to their lovers without screening. Later, when either partner feels the need for privacy or separate thoughts, the other partner may feel rejected or abandoned. Sharing every thought and feeling may feel temporarily sweetly blending but, over time, can result in the loss of mystery and challenge.

Fear of Loss

The more a partner is attached to a relationship, the more he or she will fight for it if it seems threatened in any way. Being attached is not the same as being involved, interdependent, or deeply connected. Those are three healthy responses to a non-ownership relationship. Intense attachment, like a child might feel on the other end of a potentially abandoning parent, produces a feeling of anticipatory grief at the thought of losing the relationship. It can drive the person feeling threatened into a desperate grappling to hold on to it at any cost.

The sadness of that kind of response is that it usually has the opposite effect; it ultimately pushes the desired partner away. To stop the anxious partner's terror, he or she must be able to self-soothe, ease off, and focus on attending to the needs of that partner. If love is strong enough, those behaviors might be alright for a while, but no one wants to be on a shelf, waiting to be needed on demand.

How Dysfunctional Is Your Intimate Relationship?

If you willingly take a look at the ways your relationship is not functioning well, you can change those behaviors in the opposite direction and get back on track.

Take this short quiz to determine your relationship dysfunctional quotient. Give yourself an answer ranging from 1 to 5 based on the following definitions.

Never 1
Occasionally 2
A little too much 3
Frequently 4
Always 5

1. When you and your partner have a conflict, do you spend a lot of time determining who the bad guy is and making sure he or she is "properly punished?" _____
2. When you feel hurt, angry, or threatened, do you threaten your partner with exile or abandonment? _____
3. Does one of you always have to have the last word and the right to determine the outcome? _____
4. Does either of you hold grudges against the other for long periods of time and then erupt in a fight with held-back feelings of resentment? _____
5. Do you feel you have the right to tell your partner how he or she must behave in the relationship? _____
6. Does either of you share confidences about the other without permission? _____
7. When you have a fight, does someone always have to win at the expense of the other? _____
8. Do you forget the past mistakes and continue making them in the future? _____
9. Do you disrespect each other's boundaries and violate them for your own comfort? _____
10. Do you react strongly and fight in whatever way you can if you think the relationship is threatened? _____

Add up your scores.

1–10 Your relationship is not dysfunctional
11–20 You are practicing some dysfunctional interactions
21–30 You are entering the danger zone of too many dysfunctional interactions
31–40 Your relationship is in trouble
41–50 If you don't begin soon to do things differently, your relationship might fall apart

Remember, the reason to approach this from a negative point of view is for you to stop these behaviors and move them in a positive direction. Even just diminishing them will give you a head start and will result in your seeing what you could do better.

Critical Thinking

1. The author states that "All relationships are more or less dysfunctional in different ways and at different times." Do you agree or disagree? Justify your response.

2. Of the dysfunctional behaviors listed, which do you see as the most damaging and destructive to relationships and why? Why do you think couples continue to engage in these behaviors and patterns even though they are damaging their relationships?

3. Take the short quiz at the end of the article. How did you do? Given your survey results, what can you do to improve the quality of your relationship with your partner? Why is changing patterns in relationships so difficult?

Internet References

Love is Respect
www.loveisrespect.org
National Healthy Marriage Resource Center
http://www.healthymarriageinfo.org
The Bowen Center for the Study of the Family
www.thebowencenter.org
Two of Us
www.twoofus.org

Dr. Randi Gunther is a counselor specializing in singles and couples counseling for over 40 years. Gunther has a free advice e-newsletter, "Heroic Love," which focuses on how to avoid the common pitfalls that keep people from finding and keeping romantic love, how to find the right partner, avoid the dreaded "honeymoon is over" phenomenon, and prevent relationships from boredom. www.heroiclove.com

Article   Prepared by: Patricia Hrusa Williams, *University of Maine at Farmington*

Ten Reasons Why Texting Is Awful for Society and Ruining It Too

ALEXIA LAFATA

Learning Outcomes

After reading this article, you will be able to:

- Identify distinct features of text messaging as a form of communication.

- Recognize challenges in utilizing text-based communications with friends and romantic partners.

- Analyze the role that both verbal and nonverbal communication play in relationships.

On December 3, 1992—when the first "Merry Christmas" SMS text message was sent from the computer of 22-year-old engineer Neil Papworth to the cell phone of Vodafone user Richard Jarvis—society created a new communication need: The Text. And after that fateful day in 1992, gone were the days of instant, real-time interaction, as they had been replaced by this mode of communication that will be fundamentally flawed for as long as it prevails. Here's why.

1. Men and Women Communicate Differently

According to various psychological studies and my Interpersonal Communications class at Boston College, men and women value communication differently. They see communication as having different significances, and oftentimes, those significances are not aligned. Men see communication as a way to exchange information. Once information is exchanged, men feel as if they have nothing more to talk about. The scope of conversation for women, on the other hand, is unlimited, as women see communication as a tool to connect, relate, and share. For the average

woman, communication is essential to creating lasting bonds. Men bond by doing activities together, like participating in sports, watching movies or TV shows, or playing video games.

Texting is important to a woman because she loves that she has the ability to talk to her friends about anything without the limitations of "where" and "when"—a few strokes of her fingers on her keyboard, and her thought is in someone else's hands. And women will text back and forth for hours about absolutely nothing. However, for men, texting doesn't count as an "activity" over which to bond. Texting is just communicating, and this is not a man's preferred method of connecting with others.

When you are with your boyfriend in person, communication is an addendum to doing other things, even if other things are as simple as touching or eating a meal. But texting is communication for the sake of communication. And if a man doesn't text a woman as similarly or enthusiastically as she texts him, she becomes insulted and thinks he has no interest in her. She sees his lack of fervent texting as him not wanting to bond, and this will forever be a dilemma between men and women when they text. He'd just rather you come over, make Ramen noodles, and watch Safety Not Guaranteed with him instead.

2. It Associates Periods with Meanness

What was once a common, harmless punctuation mark has now become a symbol of hatred. It's acceptable—no, preferred—to use all other forms of perfect grammar when constructing a text message: capitalization of names and of "I," commas, and minimal chat speak and abbreviations. Break out the period at the end of a sentence, though, and it's guaranteed that the recipient of your message will think he/she did something terribly wrong.

In real life communication, you can rely on things like tone, speed, and volume to determine implications and connotations in other people's words. When we text, all of these vital nonverbal aspects of verbal communication become a mystery, so we are forced to infer them. The period, in all of its rigid grammatical finality, has become equivalent to a stern tone of voice.

The desired method is now a lack of punctuation at all. It's noncommittal and implies a more relaxed tone, which is certainly preferred in a conversation. And now, when I want to convey anger, I actually do use a period. Sorry, periods. You were so innocent before texting.

3. It Makes It Easy for Charming In-person Traits to Be Misconstrued

What's more charming than self-deprecating humor, witty sarcasm, or quirky personality traits that rely on voice inflections or volume changes? Few things, that's what. And texting is the ultimate enemy for people who rely on these things to make friends or meet lovers. As the old saying goes, it truly isn't what you say, but how you say it, and texting only leaves us with the "what." It's far too easy for a sarcastic comment to be misconstrued as genuinely hurtful, and it's far too difficult to make a successful joke without any voice inflection. Texting makes quirky personality traits blend into the background and leaves us with a boring society of homogeneity.

If you are gullible or aren't completely attuned to the texting style of the person with whom you are texting, you can easily make lots of mistakes when determining the meaning of certain messages. And if you are really unsure whether or not something was a joke, well—that's even worse.

4. It Makes Us Secretly Operate in Extremes All the Time

Nowadays, it seems as though we are always communicating with someone. Whether you are typing a text message as you read this or if you are currently letting someone linger (purposefully or not) before you give a response, you are involved in an interaction. And something about being in the middle of a text message interaction conjures up strange hidden feelings.

When we're waiting for a response from someone or waiting to continue an interaction, we're in limbo. Our feelings are dormant, waiting. Finally, when we get a response (or lack thereof), the aforementioned deep feelings come to fruition, and they are always on either extreme end: soaring happiness or intense rejection. And not knowing which end of the spectrum you will feel and when you will feel it is incredibly stressful.

Seriously, who doesn't experience that sudden excited feeling when they get a new text message? And who doesn't feel the immense pain that comes with not receiving a desired text message response? This brings us to #5.

5. It Makes Ignoring Easier and More Commonplace

Imagine someone ignored you in real life, or perhaps took a few extra awkward moments to respond to one of your thoughts. Would you feel bad? Sure, you might. But you wouldn't really have as much time to feel as bad if you were ignored in person as you would if you were ignored via text. In person, ignoring is pretty instant. However, since texting doesn't happen in real-time, you won't realize that you were ignored until several hours later when you still haven't received a response. The anxiety just builds upon itself for hours and hours until it topples over in a feeling of entrenched abandonment. At that point, you will have had far too much time to mull over your rejection, and you will just feel really, really awful.

It's easy to ignore someone when they text you. You can just put your phone down and remove that person from your current train of thought. You can't do this when they are right in front of your face. And if you're not face-to-face, you also can't see how that person is reacting to your ignore. As Louis C.K. stated in a genius rant on Conan O'Brien about the dangers of technology, we now have the ability to say or do something mean without seeing the result of our actions. Thus, we cannot build sympathy. If you're mean to someone in person, you can see that it makes them sad, so you learn that this action = this result. If you're mean to or ignore someone via text message, you can't see how they're responding, so you'll never learn what happens when you ignore them. Which is that they cry to their friends and spend hours analyzing what they did wrong.

6. It Gives Us False Senses of Power

Throughout history, power has involved the ability to influence the behavior of a people through an authority perceived as legitimate by a social structure. Power is present in the workplace if you achieve a higher-ranking position, in the government if you are politically influential, in the military, and more. Now, in the twenty-first century, power is also equivalent to someone waiting on you for a text message response.

There is always a power struggle during a texting conversation (especially in one of romantic pursuits), and if you say you don't actually physically feel it, you're lying. Once you send a text message of any kind, there is a very real chance that you will not receive a response. You are being vulnerable to the possibility that someone will put their phone away for a long period of time and ignore you. And because we live in a society where vulnerability is seen as weakness which is seen as lack of power, the person who sends the text message has lost just the tiniest amount of power in a conversation. The person who receives the text—who holds the sender's vulnerability in his/her hands—has the power. The more time that passes, the more power that person has.

This kind of power struggle doesn't exist in real life. It might exist if there's some kind of confessional conversation, like if someone is sharing feelings for the first time or if they are admitting they did something wrong. Other than that, though, regular back-and-forth conversations do not involve long pauses, power, or legitimate possibilities of being ignored. In real life, the definition of power does not include it being your turn to speak.

7. Emotions Are No Longer Emotions Unless They're Extreme

Laughter is no longer just laughter. Excitement is no longer just excitement. Sadness is no longer just sadness. You must sprinkle your laughter with Emojis and ALL CAPITAL LETTERS and endless amounts of HAHAs. A simple "lol" will never cut it ever again. Conveying sadness involves some uncertain . . .'s, some sad faces, some sentences in all lowercase (to convey smallness, of course). It's hard to trust someone who claims to actually be laughing when they only type "lol." Nobody believes you when you simply say that you're laughing. You now must prove it.

But what if something is ridiculously gut-splittingly funny? I've wasted HAHA for something funny but not funny enough to be ridiculous and gut-splitting, so I've prematurely set my laughter bar too high. Now, when I'm laughing hysterically, I don't have many options except to be really annoying and say HAHAHAHAHAHAHAHAHAHAHAHAHAHA about a million times, and this takes a lot of energy. Ugh, texting.

This might seem to apply to instant messaging as well, but with instant messaging I can easily convey my excitement for something via a constant flow of instant, real-time IMs. I simply cannot do that for texting (see #9).

8. It Has Caused Greetings to Become a Thing of the Past

Starting your conversation with something like "Hey," "Hello," "Hi," or any variation of "Normal Greeting" is the biggest buzz kill. To be considered interesting and/or worth responding to,

we have to think of a reason to text someone—a silly observation, a random thought, a funny memory. It is fundamentally bizarre if I text someone with a simple "Hi," even if I really do just want to say hi and talk without having anything to say yet.

Along the same lines, texting conversations only end with cliffhangers. Nobody ever says "Goodbye." I have one friend that actually makes a point to say goodbye when she is ending a texting conversation, and it confuses everyone. It's more normal to just stop responding, we all say. But she's probably a better person than all of us because we know when we're done talking to her. She respectfully picks up and leaves the conversation like one would in real life.

Not saying goodbye makes us wonder if a conversation is actually over. Without a goodbye, what designates the end of a conversation? An Emoji? The amount of hours gone without a response? Because just when you think a conversation is over, you get a response two hours later. Texting is messing up the basic dynamics of greetings and departures.

9. It Makes Us Insecure about Having More Than One Thought

What is the #1 No-No of texting? Double texting. The evils of double texting are rooted back to the days where text messages were not set up like an Instant Message like they are on smartphones today. Before smartphones, if someone double texted you, it was absolutely the most irritating thing for two reasons: 1) it disrupted the flow of the current message you were reading and 2) you couldn't view the follow up message and connect it immediately to the previous one. You had to exit out of the current message and go back into your Messages folder on your phone, and then piece together the two messages manually. So much work.

Now, because nothing is worse than a blue bubble to white bubble ratio of 3:1, double texting has taken on a new meaning. Once you send one text, you better hope that you have nothing more to contribute to that part of the conversation because then you will seem too excited, or too annoying, or too pushy. When we double text, we feel like the recipient becomes irritated with us. Double texting implies that we are more excited to talk to someone than they are to talk to us because we're giving more ideas and contributing more to the conversation—and who wants to be perceived as more excited than another person? It has made us insecure to put forth a second thought. This is what texting has done to us.

10. It Is Becoming Unnecessary

As technology progresses, texting is slowly becoming more and more unnecessary. All it does is give us another way to interact with others with a lot of added nuances. That's literally it.

And frankly, we need another way to interact with others like we need a bullet through our heads: not at ALL.

Critical Thinking

1. The author suggests that texting is a poor form of communication to use and fraught with a variety of problems. Do you agree or disagree? Why?

2. Have you ever had a miscommunication when communicating with another person via text, e-mail, or social media? If so what happened? Does the miscommunication or problem experienced relate to any of the 10 issues discussed by the author? If so, which one(s)?

3. If you choose to communicate with someone via text message, e-mail, or social media what are three things you should keep in mind to ensure communication is effective, clear, and sensitive to the other person's needs and perspective?

Internet References

Livestrong: Verbal versus Nonverbal Communication
http://www.livestrong.com/article/157893-verbal-communication-vs-nonverbal-communication/

Pew Research Center: Internet, Science, and Tech
www.pewinternet.org

Technology and Communication in Romantic Relationships: A Fact Sheet
www.healthymarriageinfo.org/download.aspx?id=2088

The New Era of Communication Among Americans
www.gallup.com/poll/179288/new-era-communication-americans.aspx

Article   Prepared by: Patricia Hrusa Williams, *University of Maine at Farmington*

Secrets: Are Yours Slowly Killing You?

BRIAN SMITH

Learning Outcomes

After reading this article, you will be able to:

- Define what the word secret means.

- Identify ways the stress of keeping a secret can influence your physical and emotional health.

- Recognize reasons individuals sometimes keep information private or concealed from people in their life.

Taking a secret to your grave could actually hasten your arrival at the cemetery. So stop holding it in—unburden yourself to boost your health and well-being.

Technically, he hadn't cheated on her. Jason had seen Stephanie only a few times, and even then, the "dates" were more like nights out with a good friend, sometimes ending with a kiss on the cheek, other times a hug, and occasionally, feeling silly, a high five. During this period, an old girlfriend came to town one weekend and Jason slept with her. How could he have known that Stephanie would wind up being the love of his life, the mother of his children, the person he would never dream of keeping secrets from?

"I felt horribly guilty about it," says Jason, 42, who was 27 at the time. "Especially when it seemed like we had a future together."

He wanted—and needed—to tell Steph about that weekend, but first it felt too soon and then it felt too late. "I built it up in my mind as the worst thing ever, and the longer I waited, the harder it became to tell her." The torment he experienced was more than mental. He felt physically awful, teeth always on edge, a low dull ache behind the eyes. "This went way beyond the usual Jewish guilt that I felt 24 hours a day," he says. "This was like a hole eating through my stomach."

We'll let you in on a little secret: Vowing to keep certain things in your life hidden—harmful lies you've told and never

copped to, hurt that you've caused others and haven't acknowledged, embarrassing or traumatic experiences buried in your brain—may eat away at you in ways and to a degree you never realized.

"Unless you're a sociopath, keeping negative secrets absolutely impacts your health," says Reef Karim, MD, an assistant clinical professor of psychiatry at the UCLA Semel Institute for Neuroscience and Human Behavior.

"No question," agrees James Pennebaker, PhD, a psychologist at the University of Texas. "Each year brings fresh evidence about the health risks of keeping dark secrets."

Researchers have discovered, for instance, that harboring secrets can set off a chronic surge of stress hormones, specifically cortisol, that can lead to all types of nasty health issues, including gastrointestinal problems, a weakened immune system, high blood pressure, and memory loss. Your brain must struggle to perform normal functions while diverting the resources necessary to maintain the secret, explains neurosurgeon Gopal Chopra, MD, an adjunct associate professor at Duke University.

"To manage a mismatch between reality and the world around you requires the additional use of the prefrontal cortex and amygdala," Dr. Chopra says. "When your brain is working at cross-purposes, the conflict creates stress."

Not only does stress erode your physical health, but it also takes an emotional toll that can affect all of your relationships.

"That's because we are holding on to something that's a lie, that's misleading, or that elicits negative energy," says Dr. Karim. "Our internal sense of guilt, feelings for the person we are keeping the secret from, or feelings about ourselves will cause us to feel disconnected in some way. Often, we don't realize this is happening, but it eventually catches up to us."

The notion of secrets as toxic reaches back to the days of sandal-wearing thinkers in ancient plazas. The third-century A.D. scholar and theologian Origen considered secrets to be poison—literally—and insisted the only way to suck out the toxins was to draw them into the open. Early Christian litera-ture refers to confession as medicine for the soul, and the priest as a physician for the soul. And in the 1930s, a predecessor of Alcoholics Anonymous, the Oxford Group, turned the notion of confession as healing into one of its most enduring slogans and the very key to recovery: "You're only as sick as your secrets."

We all have our skeletons. In fact, according to researchers at the University of Iowa, about 95 percent of people are hiding at least a few femurs in their closets.

I'm not harboring anything remotely scandalous (and if I were, I wouldn't confess it to 13 million *Men's Health* read-ers). But based on how I've suffered from keeping even a small secret, I can only imagine what a doozy would do to a guy.

On Black Friday last year, my wife and I went shopping to prepare for visits from a dozen family members for a three-day Christmas extravaganza. We snagged some great deals but still dropped a lot of cash. To my shame, while my wife was off hunt-ing for hangers and a cute knickknack, a cashier was sliding my credit card for a new GoPro video camera that was on sale. Knowing how much my wife hates when I buy electronic gadgets, I slipped it into the backseat of the car without saying anything.

I let a few days pass without mentioning the purchase, hid-ing the camera until I could work up the nerve. After two weeks of stomachaches and guilt-induced anxiety, I finally came clean. She was only mildly miffed (and would have been less so, she said, if I'd told her up front). I, on the other hand, felt like I could finally take a deep breath. What's more, I was at last able to use the damn thing and filmed a family Christmas movie that became the hit of the weekend.

When I shared this with Dale Larson, PhD, a psychologist who has spent much of his career delving into the impact of self-concealment and secrets, his reaction made me wince a little.

"This is a classic example of the kind of secret that can be harmful," Larson, a professor at Santa Clara University, told me. "The obsession over it leads to shame and rumination, and then, when the secret is eventually revealed, it can undermine trust in the romantic relationship."

And boy, do we obsess. Back in the 1990s, researchers at the University of Virginia found that keeping secrets, even seem-ingly inconsequential ones, can crowd out other thoughts to the point of "provoking psychopathology."

The word "secret" means "withdrawn, set apart, con-cealed, private." It should be no surprise, then, that shedding the burden of concealment can bring people together. It was precisely that metaphor, in fact—the burden of secrets—that intrigued researchers at Tufts University and three other major colleges enough to find out if people felt a literal weight from withholding information. To answer that question, the scientists crafted a set of experiments.

In the first experiment, 40 people were asked to think of either a "major" or a "small" secret and then to estimate the steepness of a hill. The result: The bigger the secret was, the steeper the hill seemed to them.

A second group of participants thought of either "meaning-ful" or "trivial" secrets while tossing a beanbag at a target about 9 feet away. People with the meaningful secrets overthrew, sug-gesting that they perceived the target as being farther away. The third test involved people who'd cheated on their partner but hadn't fessed up. Asked to guess how much effort and energy it would take to complete six tasks, the people who dwelled more often on their straying found the tasks more physically burdensome.

None of this surprises family counselor Deborah Corley, PhD, the coauthor of *Disclosing Secrets: When, to Whom, & How Much to Reveal.* She says she's had plenty of clients tell her they're really anxious, can't sleep, or feel depressed. "After asking more questions, I find their symptoms stem from being unable to share something they've been withholding."

If all this is true—if clinging to secrets is hurting us physi-cally, emotionally, and spiritually—then the answer should be simple: We need to man up and cop to what we're hiding.

It *can* be that simple. In 2013, following up on their first "burden" studies, Stanford University visiting scholar Michael Slepian, PhD, and fellow researchers tested whether coming clean would bring relief. The answer was yes. In each case, participants felt their psychic load lifted, giving them the very real sense that an actual physical weight had also been removed.

There is, however, the danger that in unburdening yourself, you drop an emotional anvil on someone else. Take a one-time instance of marital infidelity. If you want to spill your guts just to soothe your conscience—knowing you'll never cheat again—keep your mouth (and pants) zipped, suggests Bruce Stevens, PhD, an associate professor of clinical psychology at the University of Canberra in Australia.

"When there is a very high likelihood of it being a final blow to the marriage, I think keeping it secret is best—if the affair is over, past tense," he says. (Of course, there are circumstances when a cheater has no choice: if you've put a partner at risk for a sexually transmitted disease, for example.)

But what about the corrosive effects of keeping quiet? Those can still be addressed if you confide in someone else, such as a therapist, who can help you work through the guilt and shame as well as address any underlying issues that may have led to cheating in the first place.

The University of Texas's Pennebaker has spent two decades experimenting with "writing to heal," a program that has par-ticipants bare their souls on paper for 15 to 20 minutes a day for four straight days. Putting the experience into language,

Pennebaker says, imposes "some organization on it, some structure, something that is just very difficult to do without words".

"People sleep better after they write," he continues. "Students' grades improve. People go to the doctor less. Their immune function improves. People will tell us months afterward that it was a life-changing experience."

Jason recalls when the weight of his own secret finally became too much to bear. He and Stephanie were still in the lounging-in-bed-on-Sundays phase, deeply in love and spending almost every day and night together. There was no doubt where things were headed, and Jason couldn't have been happier about it. Still . . . there was The Secret.

It was then, tangled up in the sheets, that Stephanie looked at him and said, "I'm so glad we don't keep secrets from each other."

That was it.

"I knew it was now or never," he says. "The guilt bubbled over, and I told her. Simple as that. She wasn't exactly pleased, but the whole thing was pretty anticlimactic." His conscience now clear, he asked her to marry him soon after.

Not only that, but he's still friends with the old girlfriend—and "Stephanie really likes her."

Critical Thinking

1. Have you ever kept a secret from someone? If so, why did you keep the secret?

2. How does it feel to lie to someone or to keep a secret from important people in your life? Did you ever experience any of the physical and emotional effects discussed in the article? If so, which ones?

3. What are some negative consequences of revealing a secret? Are there times it is better not to reveal something that you have concealed or chosen to keep private? What is a healthy way to handle the situation?

Internet References

Love is Respect
www.loveisrespect.org
National Healthy Marriage Resource Center
www.healtymarriageinfo.org
Secrets, Lies, and Relationships
www.blogs.psychcentral.com/healing-together/2009/12/secrets-lies-and-relationships/

Article

Prepared by: Patricia Hrusa Williams,
University of Maine at Farmington

Are You with the Right Mate?

REBECCA WEBBER

Learning Outcomes

After reading this article, you will be able to:

- Understand factors important to compatibility and marital satisfaction.

- Describe the personality characteristics associated with being a good mate or partner.

- Recognize reasons for growth and change in marital relationships over time.

Elliott Katz was stunned to find himself in the middle of a divorce after two kids and 10 years of marriage. The Torontonian, a policy analyst for the Ottawa government, blamed his wife. "She just didn't appreciate all I was doing to make her happy." He fed the babies, and he changed their diapers. He gave them baths, he read them stories, and put them to bed. Before he left for work in the morning, he made them breakfast. He bought a bigger house and took on the financial burden, working evenings to bring in enough money so his wife could stay home full-time.

He thought the solution to the discontent was for her to change. But once on his own, missing the daily interaction with his daughters, he couldn't avoid some reflection. "I didn't want to go through this again. I asked whether there was something I could have done differently. After all, you can wait years for someone else to change."

What he decided was, indeed, there were some things he could have done differently—like not tried as hard to be so non-controlling that his wife felt he had abandoned decision-making entirely. His wife, he came to understand, felt frustrated, as if she were "a married single parent," making too many of the plans and putting out many of the fires of family life, no matter how many chores he assumed.

Ultimately, he stopped blaming his wife for their problems. "You can't change another person. You can only change yourself," he says. "Like lots of men today" he has since found, "I was very confused about my role as partner." After a few post-divorce years in the mating wilderness, Katz came to realize that framing a relationship in terms of the right or wrong mate is by itself a blind alley.

"We're given a binary model," says New York psychotherapist Ken Page. "Right or wrong. Settle or leave. We are not given the right tools to think about relationships. People need a better set of options."

Sooner or later, there comes a moment in *all* relationships when you lie in bed, roll over, look at the person next to you and think it's all a dreadful mistake, says Boston family therapist Terrence Real. It happens a few months to a few years in. "It's an open secret of American culture that disillusionment exists. I go around the country speaking about 'normal marital hatred.' Not one person has ever asked what I mean by that. It's extremely raw."

What to do when the initial attraction sours? "I call it the first day of your real marriage," Real says. It's not a sign that you've chosen the wrong partner. It is the signal to grow as an individual—to take responsibility for your own frustrations. Invariably, we yearn for perfection but are stuck with an imperfect human being. We all fall in love with people we think will deliver us from life's wounds but who wind up knowing how to rub against us.

A new view of relationships and their discontents is emerging. We alone are responsible for having the relationship we want. And to get it, we have to dig deep into ourselves while maintaining our connections. It typically takes a dose of bravery—what Page calls "enlightened audacity." Its brightest possibility exists, ironically, just when the passion seems most totally dead. If we fail to plumb ourselves and speak up for our deepest needs, which admittedly can be a scary prospect, life will never feel authentic, we will never see ourselves with any clarity, and everyone will always be the wrong partner.

The Way Things Are

Romance itself seeds the eventual belief that we have chosen the wrong partner. The early stage of a relationship, most marked by intense attraction and infatuation, is in many ways akin to cocaine intoxication, observes Christine Meinecke, a clinical psychologist in Des Moines, Iowa. It's orchestrated, in part, by the neurochemicals associated with intense pleasure. Like a cocaine high, it's not sustainable.

But for the duration—and experts give it nine months to four years—infatuation has one overwhelming effect: Research shows that it makes partners overestimate their similarities and idealize each other. We're thrilled that he loves Thai food, travel, and classic movies, just like us. And we overlook his avid interest in old cars and online poker.

Eventually, reality rears its head. "Infatuation fades for everyone," says Meinecke, author of *Everybody Marries the Wrong Person*. That's when you discover your psychological incompatibility, and disenchantment sets in. Suddenly, a switch is flipped, and now all you can see are your differences. "You're focusing on what's wrong with *them*. They need to get the message about what *they* need to change."

You conclude you've married the wrong person—but that's because you're accustomed to thinking, Cinderella-like, that there *is* only one right person. The consequences of such a pervasive belief are harsh. We engage in destructive behaviors, like blaming our partner for our unhappiness or searching for someone outside the relationship.

Along with many other researchers and clinicians, Meinecke espouses a new marital paradigm—what she calls "the self-responsible spouse." When you start focusing on what isn't so great, it's time to shift focus. "Rather than look at the other person, you need to look at yourself and ask, 'Why am I suddenly so unhappy and what do I need to do?'" It's not likely a defect in your partner.

In mature love, says Meinecke, "we do not look to our partner to provide our happiness, and we don't blame them for our unhappiness. We take responsibility for the expectations that we carry, for our own negative emotional reactions, for our own insecurities, and for our own dark moods."

But instead of looking at ourselves, or understanding the fantasies that bring us to such a pass, we engage in a thought process that makes our differences tragic and intolerable, says William Doherty, professor of psychology and head of the marriage and family therapy program at the University of Minnesota. It's one thing to say, "I wish my spouse were more into the arts, like I am." Or, "I wish my partner was not just watching TV every night but interested in getting out more with me." That's something you can fix.

It's quite another to say, "This is intolerable. I need and deserve somebody who shares my core interests." The two thought processes are likely to trigger differing actions. It's possible to ask someone to go out more. It's not going to be well received to ask someone for a personality overhaul, notes Doherty, author of *Take Back Your Marriage*.

No one is going to get all their needs met in a relationship, he insists. He urges fundamental acceptance of the person we choose and the one who chooses us. "We're all flawed. With parenting, we know that comes with the territory. With spouses, we say 'This is terrible.'"

The culture, however, pushes us in the direction of discontent. "Some disillusionment and feelings of discouragement are normal in the love-based matches in our culture," explains Doherty. "But consumer culture tells us we should not settle for anything that is not ideal for us."

As UCLA psychologist Thomas Bradbury puts it, "You don't have a line-item veto when it comes to your partner. It's a package deal; the bad comes with the good."

Further, he says, it's too simplistic an interpretation that your partner is the one who's wrong. "We tend to point our finger at the person in front of us. We're fairly crude at processing some information. We tend not to think, 'Maybe I'm not giving her what she needs.' 'Maybe he's disgruntled because I'm not opening up to him.' Or, 'Maybe he's struggling in his relationships with other people.' The more sophisticated question is, 'In what ways are we failing to make one another happy?'"

Now in a long-term relationship, Toronto's Katz has come to believe that "Marriage is not about *finding* the right person. It's about *becoming* the right person. Many people feel they married the wrong person, but I've learned that it's truly about growing to become a better husband."

Eclipsed by Expectations

What's most noticeable about Sarah and Mark Holdt of Estes Park, Colorado, is their many differences. "He's a Republican, I'm a Democrat. He's a traditional Christian, I'm an agnostic. He likes meat and potatoes, I like more adventurous food," says Sarah. So Mark heads off to church and Bible study every week, while Sarah takes a "Journeys" class that considers topics like the history of God in America. "When he comes home, I'll ask, 'What did you learn in Bible Study?'" she says. And she'll share her insights from her own class with him.

But when Sarah wants to go to a music festival and Mark wants to stay home, "I just go," says Sarah. "I don't need to have him by my side for everything." He's there when it matters most—at home, at the dinner table, in bed. "We both thrive on touch," says Sarah, "so we set our alarm a half hour early every morning and take that time to cuddle." They've been married for 14 years.

It takes a comfortable sense of self and deliberate effort to make relationships commodious enough to tolerate such differences. What's striking about the Holdts is the time they take to share what goes on in their lives—and in their heads—when they are apart. Research shows that such "turning toward" each other and efforts at information exchange, even in routine matters, are crucial to maintaining the emotional connection between partners.

Say one partner likes to travel and the other doesn't. "If you view this with a feeling of resentment, that's going to hurt, over and over again," says Doherty. If you can accept it, that's fine—provided you don't start living in two separate worlds.

"What you don't want to do," he says, "is develop a group of single travel friends who, when they are on the road, go out and flirt with others. You start doing things you're not comfortable sharing with your mate." Most often, such large differences are accompanied by so much disappointment that partners react in ways that do not support the relationship.

The available evidence suggests that women more than men bring some element of fantasy into a relationship. Women generally initiate more breakups and two-thirds of divorces, becoming more disillusioned than men. They compare their mates with their friends much more than men do, says Doherty.

He notes, "They tend to have a model or framework for what the relationship should be. They are more prone to the comparison between what they have and what they think they should have. Men tend to monitor the gap between what they have and what they think they deserve only in the sexual arena. They don't monitor the quality of their marriage on an everyday basis."

To the extent that people have an ideal partner and an ideal relationship in their head, they are setting themselves up for disaster, says family expert Michelle Givertz, assistant professor of communication studies at California State University, Chico. Relationship identities are negotiated between two individuals. Relationships are not static ideals; they are always works in progress.

To enter a relationship with an idea of what it should look like or how it should evolve is too controlling, she contends. It takes two people to make a relationship. One person doesn't get to decide what it should be. And to the extent that he or she does, the other partner is not going to be happy.

"People can spend their lives trying to make a relationship into something it isn't, based on an idealized vision of what should be, not what is," she says. She isn't sure why, but she finds that such misplaced expectations are increasing. Or, as Doherty puts it, "A lot of the thinking about being married to the wrong mate is really self-delusion."

Yes, Virginia, Some Mates Really *Are* Wrong

Sometimes, however, we really do choose the wrong person—someone ultimately not interested in or capable of meeting our needs, for any of a number of possible reasons. At the top of the list of people who are generally wrong for *anyone* are substance abusers—whether the substance is alcohol, prescription drugs, or illicit drugs—who refuse to get help for the problem.

"An addict's primary loyalty is not to the relationship, it's to the addiction," explains Ken Page. "Active addicts become cheaper versions of themselves and lose integrity or the ability to do the right thing when it's hard. Those are the very qualities in a partner you need to lean on." Gamblers fall into the same compulsive camp, with the added twist that their pursuit of the big win typically lands them, sooner or later, into deep debt that threatens the foundations of relationship life.

People who cheated in one or more previous relationships are not great mate material. They destroy the trust and intimacy basic to building a relationship. It's possible to make a case for a partner who cheats once, against his own values, but not for one who compulsively and repeatedly strays. Doherty considers such behavior among the "hard reasons" for relationship breakup, along with physical abuse and other forms of over controlling. "These are things that nobody should have to put up with in life," he says.

But "drifting apart," "poor communication," and "we're just not compatible anymore" are in a completely different category. Such "soft reasons," he insists, are, by contrast, always two-way streets. "Nobody gets all the soft goodies in life," he finds. "It's often better to work on subtle ways to improve the relationship."

A Critical Difference

There's a difference between fighting for what you want in your relationship and being in direct control of your partner, demanding that he or she change, says Real.

Firmly stand up for your wants and needs in a relationship. "Most people don't have the skill to speak up for and fight for what they want in a relationship," he observes. "They don't speak up, which preserves the love but builds resentment. Resentment is a choice; living resentfully means living unhappily. Or they speak up—but are not very loving." Or they just complain.

The art to speaking up, he says, is to transform a complaint into a request. Not "I don't like how you're talking to me," but "Can you please lower your voice so I can hear you better?" If you're trying to get what you want in a relationship, notes Real, it's best to keep it positive and future-focused.

In an ongoing marriage, he adds, "incompatibility is never the real reason for a divorce." It's a reason for breakup of a dating relationship. But when people say "she's a nice person but we're just not compatible," Doherty finds, something happened in which both were participants and allowed the relationship to deteriorate. It's a nice way to say you're not blaming your partner.

The real reason is likely to be that neither attended to the relationship. Perhaps one or both partners threw themselves into parenting. Or a job. They stopped doing the things that they did when dating and that couples need to do to thrive as a partnership—take time for conversation, talk about how their day went or what's on their mind. Or perhaps the real love was undermined by the inability to handle conflict.

"If you get to the point where you're delivering an ultimatum," says Bradbury, you haven't been maintaining your relationship properly. "It's like your car stopping on the side of the road and you say, 'It just isn't working anymore'—but you haven't changed the oil in 10 years." The heart of any relationship, he insists—what makes people the right mates for each other—is the willingness of both partners to be open and vulnerable; to listen and care about each other.

Although there are no guarantees, there are stable personal characteristics that are generally good and generally bad for relationships. On the good side: sense of humor; even temper; willingness to overlook your flaws; sensitivity to you and what you care about; ability to express caring. On the maladaptive side: chronic lying; chronic worrying or neuroticism; emotional over reactivity; proneness to anger; propensity to harbor grudges; low self-esteem; poor impulse control; tendency to aggression; self-orientation rather than an other-orientation. Situations, such as chronic exposure to nonmarital stress in either partner, also have the power to undermine relationships.

In addition, there are people who are specifically wrong for *you*, because they don't share the values and goals you hold most dear. Differences in core values often plague couples who marry young, before they've had enough life experience to discover who they really are. Most individuals are still developing their belief systems through their late teens and early 20s and still refining their lifestyle choices. Of course, you have to know what you hold most dear, and that can be a challenge for anyone at any age, not just the young.

One of the most common reasons we choose the wrong partner is that we do not know who we are or what we really want. It's hard to choose someone capable of understanding you and meeting your most guarded emotional needs and with whom your values are compatible when you don't know what your needs or values are or haven't developed the confidence to voice them unabashedly.

Maria Lin is a nonpracticing attorney who married a chef. "I valued character, connection, the heart," she says. "He was charming, funny, treated me amazingly well, and we got along great." But over time, intellectual differences got in the way. "He couldn't keep up with my analysis or logic in arguments or reasoning through something, or he would prove less capable at certain things, or he would misspell or misuse terms. It was never anything major, just little things."

Lin confides that she lost respect for her chef-husband. "I didn't realize how important intellectual respect for my partner would end up being to me. I think this was more about not knowing myself well enough, and not knowing how being intellectually stimulated was important to me, and (even worse) how it would tie to that critical factor of respect."

The Signal to Grow

It is a fact that like the other basic pillars of life, such as work and children, marriage is not always going to be a source of satisfaction. No one is loved perfectly; some part of our authentic self is never going to be met by a partner. Sure, you can always draw a curtain over your heart. But that is not the only or the best response.

"Sometimes marriage is going to be a source of pain and sorrow," says Givertz. "And that's necessary for personal and interpersonal growth." In fact, it's impossible to be deliriously happy in marriage every moment if you are doing anything at all challenging in life, whether raising children, starting a business, or taking care of an aging parent.

Disillusionment becomes an engine for growth because it forces us to discover our needs. Knowing oneself, recognizing one's needs, and speaking up for them in a relationship are often acts of bravery, says Page. Most of us are guarded about our needs, because they are typically our areas of greatest sensitivity and vulnerability.

"You have to discover—and be able to share—what touches you and moves you the most," he observes. "But first, of course, you have to accept that in yourself. Few of us are skilled at this essential process for creating passion and romance. We'd rather complain." Nevertheless, through this process, we clarify ourselves as we move through life.

At the same time, taking the risk to expose your inner life to your partner turns out to be the great opportunity for expanding intimacy and a sense of connection. This is the great power of relationships: Creating intimacy is the crucible for growing into a fully autonomous human being while the process of becoming a fully realized person expands the possibility for intimacy and connection. This is also the work that transforms a partner into the right partner.

Another crucial element of growth in relationships, says Givertz, is a transformation of motivation—away from self-centered preferences toward what is best for the relationship and its future. There is an intrapsychic change that sustains long-term relationships. Underlying it is a broadening process in which response patterns subtly shift. Accommodation (as opposed to retaliation) plays a role. So does sacrifice. So do willingness and ability to suppress an impulse to respond negatively to a negative provocation, no matter how personally satisfying it might feel in the moment. It requires the ability to hold in mind the long-term goals of the relationship. With motivation transformed, partners are more apt to take a moment to consider how to respond, rather than react reflexively in the heat of a moment.

In his most recent study of relationships, UCLA's Bradbury followed 136 couples for 10 years, starting within six months of their marriage. All the couples reported high levels of satisfaction at the start and four years later. What Bradbury and his colleague Justin Lavner found surprising was that some couples who were so satisfied at the four-year pass eventually divorced, despite having none of the risk factors identified in previous studies of relationship dissolution—wavering commitment, maladaptive personality traits, high levels of stress.

The only elements that identified those who eventually divorced were negative and self-protective reactions during discussions of relationship difficulties and nonsupportive reactions in discussing a personal issue. Displays of anger, contempt, or attempts to blame or invalidate a partner augured poorly, even when the partners felt their marriage was functioning well overall, the researchers report in the *Journal of Family Psychology*. So did expressions of discouragement toward a partner talking about a personality feature he or she wanted to change.

In other words, the inability or unwillingness to suppress negative emotions in the heat of the moment eliminates the possibility of a transformation of motivation to a broader perspective than one's own. Eventually, the cumulative impact of negative reactivity brings the relationship down.

"There is no such thing as two people meant for each other," says Michelle Givertz. "It's a matter of adjusting and adapting." But you have to know yourself so that you can get your needs for affection, inclusion, and control met in the ways that matter most for you. Even then, successful couples redefine their relationship many times, says Meinecke. Relationships need to continually evolve to fit ever-changing circumstances. They need to incorporate each partner's changes and find ways to meet their new needs.

"If both parties are willing to tackle the hard and vulnerable work of building love and healing conflict, they have a good chance to survive," says Page. If one party is reluctant, "you might need to say to your partner, 'I need this because I feel like we're losing each other, and I don't want that to happen.'"

In the end, says Minnesota's Doherty, "We're all difficult. Everyone who is married is a difficult spouse. We emphasize that our spouse is difficult and forget how we're difficult for them." If you want to have a mate in your life, he notes, you're going to have to go through the process of idealization and disillusionment—if not with your current partner then with the next. And the next. "You could really mess up your kids as you pursue the ideal mate." What's more, studies show that, on average, people do not make a better choice the second time around. Most often, people just trade one set of problems for another.

Boston's Real reports that he attended an anniversary party for friends who had been together 25 years. When someone commented on the longevity of the relationship, the husband replied: "Every morning I wake up, splash cold water on my face, and say out loud, 'Well, you're no prize either.'" While you're busy being disillusioned with your partner, Real suggests, you'll do better with a substantial dose of humility."

Critical Thinking

1. Is it "normal" to be discontented and disillusioned about your marriage and your partner?
2. What factors are most important to compatibility in relationships?
3. Does what bothers you about your relationship say more about you than your partner?

Create Central

www.mhhe.com/createcentral

Internet References

Coalition for Marriage, Family, and Couples Education
www.smartmarriages.com
National Council on Family Relations
www.ncfr.com

REBECCA WEBBER is a freelance writer based in New York.

Webber, Rebecca. From *Psychology Today*, January/February 2012. Copyright © 2012 by Sussex Publishers, LLC. Reprinted by permission.

Article   Prepared by: Patricia Hrusa Williams, *University of Maine at Farmington*

Masters of Love

Emily Esfahani Smith

Learning Outcomes

After reading this article, you will be able to:

- Identify practices couples associate with marital satisfaction and dissatisfaction.

- Recognize the impact of Gottman's work on relationships.

- Explain what kindness is and why it is important in marital relationships.

Every day in June, the most popular wedding month of the year, about 13,000 American couples will say "I do," committing to a lifelong relationship that will be full of friendship, joy, and love that will carry them forward to their final days on this earth.

Except, of course, it doesn't work out that way for most people. The majority of marriages fail, either ending in divorce and separation or devolving into bitterness and dysfunction. Of all the people who get married, only three in ten remain in healthy, happy marriages, as psychologist Ty Tashiro points out in his book *The Science of Happily Ever After,* which was published earlier this year.

Social scientists first started studying marriages by observing them in action in the 1970s in response to a crisis: Married couples were divorcing at unprecedented rates. Worried about the impact these divorces would have on the children of the broken marriages, psychologists decided to cast their scientific net on couples, bringing them into the lab to observe them and determine what the ingredients of a healthy, lasting relationship were. Was each unhappy family unhappy in its own way, as Tolstoy claimed, or did the miserable marriages all share something toxic in common?

Psychologist John Gottman was one of those researchers. For the past four decades, he has studied thousands of couples in a quest to figure out what makes relationships work. I recently had the chance to interview Gottman and his wife Julie, also a psychologist, in New York City. Together, the renowned experts on marital stability run The Gottman Institute, which is devoted to helping couples build and maintain loving, healthy relationships based on scientific studies.

John Gottman began gathering his most critical findings in 1986, when he set up "The Love Lab" with his colleague Robert Levenson at the University of Washington. Gottman and Levenson brought newlyweds into the lab and watched them interact with each other. With a team of researchers, they hooked the couples up to electrodes and asked the couples to speak about their relationship, like how they met, a major conflict they were facing together, and a positive memory they had. As they spoke, the electrodes measured the subjects' blood flow, heart rates, and how much they sweat they produced. Then the researchers sent the couples home and followed up with them six years later to see if they were still together.

From the data they gathered, Gottman separated the couples into two major groups: the *masters* and the *disasters*. The masters were still happily together after six years. The disasters had either broken up or were chronically unhappy in their marriages. When the researchers analyzed the data they gathered on the couples, they saw clear differences between the masters and disasters. The disasters looked calm during the interviews, but their physiology, measured by the electrodes, told a different story. Their heart rates were quick, their sweat glands were active, and their blood flow was fast. Following thousands of couples longitudinally, Gottman found that the more physiologically active the couples were in the lab, the quicker their relationships deteriorated over time.

But what does physiology have to do with anything? The problem was that the disasters showed all the signs of arousal—of being in fight-or-flight mode—in their relationships. Having a conversation sitting next to their spouse was, to their bodies, like facing off with a saber-toothed tiger. Even when they were talking about pleasant or mundane facets of their relationships, they were prepared to attack and be attacked. This sent their heart rates soaring and made them more aggressive toward each other. For example, each member of a couple could be talking about how their days had gone, and a highly aroused husband might say to his wife, "Why don't you start talking about your day. It won't take you very long."

The masters, by contrast, showed low physiological arousal. They felt calm and connected together, which translated into warm and affectionate behavior, even when they fought. It's not that the masters had, by default, a better physiological make-up than the disasters; it's that masters had created a climate of trust and intimacy that made both of them more emotionally and thus physically comfortable.

Gottman wanted to know more about how the masters created that culture of love and intimacy, and how the disasters squashed it. In a follow-up study in 1990, he designed a lab on the University of Washington campus to look like a beautiful bed and breakfast retreat. He invited 130 newlywed couples to spend the day at this retreat and watched them as they did what couples normally do on vacation: cook, clean, listen to music, eat, chat, and hang out. And Gottman made a critical discovery in this study—one that gets at the heart of why some relationships thrive while others languish.

Throughout the day, partners would make requests for connection, what Gottman calls "bids." For example, say that the husband is a bird enthusiast and notices a goldfinch fly across the yard. He might say to his wife, "Look at that beautiful bird outside!" He's not just commenting on the bird here: he's requesting a response from his wife—a sign of interest or support—hoping they'll connect, however momentarily, over the bird.

The wife now has a choice. She can respond by either "turning toward" or "turning away" from her husband, as Gottman puts it. Though the bird-bid might seem minor and silly, it can actually reveal a lot about the health of the relationship. The husband thought the bird was important enough to bring it up in conversation and the question is whether his wife recognizes and respects that.

People who turned toward their partners in the study responded by engaging the bidder, showing interest and support in the bid. Those who didn't—those who turned away—would not respond or respond minimally and continue doing whatever they were doing, like watching TV or reading the paper. Sometimes they would respond with overt hostility, saying something like, "Stop interrupting me, I'm reading."

These bidding interactions had profound effects on marital well-being. Couples who had divorced after a six-year follow up had "turn-toward bids" 33 percent of the time. Only three in ten of their bids for emotional connection were met with intimacy. The couples who were still together after

six years had "turn-toward bids" 87 percent of the time. Nine times out of ten, they were meeting their partner's emotional needs.

* * *

By observing these types of interactions, Gottman can predict with up to 94 percent certainty whether couples—straight or gay, rich or poor, childless or not—will be broken up, together and unhappy, or together and happy several years later. Much of it comes down to the spirit couples bring to the relationship. Do they bring kindness and generosity; or contempt, criticism, and hostility?

"There's a habit of mind that the masters have," Gottman explained in an interview, "which is this: they are scanning social environment for things they can appreciate and say thank you for. They are building this culture of respect and appreciation very purposefully. Disasters are scanning the social environment for partners' mistakes."

"It's not just scanning environment," chimed in Julie Gottman. "It's scanning the *partner* for what the *partner* is doing right or scanning him for what he's doing wrong and criticizing versus respecting him and expressing appreciation."

Contempt, they have found, is the number one factor that tears couples apart. People who are focused on criticizing their partners miss a whopping 50 percent of positive things their partners are doing and they see negativity when it's not there. People who give their partner the cold shoulder—deliberately ignoring the partner or responding minimally—damage the relationship by making their partner feel worthless and invisible, as if they're not there, not valued. And people who treat their partners with contempt and criticize them not only kill the love in the relationship, but they also kill their partner's ability to fight off viruses and cancers. Being mean is the death knell of relationships.

Kindness, on the other hand, glues couples together. Research independent from theirs has shown that kindness (along with emotional stability) is the most important predictor of satisfaction and stability in a marriage. Kindness makes each partner feel cared for, understood, and validated—feel loved. "My bounty is as boundless as the sea," says Shakespeare's Juliet. "My love as deep; the more I give to thee, / The more I have, for both are infinite." That's how kindness works too: there's a great deal of evidence showing the more someone receives or witnesses kindness, the more they will be kind themselves, which leads to upward spirals of love and generosity in a relationship.

There are two ways to think about kindness. You can think about it as a fixed trait: either you have it or you don't. Or you could think of kindness as a muscle. In some people, that muscle is naturally stronger than in others, but it can grow stronger in everyone with exercise. Masters tend to think about kindness as a muscle. They know that they have to exercise it to keep it in shape. They know, in other words, that a good relationship requires sustained hard work.

"If your partner expresses a need," explained Julie Gottman, "and you are tired, stressed, or distracted, then the generous spirit comes in when a partner makes a bid, and you still turn toward your partner."

In that moment, the easy response may be to turn away from your partner and focus on your iPad or your book or the television, to mumble "Uh huh" and move on with your life, but neglecting small moments of emotional connection will slowly wear away at your relationship. Neglect creates distance between partners and breeds resentment in the one who is being ignored.

The hardest time to practice kindness is, of course, during a fight—but this is also the most important time to be kind. Letting contempt and aggression spiral out of control during a conflict can inflict irrevocable damage on a relationship.

"Kindness doesn't mean that we don't express our anger," Julie Gottman explained, "but the kindness informs how we choose to express the anger. You can throw spears at your partner. Or you can explain why you're hurt and angry, and that's the kinder path."

John Gottman elaborated on those spears: "Disasters will say things differently in a fight. Disasters will say 'You're late. What's wrong with you? You're just like your mom.' Masters will say 'I feel bad for picking on you about your lateness, and I know it's not your fault, but it's really annoying that you're late again.'"

* * *

For the hundreds of thousands of couples getting married this month—and for the millions of couples currently together, married or not—the lesson from the research is clear: If you want to have a stable, healthy relationship, exercise kindness early and often.

When people think about practicing kindness, they often think about small acts of generosity, like buying each other little gifts or giving one another back rubs every now and then. While those are great examples of generosity, kindness can also be built into the very backbone of a relationship through the way partners interact with each other on a day-to-day basis, whether or not there are back rubs and chocolates involved.

One way to practice kindness is by being generous about your partner's intentions. From the research of the Gottmans, we know that disasters see negativity in their relationship even when it is not there. An angry wife may assume, for example, that when her husband left the toilet seat up, he was deliberately trying to annoy her. But he may have just absent-mindedly forgotten to put the seat down.

Or say a wife is running late to dinner (again), and the husband assumes that she doesn't value him enough to show up to their date on time after he took the trouble to make a reservation and leave work early so that they could spend a romantic evening together. But it turns out that the wife was running late because she stopped by a store to pick him up a gift for their special night out. Imagine her joining him for dinner, excited to deliver her gift, only to realize that he's in a sour mood because he misinterpreted what was motivating her behavior. The ability to interpret your partner's actions and intentions charitably can soften the sharp edge of conflict.

"Even in relationships where people are frustrated, it's almost always the case that there are positive things going on and people trying to do the right thing," psychologist Ty Tashiro told me. "A lot of times, a partner is trying to do the right thing even if it's executed poorly. So appreciate the intent."

Another powerful kindness strategy revolves around shared joy. One of the telltale signs of the disaster couples Gottman studied was their inability to connect over each other's good news. When one person in the relationship shared the good news of, say, a promotion at work with excitement, the other would respond with wooden disinterest by checking his watch or shutting the conversation down with a comment like, "That's nice."

We've all heard that partners should be there for each other when the going gets rough. But research shows that being there for each other when things go *right* is actually more important for relationship quality. How someone responds to a partner's good news can have dramatic consequences for the relationship.

In one study from 2006, psychological researcher Shelly Gable and her colleagues brought young adult couples into the lab to discuss recent positive events from their lives. They psychologists wanted to know how partners would respond to each other's good news. They found that, in general, couples responded to each other's good news in four different ways that they called: *passive destructive, active destructive, passive constructive,* and *active constructive.*

Let's say that one partner had recently received the excellent news that she got into medical school. She would say something like "I got into my top choice med school!"

If her partner responded in a *passive destructive* manner, he would ignore the event. For example, he might say something like: "You wouldn't believe the great news I got yesterday! I won a free t-shirt!"

If her partner responded in a *passive constructive* way, he would acknowledge the good news, but in a half-hearted, understated way. A typical passive constructive response is saying "That's great, babe" as he texts his buddy on his phone.

In the third kind of response, *active destructive,* the partner would diminish the good news his partner just got: "Are you sure you can handle all the studying? And what about the cost? Med school is so expensive!"

Finally, there's *active constructive* responding. If her partner responded in this way, he stopped what he was doing and engaged wholeheartedly with her: "That's great! Congratulations! When did you find out? Did they call you? What classes will you take first semester?"

Among the four response styles, active constructive responding is the kindest. While the other response styles are joy-killers, active constructive responding allows the partner to savor her joy and gives the couple an opportunity to bond over the good news. In the parlance of the Gottmans, active constructive responding is a way of "turning toward" your partners bid (sharing the good news) rather than "turning away" from it.

Active constructive responding is critical for healthy relationships. In the 2006 study, Gable and her colleagues followed up with the couples two months later to see if they were still together. The psychologists found that the only difference between the couples who were together and those who broke up was active constructive responding. Those who showed genuine interest in their partner's joys were more likely to be together. In an earlier study, Gable found that active constructive responding was also associated with higher relationship quality and more intimacy between partners.

There are many reasons why relationships fail, but if you look at what drives the deterioration of many relationships, it's often a breakdown of kindness. As the normal stresses of a life together pile up—with children, career, friend, in-laws, and other distractions crowding out the time for romance and intimacy—couples may put less effort into their relationship and let the petty grievances they hold against one another tear them apart. In most marriages, levels of satisfaction drop dramatically within the first few years together. But among couples who not only endure, but live happily together for years and years, the spirit of kindness and generosity guides them forward.

Critical Thinking

1. In Gottman's research on marriage he identified two groups, the masters and the disasters. Briefly describe the characteristics of each group and how they look in interaction with their partners.

2. Which characteristics did Gottman identify that predicted whether couples would divorce or not? Why do you think these characteristics or practices are important to maintaining a satisfying marriage?

3. The research cited in the article discusses the value of practicing kindness in relationships. What does it mean to be kind? What does kindness look like in interactions between partnerrs?

Internet References

Love is Respect
www.loveisrespect.org
National Healthy Marriage Resource Center
www.healtymarriageinfo.org
The Gottman Institute
www.gottman.com

Article

Prepared by: Patricia Hrusa Williams,
University of Maine at Farmington

How to Stay Married

ANNE KINGSTON

Learning Outcomes

After reading this article, you will be able to:

- Explain how men's and women's views and expectations for relationships and marriage differ.
- Describe the reasons behind women's adulterous behavior.
- Understand factors important to marital longevity.

Cynthia is a 68-year-old woman in a 45-year "committed marriage" who has figured out how to keep it that way. Every other month or so she goes out to lunch with her college boyfriend Thomas, who is also married and has no intention of leaving his wife. Usually their outings end in a hot and heavy "petting session" in his Mercedes. Sometimes, he rubs Jean Naté lotion, the scent Cynthia wore in college, onto her legs and compliments her beautiful feet. They've never consummated their relationship, nor do they intend to. Being with Thomas is "like a balloon liftoff," Cynthia reports, one that eases some of the tensions between her and her 74-year-old physics professor husband. "I'm a nicer, more tolerant person because of this affair," she says.

Cynthia's story is one of more than 60 confessionals from long-time wives that punctuate Iris Krasnow's new book *The Secret Lives of Wives: Women Share What It Really Takes to Stay Married.* And what their stories reveal is that marital longevity requires wives to establish strong, separate identities from their husbands through creative coping mechanisms, some of them covert. Krasnow spoke with more than 200 women, married between 15 and 70 years, who report taking separate holidays, embarking on new careers, establishing a tight circle of female friends, dabbling in *Same Time, Next Year*-style liaisons and adulterous affairs, and having "boyfriends with boundaries." Yoga and white wine also feature predominately.

The 58-year-old Krasnow, an author and journalism professor at American University, writes she was "stunned by the secrets and shenanigans" in her journalistic journey through American marriages. She comes to the subject from the vantage point of her own 23-year marriage to an architect she loves but admits to "loathing" occasionally. She credits summers spent apart, separate hobbies and her close relationships with male buddies for some of their marital stability.

It's a theory that builds on her previous books, *Surrendering to Motherhood* and *Surrendering to Marriage,* which extol the virtues of sublimating the self to a higher ideal.

Krasnow embraces the modern expectation that individuals experience perpetual personal growth and reinvention but dismisses the notion that partners must share each of these stages: "The reality is that for many wives, attaining longevity requires getting growth spurts elsewhere and experimenting with alternative routes," she writes.

First, however, women must lower their expectations of what marriage can provide, she advises: "Wives who don't rely on their husbands for happiness end up having the happiest marriages." Speaking on her phone from her home in Maryland, she echoes the sentiment: "You have to be partners on the level of the soul," she says of marriage. "But you are your own soulmate. Everybody needs a source of passion and purpose within. When you have that you can make any relationship work. You're not depending on anyone else to make you happy."

Krasnow paints a rosy picture of what a long-lasting marriage can provide women—better health, a rich shared history, the comfort of having someone who has your back, and personal and economic stability amid global uncertainty. Many of her testimonials suggest marriages can be regenerated over time, like a liver, with longer-married couples reporting the greatest happiness of all. There's also practical considerations, writes Krasnow, who admits online dating or disrobing in front of someone new horrifies her.

The book is destined to strike a nerve at a time when expectations of marriage and divorce are under scrutiny. Both the marriage rate and the divorce rate are dropping, with the exception of "grey divorce" among people over 50, embodied by Al and Tipper Gore who split after 40 years of marriage. We're in the midst of a divorce backlash, fuelled by the conservative-marriage movement and books like Judith Wallerstein's *The Unexpected Legacy of Divorce,* which raised consciousness about how divorce fractures families. Krasnow rejects the popular notion that divorce offers an opportunity for reinvention, as propagated by the booming divorce memoir genre. We should call it what it is: "a failure," she writes.

Yet it's clear the old script doesn't fit at a time women are increasingly out-earning their husbands and people are living into their 80s. "Women want to redefine how they navigate marriage," Krasnow says.

And the happily-ever-after prescription she offers will resonate. Many of the women Krasnow interviewed are like her—educated, smart, with enough disposable income to spend summers painting in Italy or travelling to ashrams. Most have financial autonomy: even a woman in a traditional arranged marriage has a thriving career and a helpful husband who gives her her own "space."

The directive that couples should give each other "space" for marriages to thrive is far from new, of course. Krasnow quotes from Kahlil Gibran's *The Prophet,* "Let there be space in your togetherness," published in 1923. In 1929, Virginia Woolf famously wrote of the need for women to have "money and a room of one's own" to create art. In 1954, Anne Morrow Lindbergh, wife of Charles Lindbergh, wrote *Gift From the Sea* on a summer retreat from her husband and children, which espoused the importance of solitude and self-reflection for women. It was an instant bestseller. And Johnny Cash attributed part of the success of his 32-year union with June Carter Cash to separate bathrooms: "The lady needs her space," he said.

Yet that sentiment runs counter to a popular culture in thrall to a "happily ever after" fairy-tale narrative and the "you complete me" message espoused in the movie *Jerry Maguire.* It's precisely the disconnect between the expectation that husband and wife be everything to one another and the reality of marriage that causes women to keep secrets, says Susan Shapiro Barash, a professor of gender studies at Marymount Manhattan College whose books include *Little White Lies, Deep Dark Secrets: The Truth About Why Women Lie.*

As time goes on, she says a lot of women feel trapped and that they've grown apart. "But because the culture so endorses marriage as a means and an end—children, a family, a partner for life (at least 60 per cent of the time). When it doesn't, "it's sometimes such a rude awakening for women they cover it up. Longevity does not lend itself to living happily as a wife."

That's a problem in a society in which women over 80 are the fastest-growing demographic.

Krasnow's examples indicate the wives most likely to live happily ever after into old age are those who can carve happily ever after out for themselves. It's the next iteration of the wife script that has traditionally called for a wifely sacrifice.

"We are the caregivers, the softies, the gender programmed to take care of the needs of everybody else before we care for ourselves," writes Krasnow. As a respite, she describes going out with her female friends for freewheeling bimonthly dinners where she can let loose as the "unmom" and "unwife."

Krasnow quotes 77-year-old sex and relationship therapist Marilyn Charwat, who says the American standard of sexual morality—that you marry one person and stay sexually and emotionally true and connected to that person—is "inhumane and impossible."

Yet the book reflects a broad view that sexual secrecy in marriage is rampant, from a woman buoyed by the memory of a furtive kiss with a neighbour to long-term sexual liaisons.

Not that Krasnow is advocating infidelity, though flirting is fine: "I say ride that hormonal surge straight to your own bedroom and initiate great sex with your spouse," she writes. Charwat's advice is more practical. She recommends women use vibrators, which releases them from relationship "tyranny."

The infidelity chapter, in which Krasnow spoke to 14 women conducting affairs, is coyly titled "Naughty Girls," a sensibility reflected in the cautionary references to 19th-century fictional heroines Emma Bovary and Anna Karenina. In one cautionary story, which reinforces Krasnow's theory that women should stick with their marriages, Lucy leaves her husband for a man she met on a plane and regrets her mistake.

Unlike husbands, wives are driven to extramarital affairs not as a way of exiting their marriage but remaining in them. One woman says her husband's sexual unresponsiveness justified her cheating. Mimi, a Lilly Pulitzer-wearing, 57-year-old conservative who's a secret swinger with her husband, practises an odd form of monogamy by saying he is the only man able to bring her to orgasm.

Shapiro Barash, who explored adultery in *A Passion for More: Wives Reveal the Affairs That Make or Break Their Marriages,* agrees unrealistic expectations usually fuel adultery. "The affair is always about what's missing from a marriage. I have rarely heard a woman speak of her lover being similar to her husband."

Krasnow's husband isn't a talker, so she craves extramarital conversation, not sex, a need sated by her various "boyfriends with boundaries." But seeking male friendship can be more fraught with peril than sexual affairs, the book reveals. One woman interviewed felt compelled to lie about her intense platonic relationship with a man; when her husband found out, he created a scene and demanded she never see him again. Krasnow admits there can be "danger zones": such as when participants text each other every 20 minutes. "Any man in my life, I immediately make sure my husband meets him."

What Krasnow is providing is a much-needed middle-aged fairy tale that begins years after the prince grows a paunch. Her prescriptions are both surprisingly banal and brilliant sound bites. "The real secret to staying married is not getting divorced," Krasnow writes, in a tautology. Save abuse or serial adultery, every marriage is salvageable with a big caveat that there's "trust, respect and intimacy, both emotional and physical."

As long as there's "a spittle of love," there's hope, she writes. Shelley, a woman whose marriage survived her husband's affair with her best friend, blames the woman more than her husband in a telling statement: "There's something sacred with the bond of women."

Then there's 48-year-old Julia, locked in a marriage "bound by the endless need" of her seriously ill daughter, who craves an "equal partner" but feels her husband is giving up. Her solution is to take up painting.

The focus on personal happiness would seem at odds with the notion espoused in Krasnow's other books. It's a perspective voiced by Phil and Pat Denniston, a happily married California couple even though they live and work together 24-7. They speak about the risks of separate directions and observe that marriages in which participants speak in terms of "me" not "us" are doomed.

In order to get to the happy "us," it's up to the wife to make the right choices from the get-go, Krasnow writes. She recalls she once asked Barbara Bush senior the secret to a happy marriage: "Pick the right husband in the first place."

The author agrees. "You should marry someone who's flexible, confident and trusts you: if you can't count on your husband or wife in a crazy unstable world then you're marrying the wrong person. But if you do marry the wrong person, you can always fall back on your secret life."

Critical Thinking

1. What do we hope to gain from getting married?
2. How do men's and women's views of marriage differ?
3. In *The Secret Lives of Women: What It Really Takes to Stay Married,* Iris Krasnow suggests that women need to lower their expectations of what marriage can provide. Do you agree or disagree? Why?

4. Is it a reasonable expectation in marriage to find someone who "completes you?"

Create Central

www.mhhe.com/createcentral

Internet References

Coalition for Marriage, Family, and Couples Education
www.smartmarriages.com
National Council on Family Relations
www.ncfr.com

Article   Prepared by: Patricia Hrusa Williams, *University of Maine at Farmington*

The Gay Guide to Wedded Bliss

Research finds that same-sex unions are happier than heterosexual marriages. What can gay and lesbian couples teach straight ones about living in harmony?

LIZA MUNDY

Learning Outcomes

After reading this article, you will be able to:

- Define the Defense of Marriage Act.

- Explain trends in marriage in the United States.

- Identify and discuss the role which gender plays in couple's relationships and marital unions.

It is more than a little ironic that gay marriage has emerged as the era's defining civil-rights struggle even as marriage itself seems more endangered every day. Americans are waiting longer to marry: according to the U.S. Census Bureau, the median age of first marriage is 28 for men and 26 for women, up from 23 and 20, respectively, in 1950. Rates of cohabitation have risen swiftly and sharply, and more people than ever are living single. Most Americans still marry at some point, but many of those marriages end in divorce. (Although the U.S. divorce rate has declined from its all-time high in the late '70s and early '80s, it has remained higher than those of most European countries.) All told, this has created an unstable system of what the UCLA sociologist Suzanne Bianchi calls "partnering and repartnering," a relentless emotional and domestic churn that sometimes results in people forgoing the institution altogether.

[. . .]

College graduates enjoy relatively stable unions, but for every other group, marriage is collapsing. Among "middle American" women (those with a high-school degree or some college), an astonishing 58 percent of first-time mothers are unmarried. The old Groucho Marx joke—"I don't care to belong to any club that will have me as a member"—applies a little differently in this context: you might well ask why gays and lesbians want to join an institution that keeps dithering about whether to admit them even as the repo men are coming for the furniture and the fire marshal is about to close down the clubhouse.

Against this backdrop, gay-marriage opponents have argued that allowing same-sex couples to wed will pretty much finish matrimony off. This point was advanced in briefs and oral arguments before the Supreme Court in March, in two major same-sex-marriage cases. One of these is a constitutional challenge to a key section of the Defense of Marriage Act, the 1996 law that defines marriage as a union between a man and a woman, and bars the federal government from recognizing same-sex marriages. The other involves California's Proposition 8, a same-sex-marriage ban passed by voters in 2008 but overturned by a federal judge in 2010. Appearing before the high court in March, Charles J. Cooper, the lawyer defending the California ban, predicted that same-sex marriage would undermine traditional marriage by eroding "marital norms."

The belief that gay marriage will harm marriage has roots in both religious beliefs about matrimony and secular conservative concerns about broader shifts in American life. One prominent line of thinking holds that men and women have distinct roles to play in family life; that children need both a mother and a father, preferably biologically related to them; and that a central purpose of marriage is abetting heterosexual procreation. During the Supreme Court arguments over Proposition 8, Justice Elena Kagan asked Cooper whether the essence of his argument against gay marriage was that opposite-sex couples can procreate while same-sex ones cannot. "That's the essential thrust of our position, yes," replied Cooper. He also warned that "redefining marriage as a genderless institution could well lead over time to harms to that institution."

Threaded through this thinking is a related conviction that mothers and fathers should treat their union as "permanent and exclusive," as the Princeton professor Robert P. George and his co-authors write in the new book *What Is Marriage? Man and Woman: A Defense*. Marriage, seen this way, is a rigid institution that exists primarily for the rearing of children and that powerfully constrains the behavior of adults (one is tempted to call this the "long slog 'til death" view of marriage), rather than an emotional union entered into for pleasure and companionship between adults. These critics of gay marriage are, quite validly, worried that too many American children are being raised in unstable homes, either by struggling single parents or by a transient succession of live-in adults. They fear that the spread of gay marriage could help finally sever the increasingly tenuous link between children and marriage, confirming that it's okay for dads, or moms, to be deleted from family life as hedonic fulfillment dictates.

In mounting their defense, advocates of same-sex marriage have argued that gays and lesbians who wish to marry are committed to family well-being; that concern for children's welfare is a chief reason many do want to marry; that gay people are being discriminated against, as a class, in being denied rights readily available to any heterosexual. And to the charge that same-sex marriage will change marriage, they tend to argue that it will not—that married gays and lesbians will blend seamlessly with the millions of married straight Americans. "The notion that this group can somehow fundamentally change the institution of marriage—I find it difficult to wrap my head around," says Gary Gates, a demographer with the Williams Institute, a research center affiliated with the UCLA School of Law.

But what if the critics are correct, just not in the way they suppose? What if same-sex marriage does change marriage, but primarily for the better? For one thing, there is reason to think that, rather than making marriage more fragile, the boom of publicity around same-sex weddings could awaken among heterosexuals a new interest in the institution, at least for a time. But the larger change might be this: by providing a new model of how two people can live together equitably, same-sex marriage could help haul matrimony more fully into the 21st century. Although marriage is in many ways fairer and more pleasurable for both men and women than it once was, it hasn't entirely thrown off old notions and habits. As a result, many men and women enter into it burdened with assumptions and stereotypes that create stress and resentment. Others, confronted with these increasingly anachronistic expectations—expectations at odds with the economic and practical realities of their own lives—don't enter into it at all.

Same-sex spouses, who cannot divide their labor based on preexisting gender norms, must approach marriage differently than their heterosexual peers. From sex to fighting, from child-rearing to chores, they must hammer out every last detail of domestic life without falling back on assumptions about who will do what. In this regard, they provide an example that can be enlightening to all couples. Critics warn of an institution rendered "genderless." But if a genderless marriage is a marriage in which the wife is not automatically expected to be responsible for school forms and child care and dinner preparation and birthday parties and midnight feedings and holiday shopping, I think it's fair to say that many heterosexual women would cry "Bring it on!"

Beyond that, gay marriage can function as a controlled experiment, helping us see which aspects of marital difficulty are truly rooted in gender and which are not. A growing body of social science has begun to compare straight and same-sex couples in an attempt to get at the question of what is female, what is male. Some of the findings are surprising. For instance: we know that heterosexual wives are more likely than husbands to initiate divorce. Social scientists have struggled to explain the discrepancy, variously attributing it to the sexual revolution; to women's financial independence; to men's failure to keep modern wives happy. Intriguingly, in Norway and Sweden, where registered partnerships for same-sex couples have been in place for about two decades (full-fledged marriage was introduced several years ago), research has found that lesbians are twice as likely as gay men to split up. If women become dissatisfied even when married to other women, maybe the problem with marriage isn't men. Maybe women are too particular. Maybe even women don't know what women want. These are the kinds of things that we will be able to tease out.

[. . .]

Whatever happens with the high court, it seems likely that gay marriage will continue its spread through the land. So what happens, then, to the institution of marriage? The impact is likely to be felt near and far, both fleetingly and more permanently, in ways confounding to partisans on both sides.

Rules for a More Perfect Union

Not all is broken within modern marriage, of course. On the contrary: the institution is far more flexible and forgiving than it used to be. In the wake of women's large-scale entry into the workplace, men are less likely than they once were to be saddled with being a family's sole breadwinner, and can carve out a life that includes the close companionship of their children. Meanwhile, women are less likely to be saddled with the sole responsibility for child care and housework, and can envision a life beyond the stove top and laundry basket.

And yet for many couples, as Bianchi, the UCLA sociologist, has pointed out, the modern ideal of egalitarianism has proved "quite difficult to realize." Though men are carrying more of a domestic workload than in the past, women still bear the brunt of the second shift. Among couples with children, when both spouses work full-time, women do 32 hours a week of housework, child care, shopping, and other family-related services, compared with the 21 hours men put in. Men do more paid work—45 hours, compared with 39 for women—but still have more free time: 31 hours, compared with 25 for women. Betsey Stevenson and Justin Wolfers, economists and professors of public policy at the University of Michigan, have shown that happiness rates among women have dropped even as women have acquired more life options. One possible cause is the lingering inequity in male-female marriage: women's at-home workload can become so burdensome that wives opt out of the paid workforce—or sit at the office making mental lists of the chores they do versus the chores their husbands do, and bang their heads on their desks in despair.

Not that everything is easy for fathers in dual-earner couples, who now feel afflicted by work-life conflict in even greater numbers than their wives (60 percent of men in such couples say they experience this conflict, versus 47 percent of women, according to a 2008 study by the Families and Work Institute). And men face a set of unfair expectations all their own: the Pew Research Center found in 2010 that 67 percent of Americans still believe it's "very important" that a man be ready to support a family before getting married, while only 33 percent believe the same about women.

This burden, exacerbated by the economic realities facing many men today, has undoubtedly contributed to marriage's recent decline. As our economy has transitioned away from manufacturing and industry, men with a high-school education can no longer expect the steady, well-paying union jobs that formerly enabled many to support their families. Outdated assumptions that men should bring something to the table, and that this something should be money, don't help. Surveying their prospects, many working-class mothers reject marriage altogether, perhaps reasoning that they can support a child, but don't want a dependent husband.

It's not that people don't want to marry. Most never-married Americans say they still aspire to marriage, but many of them see it as something grand and out of reach. Getting married is no longer something you do when you are young and foolish and starting out; prosperity is not something spouses build together. Rather, marriage has become a "marker of prestige," as the sociologist Andrew Cherlin puts it—a capstone of a successful life, rather than its cornerstone. But while many couples have concluded that they are not ready for marriage, they have things backwards. It's not that they aren't ready for marriage; it's that marriage isn't ready for the realities of 21st-century life. Particularly for less affluent, less educated Americans, changing economic and gender realities have dismantled the old institution, without constructing any sort of replacement.

As we attempt to come up with a more functional model, research on same-sex unions can provide what Gary Gates of the Williams Institute calls an "important counterfactual." Although gays and lesbians cannot solve all that ails marriage, they seem to be working certain things out in ways straight couples might do well to emulate, chief among them a back-to-the-drawing-board approach to divvying up marital duties. A growing body of scholarship on household division of labor shows that in many ways, same-sex couples do it better.

This scholarship got its start in the late 1960s, with a brilliant insight by the sociologist Pepper Schwartz. [. . .] Like many of her peers, she was keen to figure out what women were and what men were: which traits were biological and which social, and where there might be potential for transformational change. "It occurred to me," she says, that "a naturally occurring experiment" could shed light on these issues. Actually, two experiments: the rise of unmarried heterosexual cohabitation, and the growing visibility of gay and lesbian couples. If she surveyed people in three kinds of relationships—married; straight and cohabiting; and gay and cohabiting—and all showed similarity on some measures, maybe this would say something about both men and women. If the findings didn't line up, maybe this would say something about marriage.

After taking a teaching position at the University of Washington (where she remains a faculty member), Schwartz teamed up with a gay colleague, the late Philip Blumstein, to conduct just such a survey, zeroing in on the greater San Francisco, New York City, and Seattle metropolitan areas. It was a huge effort. Unmarried cohabiting couples were not yet easy to find, and gays and lesbians were so leery of being outed that when Schwartz asked a woman who belonged to a lesbian bridge group whether she could interview the other players about their relationships, the woman said, "We don't even talk about it ourselves." Schwartz and Blumstein collected responses to 12,000 questionnaires and conducted hundreds of interviews; at one point, they had 20 graduate students helping tabulate data. The project took about a decade, and resulted in a groundbreaking piece of sociology, the book *American Couples: Money, Work, Sex.*

What Schwartz and Blumstein found is that gay and lesbian couples were fairer in their dealings with one another than straight couples, both in intent and in practice. The lesbians in the study were almost painfully egalitarian—in some cases putting money in jars and splitting everything down to the penny in a way, Schwartz says, that "would have driven me crazy." Many unmarried heterosexual cohabitators were also careful about divvying things up, but lesbian couples seemed to take the practice to extremes: "It was almost like 'my kitty, your litter.'" Gay men, like lesbians, were more likely than straight couples to share cooking and chores. Many had been in heterosexual marriages, and when asked whether they had helped their wives with the housework in those prior unions, they usually said they had not. "You can imagine," Schwartz says, "how irritating I found this."

There were still some inequities: in all couples, the person with the higher income had more authority and decision-making power. This was least true for lesbians; truer for heterosexuals; and most true for gay men. Somehow, putting two men together seemed to intensify the sense that "money talks," as Schwartz and Blumstein put it. They could not hope to determine whether this tendency was innate or social—were men naturally inclined to equate resources with power, or had our culture ingrained that idea in them?—but one way or another, the finding suggested that money was a way men competed with other men, and not just a way for husbands to compete with their wives. Among lesbians, the contested terrain lay elsewhere: for instance, interacting more with the children could be, Schwartz says, a "power move."

Lesbians also tended to discuss things endlessly, achieving a degree of closeness unmatched by the other types of couples. Schwartz wondered whether this might account for another finding: over time, sex in lesbian relationships dwindled—a state of affairs she has described as "lesbian bed death." [. . .] She posits that lesbians may have had so much intimacy already that they didn't need sex to get it; by contrast, heterosexual women, whose spouses were less likely to be chatty, found that "sex is a highway to intimacy." As for men, she eventually concluded that whether they were straight or gay, they approached sex as they might a sandwich: good, bad, or mediocre, they were likely to grab it.

RULE 1: Negotiate in advance who will empty the trash and who will clean the bathroom. Other studies have since confirmed Schwartz and Blumstein's findings that same-sex couples are more egalitarian. In 2000, when Vermont became the first state to legalize same-sex civil unions, the psychologist Esther Rothblum saw an opportunity to explore how duties get sorted among a broad swath of the same-sex population. Rothblum, now at San Diego State University, is herself a lesbian and had long been interested in the relationships and mental health of lesbians. She also wanted to see how legal recognition affected couples.

As people from around the country flocked to Vermont to apply for civil-union licenses, Rothblum and two colleagues got their names and addresses from public records and asked them to complete a questionnaire. Then, they asked each of the civil-union couples to suggest friends in same-sex couples who were not in civil unions, and to identify a heterosexual sibling who was married, and wrote those people asking them to participate. This approach helped control for factors like background and upbringing among the subjects. The researchers asked people to rate, on a scale of one to nine, which partner was

more likely to do the dishes, repair things around the house, buy groceries. They asked who was more likely to deal with the landlord, punish the children, call the plumber, drive the kids to appointments, give spontaneous hugs, pay compliments. They also asked who was more likely to appreciate the other person's point of view during an argument.

They found that, even in the new millennium, married heterosexual couples were very likely to divide duties along old-fashioned gender lines. Straight women were more likely than lesbians to report that their partner paid the mortgage or the rent and the utility bills, and bought groceries, household appliances, even the women's clothing. These wives were also more likely to say they did the bulk of the cooking, vacuuming, dishes, and laundry. Compared with their husbands, they were far, far more likely to clean the bathroom. They were also more likely than their husbands to perform "relationship maintenance" such as showing affection and initiating serious conversations. When Rothblum and her colleagues held the heterosexual husbands up against the gay men, they found the same pattern. The straight guys were more likely to take care of the lawn, empty the trash, and make household repairs than their partners. They were the ones to fix drinks for company and to drive when the couple went out. They cooked breakfast reasonably often, but not dinner. On all these measures and more, the same-sex couples were far more likely to divide responsibilities evenly. This is not to say that the same-sex couples split each duty half-and-half. One partner might do the same chore regularly, but because there was no default assignment based on gender, such patterns evolved organically, based on preferences and talents.

Rothblum's observations are borne out by the couples I interviewed for this piece. "I'm a better cook, so I take on most of that responsibility," said Seth Thayer, who lives in a small coastal town in Maine. His husband, Greg Tinder, "is a better handyman." Others spoke of the perils of lopsided relationships. Chris Kast, a Maine newlywed, told me that he and his husband, Byron Bartlett, had both been married to women. In Bartlett's first marriage, it was tacitly assumed that he would take out the garbage. Now the two men divide tasks by inclination. "I'm more of a Felix Ungar—I notice when something's dirty—but we both clean," Kast said. "With Chris and I," Bartlett added, "we have to get *everything* done." Isabelle Dikland, a Washington, D.C., business consultant who is married to Amy Clement, a teacher, told me about a dinner party she recently attended with a group of mostly straight parents. Dikland and Clement, who had just had a second daughter, were extolling the virtues of having two children. The straight mother they were talking with seemed dubious, "if we had a second kid, guess who would do all the work," she told them. "I'd have to give up my career; I'm already doing everything." The woman glanced surreptitiously at her husband, at which point Dikland "dropped the subject really quickly."

RULE 2: When it comes to parenting, a 50-50 split isn't necessarily best. Charlotte J. Patterson, a psychologist at the University of Virginia, has arresting visual evidence of the same egalitarianism at work in parenting: compared with husband-and-wife pairs, she has found, same-sex parents tend to be more cooperative and mutually hands-on. Patterson and a colleague, Rachel Farr, have conducted a study of more than 100 same-sex and heterosexual adoptive parents in 11 states and the District of Columbia; it is among the first such studies to include gay fathers. As reported in an article in a forthcoming issue of the journal *Child Development*, the researchers visited families in their homes, scattered some toys on a blanket, invited the subjects to play with them any way they chose, and videotaped the interactions. "What you see is what they did with that blank slate," Patterson says. "One thing that I found riveting: the same-sex couples are far more likely to be in there together, and the opposite-sex couples show the conventional pattern—the mom more involved, the dad playing with Tinkertoys by himself." When the opposite-sex couples did parent simultaneously, they were more likely to undermine each other by talking at cross-purposes or suggesting different toys. The lesbian mothers tended to be egalitarian and warm in their dealings with one another, and showed greater pleasure in parenting than the other groups did. Same-sex dads were also more egalitarian in their division of labor than straight couples, though not as warm or interactive as lesbian moms. (Patterson says she and her colleagues may need to refine their analysis to take into account male ways of expressing warmth.)

By and large, all of the families studied, gay and straight alike, were happy, high functioning, and financially secure. Each type of partner—gay, straight; man, woman—reported satisfaction with his or her family's parenting arrangement, though the heterosexual wife was less content than the others, invariably saying that she wanted more help from her husband. "Of all the parents we've studied, she's the least satisfied with the division of labor," says Patterson, who is in a same-sex partnership and says she knows from experience that deciding who will do what isn't always easy.

Even as they are more egalitarian in their parenting styles, same-sex parents resemble their heterosexual counterparts in one somewhat old-fashioned way: a surprising number establish a division of labor whereby one spouse becomes the primary earner and the other stays home. Lee Badgett, an economist at the University of Massachusetts at Amherst, told me that, "in terms of economics," same-sex couples with children resemble heterosexual couples with children much more than they resemble childless same-sex couples. You might say that gay parents are simultaneously departing from traditional family structures and leading the way back toward them.

In his seminal book *A Treatise on the Family*, published in 1981, the Nobel Prize–winning economist Gary Becker argued that "specialization," whereby one parent stays home and the other does the earning, is the most efficient way of running a household, because the at-home spouse enables the at-work spouse to earn more. Feminists, who had been fighting for domestic parity, not specialization, deplored this theory, rightly fearing that it could be harnessed to keep women at home. Now the example of gay and lesbian parents might give us all permission to relax a little: maybe sometimes it really is easier when one parent works and the other is the supplementary or nonearning partner, either because this is the natural order of things or because the American workplace is so greedy and unforgiving that something or somebody has to give. As Martha Ertman, a University of Maryland law professor, put it to me, many families just function better when the same person is consistently "in charge of making vaccinations happen, making sure the model of the World War II monument gets done, getting the Christmas tree home or the challah bought by 6 o'clock on Friday." The good news is that the decision about which parent plays this role need not have anything to do with gender.

More surprising still, guess who is most likely to specialize. Gay dads. Using the most recent Census Bureau data, Gary Gates found that 32 percent of married heterosexual couples with children have only one parent in the labor force, compared with 33 percent of gay-male couples with children. (Lesbians also specialize, but not at such high rates, perhaps because they are so devoted to equality, or perhaps because their earnings are lower—women's median wage is 81 percent that of men—and not working is an unaffordable luxury.) While the percentage point dividing gay men from straight couples is not statistically significant, it's intriguing that gay dads are as likely as straight women to be stay-at-home parents.

Gay men's decisions about breadwinning can nonetheless be fraught, as many associate employment with power. A study published in the *Journal of GLBT Family Studies* in 2005 by Stephanie Jill Schacher and two colleagues found that when gay men do specialize, they don't have an easy time deciding who will do what: some stay-at-home dads perceived that their choice carried with it a loss in prestige and stature. As a result, gay men tended to fight not over who got to stay home, but over who didn't have to. "It's probably the biggest problem in our relationship," said one man interviewed for that study. Perhaps what Betty Friedan called "the problem that has no name" is inherent in child-rearing, and will always be with us.

RULE 3: Don't want a divorce? Don't marry a woman. Three years after they first gathered information from the couples who received licenses in Vermont, Esther Rothblum and her colleagues checked back to evaluate the condition of their relationships. Overall, the researchers found that the quality of gay and lesbian relationships was higher on many measures than that of the straight control group (the married heterosexual siblings), with more compatibility and intimacy, and less conflict.

Which is not to say same-sex couples don't have conflict. When they fight, however, they fight fairer. They can even fight funny, as researchers from the University of Washington and the University of California at Berkeley showed in an article published in 2003, based on a study of couples who were navigating potentially tense interactions. Recruiting married straight couples as well as gays and lesbians in committed relationships, the researchers orchestrated a scenario in which one partner had to bring up an area of conflict to discuss with the other. In same-sex couples, the partner with the bone to pick was rated "less belligerent and less domineering" than the straight-couple counterpart, while the person on the receiving end was less aggressive and showed less fear or tension. The same-sex "initiator" also displayed less sadness and "whining," and more affection, joy, and humor. In trying to make sense of the disparity, the researchers noted that same-sex couples valued equality more, and posited that the greater negativity of straight couples "may have to do with the standard status hierarchy between men and women." Which perhaps boils down to something like this: straight women see themselves as being less powerful than men, and this breeds hostility.

When it comes to conflict, a crucial variable separates many gay and lesbian couples from their straight counterparts: children. As Rothblum points out, for married heterosexual parents, happiness tends to be U-shaped: high at the beginning of marriage, then dipping to a low, then high again. What happens in that low middle is child-rearing. Although the proportion of gay and lesbian couples with children is increasing, same-sex couples are still less likely than straight couples to be parents. Not all research comparing same-sex and married straight couples has done an adequate job of controlling for this important difference. One that did, a 2008 study in the *Journal of Family Psychology*, looked at couples during their first 10 years of cohabitation. It found that childless lesbians had a higher "relationship quality" than their child-free gay-male and heterosexual counterparts. And yet a 2010 study in the same journal found that gay-male, lesbian, and straight couples alike experienced a "modest decline in relationship quality" in the first year of adopting a child. As same-sex couples become parents in greater numbers, they could well endure some of the same strife as their straight peers. It remains to be seen whether the different parenting styles identified by Charlotte Patterson might blunt some of the ennui of child-rearing.

As for divorce, the data are still coming in. A 2006 study of Sweden and Norway found higher dissolution rates among same-sex couples in registered partnerships than among married straight people. Yet in the United States, a study by the Williams Institute has found that gay unions have lower dissolution rates than straight ones. It is simply too soon to tell with any certainty whether gay marriages will be more or less durable in the long run than straight ones. What the studies to date do (for the most part) suggest is this: despite—or maybe because of—their perfectionist approach to egalitarianism, lesbian couples seem to be more likely to break up than gay ones. Pepper Schwartz noted this in the early 1980s, as did the 2006 study of same-sex couples in Sweden and Norway, in which researchers speculated that women may have a "stronger general sensitivity to the quality of relationships." Meaning maybe women are just picky, and when you have two women, you have double the pickiness. So perhaps the real threat to marriage is: women.

The Contagion Effect

Whatever this string of studies may teach us about marriage and gender dynamics, the next logical question becomes this: Might such marriages do more than merely inform our understanding of straight marriage—might their attributes trickle over to straight marriage in some fashion?

In the course of my reporting this year in states that had newly legalized same-sex marriage, people in the know—wedding planners, officiants, fiancés and fiancées—told me time and again that nuptial fever had broken out around them, among gay and straight couples alike. Same-sex weddings seemed to be bestowing a new frisson on the idea of getting hitched, or maybe restoring an old one. At the Gay and Lesbian Wedding Expo in downtown Baltimore, just a few weeks after same-sex marriage became legal in Maryland, Drew Vanlandingham, who describes himself as a "wedding planner designer," was delighted at how business had picked up. Here it was, January, and many of his favorite venues were booked into late summer—much to the consternation, he said, of his straight brides. "They're like, 'I better get a move on!'" It was his view that in Maryland, both teams were now engaged in an amiable but spirited race to the altar.

Ministers told me of wedding booms in their congregations. In her years as the pastor of the Unitarian church in Rockville, Maryland, Lynn Strauss said she had grown accustomed to a thin wedding roster: some years she might perform one or two services; other years, none. But this year, "my calendar is full of weddings," she said. "Two in March, one in April, one in May, one in September, one in October—oh, and one in July." Three were same-sex weddings, but the rest were heterosexual. When I attended the church's first lesbian wedding, in early March, I spoke with Steve Greene and Ellen Rohan, who had recently been married by Strauss. It was Steve's third marriage, Ellen's second. Before he met Ellen, Steve had sworn he would never marry again. Ellen said the arrival of same-sex marriage had influenced their feelings. "Marriage," she said simply, "is on everyone's mind."

Robert M. Hardies, who is a pastor at the Unitarian All Souls Church in Washington, D.C., and who is engaged to be married to his longtime partner and co-parent, Chris Nealon, told me that he has seen "a re-enchantment of marriage" among those who attend same-sex ceremonies: "Straight folks come to [same-sex] weddings, and I watch it on their face—there's a feeling that this is really special. Suddenly marriage is sexy again." We could chalk these anecdotes up to the human desire to witness love that overcomes obstacles—the same desire behind all romantic comedies, whether Shakespeare's or Hollywood's. But could something a bit less romantic also be at work?

There is some reason to suppose that attitudes about marriage could, in fact, be catching. The phenomenon known as "social contagion" lies at the heart of an increasingly prominent line of research on how our behavior and emotions affect the people we know. One famous example dates from 2008, when James H. Fowler and Nicholas A. Christakis published a study showing that happiness "spreads" through social networks. They arrived at this conclusion via an ingenious crunching of data from a long-running medical study involving thousands of interconnected residents—and their children, and later their grandchildren—in Framingham, Massachusetts. "Emotional states can be transferred directly from one individual to another," they found, across three degrees of separation. Other studies have shown that obesity, smoking habits, and school performance may also be catching.

Most relevant, in a working paper that is under submission to a sociology journal, the Brown University political scientist Rose McDermott, along with her co-authors, Fowler and Christakis, has identified a contagion effect for divorce. Divorce, she found, can spread among friends. She told me that she also suspects that tending to the marriages of friends can help preserve your own. McDermott says she readily sees how marriage could itself be contagious. Intriguingly, some of the Scandinavian countries where same-sex unions have been legal for a decade or more have seen a rise, not a fall, in marriage rates. In response to conservative arguments that same-sex marriage had driven a stake through the heart of marriage in northern Europe, the Yale University law professor William N. Eskridge Jr. and Darren Spedale in 2006 published an analysis showing that in the decade since same-sex partnerships became legal, heterosexual marriage rates had increased 10.7 percent in Denmark, 12.7 percent in Norway, and 28.8 percent in Sweden. Divorce rates had dropped in all three countries. Although there was no way to prove cause and effect, the authors allowed, you could safely say that marriage had not been harmed.

So let's suppose for a moment that marital behavior is catching. How, exactly, might it spread? I found one possible vector of contagion inside the Washington National Cathedral, a neo-Gothic landmark that towers watchfully over the Washington, D.C., skyline. The seat of the bishop of an Episcopal diocese

that includes D.C. and parts of Maryland, the cathedral is a symbol of American religious life, and strives to provide a spiritual home for the nation, frequently hosting interfaith events and programs. Presiding over it is the Very Reverend Gary Hall, an Episcopal priest and the cathedral's dean. Earlier this year, Hall announced that the cathedral would conduct same-sex weddings, a declaration that attracted more attention than he expected. Only people closely involved with the church and graduates of the private schools on its grounds can marry there. Even so, it is an influential venue, and Hall used the occasion to argue that same-sex couples offer an image of "radical" equality that straight couples can profitably emulate. He believes, moreover, that their example can be communicated through intermediaries like him: ministers and counselors gleaning insights from same-sex couples, and transmitting them, as it were, to straight ones. Hall says that counseling same-sex couples in preparation for their ceremonies has already altered the way he counsels men and women.

"I have a list of like 12 issues that people need to talk about that cause conflict," said Hall, who is lanky, with short gray hair and horn-rims, and who looks like he could be a dean of pretty much anything: American literature, political philosophy, East Asian studies. As we talked in his office one morning this spring, sunlight poured through a bank of arched windows onto an Oriental rug. Over the years, he has amassed a collection of cheesy 1970s paperbacks with names like *Open Marriage* and *Total Woman*, which he calls "books that got people into trouble." The dean grew up in Hollywood, and in the 1990s was a priest at a church in Pasadena where he did many same-sex blessings (a blessing being a ceremony that stops short of legal marriage). He is as comfortable talking about Camille Paglia and the LGBT critique of marriage as he is about Holy Week. He is also capable of saying things like "The problem with genital sex is that it involves us emotionally in a way that we're not in control of."

When Hall sees couples for premarital preparation, he gives them a list of hypothetical conflicts to take home, hash out, and report back on. Everybody fights, he tells them. The people who thrive in marriage are the ones who can handle disagreement and make their needs known. So he presents them with the prime sticking points: affection and lovemaking; how to deal with in-laws; where holidays will be spent; outside friendships. He talks to them about parenting roles, and chores, and money—who will earn it and who will make decisions about it.

Like Esther Rothblum, he has found that heterosexual couples persist in approaching these topics with stereotypical assumptions. "You start throwing out questions for men and women: 'Who's going to take care of the money?' And the guy says, 'That's me.' And you ask: 'Who's responsible for birth control?' And the guy says, 'That's her department.'" By contrast, he reports, same-sex couples "have thought really hard about how they're going to share the property, the responsibilities, the obligations in a mutual way. They've had to devote much more thought to that than straight couples, because the straight couples pretty much still fall back on old modes."

Now when Hall counsels heterosexuals, "I'm really pushing back on their patriarchal assumptions: that the woman's got to give up her career for the guy; that the guy is going to take care of the money." Every now and then, he says, he has a breakthrough, and a straight groom realizes that, say, contraception is his concern too. Hall says the same thing is happening in the offices of any number of pastors, rabbis, and therapists. "You're not going to be able to talk to heterosexual couples where there's a power imbalance and talk to a homosexual couple where there is a power mutuality," and not have the conversations impact one another. As a result, he believes there will be changes to marriage, changes that some people will find scary. "When [conservatives] say that gay marriage threatens my marriage, I used to say, 'That's ridiculous.' Now I say, 'Yeah, it does. It's asking you a crucial question about your marriage that you may not want to answer: If I'm a man, am I actually sharing the duties and responsibilities of married life equally with my wife?' Same-sex marriage gives us another image of what marriage can be."

Hall argues that same-sex marriage stands to change even the wedding service itself. For a good 1,000 years, he notes, the Christian Church stayed out of matrimony, which was primarily a way for society to regulate things like inheritance. But ever since the Church did get involved, the wedding ceremony has tended to reflect the gender mores of the time. For example, the Book of Common Prayer for years stated that a wife must love, honor, and obey her husband, treating him as her master and lord. That language is long gone, but vestiges persist: the tradition of the father giving away the bride dates from an era when marriage was a property transfer and the woman was the property. In response to the push for same-sex marriage, Hall says, the General Convention, the governing council of the entire Episcopal Church, has devised a liturgy for same-sex ceremonies (in most dioceses, these are blessings) that honors but alters this tradition so that both spouses are presented by sponsors.

"The new service does not ground marriage in a doctrine of creation and procreation," Hall says. "It grounds marriage in a kind of free coming-together of two people to live out their lives." A study group has convened to look at the Church's teachings on marriage, and in the next couple of years, Hall expects, the General Convention will adopt a new service for all Episcopal weddings. He is hopeful that the current same-sex service will serve as its basis.

The legalization of same-sex marriage is likely to affect even members of churches that have not performed such ceremonies. Delman Coates, the pastor of Mt. Ennon Baptist, a predominantly African American mega-church in southern Maryland, was active in his state's fight for marriage equality, presenting it to his parishioners as a civil-rights issue. The topic has also led to some productive, if difficult, conversations about "what the Scriptures are condemning and what they're confirming." In particular, he has challenged his flock over what he calls the "typical clobber passages": certain verses in Leviticus, Romans, and elsewhere that many people interpret as condemnations of homosexuality. These discussions are part of a long-standing effort to challenge people's thinking about other passages having to do with divorce and premarital sex—issues many parishioners have struggled with at home. Coates preaches that what the Bible is condemning is not modern divorce, but a practice, common in biblical times, whereby men cast out their wives for no good reason. Similarly, he tells them that the "fornication" invoked is something extreme—rape, incest, prostitution. He does not condone illicit behavior or familial dissolution, but he wants the members of his congregation to feel better about their own lives. In exchanges like these, he is making gay marriage part of a much larger conversation about the way we live and love now.

Gay marriage's ripples are also starting to be felt beyond churches, in schools and neighborhoods and playgroups. Which raises another question: Will gay and lesbian couples be peacemakers or combatants in the "mommy wars"—the long-simmering struggle between moms who stay at home and moms who work outside it? If you doubt that straight households are paying attention to same-sex ones, consider Danie, a woman who lives with her husband and two children in Bethesda, Maryland. (Danie asked me not to use her last name out of concern for her family's privacy.) Not long after she completed a master's degree in Spanish linguistics at Georgetown University, her first baby was born. Because her husband, Jesse, works long hours as a litigator, she decided to become a full-time parent—not an easy decision in work-obsessed Washington, D.C. For a while, she ran a photography business out of their home, partly because she loves photography but partly so she could assure people at dinner parties that she had paying work. Whenever people venture that women who work outside the home don't judge stay-at-home moms, Danie thinks: *Are you freaking kidding me?*

She takes some comfort, however, in the example of a lesbian couple with whom she is friendly. Both women are attorneys, and one stays home with their child. "Their life is exactly the same as ours," Danie told me, with a hint of vindication. If being a stay-at-home mother is "good enough for her, then what's my issue? She's a huge women's-rights activist." But while comparing herself with a lesbian couple is liberating in some ways, it also exacerbates the competitive anxiety that afflicts so many modern mothers. The other thing about these two mothers, Danie said, is that they are so relaxed, so happy, so present. Even the working spouse manages to be a super-involved parent, to a much greater extent than most of the working fathers she knows. "I'm a little bit obsessed with them," she says.

Related to this is the question of how gay fatherhood might impact heterosexual fatherhood—by, for example, encouraging the idea that men can be emotionally accessible, logistically capable parents. Will the growing presence of gay dads in some communities mean that men are more often included in the endless e-mail chains that go to parents of preschoolers and birthday-party invitees? As radically as fatherhood has changed in recent decades, a number of antiquated attitudes about dads have proved strangely enduring: Rob Hardies, the pastor at All Souls, reports that when his partner, Chris, successfully folded a stroller before getting on an airplane with their son, Nico, he was roundly congratulated by passersby, as if he had solved a difficult mathematical equation in public. So low are expectations for fathers, even now, that in Stephanie Schacher's study of gay fathers and their feelings about care-giving, her subjects reported that people would see them walking on the street with their children and say things like "Giving Mom a break?" Hardies thinks that every time he and Chris take their son to the playground or to story hour, they help disrupt this sort of thinking. He imagines moms seeing a man doing this and gently—or maybe not so gently—pointing it out to their husbands. "Two guys somehow manage to get their act together and have a household and cook dinner and raise a child, without a woman doing all the work," he says. Rather than setting an example that fathers don't matter, gay men are setting an example that fathers do matter, and that marriage matters, too.

The Sex Problem

When, in the 1970s and early 1980s, Pepper Schwartz asked couples about their sex lives, she arrived at perhaps her most explosive finding: non-monogamy was rampant among gay men, a whopping 82 percent of whom reported having had sex outside their relationship. Slightly more than one-third of gay-male couples felt that monogamy was important; the other two-thirds said that monogamy was unimportant or that they were neutral on the topic. In a funny way, Schwartz says, her findings suggested that same-sex unions (like straight ones) aren't necessarily about sex. Some gay men made a point of telling her they loved their partners but weren't physically attracted to them. Others said they wanted to be monogamous but were unsupported in that wish, by their partner, gay culture, or both.

Schwartz believes that a move toward greater monogamy was emerging among gay men even before the AIDS crisis. Decades later, gay-male couples are more monogamous than they used to be, but not nearly to the same degree as other kinds of couples. In her Vermont research, Esther Rothblum found

that 15 percent of straight husbands said they'd had sex outside their relationship, compared with 58 percent of gay men in civil unions and 61 percent of gay men who were partnered but not in civil unions. When asked whether a couple had arrived at an explicit agreement about extra-relational sex, a minuscule 4 percent of straight husbands said they'd discussed it with their partner and determined that it was okay, compared with 40 percent of gay men in civil unions and 49 percent of gay men in partnerships that were not legally recognized. Straight women and lesbians, meanwhile, were united in their commitment to monogamy, lesbians more so than straight women: 14 percent of straight wives said they had had sex outside their marriage, compared with 9 percent of lesbians in civil unions and 7 percent of lesbians who were partnered but not in civil unions.

The question of whether gays and lesbians will change marriage, or vice versa, is at its thorniest around sex and monogamy. Private behavior could well stay private: when she studied marriage in the Netherlands, Lee Badgett, the University of Massachusetts economist, found that while many same-sex couples proselytize about the egalitarianism of their relationships, they don't tend to promote non-monogamy, even if they practice it. Then again, some gay-rights advocates, like the writer and sex columnist Dan Savage, argue very publicly that insisting on monogamy can do a couple more harm than good. Savage, who questions whether most humans are cut out for decades of sex with only one person, told me that "monogamy in marriage has been a disaster for straight couples" because it has set unrealistic expectations. "Gay-male couples are much more likely to be realistic about what men are," he said. Savage's own marriage started out monogamous; the agreement was that if either partner cheated, this would be grounds for ending the relationship. But when he and his husband decided to adopt a child, Savage suggested that they relax their zero-tolerance policy on infidelity. He felt that risking family dissolution over such an incident no longer made sense. His husband later suggested they explicitly allow each other occasional dalliances, a policy Savage sees as providing a safety valve for the relationship. If society wants marriage to be more resilient, he argues, we must make it more "monagamish."

This is, to be sure, a difficult argument to win: a husband proposing non-monogamy to his wife on the grounds that it is in the best interest of a new baby would have a tough time prevailing in the court of public opinion. But while most gay-marriage advocates stop short of championing Savage's "wiggle room," some experts say that gay men are better at talking more openly about sex. Naveen Jonathan, a family therapist and a professor at Chapman University, in California, says he sees many gay partners hammer out an elaborate who-can-do-what-when sexual contract, one that says, "These are the times and the situations where it's okay to be non-monogamous, and these are the times and the situations where it is not." While some straight couples have deals of their own, he finds that for the most part, they simply presume monogamy. A possible downside of this assumption: straight couples are far less likely than gay men to frankly and routinely discuss sex, desire, and the challenges of sexual commitment.

Other experts question the idea that most gay males share a preference for non-monogamous relationships, or will in the long term. Savage's argument that non-monogamy is a safety valve is "very interesting, but it really is no more than a claim," says Justin Garcia, an evolutionary biologist at the Kinsey Institute for Research in Sex, Gender, and Reproduction. Garcia points out that not all men are relentlessly sexual beings, and not all men want an open relationship, "in some ways, same-sex couples are healthier—they tend to have these negotiations more," he says. But negotiating can be stressful: in many cases, Garcia notes, one gay partner would prefer to be monogamous, but gives in to the other partner.

So which version will prevail: non-monogamous marriage, or marriage as we conventionally understand it? It's worth pointing out that in the U.S., same-sex unions are slightly more likely between women, and non-monogamy is not a cause women tend to champion. And some evidence suggests that getting married changes behavior: William Eskridge and Darren Spedale found that in the years after Norway, Sweden, and Denmark instituted registered partnerships, many same-sex couples reported placing a greater emphasis on monogamy, while national rates of HIV infections declined.

Sex, then, may be one area where the institution of marriage pushes back against norms that have been embraced by many gay couples. Gary Hall of the National Cathedral allows that in many ways, gay relationships offer a salutary "critique" of marriage, but argues that the marriage establishment will do some critiquing back. He says he would not marry two people who intended to be non-monogamous, and believes that monogamy will be a "critical issue" in the dialogue between the gay community and the Church. Up until now, he says, progressive churches have embraced "the part of gay behavior that looks like straight behavior," but at some point, churches also have to engage gay couples whose behavior doesn't conform to monogamous ideals. He hopes that, in the course of this give-and-take, the church ends up reckoning with other ongoing cultural changes, from unmarried cohabitation to the increasing number of adults who choose to live as singles. "How do we speak credibly to people about their sexuality and their sexual relationships?" he asks. "We really need to rethink this."

So yes, marriage will change. Or rather, it will change again. The fact is, there is no such thing as traditional marriage. In various places and at various points in human history, marriage has been a means by which young children were betrothed,

uniting royal houses and sealing alliances between nations. In the Bible, it was a union that sometimes took place between a man and his dead brother's widow, or between one man and several wives. It has been a vehicle for the orderly transfer of property from one generation of males to the next; the test by which children were deemed legitimate or bastard; a privilege not available to black Americans; something parents arranged for their adult children; a contract under which women, legally, ceased to exist. Well into the 19th century, the British common-law concept of "unity of person" meant a woman *became* her husband when she married, giving up her legal standing and the right to own property or control her own wages.

Many of these strictures have already loosened. Child marriage is today seen by most people as the human-rights violation that it is. The Married Women's Property Acts guaranteed that a woman could get married and remain a legally recognized human being. The Supreme Court's decision in *Loving v. Virginia* did away with state bans on interracial marriage. By making it easier to dissolve marriage, no-fault divorce helped ensure that unions need not be lifelong. The recent surge in single parenthood, combined with an aging population, has unyoked marriage and child-rearing. History shows that marriage evolves over time. We have every reason to believe that same-sex marriage will contribute to its continued evolution.

The argument that gays and lesbians are social pioneers and bellwethers has been made before. Back in 1992, the British sociologist Anthony Giddens suggested that gays and lesbians were a harbinger of a new kind of union, one subject to constant renegotiation and expected to last only as long as both partners were happy with it. Now that these so-called harbingers are looking to commit to more-binding relationships, we will have the "counterfactual" that Gary Gates talks about: we will be better able to tell which marital stresses and pleasures are due to gender, and which are not.

In the end, it could turn out that same-sex marriage isn't all that different from straight marriage. If gay and lesbian marriages are in the long run as quarrelsome, tedious, and unbearable; as satisfying, joyous, and loving as other marriages, we'll know that a certain amount of strife is not the fault of the alleged war between men and women, but just an inevitable thing that happens when two human beings are doing the best they can to find a way to live together.

Critical Thinking

1. How do you think the legalization of same-sex marriage may change what it means to be married in the United States?

2. What are some of the differences in the gender roles, division of labor, and decision-making practices in same-sex and heterosexual couples?

3. Given the insights noted in this article, what are three ways marriage in the United States may change in the next 30 years? Why do you think these changes will occur? Do you think these changes will strengthen or weaken the institution of marriage?

Create Central

www.mhhe.com/createcentral

Internet References

Coalition for Marriage, Family, and Couples Education
www.smartmarriages.com

Council on Contemporary Families
www.contemporaryfamilies.org

National Council of State Legislatures, Defining Marriage
www.ncsl.org/issues-research/human-services/same-sex-marriage
-overview.aspx

The Pew Forum on Religion and Public Life: Gay Marriage and Homosexuality
www.pewforum.org/Topics/Issues/Gay-Marriage-and-Homosexuality

Article Prepared by: Patricia Hrusa Williams, *University of Maine at Farmington*

Multiple Lovers, Without Jealousy

Polyamorous people still face plenty of stigmas, but some studies suggest they handle certain relationship challenges better than monogamous people do.

OLGA KHAZAN

Learning Outcomes

After reading this article, you will be able to:

- Define polyamory.
- Identify the origins and history of polyamory.
- Analyze the strengths and challenges of monogamy and polyamorous relationships.
- Explain the role and causes of jealousy in relationships.

When I met Jonica Hunter, Sarah Taub, and Michael Rios on a typical weekday afternoon in their tidy duplex in Northern Virginia, a very small part of me worried they might try to convert me.

All three live there together, but they aren't roommates—they're lovers.

Or rather, Jonica and Michael are. And Sarah and Michael are. And so are Sarah and whomever she happens to bring home some weekends. And Michael and whomever he might be courting. They're polyamorous.

Michael is 65, and he has a chinstrap beard that makes him look like he just walked off an Amish homestead. Jonica is 27, with close-cropped hair, a pointed chin, and a quiet air. Sarah is 46 and has an Earth Motherly demeanor that put me at relative ease.

Together, they form a polyamorous "triad"—one of the many formations that's possible in this jellyfish of a sexual preference. "There's no one way to do polyamory" is a common refrain in "the community." Polyamory—which literally means "many loves"—can involve any number of people, either cohabiting or not, sometimes all having sex with each other, and sometimes just in couples within the larger group.

Sarah and Michael met 15 years ago when they were both folk singers and active in the polyamorous community. Both of them say they knew from a young age that there was something different about their sexuality. "Growing up, I never understood why loving someone meant putting restrictions on relationships," Michael said.

"What I love about polyamory is that everything is up for modification," Sarah says. "There are no 'shoulds.' You don't have to draw a line between who is a lover and who is a friend. It's about what is the path of my heart in this moment."

They've been "nesting partners" for 12 years, but they've both had other relationships throughout that time. Jonica moved in three years ago after meeting Michael on OkCupid. She describes the arrangement's appeal as "more intimacy, less rules. I don't have to limit my relationship with other partners."

The house is, as they describe, an "intentional community"—a type of resource-sharing collectivist household. They each have their own room and own bed. Sarah is a night owl, so she and Michael spend time together alone late at night. Jonica sees him alone in the early morning. They all hang out together throughout the day. The house occasionally plays host to a rotating cast of outside characters, as well—be they friends of the triad or potential love interests.

The triad works together, too, running a consulting nonprofit that puts on events "that teach skills for living together peacefully, such as clear communication, boundaries, what to do when you get upset," Sarah said. An added bonus of the living arrangement is that it cuts down on commuting time.

I initially expected the polyamorous people I met to tell me that there were times their relationships made them sick with envy. After all, how could someone listen to his significant other's stories of tragedy and conquest in the dating world, as Michael regularly does for Sarah, and not feel possessive? But it became clear to me that for "polys," as they're sometimes known, jealousy is more of an internal, negligible feeling than a partner-induced, important one. To them, it's more like a passing head cold than a tumor spreading through the relationship.

Of the three people living in the Northern Virginia duplex, Sarah volunteers that she's the one most prone to jealousy. "It can be about feeling like you're not special, or feeling like this thing belonged to me and now someone's taken it."

She said it was rough for her when Jonica first moved in. Sarah had been accustomed to seeing Michael whenever she wanted, but she started to feel a pang when he spent time with Jonica.

"At first I thought, 'Is something bad happening, something I don't want to support?' she said. "No, I want to support Michael and Jonica in being together. From there, I look at my own reaction. I can be an anxious person, so maybe I was feeling anxious. I find other ways of getting grounded. I might go for a walk or play guitar."

"It's part of learning a healthy self-awareness and the ability to self-soothe," she added. "I notice what I'm feeling, and do a dive inward."

Two-person marriage, be it gay or straight, is still such the norm that even the most progressive among us do a double-take when someone says they like their relationships a little more populous. (This stigma is also why, with the exception of the Northern Virginia triad, all of the other polyamorous sources in this article asked to go either by their first names or pseudonyms).

Increasingly, polyamorous people—not to be confused with the prairie-dress-clad fundamentalist polygamists—are all around us. By some estimates, there are now roughly a half-million polyamorous relationships in the U.S., though underreporting is common. Some sex researchers put the number even higher, at 4 to 5 percent of all adults, or 10 to 12 million people. More often than not, they're just office workers who find standard picket-fence partnerships dull. Or, like Sarah, they're bisexuals trying to fulfill both halves of their sexual identities. Or they're long-term couples who don't happen to think sexual exclusivity is the key to intimacy.

Elisabeth Sheff, a sociologist who interviewed 40 polyamorous people over the course of several years for her recent book, *The Polyamorists Next Door,* says that polyamorous configurations with more than three people tend to be rarer and have more turnover. "Polys" are more likely to be liberal and educated, she said, and in the rare cases that they do practice religion, it's usually paganism or Unitarian Universalism.

Polys differentiate themselves from swingers because they are emotionally, not just sexually, involved with the other partners they date. And polyamorous arrangements are not quite

the same as "open relationships" because in polyamory, the third or fourth or fifth partner is just as integral to the relationship as the first two are.

Polyamory overlaps somewhat with geek culture, such as cosplay, or the kink world, such as BDSM. Many couples who become interested in polyamory start by looking for a single, bisexual woman to add to the relationship. In fact, this quest has become so common (and its object has remained so elusive) that it's known as "hunting the unicorn."

But Sheff cautions that once said unicorn is caught, "the men are sometimes not as well-tended as they hoped to be. During the actual sex, the women get interested in each other, and the men describe it as 'not all that.'"

Even many devout monogamists admit that it can be hard for one partner to supply the full smorgasbord of the other's sexual and emotional needs. When critics decry polys as escapists who have simply "gotten bored" in traditional relationships, polys counter that the more people they can draw close to them, the more self-actualized they can be.

In the course of her research, Sheff met one couple in which the man was as "as kinky as a cheap garden hose." "It didn't do it for [his wife], the whole kink thing," Sheff told me. "So he started going to local [BDSM] dungeons and playing with other women. She was not that into that, either. She loved the theater, but she stopped going as much because he thought it was boring and stupid and expensive."

So the couple went poly: "He started dating kinky women. She ended up hooking up with her old high school friend she found on Facebook, and they enjoyed the theater together. And she ended up enjoying time with her husband but not feeling so much pressure about the kinky sex."

I asked the logical, mono-normative question: Why didn't the wife just ditch the garden hose for the theater man? "She gets stuff from the garden-hose guy that she doesn't get from the intellectual guy," Sheff explained. "They do fun things together, and the theater guy is too needy for her. She doesn't want him all to herself, because he would be too much work."

When I went to visit polyamorists in Baltimore, I brought my 6-foot-3 boyfriend with me. The organizer of the local social group BmorePoly, a middle-aged software engineer named Barry, opened the door and said, "Is that your bodyguard?"

I laughed a little too loud.

(We're not polyamorous, by the way. I feel the need to clarify that, as did the scientists I spoke with who study polyamory. One such professor told me that when she describes her research to her peers at academic conferences, they often ask her if she herself is in an open relationship. "Would you ask a cancer researcher if they had cancer?" she told me recently.)

One of the Baltimore couples, Josh and Cassie, represents a typical approach to polyamory: They met a decade ago through a mutual friend, and they dated monogamously for several years before Cassie, who is bisexual, raised the idea of adding another woman to the relationship. They've since had several committed triad relationships lasting from a few months to several years. The "other woman" becomes a full partner in the relationship, and ideally, she complements them both in some way. Cassie always hopes that it'll be a fellow horror-movie lover, while Josh keeps his fingers crossed for an anime fanatic.

"She can go running at 5 A.M. with him," Cassie said. "I'm fine sleeping in."

The only restrictions are that Josh and Cassie spend their wedding anniversary alone together, and that all parties undergo a full STD check before any kind of "fluid bonding" takes place.

Expanding the group beyond three people hasn't been an option so far, Josh says. "When we date together, it's a closed group," Josh said. "That's what works best for us in terms of time and energy. I have a very demanding job."

When monogamous people discover that Josh and Cassie are involved with a third partner, they ask questions that suggest it's just a fling. "Like, 'How far is this gonna go or how long will you be with them?'" Cassie recalls. The answer she gives: "We let it have a natural growth, like any other relationship."

Another Baltimore couple, Erin and Bill, has so far mostly had shorter-term triad arrangements. When Erin and Bill met in the summer of 2012, Bill confessed that he had always fantasized about having sex with a woman and another man at the same time. "I'm heteroflexible," Bill said. "It's like saying you're mostly straight. You're like 70-30."

As it turns out, Erin's fantasy was to have sex with two men at the same time.

When Erin and Bill meet a man they like, all three go out together, with the two men sitting on either side of Erin and holding one of each of her hands.

Bill says watching his wife have sex with another man is anything but unsettling. Instead, it sometimes induces *compersion*—the poly principle of basking in the joy of a partner's success in romance, just as you would with his or her success in work or sports.

"There are so many societal norms that say, 'He looked the wrong way at someone so I'm gonna go all Carrie Underwood on his vehicle,'" Erin said. "Polyamory is about the idea that having their undivided attention isn't the end all, be all."

Though some ancient civilizations permitted polygamy, or multiple wives, the idea of monogamous marriage has been deeply rooted in Western society since the time of the Ancient Greeks. (Although monogamous Hellenic men were free to have their way with their male and female slaves.)

Monogamy quickly became the norm—and social norms influence our psychology. The process of adhering to social rules and punishing rule violators tickles the reward circuits of our brains. Some studies suggest that each time you think to yourself that polyamory is icky, an oxytocin molecule gets its wings.

In its history, America saw only a handful of collective dalliances away from two-person marriage model. In the 1840s in upstate New York, the Oneida commune practiced "complex marriage," in which the 300 members were encouraged to have consensual intercourse with whomever they desired. As its leader, the lawyer John Humphrey Noyes, put it in his proposal letter to his wife, Harriet: "I desire and expect my [wife] will love all who love God . . . with a warmth and strength of affection which is unknown to earthly lovers, and as free as if she stood in no particular connection with me. In fact the object of my connection with her will not be to monopolize and enslave her heart or my own, but to enlarge and establish both in the free fellowship of God's universal family."

By some accounts, the Oneida way of life was far more feminist than traditional marriage was at the time: The women only had sex when they wanted to, for example, and some of the female members relished having multiple sex partners.

But this was no erotic utopia. The commune's elderly true believers regularly initiated its less-experienced teenagers into sex in order to strengthen the younger generation's devotion to Noyes. Members were publicly chastised if they were discovered carrying on exclusive relationships. People who wanted to be parents were matched in arranged marriages and prevented from bonding with their children, all as part of Noyes' plan to create a superior uber-race. In 1879, Noyes, fearing arrest for statutory rape, fled the country and wrote to his followers that they should abandon complex marriage. The 70 remaining commune members entered traditional marriages with whomever they happened to be living with at the time.

From there, "free love" experiments largely became the private domain of lefty academics, anarchists, and artists. London's "Bloomsbury Set," for example, was famously a jungle gym of affairs and attractions.

The practice of "swinging" first became common among American military members during World War II, with the tacit understanding that the wives of the men who did not survive would be taken in by those who did. Group marriage saw a limited rebirth in the communes of the 1960s, and open relationships, too, had a heyday in the permissive 1970s. The specter of AIDS put a damper on the free-love movement in the 1980s and early 1990s, but when the Internet came along, the poly-inclined found new and improved ways to connect with one another.

When Sarah Taub was a teenager in the 1980s, "if I wanted to look for anything about open relationships, there was some science fiction. There was no one you could talk to about it. I felt like I was crazy or that there was something wrong with me."

In her youth, she entered a sexless monogamous relationship that puttered along for a few years before she discovered the poly world. "These days, someone wanting to be poly can easily find a huge group on the Internet," she said. "Poly people are very happy and communicative—there is huge support now that there never was before."

In 1990, Morning Glory Zell, the High Priestess of the Oregon-based pagan Church of All Worlds, wrote an article called "A Bouquet of Lovers," which laid out a vision for transparent, consensual open relationships. Some think it was one of the first modern uses of the word "polyamorous."

"I feel that this whole polyamorous lifestyle is the *avante garde* of the 21st century," Zell wrote. "Polyamorous extended relationships mimic the old multi-generational families before the Industrial Revolution, but they are better because the ties are voluntary and are, by necessity, rooted in honesty, fairness, friendship and mutual interests. Eros is, after all, the primary force that binds the universe together." Zell died—or rather, "crossed the veil into the Summerlands"—in May of this year, but her legacy lives on.

Despite lingering disapproval, there's some evidence that Americans are growing increasingly accepting of open relationships. To be sure, the sanctity of two-person marriage still looms large: For decades now, most Americans—90 percent, give or take—have told Gallup that having an affair is unacceptable. In a 1975 survey conducted in a Midwestern town, only 7 percent of the residents said they would ever participate in mate-swapping. Only 2 percent said they ever had. As recently as 2005, college women ranked open marriage as one of the least desirable partnership options: 95 percent of one study's participants said "One man married to two or more wives" was the one of the most undesirable forms of marriage, while 91 percent said "group marriage" was.

However, an April study asked 1,280 heterosexuals how willing they would be, on a scale from one to seven, to commit various non-monogamous acts, such as swinging or adding a third party to the relationship. Depending on the scenario, up to 16 percent of women and up to 31 percent of men chose a four or higher on the scale when asked whether they'd willing, while still with their partners, to do things like have a third person join the relationship, or have "casual sex with whomever, no questions asked."

Polyamory might seem like the bailiwick of the young and carefree, but many of its practitioners have children. The idea of parents having live-in third, fourth, or fifth partners isn't frowned upon.

Bill and Erin don't hide their outside relationships from Erin's 17-year-old daughter. One day, the couple was watching the television show *Sister Wives,* which documents a polygamous family in Utah, when the daughter remarked that it was an interesting system.

"She was talking about *Sister Wives,* and I said, 'What about brother husbands?'" Bill asked her. "I said, 'Your mom and I date a guy.' And she was like, 'Cool.'"

Sheff said that most polyamorous parents date outside the home, much like divorced parents do. And how much they share with their children depends on their ages—a 4-year-old doesn't need to know as much as a 14-year-old does. "It's much more like, 'This is a friend,' not 'This is your new dad of the month,'" she said.

Cassie and Josh said their son, who is now 10, has grown up around his parents' girlfriends, so he doesn't find it unusual. He calls the women the couple dates "Ms. 'Anne,'" and refers to them as "my dad's [or sometimes mom's] girlfriend" to others.

"We have friends who are poly, mono, gay, and lesbian," Cassie said. "He doesn't understand why people have a problem with people caring for and loving each other."

Some marriage experts don't agree that polyamory's impact on children is neutral, though. "We know that kids thrive on stable routines with stable caregivers," said W. Bradford Wilcox, a sociologist and the director of the National Marriage Project at the University of Virginia. Polyamory can be like a "marriage-go-round," Wilcox said. "When kids are exposed to a revolving carousel of spouses, that experience of instability and transition can be traumatic." (Wilcox, who has contributed to *The Atlantic,* is known for having rather conservative views: He recently penned a *Washington Post* op-ed about how marriage ostensibly protects women, and he consulted on a much-contested study about the children of same-sex couples.)

Wilcox also assumes that polyamorous people must struggle to devote enough time and attention to each partner and child. "It's a challenge for me as a husband and father to give my wife and kids enough attention," Wilcox said. "I can't imagine how challenging it would be to add another partner. There are limits to time and space."

There's some evidence that polygamy, in particular, can be harmful, not only to children but to women and men. The anthropologist Joseph Henrich has found that the world's polygamous societies gradually evolved toward monogamous marriage because doing so resolved many of the problems created when powerful men hoarded all the wives for themselves. Meanwhile, these societies' mobs of horny, angry, low-status single men would lead to "significantly higher levels [of] rape, kidnapping, murder, assault, robbery and fraud," as Henrich and fellow researchers wrote in a recent study.

By easing the competition to scoop up as many wives as possible, monogamy allows men to instead focus on things like child-rearing, long-term planning, and saving money. It also increases the age at first marriage and lowers fertility rates, Henrich found. He suggests that's one reason polygamy was outlawed in Japan in 1880, in 1953 in China, and in 1955 in India, for most religious groups. But the welfare of children living in today's polyamorous households won't be knowable until there are more long-term studies on that (tiny) cohort.

In fact, there's a paucity of any sort of research on consensual, Western non-monogamy. A 2005 study that examined 69 polygamous families found that there often was a "deep-seated feeling of angst that arises over competing for access to their mutual husband." Conflict between the co-wives, the researchers wrote, is "pervasive and often marked by physical or verbal violence." But that analysis was based on predominantly African cultures where men take several wives, not the more egalitarian polyamorous community in the developed world.

The nascent research that does exist suggests these modern polyamorous relationships can be just as functional—and sometimes even more so—than traditional monogamous pairings.

Perhaps most obviously, people who have permission to "cheat"—that is, through a planned, non-monogamous arrangement—are more likely to use condoms and have frequent STI tests than clandestine cheaters are. Apparently, sneaking around is already so morally torturous that a stop at Walgreens for Trojans would simply be too much to handle.

Terri Conley, a professor of psychology and women's studies at the University of Michigan who studies polyamory, has analyzed a sample of 1,700 monogamous individuals, 150 swingers, 170 people in open relationships, and 300 polyamorous individuals for a forthcoming study. She said that while people in "open relationships" tend to have lower sexual satisfaction than their monogamous peers, people who described themselves as "polyamorous" tended to have equal or higher levels of sexual satisfaction.

What's more, polyamorous people don't seem to be plagued by monogamous-style romantic envy. Bjarne Holmes, a psychologist at Champlain College in Vermont has found that polyamorous people tend to experience less overall jealousy, even in situations that would drive monogamous couples to Othello-levels of suspicion. "It turns out that, hey, people are not reacting with jealousy when their partner is flirting with someone else," Holmes told LiveScience.

Sheff agreed. "I would say they have lower-than-average jealousy," she said. "People who are very jealous generally don't do polyamory at all."

Conley found that jealousy is "much higher" among monogamous pairs than non-monogamous ones. Polyamorous people also seemed to trust each other more. "For a long time I've been interested in whether monogamous relationships are all they're cracked up to be," Conley said.

Her findings, like Holmes' and Sheff's, are preliminary and limited. But if they hold up, it could mean that at least in some ways, polyamory is a more humane way to love.

Then again, most people aren't biologically predisposed to share their lovers. With limited resources, the only way for our caveman forbears to be sure they weren't raising someone else's children was to ensure their cave-ladies never strayed.

"The men who were happy to have their partner have sex with other men were not our ancestors, because they were more likely to be raising offspring that were not their own," Todd K. Shackelford, an evolutionary psychologist at Oakland University, told me. "They did not pass on the genes that built their greater liberalness."

Although women did not face the risk of accidentally raising a rival's offspring, they similarly had to sweat over whether their partners were cheating—and thus wasting their time and efforts on another woman's children.

These divergent infidelity anxieties, Shackelford says, forged the differences in how modern men and women experience relational jealousy today. Women get more upset about emotional unfaithfulness, while men are more concerned with sexual cheating.

"There's a phenomenon within psychology called obsessional review, which refers to the kinds of questions that the partner that finds out about the infidelity asks the unfaithful partner," Shackelford said. "Men ask, 'Did you have sex with him? How many orgasms did you have?' etc. Women ask, 'Are you in love with her? Did you buy her gifts? Did you take her to *our* restaurant?' and so on."

Beyond the broad strokes of gender, individual differences further shape our jealous reactions. In a 2005 study, Shackelford found that men who had previous long-term relationship experience were more jealous in their current romances.

Modern forms of dating also have the potential to foment jealousy to a greater degree than the steadier, simpler courtships of yore. We're no longer settling down with our high-school sweethearts: In 1970, the average first-time bride was 21; today, she's 26. And women now have sex for the first time nearly 10 years before they give birth for the first time. In 1945, that span was only four years.

Later marrying and child-rearing ages have opened up a bevy of potential mate options at work, among friends, and online. But with great choice often comes great envy. "What's the new sexual etiquette for the way people flow into relationships over the course of a longer adulthood?" asked

Virginia Rutter, professor of Sociology at Framingham State University. "And how does a lifetime of having opposite-sex close relationships affect the boundaries around heterosexual relationships?"

Social media tends to pump steroids into existing romantic discontent. Tara Marshall, a psychology professor at Brunel University in London, has found that people who are naturally anxious tend to stalk their partners on Facebook, scouring their partners' digital footprints for hints of dishonesty. Through the filter of jealousy, even the most neutral, sideways-hugging photos might be interpreted as threatening.

And there's something uniquely crazy-making about online dating—the way these arranged romances lurch from "just sex" to "getting serious" and back again, unpredictably fizzling or heating up, depending on who's available.

According to Jennifer Theiss, a communications professor at Rutgers University who studies relationships, uncertainty over the status of a romantic relationship tends to increase angst—as does transitioning from casual dating to a more committed state. There's nothing longer than the pause after one partner asks, "Where are we?"

"That's when people have uncertainty over how the partner feels about them—they're having a hard time reading their partner," Theiss told me. "At any other time, the fact that X commented on a Facebook post wouldn't bother me, but today you didn't kiss me before work, so now when I see that X commented, I'm much more sensitive."

When a couple meets online, there's little to stop one party from keeping her online options open—and her profile up to date. In that way, it can be a sort of involuntary polyamory, with a horde of would-be monogamists all vying for each others' attention over Tinder's siren call. "Before this kind of technology took off, people were meeting in bars or at work ," Theiss said. "You probably would have escalated your relationship more quickly to monogamy."

Our dating options may be increasing, Theiss and other researchers suggest, but so are our occasions to be suspicious and envious. "Peoples' eyes are opened to the possibility that people are maintaining emotional connections to a lot of people through technology," Theiss said. "The ability to connect with old partners and to still be online friends with them can create new opportunities for jealousy that didn't exist 30 or 40 years ago."

Stew, a Maryland man who is in an open relationship with his "main partner," M, said that even though he tries to be open-minded, he still sometimes feel uneasy when others flirt with his "beloveds" on Facebook.

"Sometimes I feel pangs of envy or insecurity," he said. "Maybe [the men doing the flirting] are really good at something I'm not, or they have an awesome job, or their life is so much cooler because they are internationally renowned underwater photographers or something."

Those of us who are in monogamous relationships will probably never stop being jealous—and that's healthy. What's not healthy is the way some monogamous people manipulate their partners' jealousy and devotion. According to Shackelford, women in monogamous relationships "are more likely to use sexual assets to induce jealousy in their partner," while "men will manipulate access to resources."

By contrast, the way polyamorous people tend to resolve their conflicts is more above-board. When extramarital relations are already out in the open, it seems there's little else to hide. "A big part of what makes someone feel jealous is when their expectations for the relationship are violated," Theiss said. "In poly situations, where they've actually negotiated the ground rules—'I care about you and I also care about this other person, and that doesn't mean I care less about you'—that creates a foundation that means [they] don't have to feel jealous. They don't have uncertainty about what's happening."

For example, as Conley, the polyamory researcher, has noted, "polyamory writings explicitly advocate that people revisit and reevaluate the terms of their relationships regularly and consistently—this practice could benefit monogamous relationships as well. Perhaps a monogamous couple deemed dancing with others appropriate a year ago, but after revisiting this boundary they agree that it is stressful and should be eliminated for the interim."

People in plural relationships get jealous, too, of course. But the way polys get jealous is unique—and possibly even adaptive. Rather than blame the partner for their feelings, the polys view the jealousy as an irrational symptom of their own self-doubt.

Cassie and Josh had been dating a woman—let's call her Anne—for about a year and a half when all three went to a diner together. Josh, who doesn't like tomatoes, ordered a burger. Cassie went to the bathroom. When she came back, the burger had arrived and Anne was eating Josh's tomatoes.

Cassie loves tomatoes—and she *always* eats Josh's tomatoes.

"They were my freaking tomatoes," she said. "I had experienced the loss of my tomatoes, and that was a unique thing for me."

"I was going to be angry and scream, but then I thought, 'This is just tomatoes.'"

Rather than throw a tantrum or banish Anne from the triad, Cassie simply waited to cool off about the tomatoes, and the three moved on.

"I think everyone feels jealous," Josh said. "Us and the people we've dated and most of the people I know feel jealous. But when I think of jealousy, I think of it more as it's another emotion we *express* as jealousy. You're not actually jealous; you're feeling loss."

"I had revelations about jealousy back when I was trying to be monogamous," said Jonica, the 27-year-old living in the triad in Virginia. She realized "it's kinda silly. It produces the opposite effect that you supposedly want. If I was jealous of my lover, and I start acting out on that emotion, it's going to drive that person away from me."

Stew, the man in the open relationship, says that whenever jealousy surfaces, he and his partners recognize it as "one or more specific unmet needs, like wanting more date-like time together."

For example, his main partner, M, was recently feeling jealous that he was spending so much time with B, his girlfriend, and feared that Stew would eventually want to leave M for B. M "knows in her logical brain that this isn't the case, but thoughts like these are worries, like 'Did I leave the stove on?'" Stew said. "You can't logic them away."

So on top of reassuring M that he would never leave her, in times like these, Stew tries to lighten the mood "with a nice walk around the block, or making dinner with her, or being silly, or watching Netflix."

"We're in a place where, for the most part, we both are able to see feelings of envy and insecurity for what they are, and we have a deep bond of trust that is most often very easily accessible, which we can reach out to and touch when we need to remind ourselves that it's there," he said.

Josh and Cassie talk over and negotiate everything—"a lot more than other couples do," they think. The tomatoes were such a big deal because their allotment hadn't been previously agreed upon. (In the end, the three decided they would share all future tomatoes.)

Overall, Josh says sharing a life between three adults, rather than two, is not as kinky and complicated as some monogamous people might think. "The stuff in poly that's difficult is not the sex," he said. "It's where the goddamn spoons get put away."

In that sense, at least, poly and mono relationships are more alike than they are different.

Critical Thinking

1. Before reading the article what was your opinion of polyamorous or open relationships? Has your opinion changed? If so, how?

2. Why do people enter into polyamorous relationships? What are some potential benefits and challenges in this type of relationship?

3. Why do you think jealousy occurs in relationships? Do you think you could be in a relationship with more than one person and not feel jealous? Why or why not?

Internet References

BmorePoly
www.bmorepoly.com

Council on Contemporary Families
www.contemporaryfamilies.org

More Than Two
www.morethantwo.com

Prepared by: Patricia Hrusa Williams,
University of Maine at Farmington

Article

Parenting Wars

JANE SHILLING

Learning Outcomes

After reading this article, you will be able to:

- Recognize familial, societal, cultural, historical, and media influences on parenting.

- Understand child traits such as character and identity that are associated with positive developmental outcomes.

Recently I embarked on a long-overdue purge of my book-shelves. In the several dozen bin bags that made their way to the Oxfam bookshop (where the expressions of the staff slowly morphed from pleased gratitude, on my first visit, to unconcealed dread by the fifth) were two copies of the Communist Manifesto (*two?*); a formidable collection of works by Foucault, Sarraute, Perec and Queneau (I suppose I must once have read them—bookmarking postcards fell out of some of them—but if I did, no trace of the experience has remained); and all my parenting books. Penelope Leach's *Baby and Child,* Steve Biddulph's *Raising Boys* and *The Secret of Happy Children,* Kate Figes on *The Terrible Teens*—none of them, I realised, had been purchased by me: all had been acquired for some exercise in journalism—reviewing or interviewing, but never for private reading.

I don't know what made me think I could raise a child without an instruction manual, especially as I was the single mother of a boy, with no partner or brothers to consult about the mysteries of maleness. Sheer wilfulness, I suppose (and a certain bruised desire to avoid books that wrote of families as consisting of a child with two parents who were, in the days when I was doing my child-rearing, invariably assumed to be a mummy and a daddy). No doubt I should have made a better fist of it if I had been able to embrace Leach and Biddulph as my mentors, but my son is 21 now, and we are far into the territory for which no self-help books on parent/child relationships exist (unless you count D H Lawrence's *Sons and Lovers,* as a handy guide on what not to do).

As I began to inhabit my new identity as a mother and a lone parent, bringing up my child felt like an experience too personal and intimate to be trimmed to a template provided by experts. I was keen on babies and small children, and imagined that maternal instinct would cover the basics adequately. In this, I was faithfully replicating my own upbringing. My mother owned a copy of Dr Spock's *Baby and Child Care,* but it hadn't the air of a book that had been consulted frequently

(though oddly enough I read it avidly as a child—so perhaps my son was, by default, a Spock baby).

My mother's maternal style must in turn have been modelled on her childhood, though my maternal grandmother was the youngest of a family of 13, so there would have been lots of people to offer advice on teething and potty training, a resource that my mother, an only child, and I, the first of my close friends to have a baby, both lacked.

I don't think that any of the women in my family took a conceptual or political view of child-rearing or parenthood. We were too absorbed by the day-to-day business of reading stories and wiping bottoms to find time to analyse what we were about. (I was the only one of us to combine work with motherhood throughout my son's childhood, and that wasn't a considered decision: as a lone parent, I had no choice.)

In my childhood—and, I think, my mother's—the visionary thinking came from my grandfather, who had spent his infancy and early childhood in the St Pancras workhouse and had, not coincidentally, strong views about the necessity for setting life goals and working towards them, preferably by getting an excellent education.

Even 20 years ago, my unprofessional attitude to bringing up a child was anachronistic; these days I suspect it would be regarded as borderline negligent. Mine was certainly the last generation in which one could allow oneself to muddle along without the assistance of the experts, treating parenthood as though it were analogous to friendship—a relationship that would grow and flourish of its own accord.

I might have done my best to ignore the fact, but as a single parent I was a fragmentary factor in what has grown into an urgent social crisis around the issues of childhood and family. If ever there was a time when one could raise children unselfconsciously, it is long past. Now every aspect of parenthood, from conception and birth to the forming of intellect and character, is the subject of anxious and often agonised scrutiny.

The crisis is both personal and political. On the one hand, as engaged parents, we feel that we are in some sense our children: their successes and failures represent us almost more vividly than our own achievements. And as the condition of youth becomes ever more extended, lasting in attenuated form until middle age and beyond, our children can help to feed our vision of ourselves as perennially young. (Whenever I hear a parent say that they are "more of a friend than a parent" to their son or daughter, I wonder what privately the child might think about that.)

The inevitable consequence of seeing our children as our alter egos and friends is the sense of dread that fills us when they become opaque to us. Children and adolescents need to have parenting from somewhere, and if it isn't offered by their parents they will seek it among their peers—a group that once might have included mainly the people in their year at school, but which now, thanks to social media and the internet, comprises a global community of "friends" and acquaintances, a world in which the most adhesive parent can find it difficult to stick with its offspring.

Beyond the family, there lies society—a construct composed, alarmingly enough, of other people and their children, many of them not as conscientiously raised as one's own. The media reports are dismaying; this is a generation disaffected and resentful, alienated from education, or unable to obtain the jobs that were promised them in return for their hard-won examination results, debarred by the lack of an income from buying their own home, the dependency of childhood uneasily protracted by having to return to living in the family home as adults after a taste of freedom at college. Despite our excellent intentions and our strenuous efforts, is this the world we have made for our children?

The confusion of western attitudes to parenting is reflected in a cacophony of contradictory images. Last year the cover of *Time* magazine featured a photograph of the 26-year-old attachment parenting advocate Jamie Lynne Grumet breastfeeding her son Aram, aged nearly four, who was dressed in military-style camouflage pants and standing on a small chair to reach the magnificently tanned breast protruding from her sexy black camisole top.

While Aram suckles in his miniature army fatigues, the infant literacy movement encourages parents to believe that it is never too early to begin learning to read, with initiatives such as Reading Bear, a free online programme for tinies whose editor-in-chief is Larry Sanger, the co-founder of Wikipedia. Not that a Tiger Mother-ish enthusiasm for prodigies of infant learning is an exclusively 21st-century phenomenon. Dr Johnson's friend Hester Thrale recorded in her Family Book of 1766 the achievements of her two-year-old daughter, Queeney, who later became the disaffected protagonist of Beryl Bainbridge's splendid novel *According to Queeney:*

> She repeats the Pater Noster, the three Christian virtues, and the signs of the Zodiac in Watts' verses; she likewise knows them on the globe perfectly well. . . . She knows her nine figures and the simplest combinations of them; but none beyond a hundred; she knows all the Heathen Deities by their Attributes and counts to 20 without missing one.

Eat your heart out, Amy Chua.

It is true that there has probably never been a time when parenting was regarded as the exclusive preserve of parents. In *Dream Babies,* her 1983 study of child-rearing advice to parents from Locke to Spock, Christina Hardyment notes that the history of childcare manuals is almost as old as that of mass publication. The original manuals were booklets written by doctors for use by nurses in foundling hospitals. "It is with great Pleasure I see at last the Preservation of Children become the Care of Men of Sense," wrote William Cadogan in his *Essay*

on Nursing (1748). "In my opinion this Business has been too long fatally left to the management of Women who cannot be supposed to have a proper Knowledge to fit them for the Task, notwithstanding they look upon it to be their own Province."

The sentiment, if not the language, is curiously familiar from the plethora of modern parenting books which, even as they reassure anxious parents, cannot help but undermine their confidence with categorical but contradictory claims to know what is best for their offspring. Baby not sleeping? Gina Ford will fix that in no time. What a relief. Unless, that is, you happen to pick up Penelope Leach's most recent tome, *The Essential First Year: What Babies Need Parents to Know* (2010), from which you learn that leaving a distressed baby to cry can produce levels of the stress hormone cortisol (in the baby, that is, rather than the parent) that are toxic to its developing brain and may have long-term emotional consequences, as the anxiety of being left to weep unanswered pursues the beleaguered infant throughout childhood and adult life.

In short, you have a choice between inflicting brain damage and emotional distress if you leave little Magenta to cry herself to sleep; or an identical result if you rush to comfort her every time she wakes in the small hours and then—in an unforgivable, if perhaps understandable, episode of insomnia-induced rage—hurl her into her cot and lie on the floor beside it sobbing inconsolably and screaming, "I wish I'd never had a baby."

Still, let's not catastrophise. Somehow you and your child have both survived the essential first year, and even the essential first decade. Now you are entering the difficult hinterland of adolescence, and there are yet more things to worry about.

If you've got sons, there is the academic underperformance of boys in the overly feminised school environment, not to mention peer pressure to engage in all kinds of highly hazardous, not to say illegal, behaviour, and the long hours they spend closeted with their computer in their dark and malodorous rooms. For the parents of girls, there are problems of early sexualisation and their fragile relationship with their body image; nor is there any room for complacency about their examination results, which are likely to be affected by their desire not to be regarded as a nerd, neek, or anything other than one of the "popular girls".

For both sexes there is, besides the universal hazards of bullying and being mugged in the park for your cool stuff, the horrible complication of the way in which emergent adolescent sexuality is formed (or deformed) by online pornography.

Here, happily, Steve Biddulph the no-nonsense Australian family therapist and childcare guru can help, with his best-selling books *Raising Boys* and (most recently) *Raising Girls.* When it comes to bringing up daughters, a mother's place is invariably in the wrong, and Biddulph's warmth and wisdom will doubtless console many. Nevertheless, there is something about the spectacle of a middle-aged male expert issuing advice on raising girls that conjures a faint echo of Cadogan's conviction that the raising of children is best left to men of sense.

The happiness of children (as opposed to their moral education, which predominated in child-rearing manuals before the mid-20th century) is something to which a prodigious amount of expertise has been devoted over the past couple of generations.

Almost two decades ago, in 1994, Penelope Leach published a premonitory tract about the treatment of children in affluent western society. *Children First,* subtitled *What Our Society Must Do—and Is Not Doing—for Our Children Today,* was a scathing anatomy of the societal approach to child-rearing which saw parenting as "a universal hobby that is awkward because it cannot be shelved during the working week, interrupts important adult business and is hard on soft furnishings".

Some of Leach's most urgent priorities for a child-friendly society have been addressed in the intervening years. Yet her sunlit vision of a world in which children's needs have equal weight with those of adults remains dismayingly far from reality. In 2007, a Unicef study that assessed the well-being of children in six categories—material; health and safety; education; peer relationships; behaviours and risks; and young people's own perceptions of their happiness—placed the US second-to-last and the UK last in a league of 21 economically advanced nations.

In the introduction to his book *The Beast in the Nursery* (1998), the psychoanalyst Adam Phillips writes, "As children take for granted, lives are only liveable if they give pleasure." Yet the Unicef study suggests that despite our obsession with raising happy, successful children, many of them are trapped in lives that are, by Phillips's measure, unliveable.

So, what has gone wrong? In *Kith,* her strange, poetic book on the relationship between childhood and the natural world (to be published in May), the writer Jay Griffiths asks the intractable question: "Why are so many children in Euro-American cultures unhappy?" and concludes that, in the affluent west, childhood has become a lost realm.

Children's books are written by grownups, so it is unwise to call them in evidence when discussing styles of parenting. Nevertheless, it is striking that the fiction best loved by children—from Captain Marryat and Mark Twain, E Nesbit and Richmal Crompton to Jacqueline Wilson and J K Rowling—describes childhood as a state unencumbered by parental interference, in which children confront all kinds of challenges and dangers and survive by their own resourcefulness.

In modern America and Europe, Griffiths notes, children may read about the adventures of Huck Finn or William Brown but they are unlikely to share their experiences: "Many kids today are effectively under house arrest. . . . If there is one word which sums up the treatment of children today, it is 'enclosure'. Today's children are enclosed in school and home . . . and rigid schedules of time". Society, she adds, "has historically contrived a school system that is half factory, half prison, and too easily ignores the very education which children crave".

In *How Children Succeed,* the Canadian-American writer Paul Tough addresses the question of childhood unhappiness from a perspective that is the precise opposite of Griffiths's: her approach is lyrical, emotional and elegiac; his is logical, analytical and didactic. Nonetheless their theories converge on a single point—that, as a preparation for life, education is failing huge numbers of children.

Tough's book, as he writes, "is about an idea that is . . . gathering momentum in classrooms and clinics and labs and lecture halls across the country and around the world. According to this new way of thinking, the conventional wisdom about child development over the past few decades has been misguided. We have been focusing on the wrong skills and abilities in our children, and using the wrong strategies to nurture and teach those skills. . . ."

There is something very satisfying about an educational theory that denounces all previous theories. It seems to offer the possibility of a miraculous redemption of past errors and the hope of a certain path to a better future. The main mistake of recent years, Tough argues, has been to focus on measurable academic attainment by our children, to the exclusion of the more nebulous personal qualities (or "character") necessary to translate examination results into the kind of stable success that makes young people good citizens.

"Character" is a term with curiously Victorian overtones; the more formidable early child-rearing volumes that Christina Hardyment discusses in *Dream Babies* are keen on this quality. Yet the interdisciplinary school of thought that Tough describes,

Gurus of the Nursery

For 52 years after it was first published in 1946, **Benjamin McLane Spock**'s *Baby and Child Care* was the second-bestselling book after the Bible. A physician by training, Spock turned to psychoanalysis to examine child-rearing. His ideas were highly influential and encouraged parents to see their children as individuals.

The psychologist **Penelope Leach**'s *Baby and Child: from Birth to Age Five,* was published in 1977 and has sold more than two million copies. Much of her writing has focused on the drawbacks of childcare, a position that has attracted significant criticism.

Gina Ford, the author of *The Contented Little Baby Book* (1999), has long divided opinion, in part because she has no children (she bases her writing and advice on having looked after "over 300" babies as a maternity nurse). Some swear by her philosophy of strict routines, whereas others deplore the rigidity of her approach.

When *Battle Hymn of the Tiger Mother* was published in 2011, readers and critics were stunned at **Amy Chua**'s candid account of raising her two daughters. Chua, a Yale law professor, writes that "this was supposed to be a story of how Chinese parents are better at raising kids than western ones. But instead, it's about a bitter clash of cultures, a fleeting taste of glory, and how I was humbled by a 13-year-old. . . ."

Paul Tough is a journalist and former editor at *The New York Times* Magazine. In *How Children Succeed* (newly published by Random House), he analyses the character traits that help a child have a secure and happy future.

An endorsement by Bill Clinton gives some indication of the praise that has greeted **Andrew Solomon**'s latest book, *Far From the Tree,* in the United States. Solomon—who is also an activist and lecturer—spent years researching the work by interviewing families with diverse and challenging experiences of child-rearing.

which is based on the theories of Martin Seligman, a professor of psychology at the University of Pennsylvania, and the late Christopher Peterson of the University of Michigan, factorises the success trait into seven separate elements: grit, self-control, zest, social intelligence, gratitude, optimism and curiosity.

Armed with these attributes, the theory goes that children from all kinds of unpromising backgrounds, from the vastly affluent with no experience of character-forming misfortune to the underprivileged with a discouraging excess of "deep and pervasive adversity at home", can achieve both the academic qualifications that are the golden ticket to the security of regular employment and the qualities that will make them useful members of society.

On this side of the Atlantic, the case for character development as an element of education has been vigorously promoted by Anthony Seldon, the Master of Wellington College. In May last year, the University of Birmingham's Jubilee Centre for Character and Values was launched, with funding from the John Templeton Foundation, established by the American philanthropist.

Tough describes how the principle of teaching—and assessing—character as well as academic attainment was initially taken up by two schools, KIPP Academy Middle School in the South Bronx, whose students are mostly from low-income families, and Riverdale Country School, situated in one of the most affluent neighbourhoods of New York City, and where pre-kindergarten fees start at $40,750 a year.

KIPP was already something of a model institution after a programme of immersive schooling produced a startling improvement in its academic results. But the instigator of that programme, David Levin, a Yale graduate, was dismayed by how many of his high-achieving students subsequently dropped out of college. Meanwhile, the headmaster of Riverdale, Dominic Randolph, had begun to feel that "the push on tests" at high-achieving schools such as his was "missing out on some serious parts of what it means to be human".

For the students, the problems at both ends of the socio-economic spectrum were oddly similar: low levels of maternal attachment, high levels of parental criticism, minimal after-school adult supervision, emotional and physical isolation from parents and—in the case of the rich children—excessive pressure to succeed, resulting in anxiety, depression and chronic academic problems.

The evolution of the character development programme diverged sharply at the two schools during the course of the trial. At KIPP it leaned towards the practical and prescriptive; at Riverdale the emphasis was more moral and philosophical, on leading a good life rather than wearing the uniform correctly and paying attention in class.

As the programme has continued, the statistics on college dropout rates among KIPP students have seemed modestly encouraging. It is harder to measure the success of the experiment among Riverdale students, as their path towards academic success was always much clearer. Tough acknowledges that what he calls the "new science of adversity . . . presents a real challenge to some deeply held political beliefs on both the left

and the right". In the UK, Seldon concedes that "character" might be seen as a synonym for "middle-class" or "public-school" values. Yet both men appear convinced that it is the only means of enabling young people to alter what might otherwise appear to be a fixed destiny of failure and unhappiness.

While Tough proposes the formal exercise of grit and optimism as the key to personal success, Andrew Solomon's new book, *Far From the Tree,* is a study of families whose ideas about what constitutes "success" for their child have had to be recalibrated, sometimes very sharply. Solomon interviewed 200 families for his epic survey of identity and difference, which was a decade in the writing. Each chapter is devoted to the experiences of children and parents living with one of a dozen forms of "otherness"— deafness, dwarfism, Down's syndrome, autism, schizophrenia, prodigies, criminal children and those born of rape.

Solomon's theme is the development of identity. He argues that children acquire identity both "vertically", in the form of inherited traits such as language and ethnicity, and "horizontally", from a peer group. The greater the differences between the child and his or her parents, the more powerful the tensions between the horizontal and vertical identities.

The germ of the book sprang from an article on deaf culture that Solomon wrote in 1993 for *The New York Times.* He found that most deaf children are born to hearing parents, who often feel compelled to help their children "succeed" in a hearing world by focusing on the ability to communicate orally, often to the detriment of other aspects of their development. For such children, the discovery of a culture that celebrates deafness, regarding it as a state of being as vibrant and creative as the hearing world, often appears a liberation, a portal to an identity that does not have to be lived out against a contrasting "normality".

But within that experience of liberation lies the seed of a painful truth: that, for all children marked by difference, whatever its nature (Solomon is gay, and writes movingly about his experience of growing up in a straight family), their first experience of their otherness is almost invariably provided by their own family. He explores the complicated nexus of "normalities" which exists within the family of a child who is in some way different, and between the family and the outside world, with a dogged forensic elegance.

Solomon's account, like Tough's, is laden with anecdote, but while Tough uses his case histories to personalise his theories, Solomon's purpose in writing is narrative and exploratory, rather than ideological or didactic. Like Griffiths, he seeks the key to a universe of familial complexity, and finds it in the most obvious place of all. Love, he concludes, is all you need.

That was pretty much my guiding principle when I began my own experience of parenthood. And on the whole I'm not persuaded that the outcome would have been very different if I had spent more time consulting the experts. Which is not the same thing as feeling that I have been a success as a parent. Raising a child involves a circuitous journey of many branching routes that may lead, if parents and children are lucky, loving and tolerant, to a destination that everyone involved finds bearable.

Twenty years ago, or ten, or even five, if you had asked me whether I thought I was a good mother, I would have answered "good enough" with a degree of self-satisfaction. I had, after all, raised a kind, sane, personable grown-up with a decent clutch of exam results, an entrenched reading habit and an unusual ability to discuss with enthusiasm both West Ham's position in the League table and the nuances of female fashion; and I felt that I had done it largely contra mundum.

More recently, as my son and I have settled into our roles as adult equals and our accounts of the past have diverged, I have begun to understand that he has grown into the person he is as much despite me as because of me. My main aim as a mother had been to try to avoid the aspects of my own upbringing that had caused me pain. I thought that would be easy, but it was not.

Sometimes my son's narratives of his childhood (still so recent and fresh in his mind) make me think that almost everything I did was wrong. It is a melancholy reflection, to put it mildly. But it makes me think that perhaps the real work of parenthood is to learn to accommodate the stories that your children tell you about their upbringing.

Critical Thinking

1. Shilling's article discusses and reviews several different philosophies of rearing children. Which is closest to the style of parenting your parents used? Which style or attributes do you want to adopt as a parent? Why?

2. Why are modern parents believed to be more fearful and protective than past generations?

3. What is the single most important thing parents can do to help promote the healthy development of their children?

4. The article suggests that parents have over-emphasized academic success in children and under-emphasized character development. Do you agree or disagree? Why?

Create Central

www.mhhe.com/createcentral

Internet Reference

Health and Parenting Center
www.webmd.com/parenting

Tufts University Child and Family Webguide
www.cfw.tufts.edu

Positive Parenting
www.positiveparenting.com

The National Association for Child Development
www.nacd.org

Child Trends
www.childtrends.org

Jane Shilling is the author of *The Stranger in the Mirror*.

Shilling, Jane. From *New Stateswoman*, January 2013, pp. 27–31. Copyright © 2013 by New Statesman, Ltd. Reprinted by permission.

Article   Prepared by: Patricia Hrusa Williams, *University of Maine at Farmington*

Raising a Moral Child

ADAM GRANT

Learning Outcomes

After reading this article, you will be able to:

- Define moral behavior.

- Compare and contrast the terms guilt and shame.

- Identify parenting strategies associated with moral behavior in children.

What does it take to be a good parent? We know some of the tricks for teaching kids to become high achievers. For example, research suggests that when parents praise effort rather than ability, children develop a stronger work ethic and become more motivated.

Yet although some parents live vicariously through their children's accomplishments, success is not the No. 1 priority for most parents. We're much more concerned about our children becoming kind, compassionate and helpful. Surveys reveal that in the United States, parents from European, Asian, Hispanic, and African ethnic groups all place far greater importance on caring than achievement. These patterns hold around the world: When people in 50 countries were asked to report their guiding principles in life, the value that mattered most was not achievement, but caring.

Despite the significance that it holds in our lives, teaching children to care about others is no simple task. In an Israeli study of nearly 600 families, parents who valued kindness and compassion frequently failed to raise children who shared those values.

Are some children simply good-natured—or not? For the past decade, I've been studying the surprising success of people who frequently help others without any strings attached. As the father of two daughters and a son, I've become increasingly curious about how these generous tendencies develop.

Genetic twin studies suggest that anywhere from a quarter to more than half of our propensity to be giving and caring is inherited. That leaves a lot of room for nurture, and the evidence on how parents raise kind and compassionate children flies in the face of what many of even the most well-intentioned parents do in praising good behavior, responding to bad behavior, and communicating their values.

By age 2, children experience some moral emotions—feelings triggered by right and wrong. To reinforce caring as the right behavior, research indicates, praise is more effective than rewards. Rewards run the risk of leading children to be kind only when a carrot is offered, whereas praise communicates that sharing is intrinsically worthwhile for its own sake. But what kind of praise should we give when our children show early signs of generosity?

Many parents believe it's important to compliment the behavior, not the child—that way, the child learns to repeat the behavior. Indeed, I know one couple who are careful to say, "That was such a helpful thing to do," instead of, "You're a helpful person."

But is that the right approach? In a clever experiment, the researchers Joan E. Grusec and Erica Redler set out to investigate what happens when we commend generous behavior versus generous character. After 7- and 8-year-olds won marbles and donated some to poor children, the experimenter remarked, "Gee, you shared quite a bit."

The researchers randomly assigned the children to receive different types of praise. For some of the children, they praised the action: "It was good that you gave some of your marbles to those poor children. Yes, that was a nice and helpful thing to do." For others, they praised the character behind the action: "I guess you're the kind of person who likes to help others whenever you can. Yes, you are a very nice and helpful person."

A couple of weeks later, when faced with more opportunities to give and share, the children were much more generous after their character had been praised than after their actions had been. Praising their character helped them internalize it as part of their identities. The children learned who they were from observing their own actions: I am a helpful person. This dovetails with new research led by the psychologist Christopher J. Bryan, who finds that for moral behaviors, nouns work better than verbs. To get 3- to 6-year-olds to help with a task, rather than inviting them "to help," it was 22 to 29 percent more effective to encourage them to "be a helper." Cheating was cut in half when instead of, "Please don't cheat," participants were told, "Please don't be a cheater." When our actions become a reflection of our character, we lean more heavily toward the moral and generous choices. Over time it can become part of us.

Praise appears to be particularly influential in the critical periods when children develop a stronger sense of identity. When the researchers Joan E. Grusec and Erica Redler praised the character of 5-year-olds, any benefits that may have emerged didn't have a lasting impact: They may have been too young to internalize moral character as part of a stable sense of self. And by the time children turned 10, the differences between praising character and praising actions vanished: Both were effective. Tying generosity to character appears to matter most around age 8, when children may be starting to crystallize notions of identity.

Praise in response to good behavior may be half the battle, but our responses to bad behavior have consequences, too. When children cause harm, they typically feel one of two moral emotions: shame or guilt. Despite the common belief that these emotions are interchangeable, research led by the psychologist June Price Tangney reveals that they have very different causes and consequences.

Shame is the feeling that I am a bad person, whereas guilt is the feeling that I have done a bad thing. Shame is a negative judgment about the core self, which is devastating: Shame makes children feel small and worthless, and they respond either by lashing out at the target or escaping the situation altogether. In contrast, guilt is a negative judgment about an action, which can be repaired by good behavior. When children feel guilt, they tend to experience remorse and regret, empathize with the person they have harmed, and aim to make it right.

In one study spearheaded by the psychologist Karen Caplovitz Barrett, parents rated their toddlers' tendencies to experience shame and guilt at home. The toddlers received a rag doll, and the leg fell off while they were playing with it alone. The shame-prone toddlers avoided the researcher and did not volunteer that they broke the doll. The guilt-prone toddlers were more likely to fix the doll, approach the experimenter, and explain what happened. The ashamed toddlers were avoiders; the guilty toddlers were amenders.

If we want our children to care about others, we need to teach them to feel guilt rather than shame when they misbehave. In a review of research on emotions and moral development, the psychologist Nancy Eisenberg suggests that shame emerges when parents express anger, withdraw their love, or try to assert their power through threats of punishment: Children may begin to believe that they are bad people. Fearing this effect, some parents fail to exercise discipline at all, which can hinder the development of strong moral standards.

The most effective response to bad behavior is to express disappointment. According to independent reviews by Professor Eisenberg and David R. Shaffer, parents raise caring children by expressing disappointment and explaining why the behavior was wrong, how it affected others, and how they can rectify the situation. This enables children to develop standards for judging their actions, feelings of empathy and responsibility for others, and a sense of moral identity, which are conducive to becoming a helpful person. The beauty of expressing disappointment is that it communicates disapproval of the bad behavior, coupled with high expectations and the potential for improvement: "You're a good person, even if you did a bad thing, and I know you can do better."

As powerful as it is to criticize bad behavior and praise good character, raising a generous child involves more than waiting for opportunities to react to the actions of our children. As parents, we want to be proactive in communicating our values to our children. Yet many of us do this the wrong way.

In a classic experiment, the psychologist J. Philippe Rushton gave 140 elementary- and middle-school-age children tokens for winning a game, which they could keep entirely or donate some to a child in poverty. They first watched a teacher figure play the game either selfishly or generously, and then preach to them the value of taking, giving or neither. The adult's influence was significant: Actions spoke louder than words. When the adult behaved selfishly, children followed suit. The words didn't make much difference—children gave fewer tokens after observing the adult's selfish actions, regardless of whether the adult verbally advocated selfishness or generosity. When the adult acted generously, students gave the same amount whether generosity was preached or not—they donated 85 percent more than the norm in both cases. When the adult preached selfishness, even after the adult acted generously, the students still gave 49 percent more than the norm. Children learn generosity not by listening to what their role models say, but by observing what they do.

To test whether these role-modeling effects persisted over time, two months later researchers observed the children playing the game again. Would the modeling or the preaching influence whether the children gave—and would they even remember it from two months earlier?

The most generous children were those who watched the teacher give but not say anything. Two months later, these children were 31 percent more generous than those who observed the same behavior but also heard it preached. The message from this research is loud and clear: If you don't model generosity, preaching it may not help in the short run, and in the long run, preaching is less effective than giving while saying nothing at all.

People often believe that character causes action, but when it comes to producing moral children, we need to remember that action also shapes character. As the psychologist Karl Weick is fond of asking, "How can I know who I am until I see what I do? How can I know what I value until I see where I walk?"

Critical Thinking

1. What does it mean to be a moral child?
2. How much and what aspects of being moral are due to nature? Nurture?

3. In the article the author states "If we want our children to care about others, we need to teach them guilt rather than shame when they misbehave." Explain what they mean by this.

Internet References

Health and Parenting Center
www.webmd.com/parenting
Positive Parenting
www.positiveparenting.com
Raising a Moral Child: Ask Dr. Sears
http://www.askdrsears.com/topics/parenting/discipline-behavior/morals-manners/moral-child

---

ADAM GRANT is a professor of management and psychology at the Wharton School of the University of Pennsylvania and the author of *Give and Take: Why Helping Others Drives Our Success.*

Article   Prepared by: Patricia Hrusa Williams, *University of Maine at Farmington*

My Rules for My Kids: Eat Your Vegetables; Don't Blame the Teacher

FRANCIS L. THOMPSON

Learning Outcomes

After reading this article, you will be able to:

• Identify parenting practices associated with raising competent, independent children.

• Recognize differences in family values and how they translate into disciplinary and child rearing practices.

My wife and I had 12 children over the course of 15 and a half years. Today, our oldest is 37 and our youngest is 22. I have always had a very prosperous job and enough money to give my kids almost anything. But my wife and I decided not to.

I will share with you the things that we did, but first let me tell you the results: All 12 of my children have college degrees (or are in school), and we as parents did not pay for it. Most have graduate degrees. Those who are married have wonderful spouses with the same ethics and college degrees, too. We have 18 grandchildren who are learning the same things that our kids learned—self respect, gratitude, and a desire to give back to society.

We raised our family in Utah, Florida, and California; my wife and I now live in Colorado. In March, we will have been married 40 years. I attribute the love between us as a part of our success with the children. They see a stable home life with a commitment that does not have compromises.

Here's what we did right (we got plenty wrong, too, but that's another list):

Chores

Kids had to perform chores from age 3. A 3-year-old does not clean toilets very well but by the time he is 4, it's a reasonably good job.

They got allowances based on how they did the chores for the week.

We had the children wash their own clothes by the time they turned 8. We assigned them a wash day.

When they started reading, they had to make dinner by reading a recipe. They also had to learn to double a recipe.

The boys and girls had to learn to sew.

Study Time

Education was very important in our family.

We had study time from 6 P.M. to 8 P.M. every week day. No television, computer, games, or other activities until the two hours were up. If they had no homework, then they read books. For those too young to be in school, we had someone read books to them. After the two hours, they could do whatever they wanted as long as they were in by curfew.

All the kids were required to take every Advanced Placement class there was. We did not let entrance scores be an impediment. We went to the school and demanded our kids be let in. Then we, as parents, spent the time to ensure they had the understanding to pass the class. After the first child, the school learned that we kept our promise that the kids could handle the AP classes.

If children would come home and say that a teacher hated them or was not fair, our response was that you need to find a way to get along. You need [to] find a way to learn the material because in real life, you may have a boss that does not like you. We would not enable children to "blame" the teacher for not learning, but place[d] the responsibility for learning the material back on the child. Of course, we were alongside them for two hours of study a day, for them to ask for help anytime.

Picky Eaters Not Allowed

We all ate dinner and breakfast together. Breakfast was at 5:15 A.M. and then the children had to do chores before school. Dinner was at 5:30 P.M.

More broadly, food was interesting. We wanted a balanced diet, but hated it when we were young and parents made us eat all our food. Sometimes we were full and just did not want to eat anymore. Our rule was to give the kids the food they hated most first (usually vegetables) and then they got the next type of food. They did not have to eat it and could leave the table. If later they complained they were hungry, we would get out that food they did not want to eat, warm it up in the microwave, and provide it to them. Again, they did not have to eat it. But they got no other food until the next meal unless they ate it.

Extracurriculars

All kids had to play some kind of sport. They got to choose, but choosing none was not an option. We started them in grade school. We did not care if it was swimming, football, baseball, fencing, tennis, etc. and did not care if they chose to change sports. But they had to play something.

All kids had to be in some kind of club: Boy Scouts, Girl Scouts, history, drama, etc.

They were required to provide community service. We would volunteer within our community and at church. For Eagle Scout projects, we would have the entire family help. Once we collected old clothes and took them to Mexico and passed them out. The kids saw what life was like for many families and how their collections made them so happy and made a difference.

Independence

When the kids turned 16, we bought each a car. The first one learned what that meant. As the tow truck pulled a once "new" car into the driveway, my oldest proclaimed: "Dad, it is a wreck!" I said, "Yes, but a 1965 Mustang fastback wreck. Here are the repair manuals. Tools are in the garage. I will pay for every part, but will not pay for LABOR." Eleven months later, the car had a rebuilt engine, rebuilt transmission, newly upholstered interior, a new suspension system, and a new coat of paint. My daughter (yes, it was my daughter) had one of the hottest cars at high school. And her pride that she built it was beyond imaginable. (As a side note, none of my kids ever got a ticket for speeding, even though no car had less than 450 horsepower.)

We as parents allowed kids to make mistakes. Five years before the 16th birthday and their "new" car gift, they had to help out with our family cars. Once I asked my son, Samuel, to change the oil and asked if he needed help or instruction. "No, Dad, I can do it." An hour later, he came in and said, "Dad, does it take 18 quarts of oil to change the oil?" I asked where did he put 18 quarts of oil when normally only five were needed. His response: "That big screw on top at the front of the engine." I said "You mean the radiator?" Well, he did not get into trouble for filling the radiator with oil. He had to drain it, we bought a radiator flush, put in new radiator fluid, and then he had to change the real oil. We did not ground him or give him any punishment for doing it "wrong." We let the lesson be the teaching tool. Our children are not afraid to try something new. They were trained that if they do something wrong they will not get punished. It often cost us more money, but we were raising kids, not saving money.

The kids each got their own computer, but had to build it. I bought the processor, memory, power supply, case, keyboard, hard drive, motherboard, and mouse. They had to put it together and load the software on. This started when they were 12.

We let the children make their own choices, but limited. For example, do you want to go to bed now or clean your room? Rarely, did we give directives that were one way, unless it dealt with living the agreed-upon family rules. This let the child feel that she had some control over life.

In It Together

We required the children to help each other. When a fifth grader is required to read 30 minutes a day, and a first grader is required to be read to 30 minutes a day, have one sit next to the other and read. Those in high school calculus tutored those in algebra or grade-school math.

We assigned an older child to a younger child to teach them and help them accomplish their weekly chores.

We let the children be a part of making the family rules. For example, the kids wanted the rule that no toys were allowed in the family room. The toys had to stay either in the bedroom or playroom. In addition to their chores, they had to all clean their bedroom every day (or just keep it clean in the first place). These were rules that the children wanted. We gave them a chance each month to amend or create new rules. Mom and Dad had veto power of course.

We tried to be always consistent. If they had to study two hours every night, we did not make an exception to it. Curfew was 10 P.M. during school nights and midnight on non-school nights. There were no exceptions to the rules.

Vacation Policy

We would take family vacations every summer for two or three weeks. We could afford a hotel, or cruise, but did not choose those options. We went camping and backpacking. If it rained, then we would figure out how to backpack in the rain and survive. We would set up a base camp at a site with five or six tents, and I would take all kids age 6 or older on a three- to five-day backpack trip. My wife would stay with the little ones. Remember, for 15 years, she was either pregnant or just had a baby. My kids and I hiked across the Grand Canyon, to the top of Mount Whitney, across the Continental Divide, across Yosemite.

We would send kids via airplane to relatives in Europe or across the US for two or three weeks at a time. We started this when they were in kindergarten. It would take special treatment for the airlines to take a 5-year-old alone on the plane and required people on the other end to have special documentation. We only sent the kids if they wanted to go. However, with the younger ones seeing the older ones travel, they wanted to go. The kids learned from an early age that we, as parents, were always there for them, but would let them grow their own wings and fly.

Money and Materialism

Even though we have sufficient money, we have not helped the children buy homes, pay for education, pay for weddings (yes, we do not pay for weddings either). We have provided extensive information on how to do it or how to buy rental units and use equity to grow wealth. We do not "give" things to our children but we give them information and teach them "how" to do things. We have helped them with contacts in corporations, but they have to do the interviews and "earn" the jobs.

We give birthday and Christmas presents to the kids. We would play Santa Claus but as they got older, and would ask about it, we would not lie. We would say it is a game we play and it is fun. We did and do have lists for items that each child would like for presents. Then everyone can see what they want. With the [I]nternet, it is easy to send such lists around to the children and grandchildren. Still, homemade gifts are often the favorite of all.

The Real World

We loved the children regardless of what they did. But would not prevent consequences of any of their actions. We let them suffer consequences and would not try to mitigate the consequences because we saw them suffering. We would cry and be sad, but would not do anything to reduce the consequences of their actions.

We were and are not our kids' best friends. We were their parents.

Critical Thinking

1. How would you characterize the parenting style the author and his wife utilized with their 12 children?

2. The author feels that he and his wife have been successful in raising their children. How do they define success and what it means to be a competent adult?

3. In looking at the list of family rules used with their children, which rules do you agree with and which do you feel are harsh or inappropriate in some way? Provide a rationale for your choices and explain your reasoning.

Create Central

www.mhhe.com/createcentral

Internet References

Child Trends
www.childtrends.org

Health and Parenting Center
www.webmd.com/parenting

Tufts University Child and Family Webguide
www.cfw.tufts.edu

University of Alabama Parenting Assistance Line
http://www.pal.ua.edu/discipline/consistency.php

Article   Prepared by: Patricia Hrusa Williams, *University of Maine at Farmington*

The Science of Siblings

FRANCINE RUSSO

Learning Outcomes

After reading this article, you will be able to:

- Analyze ways siblings influence personality and development at different points of the lifespan.
- Understand the research basis behind common beliefs about the influence of siblings on behavior and personality.

Growing up in North Miami Beach, Tobi Cohen Kosanke, now 48, adored her brother Keith. Seven years older, he was a "laid-back surfer dude," while she was a "chubby, nerdy" little girl. Tobi knew she could never live up to Keith's cool persona, so while he was quitting school, experimenting with drugs, and focusing on riding the next wave, Tobi threw herself into school, with her brother's encouragement. The hard work paid off: She went on to earn her PhD and become a geologist. "I hung out with the geeky kids, the good kids, the smart kids, because of my brother," she says. "I loved Keith, and I know he was proud of me, but I owe my success to taking the road that he didn't take."

Tobi's story is not unusual. Of all the factors that shape your personality—your genes, your parents, your peers—siblings are at the top, according to one major theory of human development. If you think about it, the relationships with your sisters and brothers will likely last longer than any others in your lifetime. Research shows that even in adolescence, you spend 10 to 17 hours a week with them—and experts are finding that their impact continues long after you've left the nest. Study after study has shown that the ways you interact with each other growing up can affect your relationships, your happiness, even the way you see yourself throughout the rest of your life.

"I'm First!" "I'm the Baby!"

Some of the earliest studies of siblings focused on how birth order influences personality and fate. You're familiar with the basic types: Firstborns are said to be responsible and high-achieving, youngest siblings charmers and free spirits, and middle children lost in the mix.

It's easy to dismiss these as mere stereotypes, and indeed there are researchers who do, but others have found statistical evidence that bears them out. A Norwegian study found that firstborns had slightly higher IQs than their sibs. Other research has shown they're also more successful: According to Sandra Black, PhD, professor of economics at the University of Texas at Austin, "Firstborns earn more than secondborns, who earn more than thirdborns."

On the other hand, research has found that youngest siblings really do tend to be risk-takers. Frank Sulloway, PhD, of the Institute of Personality and Social Research at UC Berkeley, studied baseball-playing brothers—like Joe, Dom, and Vince DiMaggio—and found that the younger ones tried to steal base more often than their older brothers. Meanwhile, middle children grow up to be more peer-oriented, says Sulloway. First- and last-borns turn to parents in an emotional crisis; middle kids, to their friends. Still, birth order is hardly destiny, says Sulloway. What's more important, researchers say, is the quality and dynamics of your relationships with your siblings.

"I'm Nothing like Him!"

Within a family, children devise all sorts of strategies to increase their status and feeling of belonging, and one of the most important is what experts call "sibling de-identification." To reduce competition with brothers and sisters who may be cuter or smarter (not to mention bigger and stronger), we each carve out our own niche.

Much like Tobi Kosanke, younger siblings typically start out adoring their older brothers or sisters, says Laurie Kramer, PhD, professor of applied family studies at the University of Illinois at Urbana. "They want to mimic their strengths and talents, but over time, they realize they can't succeed at the same level. That leads them to develop their own attributes."

"You can be the smartest kid in your class or the fastest on the track team," says Susan McHale, PhD, professor of human development at Penn State University. "But if you have a brother or sister who's smarter or more athletic, it doesn't matter." In other words, your self-image is shaped at least in part by how you compare to your siblings.

And it's not just that younger kids de-identify from more capable older siblings, says McHale. In early adolescence, when we're trying to figure out who we are, it's often older siblings who emphasize their differences. For example, a boy with a feminist younger sister might adopt a more macho stance. Even among tight-knit sibs, "you want to be close but also to be your own person," says Victoria Hilkevitch Bedford, PhD, professor emerita of psychology at the University of Indianapolis.

And experts speculate that our tendency to compare ourselves to our siblings continues well into adulthood. For example, the sibling dynamic could affect what we try to achieve, says Kramer. "Asked to give a speech or do a challenging job, a less accomplished younger sibling might decline, thinking, 'If they knew my older brother, they wouldn't think I was so great.'"

"Oh, Her? She's Just One of the Guys."

When it comes to learning about the opposite sex, researchers say, there's nothing better than having an older member at home. "If you are a girl with an older brother or a boy with an older sister, you should thank them for whatever romantic success you've had," jokes William Ickes, PhD, professor of psychology at the University of Texas at Arlington.

In Ickes's now classic 1983 study, he instructed unacquainted male-female pairs to talk to each other. Girls with older brothers and boys with older sisters broke the ice more easily and were more likely to rate each other favorably.

Because the genders don't mix much in middle childhood, "kids who see opposite-sex siblings and their friends in everyday settings may come to know more about how the other sex behaves and connects," says McHale.

Melissa Payne, a 29-year-old medical industry account manager in Orlando, says her relationship with her 33-year-old brother, Dave Payne, a publicist in Tarpon Springs, Fla., not only helped pave the way for romantic connections but allowed the two to share dating advice. A few years ago, when both siblings were seeing people who did not treat them well, each reminded the other that not all women—or men—were such shabby partners. Within a year, they had broken off the relationships. "When you're dating someone, you can make excuses, but it was different hearing a guy's perspective from my brother," says Melissa.

"Hey, that's Mine!"

Young siblings fight up to eight times an *hour,* research shows. While all that squabbling may drive parents crazy, it's also how some kids learn to negotiate conflict—training ground for dealing with neighbors, bosses, and spouses down the line.

When it comes to arguing and expressing our opinions, we can take risks with our siblings because they're stuck with us, says Corinna Jenkins Tucker, PhD, associate professor of family studies at the University of New Hampshire. "Children can test which conflict resolution strategies work and which don't," she says. (Refuse to share? Just watch your brother's reaction.) And what we learn during childhood can have far-reaching effects.

Kids who learn coercive or hostile approaches to handling conflict are more likely in adolescence to join risky peer groups and engage in negative social behaviors (like smoking, drinking, or skipping school), according to McHale. But siblings can be taught to compromise—that's why parental involvement is so crucial. Reluctant referees who consider sibling aggression normal and don't help resolve clashes are making a mistake, says McHale. Their kids may end up with poorer social skills and more conflict compared with kids whose parents help them work out their disagreements.

And what about as you grow older? Some experts say that kids who learn hostile patterns of interaction with sibs may repeat those patterns with friends or coworkers. Others, however, suggest that kids who never develop close relationships with their brothers or sisters may be more likely to go out of their way to form strong connections outside the family.

"Of Course We Love You Both the Same."

It's not possible to talk about the sibling relationship without considering Mom and Dad, the central pole on the family merry-go-round. Siblings may receive a lot of things from their parents, including cues on how to treat someone in a close relationship. Good marriages tend to make for kids who get along better, says Katherine Jewsbury Conger, PhD, associate professor of human development at UC Davis.

Yet there's one parental behavior that can really make or break the sibling relationship. As every kid knows almost from his or her first breath, if Mommy or Daddy gives me less than my sister, then it's game over. Social scientists call this "differential treatment." Kids call it favoritism, and if we think Susie is Mommy's favorite, we don't like it, and sometimes maybe don't like Susie, either.

Children of different ages and abilities are bound to be treated differently, says Conger, but for kids, the real question is fairness. And if children see differential treatment as unfair, those negative feelings can last—even into the next generation, with an adult sibling resenting that Grandma gives Susie's kids better Christmas gifts.

Paige D. feels that favoritism came between her and her older brother, with whom she no longer speaks (she says their parents skipped both her college graduation and her wedding but attended her brother's graduation). "As a child, I loved my brother more than the moon and the stars," says Paige. "But I think the overt favoritism made him feel so uncomfortable that it was easier for him to block me out as a way to justify our parents' eccentricity."

Interestingly, though, while some children are highly attuned to variations in their parents' attentions, they are often mistaken about favoritism. When Deborah T. Gold, PhD, associate professor of medical sociology at Duke University, studied pairs of adult siblings, she found that in many cases each thought the *other* was their parents' favorite.

"What are We Going to do About Mom?"

How siblings get along in adulthood also depends greatly on how they manage one of the most volatile family passages—the aging and death of their parents. As grown-up sibs see their time with Mom or Dad running out, it stirs up deep childhood desires for love and approval. Research shows that in 90 percent of families, one person does most of the caregiving, and Bedford notes that if siblings grew up with a sense of unfairness, those feelings can reignite over how sisters and brothers perceive elder care. On the other hand, this passage also brings enormous opportunities to strengthen and renew sibling relationships. Putting your heads together during stressful times can help you and your siblings get to know each other as adults. Hey, my brother's not that incompetent little kid! Where did my sister acquire so much patience?

And even if things are tense (or worse), it's not impossible to repair the relationship. As young adults, Wendy Beckman and her older sister, Bonnie Nielson, were little more than cordial. Wendy, now 55 and a writer in Cincinnati, still thought of her older sister as annoyingly overprotective. But in her 30s, she made efforts to connect with Bonnie, whose marriage was unraveling.

"Bit by bit," Wendy recalls, "we started talking honestly about things in our adult lives, not just 'You took my socks when I was 12.' She actually started asking me for advice!"

Confronting their father's Alzheimer's and their mother's death from cancer, they grew even closer. "We still come at the world completely differently," says Bonnie, now 61, of Augusta, Maine. "But when you see your siblings as fully formed adults, the relationship is so much more fulfilling."

Experts say this pattern of sibling drift, followed by reconnection, is common. When siblings move away and start their own careers and families, they often have little contact except through their parents. But in middle age and beyond, as other loved ones pass away, surviving siblings can be important sources of support. In fact, research shows the healthiest, happiest, and least lonely people have warm sibling relationships.

As time passes, Patti Wood's relationship with her two older sisters has become more precious. Patti, 53, an author and speaker in Decatur, Ga., always adored her sisters, now 62 and 66. The three "military brats" stayed close during their many moves, and have bonded even more tightly after caring for their 92-year-old mother.

Despite their differences—single, long-married with grandkids, divorced with a grown child—they talk to each other nearly every day, travel together, and call each other first in a crisis. And they share a unique history. Patti's oldest sister, Robin, speaks for them all when she says, "We know we'll always be there for each other. I can't imagine not having my sisters there to count on."

Only the Lonely?

Pity the poor only child—no one to play with. (Or maybe you envied onlies, with no bratty little brother trashing their stuff.) Regardless, "there's a big misconception in American popular culture that singletons are selfish, lonely, or maladjusted," says Toni Falbo, PhD, a professor of educational psychology at the University of Texas at Austin and an only child herself. But in fact, only children have one major advantage, says Falbo: They don't have siblings competing for their parents' resources, including college funds. As a result, onlies tend to achieve high levels of education and occupational prestige.

As little kids, Falbo acknowledges, single children may be more comfortable with adults. "But peer sociability grows with experience," she says, and by high school, onlies are on par with kids who have sisters and brothers. "Every day, my mother shoved me out the door and insisted I play with other children, which forced me to develop social skills," says Falbo. "And it also helped me learn to appreciate my family, which was just the right size for me."

Critical Thinking

1. The article suggests that sibling relationships shape personality development more than other factors including genetics, parenting, or peer relationships. Do you agree or disagree and why?

2. The article presents several different stereotypes about sibling relationships and dynamics. Are there any which you feel apply to your own life and family? If so, which ones? Are there any which you do not feel are valid or based on research and why?

3. What about the outcomes of individuals who are only children, lose a sibling, or have a sibling with special needs—how might the absence, loss, or difference in their sibling connection shape their personality and development?

Internet References

Dr. Frank J. Sulloway, PhD., Birth Order Researcher
www.sulloway.org

Sibling Issues: Center for Parent Information and Resources
www.parentcenterhub.org/repository/siblings

Sibling Support Project
www.siblingsupport.org

Sibs
www.sibs.org.uk

Tufts University Child and Family Webguide
www.cfw.tufts.edu

FRANCINE RUSSO is the author of *They're Your Parents, Too! How Siblings Can Survive Their Parents' Aging Without Driving Each Other Crazy,* and frequently speaks about sibling relationships.

Francine Russo, "The Science of Siblings," from *Parade Magazine*, June 22, 2013.

Article   Prepared by: Patricia Hrusa Williams, *University of Maine at Farmington*

Birth Order May Predict Intelligence and Illness in First-Borns, but Vitality in Their Siblings

CHRIS WELLER

Learning Outcomes

After reading this article, you will be able to:

- Identify the influence of different birth order positions on health, personality, and developmental outcomes.

- Explain Sibling Niche Theory.

- Recognize challenges in studying the influence of siblings and birth order on individual adaptation.

It isn't often you hear themes of destiny in scientific literature, but birth order stands out like a sore thumb. While most research relies on people having agency in their actions, investigations into the effects of being born first, second, or someplace further down the ladder seem to say part of our future is already written.

These studies can't predict everything—we do write our own tickets, after all, at least to a certain extent (philosophers are still out on that one)—but they do help shed light on the ways in which our environments groom us to lead one type of lifestyle over another. Scientists have found links between our personalities, our health, and our ability to sustain relationships—all determined by whether the universe decided to put your core self, your essence, inside the head of one child or another.

Health Differences

As temporary only children, first-borns are given a bevy of advantages. They receive all of their parents' affection and earn all the spoils. But it comes with a price. A childhood of excess has been found to lead to several health complications later in life. First-borns are more prone to diabetes, metabolic disorders, and obesity, the last of which shouldn't come as much of a surprise. Parents who want nothing but the best for their pride and joy tend to overfeed them.

Parents also tend to helicopter over their first-borns when it comes to their vaccines. A great deal of research suggests a link between first-borns and the development of allergies, asthma, and immune-related disorders. Anxiety plays a part. Statistically speaking, worried parents of an only child will typically rush to get every shot and injection pumped into their kid's veins to prevent future illness more so than they end up doing for future children. As a result, vaccine-related emergency room visits tend to be much higher for first-borns than later siblings.

All this panic about doing parenting "right" has an upside. First-borns generally don't engage in as much risky behavior compared to their younger siblings, especially their youngest. The baby of a given family is usually more likely to exhibit addictive tendencies, such as drinking and smoking, and engage in sexual behaviors earlier. In contrast to the strict parenting styles of the first-born, last-born children tend not to get as much attention, which, again, can either be helpful or harmful to their development.

A Note on Siblings

Before discussing the personality traits that differ between siblings, it's important to keep in mind the many ways in which families operate. Health outcomes, too, come from a set of constraints. Lower-income families might not show the same preference of vaccinating their eldest child more than their youngest, simply because other things take priority, like food and paying the bills. In this sense, financial limitations skew the average data, which, it should be said, isn't a small point.

A study from Ohio State University in 2006 found older children aren't necessarily smarter than their younger siblings, as other research has suggested; rather, the majority of that research looked at large and small families, instead of siblings within the same family. When the OSU team controlled for family size, they determined intelligence levels correlated to how old mothers were when they had their first child. "In reality, if you look at these larger families, the fourth-born child is just as intelligent as the first-born," said lead author Aaron Wichman at the time. "But they all don't do as well as children from a smaller family."

Another factor psychologists have come to observe is a phenomenon called the "Sibling Niche Theory." In every family, the theory states, children look for their respective roles. Older children typically fall into a leadership role, middle children find a mediating role, and younger children settle into an introspective—and sometimes rebellious—role. At the same time, they compete for limited resources.

"They've got to differentiate themselves in some way to get the attention that they need," said Dr. Corinna Jenkins-Tucker, professor of family relations at the University of New Hampshire. Sometimes those roles are fads kids grow out of, but other times they stick around for life.

Personality Differences

Each family operates with different constraints, but psychologists have found several sweeping differences between kids born first and those thereafter. The eldest kids, for instance, are more likely to succeed in school because they learn a firmer sense of grit and determination from parents who play tough. Part of that upbringing nudges them toward the role of a leader. First-borns may face more freedom when it comes to their diets, but less so when their grades are on the line.

Kids born later in the food chain, with older siblings having already gobbled up other niches, turn to whichever spots they can get their hands on. "The baby of the family can be a little more irresponsible," Jenkins-Tucker said. "Sometimes it's conscious, sometimes it's not." A girl might see her older sister as the jock of the family, so she turns to science. Or it may simply be that soccer strikes her, at some deeper level, as "her sister's thing," so she finds her uniqueness elsewhere.

Where first-borns are the dominant forces in the house, occupying a role somewhere between parent and peer to their other siblings, and the baby of the family is avoiding an existential crisis, the middle child also merits attention. Almost in sync with their place in the family tree, middle children tend to be more even-keeled than their siblings at either pole. They mediate, Jenkins-Tucker says. Some research also finds them to be more faithful in relationships, prompting some relationship experts to suggest marrying a middle child a way to avoid divorce.

Not Written in Stone

Where you're born relative to your siblings can't predict everything about you. Bill Gates, the wealthiest person alive, is the baby of his family. If we look to his fortune and philanthropy as markers of success, he certainly breaks the mold. Kurt Cobain, meanwhile, was the oldest of his siblings and struggled with devastating heroin addiction in the years leading up to his suicide.

Birth order can't do it all. Instead, science is finding the complex relationship between nature and nurture demands we consider both sides simultaneously, not just one or the other. Our upbringing may affect our trajectory, but once we leave the nest, it's up to us to decide whether we stay on course.

Critical Thinking

1. Identify the benefits and challenges experienced by children who are the oldest, youngest, and middle children in their families.

2. What is Sibling Niche Theory? Analyze the outcomes and dynamics of the children in your family using the theory.

3. Why are the effects of siblings and birth order on individual development difficult to determine?

Internet References

Birth Order and Personality, PsychCentral
http://psychcentral.com/blog/archives/2009/07/22/birth-order-and-personality/
Dr. Frank J. Sulloway, PhD., Birth Order Researcher
www.sulloway.org
Sibling Issues: Center for Parent Information and Resources
www.parentcenterhub.org/repository/siblings/
Sibling Support Project
www.siblingsupport.org
Tufts University Child and Family Webguide
www.cfw.tufts.edu

CHRIS WELLER is a Senior Reporter at *Medical Daily,* where he covers brain health and other fun stuff.

Article   Prepared by: Patricia Hrusa Williams, *University of Maine at Farmington*

How to Make Peace With Your Sibling

Evan Imber-Black

Learning Outcomes

After reading this article, you will be able to:

- Define terms: Family dynamics and family roles.

- Identify factors which influence the relationship between siblings.

- Understand strategies for identifying and changing patterns in relationships.

You've just sat down to eat, and the phone rings. When you answer, your dining companion doesn't have to ask who it is. The expression on your face gives away the fact that it's your quarrelsome brother. You roll your eyes and think, *Here we go again.*

The topics may change—money, caring for parents, holiday plans, children—but the tension between you two is on an endless loop. You know that within two minutes you'll be having the same old fight. And the answer to the question "What can I do differently to create a different outcome?" is nowhere to be found.

It's Not the Person, It's the Pattern

Changing your sibling relationship starts with recognizing that the problem isn't one person's fault. It takes two people to create the clash—though often there are others lurking in the shadows.

Once you decide you genuinely want to improve a relationship that is distant, contentious, agitated or empty, the first step is figuring out the underlying emotional and behavioral pattern. Some examples: Your brother provokes, you seek harmony. Your sister demands, you placate. One of you is a giver, the other a taker. One aggressively confronts, the other meekly submits.

These patterns are less linear than circular in nature: Each action elicits the same response. By the time you've reached midlife, trying to figure out "who started it" is fruitless. More important are these realizations: Blame is pointless, we're in this together, and the work it takes to change is worth it.

When your sibling relationship becomes less bound by old patterns, more real and open to allowing the differences between you to peacefully exist, your lives will become richer and more meaningful. Authentic connections with people who share your history and mythologies, who speak your special family language and can laugh at common foibles, are worth their weight in gold.

The Sources of Sibling Patterns

Many believe that altering a long-standing sibling relationship requires initial agreement from both parties. But in my 35 years of practice I have found that one determined person can *initiate* a process of change. The ideas I offer in this article are derived from a well-established practice called Family Therapy With One Person, and with mindful thought and careful action, you can implement them on your own.

This work begins with *your* deliberations and reflections, proceeds to taking action and ends with having conversations with your sibling(s). Conventional wisdom suggests that communication is required, but with this approach, it comes at the *end* of the process, not the beginning.

The second step to transforming your sibling relationship is acknowledging that you are stuck in a repetitive pattern. To gain insight, assume the role of "anthropologist." However sibling dynamics are playing out today, they're usually traceable to our families as a whole, so you need to review the intergenerational "culture" of brothers and sisters in the household in which you grew up.

Many factors influence how siblings will interact. And until we question them, these become our model of relationships. Often, without realizing it, parents assign certain roles to their children: the smart one, the funny one, the beautiful one, the ditzy one. Although the roles likely contain some elements of truth, nobody is that one-dimensional. Furthermore, these roles "imprint" us, and unconsciously we all start to manifest more and more of those qualities and interact with our siblings from these "childish" starting points.

As you dig deeper, you may discover, for example, that your mother and her younger sister had a relationship characterized by one demanding and the other appeasing—and that that's exactly what happens between you and your sister. Or maybe your father and uncle were in business together and one was a methodical thinker and the other a dreamer, just like you and your brother today.

Birth Order and What to Do About It Now

Most family therapists acknowledge that birth order plays a role in sibling dynamics. The first-born is often the most responsible and the custodian of family traditions. Middle children usually need to figure out for themselves where and how they fit in. The youngest may have had more freedom and been encouraged to be carefree.

A last-born, for instance, may grow up feeling her parents trusted an older sibling with information and responsibilities, while viewing her as irresponsible. We "grow into" expected roles, and this can set up a state of permanent tension and conflict.

Changing these roles and the patterns they engender allows us to experiment with new behavior—parts of ourselves that have been submerged or sublimated in larger family expectations. As you begin to do so, your sibling will likely discover there is more room in the relationship for aspects he or she has kept hidden from you.

9 Steps to Changing Sibling Dynamics

Once you've discerned your repetitive patterns, you can begin to act differently to break a vicious cycle and inaugurate a "virtuous" cycle. As in all our important relationships, siblings often get stuck waiting for the other person to change. It's helpful to think about this as a nine-step process.

1. **Determine your repetitive sibling pattern.** Pursuing-distancing? Demanding-placating? Achieving-failing? Caretaking-care receiving? Awareness of rigid patterns is the first step to deliberate change.
2. **Identify *your* place in the pattern.** What do you do over and over again in response to your sibling? We're all good at noting what other people do, but what's *your* role in the interaction? This non-blaming recognition will help you to decide what you might change in your own behavior. Relationships improve when we stop trying to change others and take responsibility for our own actions and own a new role.
3. **Plan one small and manageable change.** If your usual dynamic with your sister is that she always needs support and you always provide it, try sharing a struggle *you're* having and ask for her help. Be specific about what she can do. Relationships are not transformed all at once, but rather with thoughtful steps.
4. **Anticipate "openings," or moments in family life when change is more likely.** These include times when other shifts are occurring, like the death of a parent, children leaving home, retirement, divorce or the birth of grandchildren. At such moments, people are more emotionally available and the dynamics more fluid.
5. **Consider who else will be impacted.** Whenever we change a pattern with one person, other relatives are often affected. If you and your mother are especially close and you begin to confide in your brother for the first time, how might your mom respond? If you and your partner have long discussed your brother's unavailability and he starts to show up, expect some changes in your primary relationship. Also, because we tend to play out these same roles in other situations (at work, with friends), you could experience some changes there too.
6. **Be prepared for positive and negative reactions.** Moving out of a familiar pattern can be highly disconcerting to others. Don't be surprised if your sibling's initial response is to try to pull you back to the tried and true. If you have always been the helper in the relationship and now you are asking for assistance, watch out for a new call for help.
7. **Maintain your new position.** Pay attention to the pull to familiar old anger and defensiveness—and resist. Think about ways to repeat your new place in the pattern, and implement them. If your older brother has always been demanding and you have always placated, your refusal of a demand will likely not be met with applause initially. Calmly let your brother know how he might help you—or himself.
8. **Watch for your sibling's new responses.** When you take a new and unexpected action in the relationship, observe what she begins to do differently. There will be more room for flexibility.
9. **Initiate a deeper conversation with your sibling.** What would each really like going forward?

Once you've demonstrated that you're genuinely committed to something new between the two of you, your sibling will be more likely to participate in the process. This may be a time to engage in some short-term family therapy.

Critical Thinking

1. The article suggests that while the topic of sibling disputes change, the tension between siblings are a consistent part of the dynamic between siblings. Do you agree? Why/why not?

2. In your own family, what are some of the patterns in relationships between siblings you have noted? Do children in your family assume different roles? How has this influenced interactions between family members? Are relationships between siblings in your family improving or do they remain the same as everyone has grown older?

3. Why is it so difficult to change patterns in relationships? What are strengths and weaknesses of the suggestions made in the article for altering these patterns and changing the dynamics of relationships?

Internet References

Family Dynamics
https://www.healthychildren.org/English/family-life/family-dynamics/Pages/default.aspx

One Person Family Therapy
https://www.ncjrs.gov/html/ojjdp/jjbul2000_04_3/pag7.html

Sibling Issues: Center for Parent Information and Resources
www.parentcenterhub.org/repository/siblings/

Sibs
www.sibs.org.uk

Tufts University Child and Family Webguide
www.cfw.tufts.edu

EVAN IMBER-BLACK is the program director of the marriage and family therapy master's degree program at Mercy College and the director of the Center for Families and Health at the Ackerman Institute for the Family. This article has been edited for style and republished with the permission of our content partner Next Avenue.

Article   Prepared by: Patricia Hrusa Williams,
                                             University of Maine at Farmington

The Accordion Family

KATHERINE S. NEWMAN

Learning Outcomes

After reading this article, you will be able to:

- Identify factors leading adult children to live with their parents.

- Understand challenges for parents and their adult children living together.

Maria Termina and her husband, Alberto, live in the northwestern city of Bra in the Piedmont region of Italy. The people of Bra are traditionalists who struggle to hold the modern world at arm's length. Proud to be the hometown of Carlo Petrini, the founder of the Slow Food Movement, Bra hosts a biennial festival that celebrates artisanal cheeses from around the world.

Alberto, now 67, has lived in Bra almost all his life and worked for the same firm as an engineer for about 40 of those years. Maria is 57. They have three grown children, the youngest of whom, 30-year-old Giovanni, has always lived with his parents and shows no signs of moving out. (All the names in this piece, which is based on interviews, are fictitious to protect privacy.)

Giovanni graduated from the local high school but went no further than that and is content with his steady blue-collar job as an electrician. He works on construction sites and picks up odd jobs on the side. It's a living, barely. His wages are modest, the building trades go up and down, and—in all honesty—his tastes in motorcycles are a bit extravagant. Though he is a skilled worker, Giovanni knows he could not enjoy himself with his friends as he does if he had to support himself entirely on his own earnings. But because he pays no rent and can eat well at his mother's table, his living expenses are low, leaving money for recreation.

Of the three children born to Maria and Alberto, only Giorgio—Giovanni's twin brother—lives on his own. (Laura, divorced, and her 5-year-old daughter recently returned to the nest.) Giorgio completed a degree in economics at a local university and moved to Turin, where he works in marketing and statistics. He is the odd man out, not only in his family but also among many of his family's neighbors. More than a third of Italian men Giovanni's age have never left home; the pattern of "delayed departure" has become the norm in Italy. And while it was common in the past for unmarried men and women to remain with their parents until they wed, the age of marriage has been climbing in the last 30 years, so much so that by the time men like Giovanni cut the apron strings, they are very nearly what we once called "middle-aged." That has made the country an international butt of jokes about the "cult of mammismo," or mama's boys.

It is no laughing matter in Italy, particularly in government circles where the economic consequences are adding up. The former prime minister Silvio Berlusconi came out in support of a campaign against mammismo, having been elected on the promise of doing away with "those hidebound aspects of Italian life which 'inhibit dynamism and growth.'" In January 2010, Renato Brunetta, then a cabinet minister, proposed making it illegal for anyone over 18 to live with his or her parents. He made the suggestion on a radio show where he also admitted that his mother made his bed until he was 30, when he left home.

Why should government officials—including those whose own family lives are hardly worthy of admiration—care one way or the other where adult children make their home? The fact is that those private choices have serious public consequences. The longer aging bambini live with their parents, the fewer new families are formed, and the evaporation of a whole generation of Italian children is knocking the social policies of the country for a loop. Plummeting fertility translates into fewer workers to add fuel to the retirement accounts in an aging society. The private calculations of families like the Terminas, who wonder how long they can support Giovanni, are becoming the public problem of prime ministers.

Does his "delayed departure" worry 30-year-old Giovanni? Not really. Expectations are changing, and there is little pressure on him to be more independent. His family isn't urging him to marry, and he leans back in his chair and opines that "nobody asks you the reason [why you stay] at home with the parents at [my] age . . . nobody obliges me to move away."

Newton, Mass., is famous for its leafy streets, New England-style colonial houses, and well-educated parents who are professionals. The nearby universities—Harvard, MIT, Tufts—and numerous liberal-arts colleges, not to mention the concentration of health-care and computer-related industries, insures a steady influx of middle- and upper-middle-class families. Immigrants—especially high-tech professionals from Israel, India, and Russia—flock to this affluent community in pursuit of opportunity.

Newton boasts first-class schools from top to bottom; graduates of its high schools turn up regularly in the Ivy League. Poor black kids are bused in from inner-city Boston through the Metco integration program to partake of the town's exemplary educational facilities, but few poor families actually live within its boundaries. All but the fairly well heeled are priced out.

William Rollo and his wife arrived in Newton in 1989 after having lived in Seattle, Philadelphia, and Summit, N.J. A Brooklyn native, William married Janet at the age of 22 and set about completing a residency in podiatry. Their elder son, John, grew up in Newton and did well enough in high school to attend Williams College, one of the nation's most selective. Even so, he beat it home after graduating and has lived with his parents for several years while preparing to apply to graduate school. "A lot of my friends are living at home to save money," he explains.

Tight finances are not all that is driving John's living arrangements. The young man had choices and decided he could opt for more of the ones he wanted if he sheltered under his parents' roof. John is saving money from his job at an arts foundation for a three-week trip to Africa, where he hopes to work on a mobile health-care project in a rural region. It's a strategic choice designed to increase his chances of being accepted into Harvard University's competitive graduate program in public health.

John needs to build up his credentials if he wants to enter a program like that. To get from here to there, he needs more experience working with patients in clinics or out in the field. It takes big bucks to travel to exotic locations, and a master's degree will cost him dearly, too. In order to make good on his aspirations, John needs his parents to cover him for the short run.

On his own, John could pay the rent on an apartment, especially if he had roommates. What he can't afford is to pay for it and travel, to support himself and save for his hoped-for future. Autonomy turns out to be the lesser priority, so he has returned to the bedroom he had before he left for college, and there he stays.

John sees few drawbacks to that arrangement. His parents don't nag him or curtail his freedom. Janet wonders if they should ask him to pay rent, to bring him down to earth a bit and teach him some life skills, like budgeting. William is not so sure. He enjoys his son's company and was happy when John moved back into his old bedroom. Having a son around to talk to is a joy, particularly since John's younger brother is out of the house now, studying at the University of Vermont. That empty nest has refilled, and thank goodness, says William, rather quietly.

If John had no goals, no sense of direction, William would not be at ease with this "boomerang arrangement." Hiding in the basement playing video games would not do. Happily, that is not on John's agenda. William is glad to help his son realize his ambitions. He approves of John's career plans and doesn't really care if they don't involve making a handsome living. What really matters is that the work means something. It will help to remake the world, something William has not felt he

could contribute to very directly as a podiatrist. Having a son who can reach a bit higher—if not financially, then morally—is an ambition worth paying for.

And it will cost this family, big time. William and Janet have invested nearly $200,000 in John's education already. They will need to do more if John is going to become a public-health specialist. They are easily looking at another $50,000, even if John attends a local graduate program and continues to live with them. Whatever it costs, they reason, the sacrifice is worth it.

What is newsworthy, throughout the developed world, is that a growing number of young adults in their 20s and 30s have never been independent. In the United States, we tend to see a boomerang pattern in the affluent upper-middle class, with young people leaving for college and then returning home. Among working-class kids, the tendency is to stay put for the duration. Only one-quarter of today's college students are full time, living on campus, and largely supported by their parents. The norm is to live at home, study part time, work to pay your share, and shelter some of the steepest costs of higher education under the parental roof.

And in most countries—outside of the social democracies—there is far less investment in dormitories and other forms of transitional housing, meager government financial aid, and a historical pattern of pursuing university degrees wherever you grew up. With the labor market turning a cold shoulder to new graduates, simply staying at home seems the only option. Hence in Italy today, 37 percent of men age 30 have never lived away from home. Their counterparts in Spain, Japan, and many other developed countries are following a similar path: Millions are staying at the Inn of Mom and Dad for years, sometimes for several decades longer than was true in earlier generations.

In the United States, we have seen a 50-percent increase since the 1970s in the proportion of people age 30 to 34 who live with their parents. As the recession of 2008–9 continued to deepen, this trend became even more entrenched. Kids who cannot find jobs after finishing college, divorced mothers who can't afford to provide a home for their children, unemployed people at their wits' end, the ranks of the foreclosed—all are beating a path back to their parents' homes to take shelter underneath the only reliable roof available.

To some degree, that has always been the way of the private safety net. Families double up when misfortune derails their members, and the generations that have been lucky enough to buy into an affordable housing market, that enjoyed stable jobs for decades, find they must open their arms (and houses) to receive these economic refugees back into the fold. Blue-collar working-class families and the poor have never known anything different: Their kids have no choice but to stay home while they try to outrun a labor market that has become increasingly inhospitable.

Their parents have had it hard as well, as layoffs have spread through the factories of the Midwest and the South; pooling income across the generations is often the only sensible survival strategy, even if the climate becomes testy.

Until relatively recently, the middle class in most prosperous countries did not need to act as an economic shock absorber for such a prolonged period in the lives of their adult children. Their households might have expanded to take in a divorced offspring or support a child who had taken a nonpaying internship, but the norm for most white-collar parents was to send young people out into the world and look on in satisfaction as they took their places in the corporate world or the professions, found their life mates, and established their own nests.

Why, in the world's most affluent societies, are young (and not-so-young) adults unable to stand on their own two feet? Is it because we have raised a "slacker generation" that is unable or unwilling to take the hard knocks that come with striking out on their own? There are questions of taste lurking here: Young people in the middle class want jobs that are meaningful, rather than a means of putting a roof over their heads. They are not as eager as the "60s generation" of yore was to sleep on floors and wear clothes with holes in exchange for their independence.

And it is not especially painful for many of them to stay at home, because they share a lot of interests with Mom and Dad. Parents and their adult children are not staring at one another over the chasm of a "generation gap," but likely share similar tastes in music, movies, and, in many households, politics. That infamous gap was a product of the disjunctures that separated the generation that came of age in World War II from their boomer children, and it loomed large. But it has not emerged in succeeding generations: The Rolling Stones and Bob Dylan perform to sell-out crowds with gray hairs and twenty-somethings in the audience.

Still, we should not overemphasize the role of taste in spurring the trend toward accordion families. There is an unmistakable structural engine at work. International competition is greater than it once was, and many countries, fearful of losing markets for their goods and services, are responding by restructuring the labor market to cut the wage bill. Countries that regulated jobs to ensure they were full time, well paid, and protected from layoffs now permit part-time, poorly paid jobs and let employers fire without restriction. That may serve the interests of businesses—a debatable low-road strategy—but it has destroyed the options for millions of new entrants to the labor market throughout advanced postindustrial societies.

Japanese workers who once looked forward to lifetime employment with a single firm have gone the way of the dinosaur. American workers have seen the emergence of contingent labor (part-time, part-year, and short-term contracts), downsizing, offshoring, and many other responses to globalization that have exposed the American work force to wage stagnation and insecurity. European labor is arguably facing a very rocky future as the global consequences of the current financial crisis weaken the economies of the European Union and threaten the social protections that made them the envy of the developed world.

Eventually, those conditions will envelop the entire work force. For the time being, though, they are most evident in the lives of the least powerful: new entrants to the labor market, immigrants, and low-skilled workers. The generation emerging from college in the first decade of this century has been struggling to find a foothold in a rapidly changing economy

that cannot absorb its members as it once did, while housing prices—foreclosure epidemics notwithstanding—are making it hard for them to stake a claim to residential independence.

They fall back into the family home because, unless they are willing to take a significant cut in their standard of living, they have no other way to manage the life to which they have become accustomed. Moreover, if they aspire to a professional occupation and the income that goes with it, a goal their parents share for them, it is going to take them a long time and a lot of money to acquire the educational credentials needed to grab that brass ring. Sheltering inside an accordion family leaves more money to pay toward those degrees.

So what's the big deal? In earlier eras, people lived at home until they married. Is there anything new here? Yes and no. For several decades now, middle-class people in the United States, at least, expected to see their children live independently for a number of years before they married, and parents expected to have empty nests once their kids passed the magical mark of 18.

That formation was so widespread that it became a national norm, and it was made possible by a rental housing market and patterns of cohabitation (romantic, roommates) that made independence affordable. And for many, it still is. Yet increasingly the forces of labor-market erosion and rising housing and educational costs have combined to put independence out of reach.

Societal norms—the expectations that people bring to the table when social change is in the air—matter for how parents around the world view these new family formations. In Japan, where I found that parents expect discipline and order, this new trajectory is disturbing and tends to be defined as personal failure. Italian families, by contrast, report that they enjoy having their grown children live with them, however vexing it may be for their government.

Spanish parents and their adult children are angry at their government for facilitating lousy labor contracts that have damaged the children's prospects, but they know that it can be a joy to be near the younger generation.

In America, we deploy a familiar cultural arsenal in crafting meaning: the work ethic and the hope of upward mobility. If Joe lives at home because it will help him get somewhere in the long run, that's fine. If he's hiding in the basement playing video games, it's not fine. The accordion family has to be in the service of larger goals or it smacks of deviance.

All of these adaptations are responses to central structural forces beyond the control of any of us. Global competition is taking us into uncharted waters, reshaping the life course in ways that would have been scarcely visible only 30 years ago. It's a brave new world, and the accordion family is absorbing the blows as best it can.

Critical Thinking

1. What does the author mean by the terms "delayed departure," "boomerang arrangement," and "accordion family?"
2. Do you live with your parents now or anticipate moving back home after college? If so, why? What kinds of

problems or challenges come with living with your parents as an adult?

3. List some historical, economic, cultural, and social factors contributing to "accordion families."

4. What are some ground rules that adult children and their parents should set around their living arrangement?

Create Central

www.mhhe.com/createcentral

Internet References

AARP Blog: Boomerang Kids
http://blog.aarp.org/tag/boomerang-kids

National Council on Family Relations
www.ncfr.com

Article

Prepared by: Patricia Hrusa Williams,
University of Maine at Farmington

Daddy Issues
Why Caring For My Aging Father Has Me Wishing He Would Die

Sandra Tsing Loh

Learning Outcomes

After reading this article, you will be able to:

- Identify the financial and emotional burdens adult children face in caring for their aging parents.

- Describe how role reversal in parent–child relationships alters family dynamics.

- Identify supports needed by adult children caring for their aging parents.

Recently, a colleague at my radio station asked me, in the most cursory way, as we were waiting for the coffee to finish brewing, how I was. To my surprise, in a motion as automatic as the reflex of a mussel being poked, my body bent double and I heard myself screaming:

"I WAAAAAAAANT MY FATHERRRRRR TO DIEEEEE!!!"

Startled, and subtly stepping back to put a bit more distance between us, my coworker asked what I meant.

"What I mean, Rob, is that even if, while howling like a banshee, I tore my 91-year-old father limb from limb with my own hands in the town square, I believe no jury of my peers would convict me. Indeed, if they knew all the facts, I believe any group of sensible, sane individuals would actually roll up their shirtsleeves and pitch in."

As I hyperventilated over the coffee-maker, scattering Splenda packets and trying to unclaw my curled fingers, I realized it had finally happened: at 49, I had become a Kafka character. I am thinking of "The Judgment," in which the protagonist's supposedly old and frail father suddenly kicks off his bedclothes with surprisingly energetic—even girlish—legs and, standing ghoulishly tall in the bed, delivers a speech so horrifying, so unexpected, and so perfectly calculated to destroy his son's spirit that his son—who until this point has been having a rather pleasant day writing a letter to a friend, amidst a not unpleasant year marked by continuing financial prosperity and a propitious engagement to a well-placed young woman— immediately *jumps off a bridge.*

Clearly, my nonagenarian father and I have what have come to be known as "issues," which I will enumerate shortly. By way of introduction, however, let us begin by considering *A Bittersweet Season,* by Jane Gross. A journalist for 29 years at *The New York Times* and the founder of a *Times* blog called The New Old Age, Gross is hardly Kafkaesque. An ultra-responsible daughter given to drawing up to-do lists for caregivers and pre-loosening caps on Snapple bottles, Gross undertook the care of her mother in as professional a way as possible. She was on call for emergencies and planned three steps ahead by consulting personally with each medical specialist. Like the typical U.S. family caregiver for an elder (who is, statistics suggest, a woman of about 50), Gross worked full-time, but (atypically) she was unencumbered by spouse or children. She had the help, too, of her child-free brother, a calm, clear-headed sort given to greeting his sister with a quiet, reassuring "The eagle has landed." What could go wrong?

Plenty. As Gross herself flatly describes it, in her introduction:

> In the space of three years . . . my mother's ferocious independence gave way to utter reliance on her two adult children. Garden-variety aches and pains became major health problems; halfhearted attention no longer sufficed, and managing her needs from afar became impossible. . . . We were flattened by the enormous demands on our time, energy, and bank accounts; the disruption to our professional and personal lives; the fear that our time in this parallel universe would never end and the guilt for wishing that it would. . . . We knew nothing about Medicaid spend-downs, in-hospital versus out-of-hospital "do not resuscitate" orders, Hoyer lifts, motorized wheelchairs, or assistive devices for people who can neither speak nor type. We knew nothing about "pre-need consultants," who handle advance payment for the funerals of people who aren't dead yet, or "feeders," whose job it is to spoon pureed food into the mouths of men and women who can no longer hold a utensil.

However ghoulish, it is a world we will all soon get to know well, argues Gross: owing to medical advancements, cancer deaths now peak at age 65 and kill off just 20 percent of older Americans, while deaths due to organ failure peak at about 75 and kill off just another 25 percent, so the norm for seniors is becoming a long, drawn-out death after 85, requiring ever-increasing assistance for such simple daily activities as eating, bathing, and moving.

This is currently the case for approximately 40 percent of Americans older than 85, the country's fastest-growing demographic, which is projected to more than double by 2035, from about 5 million to 11.5 million. And at that point, here comes the next wave—77 million of the youngest Baby Boomers will be turning 70.

Quick back-of-the-envelope calculation, for Baby Boomers currently shepherding the Greatest Generation to their final reward? Hope your aged parents have at least half a million dollars apiece in the bank, because if they are anything like Mama Gross, their care until death will absorb every penny. To which an anxious (let's say 49-year-old) daughter might respond: But what about long-term-care insurance? In fact, Gross's own mother had purchased it, and while it paid for some things, the sum was a pittance compared with a final family outlay of several hundred thousand dollars. But how about what everyone says about "spending down" in order to qualify for Medicare, Medicaid, Medi-Cal, or, ah—which exactly is it?

Unfortunately, those hoping for a kind of *Eldercare for Dummies* will get no easy answers from *A Bittersweet Season.* Chides Gross: "Medicaid is a confusing and potentially boring subject, depending on how you feel about numbers and abstruse government policy, but it's essential for you to understand." Duly noted—so I read the relevant section several times and . . . I still don't understand. All I can tell you is that the Medicaid mess has to do with some leftover historical quirks of the Johnson administration, colliding with today's much longer life expectancies, colliding with a host of federal and state regulations that intertwine with each other in such a calcified snarl that by contrast—in a notion I never thought I'd utter—public education looks hopeful. Think of the Hoyer lift that can be delivered but never repaired, or the feeder who will not push, or the pusher who will not feed.

But it gets worse. Like an unnaturally iridescent convalescent-home maraschino cherry atop this Sisyphean slag heap of woe, what actually appears to take the greatest toll on caregivers is the sheer emotional burden of this (formless, thankless, seemingly endless) project. For one thing, unresolved family dynamics will probably begin to play out: "Every study I have seen on the subject of adult children as caregivers finds the greatest source of stress, by far, to be not the ailing parent but sibling disagreements," Gross writes. Further, experts concur, "the daughter track is, by a wide margin, harder than the mommy track, emotionally and practically, because it has no happy ending and such an erratic and unpredictable course." Gross notes, I think quite rightly, that however put-upon working parents feel (and we do keeningly complain, don't we—oh the baby-proofing! oh the breast-pumping! oh the day care!), we can at least plan employment breaks around such relative foreseeables as pregnancy, the school year, and holidays. By contrast, ailing seniors trigger crises at random—falls in the bathroom, trips to the emergency room, episodes of wandering and forgetting and getting lost. Wearied at times by the loneliness of the daughter track, Gross writes, in a rare moment of black humor:

> I know that at the end of my mother's life I felt isolated in my plight, especially compared to colleagues being feted with showers and welcomed back to work with oohs and aahs at new baby pictures. I was tempted, out of pure small-mindedness, to put on my desk a photo of my mother, slumped in her wheelchair.

Those seeking a more hopeful take on this bittersweet season might turn, for momentary comparison, to *Passages in Caregiving,* by Gail Sheehy. Reading Sheehy is always a boost—even when she's rewriting some Passage she predicted 10 or 20 or 30 years ago, as is necessarily (and, given our ever-increasing life spans, probably will continue to be necessarily) the case. From her intro (as swingingly nostalgic—isn't it, almost?—as Burt Bacharach):

> In my books and speeches since 1995, when I published *New Passages* [the first update of the original *Passages*], I keep predicting liberation ahead—the advent of a Second Adulthood, starting in one's midforties and fifties. At that proud age, having checked off most "shoulds," people generally feel a new sense of mastery. Haven't you done your best to please your parents, your mentor, your boss, and your mate, and now it's time for you? The children are making test flights on their way to piloting solo. Your parents have become giddy globetrotters, piling up frequent-flier miles and e-mailing playful photos of themselves riding camels. . . . Now you can finally earn that degree, start your own business, run for office, master another language, invent something, or write that book you keep mulling.

Ominous new paragraph—to reflect tire-screeching 21st century update:

> Then you get The Call.

In Sheehy's case, The Call was a cancer diagnosis for her husband, Clay Felker, which kicked off an almost two-decade period of medical battles before his death (which was actually not, in the end, from cancer). Although Sheehy offers her book as an umbrella guide for all caregivers, weaving her personal experience together with a demographically wide range of case studies, it strikes this caregiver as less than universal. For one thing—and in fact this is a tribute to how engagingly Sheehy tells her story—even with a tube in his stomach (for which sympathetic chefs blended gourmet food at Paris bistros, whereupon he continued to charm dinner guests as usual in his handsome navy-blue blazer), Clay Felker, on the page anyway, is still pretty great company. And then, to further vanquish the blues, Sheehy and Felker rented a houseboat, spent the summer in France . . . (How is it that, no matter what, Boomers always seem to be having more fun?)

And while there is some aesthetic appeal to Sheehy's mandala-like formulation of the caregiver's journey being not a straight path but a labyrinth (whose eight turnings are Shock and Mobilization, the New Normal, Boomerang, Playing God, "I Can't Do This Anymore!", Coming Back, the In-Between Stage, and the Long Goodbye), this taxonomy feels more descriptive than helpful. Also, her take on what one learns when caring for one's failing loved one is, if not quite a Hallmark card, certainly the best possible case:

> It opens up the greatest possibilities for true intimacy and reconnection at the deepest level. The sharing of strengths and vulnerabilities, without shame, fosters love. And for some caregivers, this role offers a chance in Second Adulthood to compose a more tender sequel to the troubled family drama of our First Adulthood. We can become better than our younger selves.

Jane Gross also believes spiritual growth is possible, but her take, predictably, is far less rosy, even verging on Old Testament:

> Here we are, not just with a herculean job but with a front-row seat for this long, slow dying. We want to do all we realistically can to ease the suffering, smooth the passing, of our loved ones. But we also have the opportunity to watch what happens to our parents, listen to what they have to say to us, and use that information to look squarely at our own mortality and prepare as best we can for the end of our own lives.

For herself, insists Gross: "I can tell you now that it was worth every dreadful minute, a transformative experience." And the inspiring lesson? Here it is, as expressed in a sere opening quotation by May Sarton: "I have seen in you what courage can be when there is no hope."

Clearly, various ruminations on the meaning of the caregiver's "journey" will continue, as ever more literature is added to the caregiving genre, as ever more of us spend ever more of our days belaying loved ones in Hoyer lifts like stricken beef cattle. That said, while I do carry a datebook festooned with soothing nature photography and the proverbs of the Buddhist nun Pema Chödrön (the sort of curious artifact 50-ish women like myself receive as Christmas gifts, along with very tiny—to reduce calories—lavender-and-sea-salt-infused gourmet chocolates), I myself have yet to see any pitch for the spiritual benefit of this grim half-million-dollar odyssey that is remotely inviting. To quote Amy Winehouse, who didn't want to go to rehab: No, no, no!

No . . . No . . . No. What I propose instead is seeking comfort in what I like to call, borrowing in part from Kafka's German, *Elderschadenfreude*. On the one hand, sure, here we stand around the office coffeemaker in middle age, mixing flax into our Greek yogurt and sharing more and more tales about our elderly parents, tales that are dull ("Mom slipped in the shower—at first she said it was nothing"), slow-moving ("And then I took her to the foot doctor, but then, right there in the parking lot, she insisted she had to go to the bathroom—but the door is on the *north* side while we were on the *south*—"), and in the end, well, depressingly predictable (we already know which colleges our wards are getting into—NONE). On the other

hand, I believe it is by enduring this very suffering and tedium that one can eventually tease out a certain dark, autumnal, delightfully-bitter-as-Fernet-Branca enjoyment, best described by some dense and complicated noun-ending German word.

Elderschadenfreude is the subtle frisson of the horror tale that always begins so simply ("Mom slipped in the shower—at first she said it was nothing") but makes listeners raise eyebrows, nod knowingly, begin microwaving popcorn. It is the secret pleasure of hearing about aging parents that are even more impossible than yours. Prepare to enjoy.

My father's old age began so well. Back in his 70s, to prepare for his sunset years, this Chinese widower had taken the precaution of procuring (after some stunning misfires) his retirement plan: an obedient Chinese-immigrant wife, almost 20 years younger than himself, who, in exchange for citizenship, would—unlike American women—accept the distinctly nonfeminist role of cutting up his fruit and massaging his bunions. In addition to doing all that, said Chinese wife, Alice, helped my dad run the informal Craigslist-peopled boarding house he had turned our family home into, for which her reward would be a generous inheritance upon his death, and the right to live in the house until hers. It is a measure of my dad's frugality that he didn't even buy health insurance for Alice until she turned 65—he rolled the statistical dice against the premiums, and won! With $2,000 a month from renters, on top of a Social Security check of $1,500, he and Alice were actually *making* money. What with their habit of taking buses everywhere and a shared love of Dumpster diving, they could star in their own reality show about thrift.

This is not to say my father has been completely "well." After age 78, if you asked him "How are you?" he would exclaim: "I'm dying!" At his 80th-birthday party, when he tremulously lifted his centimeter of red wine while watching my girlfriends dance, I mourned his visible frailty. At 82, he was passing out on bus benches, hitting his head, causing his doctors to insist on a pacemaker (which he refused). By 85, battling Parkinson's, he was still hobbling down to the beach to attempt rickety calisthenics and swimming, but "he's barely *swimming* in those two feet of water," my older sister worried. "It's more like falling." By 89, he was so slowed, like a clock winding down, that, never mind going to the beach, one morning he couldn't even get out of bed.

That was when he called me, in fear and confusion, for help. A pulse-pounding hourlong drive later, arriving at his bedside, I found to my panic that I could not rouse him. He lay in that waxy, inert, folded-up pose that looks unmistakably like death (I had seen it when my mother died, of early Alzheimer's, at 69). "This is it—it's really it—Papa's dead," I wept over the phone, long-distance, to my sister. And I remember, as the dust motes danced in the familiar golden light of our family home, how my sister and I found ourselves spontaneously, tumblingly observing to each other how we were sad . . . and yet oddly at peace.

Yes, my history with this man has been checkered: in my childhood, he had been cruelly cheap (no Christmas, no heat);

in my teens, he had been unforgivably mean to my mother; in my 20s, I rebelled and fled; in my 30s, I softened and we became wry friends—why not, he couldn't harm me now; in my 40s, sensing that these were the last days of a fading elder, the memories of whom I would reflect on with increasing nostalgia, the door opened for real affection, even a kind of gratitude. After all, I had benefited professionally from using him as fodder for my writing (as he had benefited financially for years by forging my signature so I ended up paying his taxes—ah, the great circle of life).

In short, there was real grief now at seeing my father go, but I was a big girl—actually, a middle-aged woman, with some 1,000 hours of therapy behind me—and, chin up, I would get through it. Unlike in the case of my mother, who had left too early, my business here was done. I had successfully completed my Kübler-Ross stages.

The conundrum that morning in the dining room (where my father's bed was), however, was that although my father wasn't rouseable, he wasn't actually dead. (He has a lizard-like resting pulse of 36, so even in his waking state, he's sort of like the undead.) I called the Malibu paramedics, who carted him to the emergency room and stuck an IV in. An hour later, the surprisingly benign diagnosis? Simple dehydration.

With a sudden angry snort, my father woke up. I won't say I wish I had hit him over the head with a frying pan to finish the job when it seemed we were so, so close. But I will say that when my dad woke up that day, my problems really began. Because what this episode made clear was that, while nothing was wrong with my dad, although he was 89—89!—something was wrong with Alice, who was supposed to be taking care of him. Her penchant for gibbering Chinese was not, as we'd imagined, a symptom of her English skills' plateauing after 15 years in America, but of the early or middle stages of dementia. This, I hadn't expected, because, as I remind you, she is much younger than my father. Alice's age is . . . drum-roll . . . 72.

So now, aside from neglecting my elderly father, the formerly mild-mannered Alice is starting to disturb the tenants: waving butcher knives at them, hurling their things into the street. (What a fun life they're having—my father believes some of the more sturdy renters can pitch in and "help shower" him. Best to think twice before renting a room off Craigslist!) Alice is increasingly found wandering at 2 A.M. on freeways in places like Torrance (50 miles away), and is ever more routinely brought home in the dead of night by various police officers and firemen (your tax dollars at work!). And in contrast to her formerly frugal ways, Alice no longer understands money. At one point, my father called the police because she was hitting him—not to have her arrested but, as my dad says, just to "scare" her. To evade capture, she ran away with a duffel bag stuffed with their passports, marriage certificate, immigration papers, and two small, tightly packed envelopes, one with exactly 13 crisp $1 bills inside it and another with a Keystone Kops–type mélange of Chinese money, Turkish money, and . . . as I said, upon discovery, to my sister: "I didn't know Bill Nye the Science Guy *had* his own currency!"

When I gave Alice the bag (returned by the police), she accused me of stealing $2,000 from it. Meanwhile, forensic analysis reveals she had withdrawn $13,000, gone to a bank in Chinatown, and purchased a useless universal life-insurance policy, an event she cannot recall. My father does not want Alice to move to assisted living, however, because he enjoys her cooking. So the solution for Alice is a full-time Mandarin-speaking female companion. At $5,000 a month, this service is a relative bargain if it keeps Alice from withdrawing, and flinging to the winds, her next $50,000. (And who knows *where* all these mysterious accounts are? I'm trying to find out, I'm trying!) Meanwhile, armed with his own capable full-time Filipino male nurse (another $5,000 a month), my father has roared back with formidable energy. As long as he's hydrated, it appears that no bacterium can fell him—remember, he has been eating out of Dumpsters (we're talking expired sushi) for *several decades already*. (Who knows if he hasn't morphed into another life form, possibly amphibian?) Which is to say, now I have a wheelchair-bound but extremely active 91-year-old who greatly enjoys getting bathed and diapered and fed ice cream and crashing UCLA science lectures and, oh, by the way—every day he calls me now: he wants SEX. He proudly needs only 1/16th of a Viagra pill for SEX. Because Alice is no longer complying (she is unfortunately not quite that crazy), and because I have not—yet?—caved (although if one Googles this issue, one will find to one's horror the phrase *healing hands*!), my father has started to proposition Alice's lady nurse, trying to grab her breasts, begging her to touch him. Which he can't do himself, as he can barely clasp his hand around a spoon.

What would Gail Sheehy call this particular new Passage, aside from, peppily, "The New Normal"? Outdoing the "giddy globetrotters" in Sheehy's midlife Boomertopia, my father would park his wheelchair on top of the camel, then get pitched headfirst from the camel, then probably try to molest the camel. Eternally leaping up, like a ghoul, he is the über-Kafka father.

But there's more. My father's care demands an ever-changing flotilla of immigrant caregivers, of whom the chief one is Thomas. Because my father is so difficult, it's not atypical for new caregivers to quit before noon. The miraculously tolerant Thomas is the only nurse who has stuck with my father, which means that my sister, brother, and I basically work for Thomas. We've co-signed on an apartment for him and his wife and four children, who just emigrated from the Philippines; we've fixed up a beater car for him (which I've spent many a weekday smogging, re-smogging, insuring, handicapped-plating). We do all this because Thomas does an excellent job, always trying to raise the standard of my dad's care. Which is a good thing. Or is it?

Thomas is concerned about my dad's regularity. The cranberry pills and stool softeners I regularly deliver from Costco have worked to a point, yes, but now Thomas has hit upon something better: milk of magnesia. Problem is, the product is so effective that when my father is given it before bed, *although* he has finally consented to wearing an adult diaper at night, within four hours he is at capacity and begins fouling his sheets. Hence, Thomas has started finishing his 10-hour day by sleeping in my father's room at night, for which, of course, he must be given a raise, to $6,500 a month.

Thomas is optimistic. He ends conversations about the overflowing diapers with this cheerful reassurance: "I will get your Papa to 100!"

Oh my God—how could he *say* such a horrible thing? I am hyperventilating again. Okay. Never mind the question of whether, given that they have total freedom and no responsibilities, we are indulging our elders in the same way my generation has been famously indulging our overly entitled children. Never mind the question of whether there is a reasonable point at which parents lose their rights, and for the good of society we get to lock them up and medicate them.

The question that really haunts me, and that I feel I must raise now, is: At these prices, exactly how much time do I have to spend *listening to stories about my dad defecating*?

I rant to myself: He is taking everything! He is taking all the money. He's taken years of my life (sitting in doctors' offices, in pharmacies, in waiting rooms). With his horrid, selfish, grotesque behavior, he's chewed through every shred of my sentimental affection for him. He's taken the serenity I fought for—and won—in 1,000 hours of therapy centered on my family. In fact, he's destroyed my belief in "family" as a thing that buoys one up. Quite the opposite: family is like the piano around Holly Hunter's ankle, dragging me implacably down.

I have to ensure Hilton-level care for my barely Motel 6 father, the giant baby, as well as for his caregiver, the big-baby nurse, all caught up with the high-pitched drama of feeding and diapering and massaging. That's right: my family is throwing all our money away on powdering our 91-year-old dad's giant-baby ass, leaving nothing for my sweet little daughters, with their thoughts of unicorns and poetry and dance, my helpless little daughters, who, in the end, represent me! In short, on top of everything else he has taken from me, he has taken away my entire sense of self, because at age almost-50, it appears that I too have become a squalling baby!!!

The other day, my writer friend Laura was doing her own woeful monologue—and how they all just continue, like leaves falling—about her dad.

"He has learned *nothing* in 78 years. He has no wisdom. He has no soul. He insults me. He ignores his grandchildren. How much longer do I need to keep having a relationship with him?"

We were walking in the hills above Griffith Park, which turn into the grassy slopes of Forest Lawn, which put me in mind of the ending of one of the best memoirs I have ever read—and, come to think of it, perhaps the only book one will ever need—about difficult parents, Bernard Cooper's *The Bill From My Father*. The title comes from the day Cooper received a bill from his lawyer father, typed on his customary onionskin paper, demanding immediate reimbursement for parenting outlays (including an entire childhood's worth of groceries and clothing) in the amount of $2 million. Cooper Sr. escalated the pain, upon his other sons' deaths, by not just sending their widows bills but filing actual lawsuits against them.

Still, Cooper continues to have an on-again, off-again relationship with Cooper the Elder (whose history with his sons can be summed up by the progression of painted signs on the front of his law-office door, as telling as a piece of concrete poetry: COOPER; COOPER & COOPER; COOPER, COOPER & COOPER; COOPER, COOPER, COOPER & COOPER; COOPER, COOPER & COOPER; COOPER & COOPER; COOPER). Their relationship eventually drew the interest of a publisher—did Cooper want to write a book about his father? As Cooper recalls:

It would be foolish to refuse her offer because . . . Well, because money was involved, but also because the rest of my family was gone forever and Dad was all I had left, though I wasn't sure what constituted "all." Or "Dad" for that matter.

He quotes from John Cheever's short story "Reunion": " 'My father,' thinks the son, 'was my future and my doom.' " The memoir concludes with a wonderful Forest Lawn cemetery scene (his father's punchy epitaph: YOU FINALLY GOT ME).

I almost don't know what I envy Bernard Cooper for more—his incomparable literary genius or the fact that his father is *dead*. (Anti-*Elderschadenfreude*.)

The paradox is, I can't miss the good things about my father while he is alive, but I will of course miss him . . . when he is dead. By the same token—and perhaps this is the curious blessing—if my mother were alive today (what would she be, 84?), she would be driving me *insane*!!!

But then, inevitably, comes (at least in my Pema Chödrön calendar) yet another day. And indeed, inspired by my Buddhist stationery, what I decide I will let go of today is any of the previous ideas I had about future planning—the college tuitions, paying off the house, putting together some kind of retirement. . . .

Then again, in the new America, shouldn't the wealth be re-equalized from generation to generation? Is it not somewhat fitting that the Loh family's nest egg should be used to put not our children but Thomas's through college, as Andrew Carnegie advocated? ("I will get your Papa to 100!") Is that really the worst use of this money? Indeed, I muse slyly, perhaps, unlike my own Western daughters, jazz shoes and drawing pads (how useless!) spilling out of their bags, Thomas's children will actually buckle down and get real majors, leading to real jobs—doctor, engineer, or, most lucrative of all . . . *geriatric nurse*.

So I feel a little calmer today, as I deliver my raft of pills. And I find it is a rare calm day at my father's house as well. The various triaging schemes are holding. Thomas has the house smelling soapy, white sheets cover sagging couches, vases hold artificial flowers, medications are arranged on various bureaus in proud and almost spectacular displays. For today, Thomas's beater car runs. For today, Alice is medicated, and therefore pleasant. She serves a mysterious bell-pepper dish that—aside from being wildly spicy—is edible. My father's hair has never been more poofy—or black. He too is vaguely fragrant. Could be his lucky day. SEX.

I have to acknowledge, too, that in traditional China, with its notions of filial responsibility, my elders would be living with me in my home, or I in theirs. So the beautiful oh-so-Western thing is that, for today, I can drive away. And as I drive down PCH—dipping celery into Greek yogurt sprinkled with flax, dropping it all over my sweatpants—I realize that because things are not actually terrible (no cops, no paramedics, no $13,000 bank withdrawals), today qualifies as a fabulous day.

I can no longer think of my dad as my "father." But I recognize in him something as familiar to me as myself. To the end, stubborn, babyish, life-loving, he doesn't want to go to rehab, no, no, no.

Critical Thinking

1. Why does the author sometimes wish her elderly father would die? Is she being selfish in saying this? Why or why not? Do you think other adult children feel this way but do not say anything?

2. What are some of the financial and emotional burdens adult children face in caring for their aging parents?

3. How does the reversal in roles that occurs when children become caregivers for their parents alter family and relationship dynamics?

4. What types of supports do adult children need as they try to meet the needs of their own families and their aging parents?

Create Central

www.mhhe.com/createcentral

Internet References

National Center on Caregiving
www.caregiver.org

National Council on Aging
www.ncoa.org

Alzheimer's Association
www.alz.org

SANDRA TSING LOH is the author, most recently, of *Mother on Fire*.

Article   Prepared by: Patricia Hrusa Williams, *University of Maine at Farmington*

Baby Boomers Care for Grandchildren as Daughters Pursue Careers

Working mothers unanimously agree that raising children is like war. They have to fight for the spare time needed for their children, fight in a workplace inconsiderate of working mothers, and fight against the temptation to give up a career for child raising. The auxiliary troops are their baby boomer parents.

KIM EUN-HA

Learning Outcomes

After reading this article, you will be able to:

- Identify reasons why grandparents are becoming "second parents."

- Provide examples of the problems experienced in maternity leave policies and in finding high-quality child care for working families.

- Explain some of the pros and cons of grandparents providing care for their grandchildren.

Ms. Lee, 66 years old, seems to be living her life all over again. After raising her two children and seeing them get married, she has been playing the role of a mother again for the past 10 years. Her daughter, Ms. Cho, is a medical doctor at a university hospital in Seoul, and mother of two children, who are fifth and second graders. While Ms. Cho works at the hospital during the day, Ms. Lee takes care of her grandchildren. Ms. Cho leaves home at 7 A.M. and returns home around 8 P.M. at the earliest. She cannot possibly care for her children and prepare their meals. If she works a night shift or an emergency arises, her return home is even later. Her children come home from school between noon and 3 P.M. In place of Ms. Cho, her mother takes care of the children, preparing snacks and coordinating their after-school activities, such as taekwondo and piano lessons.

Learning about Childcare for First Time

Although Ms. Cho has been married 10 years, she still depends heavily on her parents. And Ms. Lee might not have imagined that she would be caring for her grandchildren all this while. She intended to help out until her daughter could place her children in daycare. But her daughter could not find a daycare center that provided extended hours of supervision. So she concluded that moving in with her parents would be the most practical solution. Her mother, understanding the situation, could not refuse. Besides, she enjoyed spending time with her lovely grandchildren.

Ms. Cho's husband, for his part, had to accept living with his parents-in-law for the sake of the children, even if such an arrangement can cause occasional discomfort. In important family matters, such as the children's education and personal pursuits, the mother-in-law's word would often hold absolute sway. The couple, however, believes that they are fortunate. They know many working couples who struggle to take care of their children because none of their parents will help out with the responsibilities.

As ever more young couples rely on their parents to care for their children, an increasing number of men in their 50s and 60s have taken on childcare roles. In Korea's aging society, with improved prospects of living until 100, middle-aged men who are retired find themselves with time on their hands and have thus come to look after their grandchildren.

Retired two years ago, 62-year-old Mr. Kim is now wholly dedicated to raising his two-year-old granddaughter. He agreed to help out because his daughter-in-law needed to work when his son decided to belatedly attend graduate school. The daughter's family lives in the same apartment complex as Mr. Kim and his wife, so the granddaughter is dropped off at their apartment in the morning and picked up in the evening. When the parents come home late, the girl stays with her grandparents overnight. Mr. Kim's wife is not as physically capable, so he takes charge of physical activity with his granddaughter. He also searches the Internet to read up about childcare.

Feeling empty after retiring from his work of 30 years, he says, "I overcame my depression by enjoying my grandchild's lovable antics." He starts and ends each day playing with his granddaughter. Sometimes he goes out to play golf or to hike with friends, but he tries to get back early enough to pick up his granddaughter from the daycare center.

Mr. Kim explains, "I don't have many memories of my own children growing up; from my 30s, I was always so busy." He adds, "I'm learning about childcare for the first time through raising my granddaughter."

New Reality Requires 'Second Parents'

Korean law provides for three months of maternity leave, and up to one year of childcare leave, so a total of 15 months can be used for staying home to care for a new baby. Korea is now facing the demographic dilemma that the world's most economically advanced countries have also experienced. The country's total fertility rate (TFR, the average number of births a woman can expect to have during her child-bearing years), which was over 6.0 in the 1960s, plunged to 1.08, one of the lowest in the world, as of 2006. The Korean government has thus implemented various policy measures to encourage families to have more children. But the changes that make a real difference, particularly in the workplace culture, are always slower to take root than intended.

Most working mothers on maternity leave get a phone call from their workplace, asking when they are coming back, far earlier than the conclusion of their childcare leave. Although companies say that they just want to know how long the position will have to be left open, they often hint that working mothers should return as soon as possible if they don't want to burden their colleagues; the implied message is they should quit if they want to stay away for so long. Undoubtedly, the situation today is far improved from that of just 10 years ago, when no such leave was offered. Few working mothers, however, will dare to use the full period of leave authorized by law, especially if the workplace's prevailing practice is for mothers to return earlier.

But, in order to return to their workplace, they have to find a reliable childcare facility. Ms. Park, a working mother, registered her child at a daycare center near her home immediately after registering the birth itself, but she received number 310 on the waiting list. Ms. Park wants to leave her child in daycare in two years, but she was told that she cannot be assured of her child's admission at that time. Ms. Park says, "If there is a good daycare center that will take my child, I am willing to move near there."

There are 39,842 daycare centers throughout the country, not a small number in light of Korea's low fertility rate (1.24 in 2011), which is far short of the replacement level of 2.01 births per female. But the number of daycare centers that mothers would prefer is far fewer as not all daycare centers provide quality childcare. Every year, accidents from unsafe conditions and child abuse incidents make the news, which make mothers even more selective. The number of reliable public daycare centers operated by the government is only 2,116, less than 5 percent of the total. That is why increasing the number of public daycare centers is one of the basic campaign pledges that politicians emphasize in every election.

The problem of childcare, however, is not entirely solved even if a child is admitted to a reputable daycare facility. Most daycare centers conclude their regular programs at 3 P.M. So for parents who have to pick up their child later in the evening, some facilities provide extended hours, but even those will close by 7 P.M.

The problem is that daycare centers strictly enforce their closing time, while this is not true of workplaces. Officially, the typical workday ends about 6 P.M., but leaving the workplace promptly at that time can be a challenge. Meetings that run late or get-togethers with co-workers can create problems for working mothers as well. A client meeting sometimes extends to dinner. There are very few family-friendly workplaces where a mother can easily call in late or be excused when a child is sick, or leave work to attend a school activity. The Ministry of Gender Equality and Family provides encouragement to such workplaces through the award of "Family-Friendly Enterprise" certificates. The fact that such an award even exists proves that there are not many companies that offer such flexibility.

Working mothers who lack "second parents" ready and able to help out at any time have little choice but to surrender. Statistics starkly show how young Korean women's career aspirations are drastically curtailed around the time they marry and start raising a family. The university entrance rate for girls in Korea is 75 percent, higher than that for boys (70.2 percent). So there is no gender discrimination in getting an education. On the other hand, the economic activity rate of Korean women stands at a mere 49.7 percent, falling far below that of Korean men (73.1 percent), and also lower than the average of OECD countries (61.8 percent). By looking at the statistical trends, you can find the reason for this situation. The economic activity rate of women in their 20s is 71.4 percent, relatively comparable to that of men, but in their 30s, the rate plummets to 55.4 percent. Between their late 20s and mid-30s, a substantial number of women exit the workforce due to marriage and childcare.

Live-in Help Not a Feasible Option

Working mothers who don't give up and keep struggling have to choose between living with parents and hiring a full-time babysitter or live-in nanny. Not all working mothers, however, can seriously consider these options. In order to live with parents, their agreement and support is required, whereas a live-in nanny is beyond the means of most families.

Take the case of 34-year-old Ms. Lee, an office worker. She has two boys, four and two years old. The end of her workday is variable. Even after her regular workday, there are evening get-togethers, and she often has to work on weekends. In her case, she has a live-in babysitter. She had hoped that her parents or her in-laws would help care for her children, but in the end everyone refused to make such a commitment. Her mother-in-law had already told her before the wedding that she doesn't want to sacrifice her mid-life freedom because of grandchildren. Ms. Lee's mother, who had already helped out her two older sisters, adamantly said, "No more sacrifices."

I don't have many memories of my own children growing up; from my 30s, I was always so busy. I'm learning about childcare for the first time through raising my granddaughter.

Ms. Lee pays her Korean-Chinese nanny 1,800,000 won (about $1,700) a month, more than a third of her salary. For a Korean babysitter, she would have to pay at least 20 percent more than that. In the past two years, she changed babysitters three times. She had to terminate the first babysitter for incompetence, while the other two quit because the job was too demanding. Ms. Lee says, "There are few choices, even if you can pay a lot. The key is to maintain a good relationship with the babysitter. Working mothers who have to put their kids in someone else's care are in a weak position."

Even for couples who can leave their children in their parent's care, things don't always go smoothly. When a mother or a mother-in-law assumes responsibility for her grandchildren, she also expects to exercise influence, which can lead to tension and conflict. The authority of the child's parents can be undermined, while placing significant demands on the grandparents. Internet communities that provide forums for working mothers are invariably swamped with complaints about the stress which results from their need for childcare and interference from their otherwise well-meaning parents and in-laws. For some women in their 50s and 60s, taking care of grandchildren can take a toll on their health; they often complain about depression.

According to "Leisure Activities of People in their 50s in Urban Areas," a study published by the Korea Institute for Health and Social Affairs, more than half (52.3 percent) of the survey respondents said they rarely engage in outdoor or sport activities, such as fishing or hiking. Only 22.7 percent have more than one or two outdoor activities every six months; even fewer, a mere 15.2 percent, have one or two activities a month. These statistics are based on a survey of 453 Korean men and women born between 1955 and 1963. The study suggests that because this generation lived their childhood immediately after the Korean War, they not only tend to care less about how to spend leisure time, but they also have little leisure time because they are busy helping to care for their grandchildren.

Return of Extended Families

Raising grandchildren can be a benefit for retired couples because it offers a helpful means to earn pocket money to supplement their income. Young couples who place their child in their parent's care are often generous in paying compensation to their parents, but it's still cheaper than having a babysitter. Many retirees prefer to babysit their grandchildren, as a source of regular income, than having to work as a security guard for an apartment complex or as a cashier at a grocery store. The childcare situation thus has led to a revival of the traditional extended family, which had been, on the whole, displaced by the nuclear family in modern Asian countries. When three or more generations can live together under one roof or close by, the family can share parenting responsibilities so that children can be nurtured in a safe environment, young couples can pursue their careers without undue worry, and elderly couples get financial aid and self-satisfaction.

Even with the government's campaign to boost the number of births, the country's fertility rate in 2011 stood at only 1.24, still at the bottom of OECD countries (a newspaper recently reported that Korea's TFR may have reached 1.3 in 2012). Although the education level and economic activity rate of women have risen dramatically, the rate of social change remains slow. Parents of the baby boomer generation have become the "reserve parents" for their grandchildren, by attending childcare classes offered by district governments and preparing themselves to care for the baby expected by their working daughter. Working mothers, in their endeavors to balance work and family, are helping to revive and redefine the traditional extended family in the 21st century, thanks to their parents' sacrifices.

Critical Thinking

1. While this article was written based on the experience of families in Korea, what are some similarities to experiences of working families here in the United States?

2. What are some challenges of having grandparents provide care for their grandchildren while their parents work?

3. Using information gained from this article, describe an intervention or support program that could be developed to facilitate the positive development of children and families when grandparents provide childcare for their grandchildren.

Create Central

www.mhhe.com/createcentral

Internet References

Alliance for Family, Friend, and Neighbor Care
http://www.familyfriendandneighbor.com/index.html

Families and Work Institute
www.familiesandwork.org

National Council on Aging
www.ncoa.org

Unit 4

UNIT

Prepared by: Patricia Hrusa Williams, *University of Maine at Farmington*

Challenges and Opportunities

Stress is life and life is stress. Sometimes stress in families gives new meaning to this statement. When a stressful event occurs in families, many processes occur simultaneously as families and their members try to cope with the stressor and its effects. One thing that can result is a reduction in family members' ability to act as resources for each other. Indeed, a stressor can overwhelm the family system, and family members may be among the least effective people in coping with each other's behavior. In this unit, we consider a wide variety of stressful life events and crises families may experience. Some are normative, stressful life events which occur as families evolve and change. Families add and lose family members. Family members age and one's health can fail. Individuals experience changes in employment and the need to balance work-family concerns as families develop and change.

There are also other non-normative, stressful life events and crises which many families experience. Marital partners may stray and grow apart. Marriages can fail and break-up. Divorced spouses remarry and create new families. A family member may be called on to serve their country and be separated from their family for a period of time. Children and adults in the family can be diagnosed with chronic illnesses or health problems. Personal, economic, relationship, and social strains can result in maladaptive coping strategies such as drug and alcohol use, mental health crises, violence, and infidelity.

The articles in this unit explore a variety of family crises, stresses, and strains. Among them are the impact of family violence, substance abuse, mental health challenges, infidelity, and economic concerns. The nature of stress resulting from a life-threatening and chronic illness, disability, loss, grief, and war are also considered. Family challenges and adaption for single-parent, divorced, and step-families are also considered. Throughout this unit the focus is not only on understanding the challenges these events and circumstances can present. An important goal is to also consider how individuals and families can best manage these crises and access supports as they navigate the stresses of life.

Article

Prepared by: Patricia Hrusa Williams,
University of Maine at Farmington

Anguish of the Abandoned Child

CHARLES A. NELSON III; NATHAN A. FOX AND CHARLES H. ZEANAH, JR.

The plight of orphaned Romanian children reveals the psychic and physical scars from first years spent without a loving, responsive caregiver.

Learning Outcomes

After reading this article, you will be able to:

- Understand the political, social, and economic reasons behind the "orphan problem" in Romania.

- Explain reasons why children become orphans worldwide.

- Identify how early experiences of deprivation impact child development and later outcomes.

- Define and explain the term "sensitive period."

In a misguided effort to enhance economic productivity, Nicolae Ceauşescu decreed in 1966 that Romania would develop its "human capital" via a government-enforced mandate to increase the country's population. Ceauşescu, Romania's leader from 1965 to 1989, banned contraception and abortions and imposed a "celibacy tax" on families that had fewer than five children. State doctors—the menstrual police—conducted gynecologic examinations in the workplace of women of child-bearing age to see whether they were producing sufficient offspring. The birth rate initially skyrocketed. Yet because families were too poor to keep their children, they abandoned many of them to large state-run institutions. By 1989 this social experiment led to more than 170,000 children living in these facilities.

The Romanian revolution of 1989 deposed Ceauşescu, and over the next 10 years his successors made a series of halting attempts to undo the damage. The "orphan problem" Ceauşescu left behind was enormous and did not disappear for many years. The country remained impoverished, and the rate of child abandonment did not change appreciably at least through 2005. A decade after Ceauşescu had been removed from power, some government officials could still be heard saying that the state did a better job than families in bringing up abandoned children and that those confined in institutions were, by definition, "defective"—a view grounded in the Soviet-inspired system of educating the disabled, dubbed "defectology."

Even after the 1989 revolution, families still felt free to abandon an unwanted infant to a state-run institution. Social scientists had long suspected that early life in an orphanage could have adverse consequences. A number of mostly small, descriptive studies that lacked control groups were conducted from the 1940s to the 1960s in the West that compared children in orphanages with those in foster care and showed that life in an institution did not come close to matching the care of a parent—even if that parent was not the natural mother or father. One issue with these studies was the possibility of "selection bias": children removed from institutions and placed into adoptive or foster homes might be less impaired, whereas the ones who remained in the institution were more disabled. The only way to counter any bias would require the unprecedented step of randomly placing a group of abandoned children into either an institution or a foster home.

Understanding the effects of life in an institution on children's early development is important because of the immensity of the orphan problem worldwide (an orphan is defined here as an abandoned child or one whose parents have died). War, disease, poverty and sometimes government policies have stranded at least eight million children worldwide in state-run facilities. Often these children live in highly structured but hopelessly bleak environments, where typically one adult oversees 12 to 15 children. Research is still lacking to gain a full understanding of what happens to children who spend their first years in such deprived circumstances.

In 1999, when we approached Cristian Tabacaru, then secretary of state for Romania's National Authority for Child Protection, he encouraged us to conduct a study on institutionalized children because he wanted data to address the question of whether to develop alternative forms of care for the 100,000 Romanian children then living in state institutions. Yet Tabacaru faced stiff resistance from some government officials, who believed for decades that children received a better upbringing in institutions than in foster care. The problem was exacerbated because some government agencies' budgets were funded, in part, by their role in making institutional care arrangements. Faced with these challenges, Tabacaru thought that scientific evidence about putative advantages of foster care for young children over state institutions would make a convincing case for reform, and so he invited us to go ahead with a study.

Infancy in an Institution

With the assistance of some officials within the Romanian government and especially with help from others who worked for SERA Romania (a nongovernmental organization), we implemented a study to ascertain the effects on a child's brain and behavior of living in a state institution and whether foster care could ameliorate the effects of being reared in conditions that run counter to what we know about the needs of young children. The Bucharest Early Intervention Project was launched in 2000, in cooperation with the Romanian government, in part to provide answers that might rectify the aftereffects of previous policies. The unfortunate legacy of Ceauşescu's tenure provided a chance to examine, with greater scientific rigor than any previous study, the effects of institutionalized care on the neurological and emotional development of infants and young children. The study was the first-ever randomized controlled study that compared a group of infants placed in foster care with another raised in institutions, providing a level of experimental precision that had been hitherto unavailable.

We recruited, from all six institutions for infants and young children in Bucharest, a group of 136 whom we considered to be free of neurological, genetic and other birth defects based on pediatric exams conducted by a member of the study team. All had been abandoned to institutions in the first weeks or months of life. When the study began, they were, on average, 22 months old—the range of ages was from six to 31 months.

Immediately after a series of baseline physical and psychological assessments, half the children were randomly assigned to a foster care intervention our team developed, maintained and financed. The other half remained in an institution—what we called the "care as usual" group. We also recruited a third group of typically developing children who lived with their families in Bucharest and had never been institutionalized. These three groups of children have been studied for more than 10 years. Because the children were randomly assigned to foster care or to remain in an institution, unlike previous studies, it was possible to show that any differences in development or behavior between the two groups could be attributed to where they were reared.

Because there was virtually no foster care available for abandoned children in Bucharest when we started, we were in the unique position of having to build our own network. After extensive advertising and background checks, we eventually recruited 53 families to foster 68 children (we kept siblings together).

Of course, many ethical issues were involved in conducting a controlled scientific study of young children, a trial in which only half the participants were initially removed from institutions. The design compared the standard intervention for abandoned children—institutional rearing—with foster care, an intervention that had never been available to these children. Ethical protections put in place included oversight by multiple Romanian- and U.S.-based institutions, implementation of "minimal risk" measures (all used routinely with young children), and noninterference with government decisions about

changes in placement when children were adopted, returned to biological parents or later placed in government-sponsored foster care that at the outset did not exist.

No child was moved back from foster care to an institution at the end of the study. As soon as the early results became available, we communicated our findings to the Romanian government at a news conference.

To ensure high-quality foster care, we designed the program to incorporate regular involvement of a social work team and provided modest subsidies to families for child-related expenses. All foster parents had to be licensed, and they were paid a salary as well as a subsidy. They received training and were encouraged to make a full psychological commitment to their foster children.

Sensitive Periods

The study set about to explore the premise that early experience often exerts a particularly strong influence in shaping the immature brain. For some behaviors, neural connections form in early years in response to environmental influences during windows of time, called sensitive periods. A child who listens to spoken language or simply looks around receives aural and visual inputs that shape neural connections during specific periods of development. The results of the study supported this initial premise of a sensitive period: the difference between an early life spent in an institution compared with foster care was dramatic. At 30, 40 and 52 months, the average IQ of the institutionalized group was in the low to middle 70s, whereas it was about 10 points higher for children in foster care. Not surprisingly, IQ was about 100, the standard average, for the group that had never been institutionalized. We also discovered a sensitive period when a child was able to achieve a maximum gain in IQ: a boy or girl placed in a home before roughly two years of age had a significantly higher IQ than one put there after that age.

The findings clearly demonstrate the devastating impact on mind and brain of spending the first two years of life within the impersonal confines of an institution. The Romanian children living in institutions provide the best evidence to date that the initial two years of life constitute a sensitive period in which a child must receive intimate emotional and physical contact or else find personal development stymied.

Infants learn from experience to seek comfort, support and protection from their significant caregivers, whether those individuals are natural or foster parents—and so we decided to measure attachment. Only extreme conditions that limit opportunities for a child to form attachments can interfere with a process that is a foundation for normal social development. When we measured this variable in the institutionalized children, we found that the overwhelming majority displayed incompletely formed and aberrant relationships with their caregivers.

When the children were 42 months of age, we made another assessment and found that the children placed in foster care displayed dramatic improvements in making emotional attachments. Almost half had established secure relationships with another person, whereas only 18 percent of the institutionalized children had done so. In the community children, those never institutionalized, 65 percent were securely attached. Children placed into foster care before the end of the 24-month sensitive period were more likely to form secure attachments compared with children placed there after that threshold.

These numbers are more than just statistical disparities that separate the institutionalized and foster groups. They translate into very real experiences of both anguish and hope. Sebastian (none of the children's names in this article are real), now 12, has spent virtually his entire life in an orphanage and has seen his IQ drop 20 points to a subpar 64 since he was tested during his fifth year. A youth who may have never formed an attachment with anyone, Sebastian drinks alcohol and displays other risk-prone behaviors. During an interview with us, he became irritable and erupted with flashes of anger.

Bogdan, also 12, illustrates the difference that receiving individualized attention from an adult makes. He was abandoned at birth and lived in a maternity ward until two months of age, after which he lived in an institution for nine months. He was then recruited into the project and randomized to the foster care group, where he was placed in the family of a single mother and her adolescent daughter. Bogdan started to catch up quickly and managed to overcome mild developmental delays within months. Although he had some behavioral problems, project staff members worked with the family, and by his fifth birthday the foster mother had decided to adopt him. At age 12, Bogdan's IQ continues to score at an above-average level. He attends one of the best public schools in Bucharest and has the highest grades in his class.

Because children raised in institutions did not appear to receive much personal attention, we were interested in whether a paucity of language exposure would have any effect on them. We observed delays in language development, and if children arrived in foster care before they reached approximately 15 or 16 months, their language was normal, but the later children were placed, the further behind they fell.

We also compared the prevalence of mental health problems among any children who had ever been institutionalized with those who had not. We found that 53 percent of the children who had ever lived in an institution had received a psychiatric diagnosis by the age of four and a half, compared with 20 percent of the group who had never been institutionalized. In fact, 62 percent of the institutionalized children approaching the age of five had diagnoses, ranging from anxiety disorders—44 percent—to attention-deficit hyperactivity disorder (ADHD)—23 percent.

Foster care had a major influence on the level of anxiety and depression—reducing their incidence by half—but did not affect behavioral diagnoses (ADHD and conduct disorder). We could not detect any sensitive period for mental health. Yet relationships were important for assuring good mental health. When we explored the mechanism to explain reduced emotional disorders such as depression, we found that the more secure the attachment between a child and foster parent, the greater probability that the child's symptoms would diminish.

We also wanted to know whether first years in a foster home affected brain development differently than living in an institution. An assessment of brain activity using electroencephalography (EEG)—which records electrical signals—showed that infants living in institutions had significant reductions in one component of EEG activity and a heightened level in another (lower alpha and higher theta waves), a pattern that may reflect delayed brain maturation. When we assessed the children at the eight-year mark, we again recorded EEG scans. We could then see that the pattern of electrical activity in children placed in foster care before two years of age could not be distinguished from that of those who had never passed time in an institution. Children taken out of an orphanage after two years and those who never left showed a less mature pattern of brain activity.

The noticeable decrease in EEG activity among the institutionalized children was perplexing. To interpret this observation, we turned to data from magnetic resonance imaging, which can visualize brain structures. Here we observed that the institutionalized children showed a large reduction in the volume of both gray matter (neurons and other brain cells) and white matter (the insulating substance covering neurons' wire-like extensions).

On the whole, all the children who were institutionalized had smaller brain volumes. Placing children in foster care at any age had no effect on increasing the amount of gray matter—the foster care group showed levels of gray matter comparable to those of the institutionalized children. Yet the foster care children showed more white matter volume than the institutionalized group, which may account for the changes in EEG activity.

To further examine the biological toll of early institutionalization, we focused attention on a crucial area of the genome. Telomeres, regions at the ends of chromosomes that provide protection from the stresses of cell division, are shorter in adults who undergo extreme psychological stresses than those who escape this duress. Shorter telomeres may even be a mark of accelerated cellular aging. When we examined telomere length in the children in our study, we observed that, on the whole, those who had spent any time in an institution had shorter telomeres than those who had not.

Lessons for All

The Bucharest Early Intervention Project has demonstrated the profound effects early experience has on brain development. Foster care did not completely remedy the profound developmental abnormalities linked to institutional rearing, but it did mostly shift a child's development toward a healthier trajectory.

The identification of sensitive periods—in which recovery from deprivation occurs the earlier the child begins to experience a more favorable living environment—may be one of the most significant findings from our project. This observation has implications beyond the millions of children living in institutions, extending to additional millions of maltreated children whose care is being overseen by child-protection authorities. We caution readers, however, not to make unwarranted assumptions that two years can be rigidly defined as a sensitive period for development. Yet the evidence suggests that the earlier children are cared for by stable, emotionally invested parents, the better their chances for a more normal development trajectory.

We are continuing to follow these children into adolescence to see if there are "sleeper effects"—that is, significant behavioral or neurological differences that appear only later in youth or even adulthood. Further, we will determine whether the effects of a sensitive period we observed at younger ages will still be observed as children enter adolescence. If they are, they will reinforce a growing body of literature that speaks to the role of early life experiences in shaping development across one's life span. This insight, in turn, may exert pressure on governments throughout the world to pay more attention to the toll that early adversity and institutionalization take on the capacity of a maturing child to traverse the emotional hazards of adolescence and acquire the needed resiliency to cope with the travails of adult life.

More to Explore

Cognitive Recovery in Socially Deprived Young Children: The Bucharest Early Intervention Project. Charles A. Nelson III et al. in Science, vol. 318, pages 1937–1940; December 21, 2007.

Effects of Early Intervention and the Moderating Effects of Brain Activity on Institutionalized Children's Social Skills at Age 8. Alisa N. Almas et al. in Proceedings of the National Academy of Sciences USA, vol. 109, Supplement no. 2, pages 17, 228–17,231; October 16, 2012.

Scientific American Online

For a video that details more about the importance of early-life caregiving, visit http://ScientificAmerican.com/apr2013/orphans.

Critical Thinking

1. Why did Romania experience an "orphan problem?"
2. Is it possible that children could receive a better upbringing in a state-run institution than they could in foster care or the care of their parents? Why or why not?
3. What do you see as ethical issues in randomly placing children to be cared for either in state-run institutions or foster families?
4. Describe some of the issues experienced by children who spent their early years in a state institution.
5. What is the best strategy to use to provide care for orphans? What should we do in situations when there are not enough foster families available to care for orphans or abused/maltreated children?

Create Central

www.mhhe.com/createcentral

Internet References

Scientific American
http://www.scientificamerican.com/article.cfm?id=orphans-how-adversity-affects-young-children

Child Rights Information Network
www.crin.org

Child Welfare Information Gateway
www.childwelfare.gov

CHARLES A. NELSON III is professor of pediatrics and neuroscience and professor of psychology in psychiatry at Harvard Medical School. He has an honorary doctorate from the University of Bucharest in Romania.

NATHAN A. FOX is Distinguished University Professor in the Department of Human Development and Quantitative Methodology at the University of Maryland, College Park.

CHARLES H. ZEANAH, JR. is professor of psychiatry and clinical pediatrics at Tulane University and executive director of the university's Institute of Infant and Early Childhood Mental Health.

Article Prepared by: Patricia Hrusa Williams, *University of Maine at Farmington*

Family Privilege

A resilience researcher and former youth in care describes the pains of family loss and provides a roadmap for restoring the powerful benefits that result from healthy families.

John R. Seita

Learning Outcomes

After reading this article, you will be able to:

- Define family privilege.
- Compare and contrast terms: virtual parents, alloparenting, and monoparenting.
- Explain the Circle of Courage Model.

For much of my life until well into my adult years, I found the idea of families to be a mysterious, wondrous, and elusive thing. Spending my first eight years in an abusive home and then being shuttled through a long string of foster homes and other residential settings, I longed for but really did not understand what I imagined to be the magic of family. My lack of real experience in a loving family caused me to wonder about how families worked, or if most were places of pain as I had experienced.

On the rare occasions I visited with friends in their homes, this social unit was a mystery to me, and it felt foreign and out of place. When sent to live with the next in a line of social worker prescribed families, I was emotionally paralyzed. I had no idea what, if anything, they expected of me, or what I expected out of them. If my own family had failed me, why would I trust these phony replacements? Yet in spite of my ambivalence, I wanted a family and instinctively understood the importance of these bonds. I felt lost and discarded, believing that my own family had abandoned me.

The strong pull for family is almost primeval. The loss of family is profoundly sad and enduring as shown in decades of research on attachment and loss. Psychologist Rosalyn

Folman (2009) recalls her own childhood growing up in an orphanage:

> The desire to be part of a family always tugged at me, even though I never consciously thought about it. It was just there, deep down in that dark place, as were all my feelings, hopes and dreams, and sometimes I could not hold it back. (p. 150)

Folman's words reflect a deep sense of pain, of loss, and of longing. Her sorrow rings true because that was once my journey as well. Now that my own wife and daughter have taught me the ropes, family is no longer foreign or fearful. But in some ways for me, and perhaps for others, family is still quite a mystery. How do families impact the well-being and development of children and young people? Moreover, if a child or adolescent lacks a stable family, is there any mechanism to compensate for this loss?

In seeking to understand family, important questions emerge. We know it is possible to articulate the tangible benefits of having a well-functioning family. Bill Buford (1955) notes that family is the essential presence—the thing that never leaves a person even if one has to leave it. An equally important quest is to explore the disadvantages of not having a well-functioning family, or any family at all.

In *Kids Who Outwit Adults* (Seita & Brendtro, 2005), the concept of *family privilege* was introduced to articulate the roles and dynamics that family plays in development of children and young people. The inspiration for family privilege was Peggy McIntosh (1990) who wrote of white privilege. Persons who have unearned advantages from either type of privilege are usually unaware of the profound assets they have gained. Few contemplate how many benefits, both hidden and seen, exist for those with solid family connections. While families have been around since the dawn of time, for most of human history they operated with backup mechanisms of intergenerational support. The phenomenon of a two-parent nuclear family—or in my case a struggling single mother—had no counterpoint in cultures where all shared in rearing the young.

Like the air we breathe, we take family for granted and do not recognize how important it is until its absence is felt.

Defining family seems straightforward enough to be easily understood by just about anyone. We presume that everyone knows what a family is and does. Yet like an onion, the more it is peeled back, the more layers are revealed, and the more potent family privilege really becomes. Like the air we breathe, we take family for granted and do not recognize how important it is until its absence is felt. This points to our obligation to cultivate family privilege, especially when no family is available.

Family Privilege

Family privilege is defined as *strengths and supports gained through primary caring relationships.* A generation ago, the typical family included two parents and a bevy of kids living under one roof. Now, every variation of blended caregiving qualifies as family. But over the long arc of human history, a real family was a multigenerational tribal community who shared responsibility for nurturing the young.

Whatever the configuration, in an increasingly fractured society, the challenge is to reclaim the spirit of family.

In our earlier resilience research (Seita, Mitchell, & Tobin, 1996), we focused on four dimensions called CCDO—Connections, Continuity, Dignity, and Opportunity. These are foundations of family privilege:

Connections underscore the need to live in relationships. Urie Bronfenbrenner distilled this to its basics, namely that every child needs at least one adult who is irrationally crazy about him or her (Bronfenbrenner, 2005).

Continuity highlights the developmental pathways that provide stability and permanence. Long-term relationships and cultural and spiritual roots give a sense of purpose and direction to life.

Dignity is grounded in the value and worth of each individual who is entitled to be treated with respect. Children deprived of *dignity* become *indignant* or descend into worthlessness.

Opportunity results as young people are able to achieve their potential, notably by meeting universal growth needs for belonging, mastery, independence, and generosity (Brendtro, Brokenleg, & Van Bockern, 2002).

The family is a child's first and principal source of these strengths and supports. However, when primary caregivers cannot deliver family privilege, others in the broader community must step forward if the child is to grow and thrive.

Virtual Family Privilege

In every culture that has ever existed, there were always some parents who were too young, immature, troubled, or clueless to properly parent their offspring. But even in supposedly primitive hunter-gatherer cultures, there was an inbuilt solution with a network of *virtual* parents in the extended family or clan. This process of sharing child rearing and backing up inadequate or overly stressed parents is called *alloparenting* (Lamb & Hewlett, 2005). Too often we are stuck with *monoparenting.*

"All kids are our kids," said Peter Benson (1997) of the Search Institute. As long as any children are at risk, then all our children reside in *at-risk communities.* Ironically, those who most need virtual family privilege from the school and community are the first to be expelled, rejected, and relegated to subsubstandard services.

Beyond the immediate family, young people live in a network of ecosystems including school, peer group, workplace, teams, youth centers, places of worship, neighborhoods, and communities. These complement family privilege when they are welcoming, safe, fair, and enriching. Young people without stability at home need support from other healthy ecosystems. Our challenge is to create caring community, organizational, and school cultures that promote virtual family privilege.

Practicing Family Privilege

How do we put family privilege into practice? The Circle of Courage model highlights four growth needs: belonging, mastery, independence, and generosity. Specific strategies are needed to build strengths in each of these areas.

Belonging: Building Trust

Belonging is the most basic biosocial need of humans. It begins with healthy parenting but can be provided by other relatives, or by adults and peers who are not biologically related. In Native American and First Nations cultures, children were reared in communities of belonging. Lakota anthropologist Ella Deloria (1998) described the core value of belonging as being related, somehow, to everyone we know. Treating others as kin forges powerful social bonds that draw all into relationships of respect.

The book *Growing Up in the Care of Strangers* (Brown & Seita, 2009) documents the gripping reflections of 11 professionals in our field who as youth were removed from their homes and placed in foster care, residential group care, or juvenile corrections. A common thread is the powerful, raw, and shameless desire to belong in a loving family. Even as adults, the confusion about family and the longing to belong remains. Social worker Claudette Braxton (2009) describes the impact of this experience of being torn from family which she and a sibling shared:

> The fact that we both grew up in placement meant that we had little personal experience with family permanence, parental role models, or unconditional love that we could include in our own philosophy of family. (p. 136)

Psychologist Rosalind Folman (2009) recalls how removal from her parents left her clueless about what a normal family provided to children:

> To this day, I have no sense of family. I cannot even imagine it. I wish that I had even vague images of my mother or father hugging or kissing me or glimpses of mundane things such as sitting at the dinner table or riding in a car with them, but I do not. The sense of family, of loving parents, is so alien to my thinking that as an adult when I walked into my neighbor's apartment and she was hugging her seven-year-old son, I asked her, "Is he sick?" When she said "No," I asked, "Is he going away on a long trip?" She said, "No." She was as puzzled by my questions as I was by her behavior. I later asked my therapist to explain it to me. He said she was hugging him because he is her son and she loves him. I sat there shocked. I said, "Parents really do that?" I just could not believe it. (p. 145)

The sense of loss of family is tangible, more real than real. Growing up without family has lifelong impact. But there are strategies to provide a sense of belonging through creating virtual family privilege. For example, schools and organizations like Big Brothers-Big Sisters enlist adults to serve as mentors for students at risk of failure. The goal is to ensure that no student is lost but has at least one advocate throughout the school year. Some schools have formed "connections committees" to reattach the most marginal students to the community bond.

Mastery: Cultivating Talent

In kinship cultures, children were reared by the village which guaranteed abundant opportunities for mastery. The young were taught to carefully observe and listen to elders and peers with more experience. Vygotsky (1978) considered the mentoring process as the foundation for competence: *the zone of proximal development* is the difference between what a person can achieve with skillful instruction versus what can be learned in isolation. In the quest for mastery, families provide modeling, practice, shared history of family lessons learned, wisdom, and pathways to competence. In short, a well-functioning family is a pathway for success.

In my own experience, I was not able to bathe in the fountain of family learning; still, many caring adults took on the role of mentor for mastery. Even though I felt inadequate, they were constantly on talent hunts to identify and nurture my untapped potentials. Mr. Wilson was an athletic instructor at my residential school who provided great encouragement. He had high expectations and constantly inspired me to strive for excellence on the basketball court. He never let me give up, no matter what the odds seemed to be. Failure was not an option.

One afternoon, we were playing one-on-one on the outdoor basketball court. As usual, the game was intense and neither Mr. Wilson nor I was giving an inch. I was playing what he called "tenacious defence" by forcing him further and further from the basket. I hounded him to the edge of the court, far beyond shooting range. In my mind's eye, I had a vision of him falling out of bounds far from the basket. But just as he was about to fulfill my fantasy and land on the grass, he turned, spun in mid-air and launched the ball toward the basket. The high, arching shot seemed to float in the air for an eternity. I stood by in astonishment as it floated through the hoop as effortlessly as a feather on the wind. "See?" he said to me with a smile on his face and a glow in his eyes, "never give up." No doubt Mr. Wilson did not view this as mastery in action, but in the end, the persistence to see a meaningful task through to its completion leads to mastery. He was teaching me a lesson for life.

Independence: Fostering Responsibility

Competence is not enough without confidence and the power to control one's destiny. Albert Bandura (1995) calls this *self-efficacy,* which is the belief in one's own ability to complete tasks and reach goals. This sense of personal power is grounded in self-control rather than the use of power to dominate others. Authentic independence is always rooted in a secure sense of belonging. In contrast, the myth of individualism ignores the interdependence of all humans. Stated succinctly by child care pioneer Henry Maier (1982), healthy development involves being both attached and free.

Young people cannot develop responsible independence through obedience models of discipline. Moral development psychologist Martin Hoffman (2001) observes that there are three types of discipline used by families: power assertion, love withdrawal, and inductive reasoning.

- *Power assertion* is part of the parental role, particularly with younger children who have not yet developed the values and capacities for self-regulation. But when force becomes the focus of discipline, it fuels powerlessness or rebellion. Such was my experience in many foster placements which were long on coercion and low on concern.

- *Love withdrawal* has no legitimate role in child rearing or teaching as it violates the principle of dignity. Feeling unloved unleashes the destructive emotion of shame, eroding the sense of self-worth. This was my story of serial rejection as my angry and defiant pain-based behavior led foster parents and so-called child care professionals to give up on me.

- *Inductive reasoning* entails using discipline problems as opportunities for learning and growth. Rather than reacting to pain-based behavior with pain-based punishment, adults treat misbehavior as a lag in learning. From the time I was removed from my mother at age eight, it took four years and 15 placements until I finally found permanency in a relationship-based residential group care center. In that setting, the more problems I presented, the more opportunities for learning ensued. The most powerful consequences were conversations with caring staff and peers who helped me see how my behavior hurt myself and others.

As I gained in self-control and responsibility, I moved from the structured residential program to a group home where I attended public school in the community. I had brief glimpses of what a real family might be on occasions when I visited in homes of fellow students, one of whom was the son of the college coach. Most of my peers from the group home and public school were college bound, and so my own progress in academics and athletics led to a college scholarship. But in spite of this success, I had spent over half of my life without family privilege. My transition to independence following a decade in foster care was treacherous. Easing into college life and its responsibilities is difficult for many young adults, but my situation was especially so because I lost my most important connections.

Without a family, I expected no phone calls from home, because there was no home. There were no requests for "care packages," for who would prepare and send them? There was no one to bail me out when I was broke, and there was no one

to help me navigate the confusing and Byzantine world of academia. I had no one to cheer me on, or if needed, to kick me in the rear as I faced the challenges of college.

While the "sink or swim" approach to independence eventually worked for me, in the short term, the pain, loss of belonging, and confusion was almost unbearable. We know enough about the science of youth development to not rely on chance. Instead, all young people need supports on the challenging pathway to independence. Given the lack of a traditional family for many youth who are at risk, constructing family privilege becomes a priority.

Generosity: Finding a Purpose

While caring for others is at the core of all ethical systems, this value was largely neglected in Western approaches to education and psychology. In contrast, most indigenous cultures are more rooted in spiritual than materialistic values; children are reared to be generous and treat all others with respect. Now modern research has begun to validate the importance of generosity. Notable is the title of brain scientist Bruce Perry's book *Born for Love: Why Empathy is Essential—and Endangered* (Perry & Szalavitz, 2011). Without concern for others, human existence has little meaning; it is in helping others that we create our own proof of worthiness.

Without experiencing love for oneself, there would appear to be little reason to care for others. Yet, it is no accident that a large number of persons who themselves had painful childhoods are committing themselves to careers in service to children with similar backgrounds. In my experience, those who heal from a love-deprived life have been blessed by the unconditional acceptance of another caring human being. Such it was with me when I first encountered Mr. Leffert, a young group worker who refused to be driven away by my insolence and adult-avoidant behavior.

He stood observing from afar my solo pursuit of basketball perfection on a hot and breezeless summer day. The cement basketball court was lonely and barren, a metaphor for much of my life. I wondered why he was watching me and what he wanted. His name was Mr. Leffert but that was all I knew. So I pretended to ignore him and finished my practice. I walked away from the courts with not even a polite nod toward my spectator—it was my coping strategy to keep my distance from all adults.

A couple days later, he showed up again, this time carrying a bag of something. As usual, I focused on basketball and on being aloof. Upon finishing my workout, I once again started to walk away without acknowledging his presence. "John," he called, "do you have a minute?" "No," I replied feeling both wary and belligerent. "Here, I have something that might improve your game. They're ankle weights and chest weights. They might help you jump higher and become quicker." I cautiously inched toward him, like a hungry stray dog might toward a stranger with scraps of food but then pulled back. Suspicious as ever, I snapped, "Why would I want these and what do you want from me?" "I've seen you working hard," he replied, "and I don't want anything except for you to have a chance to be as good a basketball player as you seem to want to be. Besides," he went on, "they're not new, I got them at a garage sale, but they are barely used, and I think they'll help you."

I was suddenly speechless, and my heart was pounding. No one had ever given me much of anything. "So," I replied sarcastically, "you're giving me someone else's used junk?" I accused. He didn't look hurt. "They're yours, John, if you want them I'll just leave them here on the side of the court." He walked away, and so did I, without his weights. But I thought about them for the next few hours and retrieved them after dark. It turns out that my goals were bigger than my anger. I decided to use his weights.

I later became both all-conference and all-state in basketball. I think Mr. Leffert's weights and his generosity both played a role in my basketball success and eventually in life. His thoughtful act and selfless generosity made a deep and long-lasting impact upon me—this happened 40 years ago. It took me a while, but that single act of generosity set the tone for a profound understanding of the power of giving which drew me into the helping profession.

Beyond Understanding to Practice

Those lacking family privilege are those most in need of it. All of us have the potential to impact the lives of these young people, often in what seem to be small ways. We help them take tentative steps toward trust. We search to discover and develop their talents and strengths. We provide coaching rather than criticism on their sometimes halting journey toward responsibility. And we model generosity so that they can pay it forward and find purpose in caring for others. Family privilege might be defined as putting the Circle of Courage into action.

My own journey from neglect, abuse, and homelessness to being a husband, father, and professional is largely a case of "luck and pluck." In other words, I was lucky to find myself in a series of serendipitous developmental opportunities. Moreover, my strong-willed and stubborn nature presented both problems and pathways to success. Using terms from resilience science, I benefited from both external and internal protective factors. It is clear what children need to grow and thrive is more than

"luck and pluck." As members of the human community, it is our responsibility to ensure that all young people experience the rich benefits of family privilege.

References

Bandura, A. (Ed.). (1995). *Self-efficacy in changing societies.* New York, NY: Cambridge University Press.

Benson, P. (1997). *All kids are our kids: What communities must do to raise caring and responsible children and adolescents.* San Francisco, CA: Jossey-Bass.

Braxton, C. (2009). Pay me now or pay me later. In W. Brown & J. Seita (Eds.), *Growing up in the care of strangers: The experiences, insights and recommendations of eleven former foster kids* (pp. 127–140). Tallahassee, FL: William Gladden Foundation.

Brendtro, L., Brokenleg, M., & Van Bockern, S. (2002). *Reclaiming youth at risk.* Bloomington, IN: Solution Tree.

Bronfenbrenner, U. (2005). *Making human beings human: Bioecological perspectives on human development.* Thousand Oaks, CA: Sage Publications.

Brown, W., & Seita, J. (2009). *Growing up in the care of strangers: The experiences, insights and recommendations of eleven former foster kids.* Tallahassee, FL: William Gladden Foundation.

Buford, B. (Ed.). (1955). *The family.* New York, NY: Granta Books.

Deloria, E. (1998). *Speaking of Indians.* Lincoln, NE: University of Nebraska Press.

Folman, R. (2009). It is how children live that matters, not where children live. In W. Brown & J. Seita (Eds.), *Growing up in the care of strangers: The experiences, insights and recommendations of eleven former foster kids* (pp. 141–158). Tallahassee, FL: William Gladden Foundation.

Hoffman, M. (2001). *Empathy and moral development: Implications for caring and justice.* New York, NY: Cambridge University Press.

Lamb, M., & Hewlett, B. (2005). *Hunter-gatherer childhoods: Evolutionary, developmental, and cultural perspectives.* Piscataway, NJ: Aldine Transaction.

Maier, H. (1982). To be attached and free: The challenge of child development. *Child Welfare, 61*(2), 67–76.

McIntosh, P. (1990). White privilege: Unpacking the invisible knapsack. *Independent School, 49,* 31–35.

Perry, B., & Szalavitz, M. (2011). *Born for love: Why empathy is essential—and endangered.* New York, NY: William Morrow.

Seita, J., & Brendtro, L. (2005). *Kids who outwit adults.* Bloomington, IN: Solution Tree.

Seita, J., Mitchell, M., & Tobin, C. (1996). *In whose best interest. One child's odyssey, a nation's responsibility.* Elizabethtown, PA: Continental Press.

Vygotsky, L. (1978). *Mind in society: The development of higher psychological processes.* Cambridge, MA: Harvard University Press.

Critical Thinking

1. What is family privilege? Explain what the author views as the foundations of family privilege and why they are important to children.

2. Why in our society do we engage in "monoparenting" instead of "virtual" parenting? What supports and systems do we have in place for "alloparenting"?

3. What are some ways we can practice family privilege and the Circle of Courage Model in our work with vulnerable children and families? All children and families?

Internet References

Child Welfare Information Gateway
www.childwelfare.gov/

Reclaiming Child and Youth Journal
www.reclaimingjournal.com

Search Institute
www.search-institute.org

JOHN R. SEITA is associate professor of social work at Michigan State University, East Lansing, Michigan, and the author of numerous publications on resilience with youth who are at risk. He may be contacted at john.seita@scc.msu.edu.

Article   Prepared by: Patricia Hrusa Williams,
                                               University of Maine at Farmington

Terrorism in the Home

Eleven myths and facts about domestic violence

VICTOR M. PARACHIN

Learning Outcomes

After reading this article, you will be able to:

- Identify the signs of domestic violence.

- Understand several causes or factors associated with the occurrence of domestic violence.

- Explain strategies which may be effective in reaching out to and assisting victims.

If anything is truly equal opportunity, it is battering. Domestic violence crosses all socioeconomic, ethnic, racial, educational, age, and religious lines.

— K. J. Wilson, *When Violence Begins At Home*

Sadly, a U.S. Department of Justice study indicates that approximately one million violent crimes are committed by former spouses, boyfriends, or girlfriends each year, with 85 percent of the victims being women. For domestic violence to be defeated, it must begin with information. Here are 11 myths and facts about domestic violence.

Myth 1: Domestic violence is only physical.

Fact: Abusive actions against another person can be verbal, emotional, sexual, and physical.
There are four basic types of domestic violence:
- Physical (shoving, slapping, punching, pushing, hitting, kicking, and restraining)
- Sexual (when one partner forces unwanted, unwelcome, uninvited sexual acts upon another)
- Psychological (verbal and emotional abuse, threats, intimidations, stalking, swearing, insulting, isolation from family and friends, forced financial dependence)
- Attacks against property and pets (breaking household objects, hitting walls, abusing or killing beloved pets)

Myth 2: Domestic violence is not common.

Fact: While precise statistics are difficult to determine, all signs indicate that domestic violence is more common than most people believe or want to believe. Here's one example: due to lack of space, shelters for battered women are able to admit only 10 to 40 percent of women who request admission. Another example is from divorced women. Though they make up less than 8 percent of the U.S. population, they account for 75 percent of all battered women and report being assaulted 14 times more often than women still living with a partner. Whatever statistics are available are believed to be low because domestic violence is often not reported.

Myth 3: Domestic violence affects only women.

Fact: Abuse can happen to anyone! It can be directed at women, men, children, the elderly. It takes place among all social classes and all ethnic groups. However, women are the most targeted victims of domestic violence. Here are some statistics:
- One in four American women report being physically assaulted and/or raped by a current or former spouse, cohabiting partner, or date at some time in their life.
- According to the FBI, a woman is beaten every 15 seconds.
- In 1996, 30 percent of all female murder victims in the United States were slain by their husbands or boyfriends.
- Around the world, at least one in every three women has been beaten, coerced into sex, or otherwise abused in her lifetime.
- While men are victims of domestic abuse, 92 percent of those subjected to violence are women.

Myth 4: Domestic violence occurs only among lower class or minority or rural communities.

Fact: Domestic violence crosses all race and class lines. Similar rates of abuse are reported in cities, suburbs, and rural areas, according to the Bureau of Justice. Abusers can be found living in mansions as well as in mobile homes. Susan Weitzman,

Ph.D., is author of the book *Not to People Like Us: Hidden Abuse in Upscale Marriages.* In her book, Dr. Weitzman presents case-by-case studies of domestic violence in families with higher than average incomes and levels of education.

Myth 5: Battered women can just leave.

Fact: A combination of factors makes it very difficult for the abused to leave. These include: family and social pressure, shame, financial barriers, children, religious beliefs. Up to 50 percent of women with children fleeing domestic violence become homeless because they leave the abuser. Also, many who are abused face psychological ambivalence about leaving. One woman recalls: "My body still ached from being beaten by my husband a day earlier. But he kept pleading through the door. 'I'm sorry. I'll never do that to you again. I know I need help.' I had a 2-week-old baby. I wanted to believe him. I opened the door." Her abuse continued for two more years before she gained the courage to leave.

Myth 6: Abuse takes place because of alcohol or drugs.

Fact: Substance abuse does not cause domestic violence. However, drugs and alcohol do lower inhibitions while increasing the level of violence, often to more dangerous levels. The U.S. Department of Health and Human Services estimates that one-quarter to one-half of abusers have substance abuse issues.

Myth 7: They can just fight back or walk away.

Fact: Dealing with domestic violence is never as simple as fighting back or walking out the door. "Most domestic abusers are men who are physically stronger than the women they abuse," notes Joyce Zoldak in her book *When Danger Hits Home: Survivors of Domestic Violence.* "In the case of elder abuse, the victims' frail condition may limit their being able to defend themselves. When a child is being abused, the adult guardian is far more imposing—both physically and psychologically—than the victim."

Myth 8: The victim provoked the violence.

Fact: The abuser is completely responsible for the abuse. No one can say or do anything which warrants being beaten and battered. Abusers often try to deflect their responsibility by blaming the victim via comments such as: "You made me angry." "You made me jealous." "This would never have happened if you hadn't done that." "I didn't mean to do that, but you were out of control." Victims need to be assured that the abuse is not their fault.

Myth 9: Domestic abuse is a private matter and it's none of my business.

Fact: We all have a responsibility to care for one another. Officials at the National Domestic Violence Hotline offer this advice to people who see or suspect domestic violence: "Yes, it is your business. Maybe he's your friend, your brother-in-law, your cousin, co-worker, gym partner, or fishing buddy. You've noticed that he interrupts her, criticizes her family, yells at her, or scares her. You hope that when they're alone, it isn't worse. The way he treats her makes you uncomfortable, but you don't want to make him mad or lose his friendship. You surely don't want to see him wreck his marriage or have to call the police. What can you do? Say something. If you don't, your silence is the same as saying abuse is OK. He could hurt someone, or end up in jail. Because you care, you need to do something—before it is too late."

Myth 10: Partners need couples counseling.

Fact: It is the abuser alone who needs counseling in order to change behavior. Social Worker Susan Schechter says couples counseling is "an inappropriate intervention that further endangers the woman." Schechter explains her position: "It encourages the abuser to blame the victim by examining her 'role' in his problem. By seeing the couple together, the therapist erroneously suggests that the partner, too, is responsible for the abuser's behavior. Many women have been brutally beaten following couples counseling sessions in which they disclosed violence or coercion. The abuser alone must take responsibility for assaults and understand that family reunification is not his treatment goal: the goal is to stop the violence."

Myth 11: Abusers are evil people.

Fact: "Anyone can find himself or herself in an abusive situation, and most of us could also find ourselves tempted to be abusive to others, no matter how wrong we know it to be," notes Joyce Zoldak. Abusers are people who may be strong and stable in some areas of their lives but weak, unreasonable and out of control in other ways. This does not excuse their behavior, because abuse is always wrong. Abusers need to be held accountable for their actions and encouraged to seek help promptly by meeting with a psychologist, psychiatrist, therapist, or spiritual leader. Abusers can also receive help from The National Domestic Violence Hotline 1-800-799-7233 or via their website: http://www.thehotline.org.

With an informed community, and with the help of family and friends, the cycle of abuse can be broken.

Critical Thinking

1. What are some impediments or reasons why women do not report domestic violence?
2. What are some reasons why domestic violence occurs in couple relationships and in families?
3. Explain why it can be difficult to identify and assist victims.
4. Why do you think some of these myths about domestic violence persist?
5. Given the information in the article, what do you think may be effective strategies which can be used to reach out to and assist victims of domestic violence?

Create Central

www.mhhe.com/createcentral

Internet References

Futures Without Violence
www.futureswithoutviolence.org
National Coalition Against Domestic Violence
www.ncadv.org
National Network to End Domestic Violence
www.nnedv.org

National Resource Center on Domestic Violence
www.nrcdv.org

VICTOR M. PARACHIN writes from Tulsa, Oklahoma.

Article Prepared by: Patricia Hrusa Williams, *University of Maine at Farmington*

Alcoholism—The Family Illness

NATIONAL ASSOCIATION FOR THE CHILDREN OF ALCOHOLICS

Learning Outcomes

After reading this article, you will be able to:

- Define term codependency.

- Understand how alcoholism may influence the family unit over time.

- Recognize roles and coping strategies adopted by family members of alcoholics.

Alcoholism is a family illness. People suffering with alcoholism organize their lives around alcohol and family life becomes organised around the alcohol-dependent family member, in an attempt to keep their problems hidden from the outside world. This results in family adaptation, creating an environment in which codependency can develop.

The unspoken family rules **don't talk, don't trust, don't feel** develop to protect the illusion of a "normal" family. As the family progressively adapts to alcoholism, they follow a similar path to the alcohol-dependent person, shown in Figure 1 below.

Family Characteristics

Although all families are different and are made up of individuals who contribute their own thoughts, behaviors and feelings, the following has been created to provide a framework to illustrate the issues which differentiate a healthy functioning family and a family struggling with alcoholism or other drug problem.

Families do not choose to become dysfunctional but adapt in order to cope with alcohol and other problems. Codependent patterns of behavior allow the family unit to balance the effects of the drinking parent's behavior. This often leads to the adoption of roles for family members to play.

Family with parental alcoholism/addiction	Healthy family
Rigid thinking—black and white	Open to change and new ideas
Low self-worth/shame	High self-worth
Compulsive behavior covers pain	Individuals choose their behavior
Rules are arbitrary—rigid or non existent and chaotic	Rules are designed to guide and protect, are age appropriate and consistent
Feelings are avoided and repressed—no risks taken because there is no safe place within the family	Feelings are expressed openly and validated. Touch is appropriate and nurturing
Denial of stress, challenging issues, and problems. Although crisis can be used as a welcome distraction from emotional pain	Expect stress and work together for mutual support
Disturbed hierarchy—one person or no one in charge, children provide parenting for siblings. Hidden coalitions, inconsistency, and chaos	Parents are in charge—strong coalition, they protect and assume responsibility for the children
Terminal seriousness—anger (often suppressed), depression, hostility, or phony happiness	Fun, humour, joy, and laughter exist in adults and children

Becomes aware using chemicals is not normal
Accepts rationalizations
Family interaction is not normal
Worries about family reputation
Protects the using pattern from others
Reacts to blackouts
Using chemicals becomes focus of anxiety
Fears that chemical problem will be known
Loses perspective on own interaction

Social contacts are strained
Increasing anxiety regarding chemical use
Social isolation increases
Feels guilty about the using
Rationalizes the using

Tries to control the using
Family grows further apart
Becomes more distrustful and resentful
Becomes more critical

Children begin to show signs of emotional problems
Feels disgust for the user
Begins to feel self-pity
Rapid mood swings

Begins to feel like a failure
Increasing irritability
Can't make decisions

Children are disturbed
Questions own sanity
Physical deterioration
Avoids sexual contact
Loses self-confidence
Children become pawns in husband/wife struggle
Makes threats
Torn loyalty to spouse and children
Growing financial problems
Compulsive efforts to control using
Crisis situations are more frequent
Assumes both parent roles
Begins to ignore user
Loses hope, quits trying to understand
Obtains control of money
May seek help
Depression, stress-related illness(IBS, migraine, etc.)
Threatens divorce
May separate or divorce
Possible hospitalizations

These roles become essential to the survival of the individual family members and the family itself. The roles are often played out with the same compulsion, delusion, and denial as the dependent plays his or her role as drinker.

Role-playing and the adoption of particular roles are not calculated behavior, but happen subconsciously; family members are unlikely to be aware that the masquerade exists. Role-playing can be destructive as it creates a false reality where there is no place for honesty/self-honesty within or outside of the family unit. Communication becomes distorted by double messages, an overt message from the role self and a covert one from the real self.

Family roles can occur in all troubled families and occasionally in healthy families in times of stress. However, in families dealing with alcoholism, the roles are more likely to be rigidly fixed and are played with greater intensity, compulsion, and delusion.

The above table has been adapted, with permission, from the work of Sharon Wegscheider Cruse, who worked with Virginia Satyr on family dysfunction, and illustrates an extremely complex adaptation process, presented for guidance only. Individuals bring their own personalities and genetic traits into the equation.

Birth order and sex also play their part. In a family where there are only two children, the roles often overlap, with one child playing two or more roles. Only children often try to play all roles, sometimes concurrently or changing to meet the needs of the family.

Roles also change when there is a change in the family group, for instance when the eldest child, often the Hero, leaves home. The family adapts in order to find homeostasis or stability. Role-playing is a way for the family to keep its secrets hidden and to continue to survive without perceived threat from the outside world.

Changes will also take place when the alcohol-dependent person finds help for his/her drinking. It is often difficult for children to give up their roles of responsibility when a parent stops drinking and wishes to resume parenting.

Role	Motivating Feeling	Identifying Symptoms	Pay Off for Individual	Pay Off for Family	Possible Price
Dependent	Shame	Chemical use	Relief of pain	None	Addiction
Enabler	Anger	Powerlessness or Martyr	Importance Righteousness	Responsibility	Illness exhaustion
Hero	Inadequacy guilt	Over-achievement	Attention (positive)	Self-worth	Compulsive drive
Scapegoat	Hurt	Delinquency	Attention (negative)	Focus away from dependent	Self-destruction addiction
Lost child	Loneliness	Solitary shyness	Escape	Relief	Social isolation
Mascot	Fear	Clowning hyperactivity	Attention (amused)	Fun	Immaturity emotional illness addiction

Recovery for the alcohol-dependent person should also include help for the family as they adapt to a new situation. The first and most important step is to face the problem with help.

Sources of Support

There are many sources of support including those listed below. Speak to a Nacoa volunteer helpline counsellor who will listen and research other avenues of support if you wish.

- **Nacoa**
  Helpline: 0800 358 3456 e-mail: helpline@nacoa.org.uk
  website: www.nacoa.org.uk
  Information, advice, and support for everyone affected by a parent's drinking.
- **ACA (Adult Children of Alcoholics)**
  Tel: 07071 781 899 website: www.adultchildrenofalco-holics.co.uk
  Support for people who have grown up in alcoholic or otherwise dysfunctional families.
- **Al-Anon Family Groups**
  Helpline: 0207 403 0888 website: www.al-anonuk.org.uk
  Support for anyone whose life is, or has been, affected by someone else's drinking.
- **Alcoholics Anonymous**
  Helpline: 0845 769 7555 website: www.alcoholics-anonymous.org.uk
  Information, support, and local meetings for alcoholics.
- **BACP**
  Tel: 01455 883300 website: www.itsgoodtotalk.org.uk
  Information about counselling and how to find a counsellor
- **COAP (Children of Addicted Parents and People)**
  website: www.coap.org.uk

Online forum for young people affected by a parent's addiction.
- **CoDA (Co-Dependents Anonymous)**
  website: www.coda-uk.org
  Self-help group interested in working through the problems codependency has caused in their lives.

Critical Thinking

1. Do you consider alcoholism an individual problem or a family illness? Why?

2. What are some ways individuals might adapt or cope with having an alcoholic member? Why might they employ these coping strategies?

3. What do you think would be the biggest challenge when a family member is an alcoholic? Visit some of the websites listed below and identify three to four supports which may help family members affected by alcoholism.

Internet References

Alcoholics Anonymous
   http://www.aa.org/

Al-Anon
   http://www.al-anon.alateen.org/

Co-dependents Anonymous
   http://coda.org/

National Association for the Children of Alcoholics
   http://www.nacoa.org/

From: The National Association for Children of Alcoholics, PO Box 64, Bristol, BS16 2UH Tel: 0117 924 8005 nacoa.org.uk, FREE Helpline 0800 358 3456, helpline@nacoa.org.uk, Registered Charity No: 1009143.

Article　　　　Prepared by: Patricia Hrusa Williams, *University of Maine at Farmington*

Keeping the Promise: Maintaining the Health of Military and Veteran Families and Children

Colonel Stephen J. Cozza, Ron Haskins, and Richard M. Lerner

Learning Outcomes

After reading this article, you will be able to:

- Identify risks of parental deployment to children and families.

- Describe factors related to the adaptability and resilience of military families.

- Summarize the types of programs and services found to be effective in assisting military families.

. . . More than two million Americans have served in the post-9/11 wars in Iraq and Afghanistan, and nearly 45 percent of them have children. Although polls show that around 90 percent of Americans recognize and appreciate the sacrifice of service members who serve the nation, the public knows little about the actual costs imposed on the health and functioning of families, including children, of service members and veterans. Research on the effects of deployment on families is still in its infancy, but it already shows that deployment leads to distress and mental health problems among parents and that these parental problems are in turn associated with elevated rates of similar social-emotional problems in children. Though military families show remarkable resilience, given the stress most of them face, we argue that the sacrifices they make place a special obligation on the nation to help these distressed families and children. After all, since 9/11, nearly 6,700 service members have died and 50,000 have been physically injured in a combat zone. Hundreds of thousands more suffer from traumatic brain injury (TBI) and posttraumatic stress disorder (PTSD). After reviewing the evidence on both the elevated levels of emotional and behavioral problems experienced by deployed service members and their families, as well as evidence on their resilience, we discuss a shared national agenda to expand and evaluate the effectiveness of preventive and treatment services for these families.

Deployment and Its Effects

Even routine military life means that families must deal with conditions that, research shows, can cause problems. Members of military families are often separated from one another; children are forced to change schools frequently; and some families, particularly those of lower rank, may face financial problems. Members of the military usually have little choice about where they are stationed, which means that spouses and children cannot decide where to live and when to move. Deployment to a combat zone adds a layer of danger to this already formidable list. The stress that family members feel when their loved one (or loved ones, in the case of families with two military parents) is in harm's way can disrupt family routines, lead to conflict between parents, and cause worry and elevated distress.

Several investigators have surveyed military families and found that combat deployment is associated with higher levels of emotional and behavioral problems in children. Anita Chandra of the RAND Corporation and her colleagues used a computer-assisted telephone interview with more than 1,500 military children aged 11 to 17 and their caretakers. Controlling for family and service member characteristics, they found that older boys and girls of all ages with a deployed parent had significantly more problems with school, family, and peers than do children the same age in the general U.S. population. Longer deployments were associated with more problems. Patricia Lester and her team at UCLA reported similar results among 272 children aged 6 to 12. Importantly, both studies found a strong relationship between the mental health of parents or caretakers and the healthy adaptation of their children to deployment stress.

Alyssa Mansfield of the University of North Carolina and her colleagues also examined how combat deployment affects children's mental health, using outpatient treatment records from 2003 to 2006 of nearly 310,000 children aged 5 to 17 with at least one parent in the Army. They compared the pediatric mental health outpatient visits of children whose parents were deployed longer than 11 months, 1 to 11 months, and not deployed at all. After controlling for children's age, gender, and mental health history, they found that both boys and girls whose parents were deployed received higher-than-normal levels of mental health diagnoses (including acute stress reaction/adjustment, depression, and behavioral disorders). Children of parents deployed more than 11 months had especially high levels of these problems. These results should be interpreted with some caution, because they are based on the procedural diagnostic codes that clinicians must enter in health care records for insurance and other purposes. Although greater use of mental health services likely indicates higher levels of distress in these military children, it should not be equated with mental illness in most of these cases.

Research also identifies an increased risk of child maltreatment among children with a deployed parent. Over the years, rates of child maltreatment in military families have been no greater, and perhaps lower, than among civilian families, and maltreatment rates in military families had been falling continuously until combat operations began in 2001. But at least three studies have now shown that parents are more likely to maltreat children during periods of deployment. A study by Deborah Gibbs of RTI International and her colleagues found that, based on confidential military records from 2001 to 2004, civilian wives of service members were four times as likely to neglect children during their husband's deployment than when he was home, and nearly twice as likely to physically abuse them. Also looking at 2001 to 2004, James McCarroll and his colleagues at the Uniformed Services University of the Health Sciences found rising rates of child maltreatment in military families, following a decline in the 1990s; most of the increase, was in neglect rather than physical abuse. Deployment may contribute to an elevated propensity for child neglect in a number of ways, for example, by temporarily creating the equivalent of a single-parent family, a known risk factor for child neglect.

We can draw two conclusions from these and similar studies on the effects of deployment on families. First, deployment leads to stress that affects both parents and children. Parental absence and parental distress are likely associated with diminished parenting capacity, greater risk for child maltreatment (particularly neglect), and greater parental dysfunction, and these in turn are associated with social-emotional and behavioral problems in children. Second, severity of exposure can make these child and family problems worse. For example, greater cumulative deployment time; a parent suffering from PTSD, as well as TBI or another injury; or a family member's death all increase the risk that a family will encounter trouble. These research findings justify concern and must lead to action by the public, by policy makers, and by senior military and other government officials.

Whatever action we take, however, we should remember that both experience and research show that combat deployment leads to a large range of reactions among military families and children. These reactions fall along a continuum from risk to resilience. Many parents and children handle the stress of deployment well, taking problems in stride and continuing to function normally. At the other end of the continuum, some parents and children struggle significantly with the challenges they face, resulting in dysfunction and risk. Most families are likely to be somewhere in the broad middle, distressed by the hardships but capable of adopting strategies that sustain their health and wellness. This range of responses suggests that we need a broad intervention strategy that supports health, screens for risk, and actively engages those who have the most trouble. To be sure, some children will need behavioral health treatment, although most can be helped with modest and relatively inexpensive interventions. But what is resilience, and do military families possess more of it than do civilian families?

Resilience in Military Families

[. . . M]ost military-connected children and parents have the attributes to be resilient in the face of parental deployment and reunification. One source of resilience is self-regulation, or a person's ability to intentionally alter her behavior, thoughts, attention, and emotions to react to and influence the environment; it is a key strength that helps people adapt and thrive in the face of adversity. A child's self-regulation is enhanced when other family members also possess self-regulation skills. For example, research shows that, when children must adapt to change, their resilience is related to their mother's adjustment and mental health. Therefore, just as in civilian families, positive relationships with close family members can help military children adapt to stress.

Other factors that protect military children and parents from stress include the perception that society appreciates the value of military service, pride in contributing to an important mission, a sense of belonging to a military culture, and awareness that networks of support don't go away when active service ends. In addition to providing a haven of safety and stability in difficult times, family relationships can help military-connected youngsters make meaning of adversity, affirm their strengths, feel connected through mutual support and collaboration, provide models and mentors, offer financial security, and frame the stressful circumstances in the context of family values and spirituality. The culture of the modern military gives families the capacity to help children see their experiences as a badge of honor rather than a burden.

What to Do

Military communities are diverse and rich with cultural heritage and resources that help sustain families and children. As a result, military communities, service members, their families, and, more specifically, their children, possess a capacity for resilience that equals or exceeds that of their civilian counterparts. But when they face deployments or other consequences of war, service members and their families are at risk for higher levels of distress, emotional and behavioral problems, child maltreatment, as well as possible deterioration in parental and family functioning, particularly when parents come home with serious disorders such as PTSD or TBI.

Combat veterans have a significant risk of developing mental disorders as a result of their wartime exposure. However, we must avoid a tendency to employ an "illness" model to understand how military spouses and children respond to wartime deployments. Though some people may develop mental disorders, they are likely to be a minority. Most other affected adults and children will experience distress. Distress is not an illness, but it can still significantly affect individuals, families, and communities. In addition to the anguish it can cause, distress can undermine occupational, social, and emotional functioning. Distressed parents are less likely to be attentive to their children and may lose some of the parenting capacity that they previously possessed. Distressed children may become withdrawn, participate in fewer extracurricular activities, find it difficult to concentrate in school, or demonstrate behavioral symptoms that are unusual or that complicate their normal development.

Interventions for mental illness differ from interventions for distress. The most successful models for helping environmentally stressed, at-risk populations emphasize prevention, particularly when these groups have previously enjoyed health and wellness. In 1994, the Institute of Medicine (IOM) outlined a model of activities that promote and sustain health. It places prevention strategies along a spectrum of intensity: universal (helpful to all), selective (useful to those at higher risk), and indicated (targeted to those who exhibit symptoms of a disorder). Beyond prevention, the IOM intervention spectrum includes more intensive activities such as case (or illness) identification, traditional treatment, and health maintenance activities. Such a model is an excellent foundation for a national plan to support and sustain military children and families.

[. . .] Universal prevention in military communities is best achieved by programs that ensure social support and make resources readily available. Such programs should also help adults, children, and families develop resilience-enhancing skills—communicating, connecting with others, being flexible, taking on new and appropriate challenges, solving problems, resolving conflicts, and building a core sense of individual and family capacity and wellness. Such skills can prepare individuals, families, and communities and sustain them through challenging times. Universal prevention programs should be available in the many settings where service members, veterans, and their children and families are likely to be found—schools, child-care programs, youth services, faith-based organizations, and health care systems, all of which have the capacity to promote health and wellness. Many such prevention programs are available in military communities, but they are less likely to be found in the civilian communities where National Guard and Reserve families often live, or where veteran families move after their service ends.

In addition to universal prevention, we need programs that target the populations who face the greatest risk, for example, those who experience multiple deployments, PTSD, TBI, or a parent's death. [. . . M]ilitary and veteran families who face long-term disability are more likely to experience disruptions in individual and family functioning. Several new preventive interventions are helping families where deployment, illness, or injury have overwhelmed family resources, disrupted family schedules and routines, or undermined previously normative parenting practices. Though deployment distress may decrease as the wars wind down, military parents' combat-related illnesses and injuries will continue to affect their families and children. Programs designed to help those who are at the most risk or are showing symptoms of distress or dysfunction are at varying stages of development, and they require further refinement and scientific study to better understand which ones are likely to be most effective, and in which circumstances.

One family-focused prevention program shows considerable promise, and it illustrates the kind of programs that should be available to all military and veteran families who need them. FOCUS (Families Overcoming Under Stress) was developed by a UCLA-Harvard team, which based its design on previous research and evaluations of programs developed to help children and families contending with parental depression, a parent's infection with HIV, and military deployment. Based on the previous research and evaluations, the UCLA-Harvard team worked with the Navy and Marine Corps to modify the program's family prevention strategies for use with military families. FOCUS includes these central elements: family education, structured communication through discussing deployment on a personal level, and development of family-level resiliency skills. This multi-session program (typically six sessions, but sometimes more) involves separate meetings with parents and children, followed by sessions with all family members, who participate in structured activities led by skilled family resilience trainers.

FOCUS has been evaluated by checking participants both before and after they took part in the program (this kind of evaluation is called a pretest-posttest design). Data were collected over 20 months from nearly 500 participating families serving at 11 military installations. Before the program began, participating parents scored higher than community norms on measures of posttraumatic stress, depression, and anxiety, and children scored higher for emotional and behavioral problems. After 20 months, parents and children alike who participated in FOCUS showed significant improvement in all these areas. They also showed improvement on measures of family functioning, such as communication, role clarity, and problem solving, all of which were targeted by the FOCUS program. These results suggest that the processes underlying family resilience can be bolstered by family-centered preventive intervention.

Pretest-posttest designs are less than rigorous, however, and evaluations that use such a design cannot be fully trusted. But some of the testing that FOCUS's creators carried out as they designed the program met the highest standard of evaluation design, and the program should continue, although it should undergo more rigorous and better controlled evaluation. Moreover, refining FOCUS specifically for families who are contending with TBI and PTSD would expand its usefulness to those who are likely to experience the highest and longest-term risk. We recommend that federal funding pay to expand, adapt, and refine the program. We also call for funding to rigorously evaluate FOCUS and similar programs, following participants for at least 10 years, to determine whether they make a long-term difference in the lives of adults and children who experience the stress associated with combat deployment and its consequences. Such a plan would require collaboration among the Department of Defense (DoD), the Department of Veterans Affairs, other federal agencies, and universities and other academic or research institutions.

We must also ensure that service members and veterans, as well as their spouses and children, can easily access evidence-based mental health treatments in the communities where they live when formal treatment is required. Since many of the disorders for which veterans are treated are chronic (for example, PTSD, substance use, depression, and TBI), treatment and health maintenance programs that support veterans' functioning and minimize relapses or complications are critical to the health and wellbeing of military and veteran families and their children. Researchers universally recognize that children's health is related to the health and wellbeing of their parents. Traditional individual treatments of service members and veterans must incorporate family-focused approaches that address the profound impact that diagnoses such as PTSD and TBI can have on families and children. Preliminary evidence suggests that such programs are helpful and well-received.

A national plan to meet the needs of military and veteran children and families will not come cheaply. As the nation debates the size of the national budget and the wars in Iraq and Afghanistan wind down, attention may shift from the needs of military children and families. This is not just an issue for the DoD. Though the DoD has developed many programs to help military children and families, civilian communities—where Guard and Reserve families live and where active-duty families will move when their service ends—remain less well equipped. An effective national plan would require us to expand and integrate systems and resources that exist outside the DoD. Families need access not only to DoD resources, but also to programs provided through other federal agencies (for example, Veterans Affairs and the Substance Abuse and Mental Health Services Administration), other health care systems (for example, TRICARE), and public mental health systems, as well as private providers and community-based programs (for example, public schools, community colleges, child-care programs, and faith-based organizations). Optimally, such a system of care would include programs that coordinate their efforts with one another, that know and respect military culture, and that include the levels of service outlined in the Institute of Medicine spectrum of preventive and treatment interventions.

It is difficult to put a price tag on our recommendations for developing and testing effective prevention and treatment programs, but it will likely be in the tens of millions of dollars. Given the dramatic sacrifices that military families have made to defend the nation, policy makers and taxpayers should honor our promise to these families with the funds necessary to restore and sustain them. To do less would disrespect their service and discredit the nation's commitment to those who serve in harm's way.

Additional Reading

Anita Chandra et al., "Children on the Homefront: The Experience of Children from Military Families," *Pediatrics* 125, no. 1 (2010): 16–25.

Stephen J. Cozza and Richard M. Lerner, eds., "Military Children and Families," special issue, *The Future of Children* 23, no. 2 (2013).

Carol S. Fullerton et al., "Child Neglect in Army Families: A Public Health Perspective," *Military Medicine* 176, no. 12 (2011): 1432–39.

Institute of Medicine, *Returning Home from Iraq and Afghanistan: Assessment of Readjustment Needs of Veterans, Service Members, and Their Families* (Washington: National Academies Press, 2013).

Patricia Lester et al., "Evaluation of a Family-Centered Prevention Intervention for Military Children and Families," *American Journal of Public Health* 102 (2012): S48–54.

Patricia Lester et al., "The Long War and Parental Combat Deployment: Effects on Military Children and Spouses," *Journal of the American Academy of Child and Adolescent Psychiatry* 49 (2010): 310–20.

Ann Masten, "Ordinary Magic: Resilience Processes in Development," *American Psychologist* 56 (2001): 227–38.

James E. McCarroll et al., "Trends in U.S. Army Child Maltreatment Reports: 1990–2004," *Child Abuse Review* 17 (2008): 108–18.

Patricia Beezley Mrazek and Robert J. Haggerty, *Reducing Risks for Mental Disorders: Frontiers for Preventive Intervention Research* (Washington, DC: Institute of Medicine, 1994).

Sean C. Sheppard, Jennifer Weil Malatras, and Allen C. Israel., "The Impact of Deployment on U.S. Military Families," *American Psychologist* 65 (6), 599–609.

Critical Thinking

1. How are challenges faced by children and the non-deployed parent when the other parent is deployed?

2. What are factors that are related to the adaptability and resilience of military families? How can these factors be utilized in interventions and supports to assist military families?

3. What strategies are the most effective in assisting military families?

Create Central

www.mhhe.com/createcentral

Internet References

Military OneSource
www.militaryonesource.mil

National Military Family Association
www.militaryfamily.org

Substance Abuse and Mental Health Services Administration
www.samhsa.gov

STEPHEN J. COZZA'S views expressed herein do not necessarily reflect those of the Uniformed Services University of the Health Sciences or the Department of Defense.

Cozza, Colonel Stephen J.; Haskins, Ron; Lerner, Richard. "Policy Brief: Keeping the Promise: Maintaining the Health of Military and Veteran Families and Children." From *The Future of Children*, a collaboration of The Woodrow Wilson School of Public and International Affairs at Princeton University and the Brookings Institution.

Article

Prepared by: Patricia Hrusa Williams,
University of Maine at Farmington

From Promise to Promiscuity

HARA ESTROFF MARANO

Learning Outcomes

After reading this article, you will be able to:

- Describe how people cheat on their partners.

- Identify why people cheat.

- Explain what happens to a relationship after infidelity.

As devastating experiences go, few events can match the emotional havoc following the discovery that one's partner is having an affair. Atop a suddenly shattered world hover pain and rejection, doubts about one's worth, and, most searingly, the rupture of trust. For Deanna Stahling, discovery struck in a hallucinatory moment that forever fractured time into Before and After. She had just stepped off a plane from the Caribbean after a week's vacation with a family friend and picked up a copy of the city's leading newspaper. There, in the lifestyles section, was a profile of a top woman executive whose name Deanna had heard a lot lately—her husband worked with the woman. Deanna had even met her—introduced by her husband a few weeks earlier at a corporate function. The exec, it was reported, was leaving the company so that she could ethically pursue a relationship with a colleague.

Deanna doesn't remember the trip home from the airport, but the house was empty and her husband's belongings were gone. A denuded bookshelf highlighted now-missing Giants memorabilia. A note on the kitchen table advised her—after 25 years, two newly fledged kids, and the recent purchase of a joint cemetery plot—to refer any questions to his attorney.

The next morning found Deanna sobbing in a therapist's office. Together they began the search for the source of the sudden defection. Like most therapists (and indeed, most everyone else), they subscribed implicitly to a deficit model of affairs: the presumption that there were fatal problems in the relationship.

Over the past several years, however, leading thinkers have begun to abandon such a pathologizing approach. No one doubts that a straying partner is alone responsible for the often disastrous decision to engage in infidelity. But a new, more nuanced perspective that puts far more emphasis on contextual and situational factors has sparked a revolution in understanding and

handling affairs. The new approach encourages as a matter of course what happens now only by chance—complete recovery without any feelings being swept under the rug and even fortification of the couple bond.

The Shifting Landscape of Illicit Love

No one knows for sure just how common affairs are. Social desirability and fear of disclosure skew survey responses significantly. In 1994, 77 percent of 3,432 people constituting a representative sample of Americans declared that extramarital sex is always wrong (although the vast majority of people also have fantasies of engaging in an affair). And the number is actually growing. Today, over 90 percent of respondents deem sexual straying unacceptable—and expect sexual monogamy.

Still, decades of studies show that affairs are common, and, at least historically, more so among men than women: Among American couples, 20 to 40 percent of heterosexual married men and 10 to 25 percent of heterosexual married women will have an affair during their lifetime. In any given year, 1.5 to 4 percent of married individuals engage in an affair.

The newest surveys also reveal a very notable shift in the demographics of deception. Among younger cohorts—those under 45—the rates of infidelity among men and women are converging. Psychologists and sociologists attribute the development to huge changes in sheer opportunity, particularly the massive movement of women out of the home and into the workplace; studies show that the majority of individuals engaged in an affair met their lover at work. The rising financial power of women renders them less risk-averse, because they are less dependent on a spouse for support. As for a longstanding belief that men are more instinctually inclined to sexual infidelity than women are? Well, it's now far more of an open question.

That doesn't mean there are no gender differences in affairs. For women, infidelity is thought to be driven more by emotional needs and is most likely when they are not satisfied in their marital relationship, especially when it is not a partnership of equals. For men, infidelity has long been more independent of the state of the marital relationship. The pioneering psychologist Shirley Glass first reported in 1985 that among individuals engaging in infidelity, 56 percent of men and 34 percent of women rate their marriage as "happy" or "very happy." However, some of these differences may be disappearing, too. In 2003, just before she died, Glass reported that 74 percent of men were emotionally (as well as sexually) involved with their affair partner.

While the landscape of illicit love has been shifting, the therapeutic world has remained fairly fixed in the belief that affairs occur because something is radically wrong with the marriage. Make no mistake—most couples stay and want to stay together after a partner has strayed, despite the enormous psychic trauma to the uninvolved spouse. And indeed, 70 percent of couples choose to rebuild the relationship after infidelity, although they may not know how. Even couples for whom the violation is so painful or incomprehensible that divorce seems the only alternative often later regret a decision made in the highly disorienting days after discovery.

Studies indeed show that relationship dissatisfaction is associated with engaging in extramarital sex. But there's evidence that in almost two-thirds of cases, marital problems are the *effect,* not the cause, of extramarital involvements. Further, affairs themselves skew perceptions of the marriage. Once infidelity has occurred, partners tend to look back on their primary relationship and see it as having been flawed all along—an attempt to reduce cognitive dissonance.

Focusing attention exclusively on relationship flaws, say the field's leading thinkers, encourages couples to get psychologically stuck, brooding on the emotional betrayal and assigning blame. There is no statute of limitations on the hurt and anger that follow a partner's affair. But for the sake of dampening emotional volatility, injured partners are often rushed into "moving on," burying distrust and resentments that fester underground, sometimes for decades, forever precluding restoration of closeness.

Context, Context, Context

Affairs, says Washington, D.C., psychologist Barry McCarthy, are "the absolutely best example of behavior being multicausal, multidimensional. There are many contributing factors. Sometimes they have nothing to do with the marriage. The most common reason for an affair is high opportunity. People fall into affairs rather than plan them." Another very common cause of affairs, he observes, is that "people do not feel desired and desirable in their marriage, and they want to see if they can be desired and desirable outside it." For others, he notes, the affair is a symptom of a mental health problem like alcohol abuse or bipolar disorder. But unless all contributing elements are openly discussed and their meaning evaluated by both partners together, injured partners cannot regain the sense of security that allows them to forgive a straying spouse and rebuild trust in their mate. "The reality is that it takes two people to continue a marriage but only one to terminate a marriage," says McCarthy.

By far the biggest predictor of affairs, experts agree, is sheer opportunity—how people vary in access and desirability to others. And the workplace is the great benefactor, providing large numbers of people with constant contact, common interests, an income to camouflage the costs of socializing outside the office, and an ironclad excuse.

In a study of more than 4,000 adults, reported in the *Journal of Family Psychology,* Donald Baucom and colleagues found that both income and employment status are indices of opportunity for affairs. "Income may not be the critical variable in itself," they offer. "Individuals with higher incomes might be considered to have higher status, to travel more, or to interact professionally with more appealing individuals." In their study, those who worked but whose spouses did not were the most likely to report being unfaithful. Opportunity at the office is most ominous when it mixes with a disparity in relationship power at home.

Travel is way up there, researchers find, especially work related travel. "Lots of elements go into that," says Kristina Coop Gordon, professor of psychology at the University of Tennessee. "You're away from your partner, maybe even missing your mate, and you're in situations where you're encountering

---

The Other Woman

She might be history's most reviled female. Or most misunderstood. She isn't all she's cracked up to be. Sex with her is generally no better than sex in the marriage. And she's not likely to be a bombshell. The most you can say for sure is that she's different from the wife, and that may be all some cheaters need. Most male affairs, which is to say most affairs, are excursions of opportunity with little emotional investment. Worth crying over, yes. But not necessarily worth bringing the house down. Fewer than 25 percent of cheaters leave a marriage for an affair partner, and those relationships are statistically extremely unlikely to endure.

However much the mystery woman incites rage and envy and dreams of malevolence, she falls short of the self-destructive comparisons made against her.

Usually, says University of Tennessee psychologist Kristina Coop Gordon, fixation on the other woman and desire for details about her are not what they seem. "It's really a test of the straying spouse by the wounded one: 'Will you be open with me about the affair?' They really don't want to know the gory details; either it will spark a fight or make them feel bad. The wounded spouse just wants proof that she's important enough."

Sometimes, however, the other woman won't let go. She may threaten retaliation or self-harm. On the other hand, the involved spouse may do a miserable job of setting firm boundaries and not make a clean break of it. "Some men are not quite letting go themselves," Gordon finds. "And they're sending mixed messages to the other woman, which both she and the wife pick up on. That may be one reason a wounded wife can become obsessed with the other woman; there's a continuing threat."

—H. E. M.

plenty of people," Gordon explains. "It certainly facilitates one-night stands." Companies that employ large cohorts of young people, especially those who socialize together after work, create an environment for affairs.

No one profession has a lock on infidelity, Gordon maintains. Most relevant is the culture within a company. "Really macho cultures, which often exist in drug enforcement and police work, can involve a 'player' phenomenon where you need to show how virile you are. They are the clearest examples of work environments that foster infidelity that I've seen."

Duplicity also has a downtown address. Living in the midst of a city abets infidelity. Not only is there exposure to large numbers of potential partners, there's more opportunity to escape detection. The larger the city one lives in, researchers have found, the greater the likelihood of an affair.

Attending religious services is generally a deterrent to infidelity, perhaps because it embeds people in a social network that promotes accountability. But it helps only those who are already happy in their relationship. If the primary relationship is less than ideal, then dissatisfaction overrides religious values. Rates of infidelity do not differ by denomination.

Education increases the propensity to infidelity. It may be a marker for more liberal attitudes toward sexuality and permissive attitudes toward adultery. Ditto a history of divorce, or having parents who divorced, especially if either one had an extramarital involvement. Women with more education than their husbands have more affairs, perhaps because they are less dependent on a spouse.

Friendships are a factor in infidelity. Peer groups may sanction or even encourage it, researchers have found. Those who engage in extramarital involvements estimate a higher prevalence of affairs in their community than those who don't and believe their friends would be relatively approving. Separate his and her friendship networks are especially risky. One way of avoiding infidelity is to share a spouse's social network. Befriending a partner's family proves particularly protective. In one study it was linked to a 26 percent decrease in the odds of sexual infidelity.

Personality differences between partners play a role as well. Spouses who are comfortable with conflict and more or less matched on that trait are less likely to have affairs, perhaps because they are most open to airing marital concerns and dissatisfactions with each other.

In general, openness is protective and a characteristic of non-cheaters. Associated with intelligence, creativity, curiosity, and insightfulness, openness makes partners more satisfied with the relationship and better able to express feelings, including love. Some researchers believe that openness is essential to commitment to and enduring satisfaction in a relationship.

Low levels of agreeableness (the tendency to be compassionate and cooperative) bode poorly for monogamy. More important, however, is whether couples are matched on that trait. Spouses who see themselves as more agreeable than their mate believe themselves to be more giving, feel exploited by their partner, and seek reciprocity through outside relationships. Many studies show that a high level of neuroticism also inclines individuals to infidelity, independent of a partner's personality.

Psychological problems factor in, too. Affairs, associated with insecurity and having low self-esteem, can be a way of seeking reassurance of desirability or of combating depression. An affair certainly provides an arousing stimulus that is an antidote, however temporary, to feeling down. Then, too, affairs are also linked to high self-regard, a sense of one's own attractiveness or entitlement, or maybe the accompaniment to narcissism.

Situations that deplete self-control—exposure to alcohol, an exhausting day of travel, doing highly challenging work—raise the risk of infidelity. They disable sexual restraint, psychologists Roy Baumeister and Matthew Gailliot have found. The two manipulated self-control by giving subjects cognitively demanding or simple word puzzles before presenting them with purely hypothetical scenarios testing their willingness to engage in infidelity. The more demanding the tasks, the more depleted self-control, the more subjects were unable to inhibit their inclination to infidelity or to stifle sexual thoughts. Of course, hypothetical infidelity is a long way from landing in bed with someone.

Hypocrisy or Hormones?

The very make-up of the human brain contributes to affairs, too, observes anthropologist Helen Fisher. She has shown in brain-imaging studies that there are separate neural systems for sex drive, romantic love, and attachment, and they can operate independently. "Everyone starts out in marriage believing they will not have an affair. Why do data from around the world consistently show that infidelity occurs even among people who are happy in their marriage? You can feel deep attachment to a partner but also feel intense romantic love for someone else while also feeling a desire for sex with other partners," she observes.

The attachment system, fueled by the neurohormones oxytocin in females and vasopressin in males, drives animals, including humans, to pair-bond to rear their offspring as a team. Both hormones are triggered by orgasm, and both trigger dopamine release in reward regions of the brain. But all animals cheat, even when they form pair bonds.

In most mammals, the bond lasts only as long as it takes to rear the young. Among prairie voles, science's favorite model of monogamy, knocking out the gene that codes for vasopressin receptors abolishes their penchant for pair-bonding. And implanting it in their notoriously promiscuous cousins, the mountain voles, leads the males to fixate on a specific female partner even when alluring others are abundantly available.

More recently, in a study of over 500 men, Swedish researchers found that variations in a gene that codes for vasopressin receptors in humans influences the very ability to form monogamous relationships. Men with two copies of a specific gene variant scored significantly lower on a questionnaire known as the Partner Bonding Scale and reported twice as many marital crises in the past year. Those with two copies of the variant were also twice as likely to be involved in outside relationships and far less likely to have ever been married than those not carrying the allele.

"Monogamy does not mean sexual fidelity. That is a separate issue," says Fisher. In fact, scientists increasingly speak of "social monogamy" to distinguish promise from promiscuity. If we are monogamous, we are also just as predictably adulterous. What's more, people jeopardize their family, their health, their safety, their social standing, their financial well-being for affairs—and violate their own strong beliefs.

Monogamy may be the norm in human culture, but it is only part of the human reproductive repertoire, contends Fisher. "We humans have a dual reproductive strategy," she argues. "We regularly appear to express a combination of lifelong (or serial) social monogamy and, in many cases, clandestine adultery."

Despite its many risks, and sometimes because of them, there are big payoffs for infidelity, Fisher argues. For men especially, genetic variation is the most obvious. But she believes that women benefit, too. Infidelity may provide a "back-up mate" to offer protection and resources when the regular guy is not around. And women may use affairs as away of "trading up" to find a more desirable partner. It's possible, too, that infidelity can serve a positive role in relationships—as a way to gain attention from one's primary partner or to signal that there are problems in the relationship that need attending to.

In a study reported in 2010 in *PLoS One,* Justin Garcia, a postdoctoral fellow at Binghamton University, outlined another payoff—pure, passionate thrill. He found that individuals with a variant of a dopamine receptor gene were more likely than those without it to have a history of "uncommitted sex, one-night stands, and adultery." The motivation, he says, "stems from a system of pleasure and reward." Fisher suspects that's just the tip of the infidelity iceberg, and more biological contributors are likely to be identified in future studies.

From Angry Victim to Proud Survivor

One of the great facts of infidelity is that it has such a wildly different emotional impact on the marital partners. The uninvolved partner is deeply traumatized and emotionally distraught over the betrayal, and desperately trying to piece together what happened. The straying partner, often because of deep shame, may get defensive and shut down or blame the spouse for not moving on, only compounding the hurt. One needs to talk about what happened; the other can't bear to. "It's as if one of them is speaking German, the other is speaking Greek, and they're not speaking English to each other," McCarthy says.

Getting them on the same track of understanding is the key to recovery from affairs, says Gordon, who along with Baucom and Douglas Snyder, professor of psychology at Texas A&M, has sparked the revolution in treating infidelity not only by focusing on the many contributing factors but by developing the first empirically validated model of recovery. As detailed in their book, *Getting Past the Affair,* the first step is for both spouses to recognize the huge emotional impact on the uninvolved partner. Gordon and company have found a powerful device: After encouraging the partners to make no decisions about the future in the immediate aftermath of discovery or disclosure, they ask that the cheated-on partner write a letter to the spouse describing what the hurt feels like.

"The cheating partner must hear, no matter how discomfiting it is," says Gordon. "The experience is very intense and usually a turning point. Partners begin to soften towards each other. It's a demonstration to the injured partner that he or she really matters."

Then together the spouses search for the meaning of the affair by exploring how the choice was made and what contributed to it. Everything is fair game—attitudes and expectations about marriage that each partner has, conflicts and anything else going on in the relationship, hidden desires, personal anxieties and insecurities, needs for excitement, the closeness and distance they feel, job demands, work ambience, flirtations, opportunities, the people and pressures around them at home and outside it. The approach short-circuits the often misguided inclination to focus on The Other Person.

From understanding flows forgiveness, which allows partners to become close again. Wild as the reaction to discovery of a partner's affair can be in the beginning, Gordon welcomes it. "At least it provides the opportunity to interact around the pain. What often happens with the 'nice' couples," she says, "is they stay together but lead parallel lives marked by great distance. There's no bond anymore."

Renewing Romance

Barry McCarthy gives the revolution in recovery from affairs another twist all his own—re-eroticizing the marriage. "A couple has to develop a new sexual style" that facilitates sexual desire both in and out of the bedroom, he says. The point is to abolish the inclination to compare marital sex with affair sex—a hopeless cause as affair partners don't have to contend with sick kids and other realities of life, and the illicitness of the liaison intensifies excitement—but to compare marital sex before the affair and after it.

For the vast majority of American couples today, sexual satisfaction plummets at the birth of the first child and reemerges, if at all, after the last child leaves home. Of course, it doesn't have to be that way. Admittedly, McCarthy says, "it's a balancing act for partners to maintain their sense of who they are as individuals, their sense of being a couple, and being parents and sexual people." But in the long run, it's in everyone's best interest. Most contemporary couples, he laments, treat sexuality with benign neglect—until an affair sets off a crisis.

In healthy marriages, sex plays what he deems "a relatively small part, a 15 to 20 percent part"—but it energizes the whole bond and allows each partner to feel desired and desirable. When couples abandon sex, they wind up draining the entire relationship of its vitality. "You not only lose the marriage connection but your sense of self," McCarthy finds. "An affair can be an attempt to regain a sense of self."

So McCarthy puts great effort into reconnecting partners both emotionally and physically. He focuses on "non-demand pleasure." "We try to reintroduce the idea of touching inside and outside the bedroom, clothed and not clothed, valuing sensual and playful touch. It can be a bridge to intercourse, but there's no demand that it has to go to intercourse." He encourages couples to find a mutually acceptable level of intimacy and come up with their own erotic scenarios.

Pacts of Prevention

Because good intentions do not prove good enough, McCarthy takes post affair repair one step further—asking couples to create an explicit pact to prevent future infidelity by either of them. Together, they lay out the terms for disclosing when their interest is straying. Having painfully reached an understanding of the complex personal, marital, and situational vulnerabilities that led to an affair, couples draft a relapse prevention agreement.

The purpose is to rob any future affair of its spontaneity and its emotional and sexual secrecy. Both partners are encouraged to articulate the types of situation, mood, and person that could draw them into an affair—and to share that information with each other.

Then they commit to alert the spouse if they are in a high-risk situation and to discuss it rather than act on it. As an incentive, the agreement, drawing on recent experience, spells out the emotional costs to both parties of an affair. Because the secrecy and cover-up of infidelity are often more damaging than the defection itself, partners agree that, if there is a sexual incident, they will disclose it within 72 hours. And it works, McCarthy finds.

The pact of prevention embodies a principle Helen Fisher enunciates most succinctly: "Predisposition isn't predestination."

Six years after her disorienting discovery, Deanna is remarried; her new husband shares her taste for travel and adventure. She can talk dispassionately (with close friends) about the thin spots that likely existed all along in her first marriage. She understands how her frequent travels as a consultant, although they never tempted *her* to stray, carried intimations of abandonment for her more anxious ex. And how, under the circumstances, his conversations with an attentive female coworker could have evolved from the collegial to the confidential almost imperceptibly over the course of a year. But there's one question that still nags at her: Why, when their marriage was about to blow apart, did her husband insist that they share eternity by purchasing a joint burial plot? She'll probably never know.

Critical Thinking

1. The article refers to infidelity as a "multicausal, multidimensional behavior." Explain what this means.

2. Who is most likely to cheat in a relationship? Why?

3. What factors contribute to cheating behavior? In what situations is someone more likely to cheat on a spouse and why?

4. What, if anything, can be done to prevent or lessen the likelihood that a spouse will cheat?

Create Central

www.mhhe.com/createcentral

Internet Reference

American Association for Marriage and Family Therapy: Infidelity
www.aamft.org/imis15/content/Consumer_Updates/Infidelity.aspx

Article   Prepared by: Patricia Hrusa Williams, *University of Maine at Farmington*

The Adultery Arms Race

Michelle Cottle

Learning Outcomes

After reading this article, you will be able to:

- Explain how technology is influencing cheating and infidelity in relationships.

- Identity different technological options and apps available to monitor partner's mobile phones and devices.

- Analyze the effects of being able to spy on a partner's activities through technology.

Jay's wife, Ann, was supposed to be out of town on business. It was a Tuesday evening in August 2013, and Jay, a 36-year-old IT manager, was at home in Indiana with their 5-year-old daughter and 9-year-old son when he made a jarring discovery. Their daughter had misplaced her iPad, so Jay used the app Find My iPhone to search for it. The app found the missing tablet right away, but it also located all the other devices on the family's plan. What was Ann's phone doing at a hotel five miles from their home?

His suspicions raised, Jay, who knew Ann's passwords, read through her e-mails and Facebook messages. (Like others in this story, Jay asked that his and Ann's names be changed.) He didn't find anything incriminating, but neither could he imagine a good reason for Ann to be at that hotel. So Jay started using Find My iPhone for an altogether different purpose: to monitor his wife's whereabouts.

Two nights later, when Ann said she was working late, Jay tracked her phone to the same spot. This time, he drove to the hotel, called her down to the parking lot, and demanded to know what was going on. Ann told him she was there posing for boudoir photos, with which she planned to surprise him for his upcoming birthday. She said the photographer was up in the room waiting for her.

Jay wanted to believe Ann. They'd been married for 12 years, and she had never given him cause to distrust her. So instead of demanding to meet the photographer or storming up to the room, Jay got in his car and drove home.

Still, something gnawed at him. According to Ann's e-mails, the boudoir photo shoot had indeed taken place—but on the previous day, Wednesday. So her being at the hotel on Tuesday and again on Thursday didn't make sense. Unless . . .

In an earlier era, a suspicious husband like Jay might have rifled through Ann's pockets or hired a private investigator. But having stumbled upon Find My iPhone's utility as a surveillance tool, Jay wondered what other apps might help him keep tabs on his wife. He didn't have to look far. Spouses now have easy access to an array of sophisticated spy software that would give Edward Snowden night sweats: programs that record every keystroke; that compile detailed logs of our calls, texts, and video chats; that track a phone's location in real time; that recover deleted messages from all manner of devices (without having to touch said devices); that turn phones into wiretapping equipment; and on and on.

Jay spent a few days researching surveillance tools before buying a program called Dr. Fone, which enabled him to remotely recover text messages from Ann's phone. Late one night, he downloaded her texts onto his work laptop. He spent the next day reading through them at the office. Turns out, his wife had become involved with a co-worker. There were thousands of text messages between them, many X-rated—an excruciatingly detailed record of Ann's betrayal laid out on Jay's computer screen. "I could literally watch her affair progress," Jay told me, "and that in itself was painful."

One might assume that the proliferation of such spyware would have a chilling effect on extramarital activities. Aspiring cheaters, however, need not despair: software developers are also rolling out ever stealthier technology to help people conceal their affairs. Married folk who enjoy a little side action can choose from such specialized tools as Vaulty Stocks, which hides photos and videos inside a virtual vault within one's phone that's disguised to look like a stock-market app, and Nosy Trap, which displays a fake iPhone home screen and takes a picture of anyone who tries to snoop on the phone. CATE (the Call and Text Eraser) hides texts and calls from certain contacts and boasts tricky features such as the ability to "quick clean" incriminating evidence by shaking your smartphone. CoverMe does much of the above, plus offers "military-grade encrypted phone calls." And in the event of an emergency, there's the nuclear option: apps that let users remotely wipe a phone completely clean, removing all traces of infidelity.

But every new app that promises to make playing around safer and easier just increases the appetite for a cleverer way to expose such deception. Some products even court both sides: a partner at CATE walked me through how a wife could install the app on her husband's phone to create a secret record of calls and texts to be perused at her leisure. Which may be great from a market-demand standpoint, but is probably not so healthy for the broader culture, as an accelerating spiral of paranoia drives an arms race of infidelity-themed weapons aimed straight at the consumer's heart.

E very tech trend has its early adopters. Justin, a 30-year-old computer programmer from Ohio, is at the vanguard of this one.

Justin first discovered CATE on the September 21, 2012, episode of *Shark Tank,* ABC's venture-capital reality show. The Call and Text Eraser, pitched specifically as a "cheating app," won $70,000 in seed money on the program. Justin knew he had to have it.

His girlfriend at the time—we'll call her Scarlett—was "the jealous type," forever poking through his smartphone and computer. Not that he could blame her, given that she'd already busted him once for having sex with another woman. "It took a lot of talking and a lot of promising that it wouldn't happen again," he told me over e-mail. (I found Justin through a user review of CATE.) "So her wanting to check up on me was understandable," he allowed. "But at the same time, it was my business and if I wanted to share I would have."

Even a not-so-jealous girlfriend might have taken exception to many of the messages on Justin's phone: "casual texting" (that is, flirting) with other women, "hard core" (explicitly sexual) texting, texts arranging "hookups." In the past, he'd been busted repeatedly for such communiqués. (Scarlett is not the only girlfriend with whom Justin has found monogamy to be a challenge.) With CATE, all Justin had to do was create a list of contacts he didn't want Scarlett to know about, and any incriminating texts and phone calls with those contacts got channeled directly into a pass-code-protected vault.

CATE is just one of many tools Justin uses to, as he puts it, "stay one step ahead." His go-to method for exchanging explicit photos is Snapchat, the popular app that causes pics and videos to self-destruct seconds after they are received. (Of course, as savvy users know, expired "snaps" aren't really deleted, but merely hidden in the bowels of the recipient's phone, so Justin periodically goes in and permanently scrubs them.) And for visuals so appealing that he cannot bear to see them vanish into the ether, he has Gallery Lock, which secretes pics and videos inside a private "gallery" within his phone.

Justin wound up cheating on Scarlett "several more times" before they finally broke up—a pattern he's repeated with other girlfriends. Oh, sure, he enjoys the social and domestic comforts of a relationship ("It's always nice to have someone to call your girl"). He understands the suffering that infidelity can cause ("I have been cheated on so I know how much it hurts"). He even feels guilty about playing around. But for him, the adrenaline kick is irresistible. "Not to mention," he adds, "no woman is the same [and] there is always going to be someone out there who can do something sexually that you have never tried." Then, of course, there's "the thrill of never knowing if you are going to get caught."

All of which makes it more than a little troubling that, while laboring to keep one semiserious girlfriend after another in the dark with privacy-enhancing apps, Justin has been equally aggressive about using spy apps to keep a virtual eye on said girlfriends.

Justin has tried it all: keystroke loggers, phone trackers, software enabling him to "see text messages, pictures, and all the juicy stuff . . . even the folder to where your deleted stuff would go." He figures he's tried nearly every spy and cheater app on the market, and estimates that since 2007, he has "kept tabs," serially, on at least half a dozen girlfriends. "The monitoring is really just for my peace of mind," he says. Plus, if he catches a girlfriend straying, "it kind of balances it out and makes it fair." That way, he explains, if she ever busts him, "I have proof she was cheating so therefore she would have no reason to be mad."

Not that Justin is immune to the occasional flash of jealousy. More than once, he has gone out to confront a girlfriend whose phone revealed her to be somewhere other than where she'd claimed to be. One relationship ended with particularly dramatic flair: "The phone went to the location off of a country road in the middle of nowhere and there she was having sex in the backseat of the car with another man." A fistfight ensued (with the guy, not the girlfriend), followed later by "breakup sex" (vice versa). One year on, Justin says, "I still don't believe that she has figured out how I found out."

Justin knows that many folks may find his playing both sides of the cheating-apps divide "twisted." But, he reasons, "I am doing it for my safety to make sure I don't get hurt. So doesn't that make it right??"

Right or wrong, cheating apps tap into a potentially lucrative market: While the national infidelity rate is hard to pin down (because, well, people lie), reputable research puts the proportion of unfaithful spouses at about 15 percent of women and 20 percent of men—with the gender gap closing fast. And while the roots of infidelity remain more or less constant (the desire for novelty, attention, affirmation, a lover with tighter glutes . . .), technology is radically altering how we enter into, conduct, and even define it. (The affairs in this piece all involved old-school, off-line sex, but there is a growing body of research on the devastation wrought by the proliferation of online-only betrayal.) Researchers regard the Internet as fertile ground for female infidelity in particular. "Men tend to cheat for physical reasons and women for emotional reasons," says Katherine Hertlein, who studies the impact of technology on relationships as the director of the Marriage and Therapy Program at the University of Nevada at Las Vegas. "The Internet facilitates a lot of emotional disclosure and connections with someone else."

At the same time, privacy has become a rare commodity. Forget the National Security Agency and Russian mobsters: in a recent survey conducted in the United Kingdom, 62 percent of men in relationships admitted to poking around in a current or ex-partner's mobile phone. (Interestingly, among women, the proportion was only 34 percent. So much for the stereotype of straying guys versus prying gals.) On the flip side, according to the Pew Research Center's Internet and American Life Project, 14 percent of adults have taken steps to hide their online activity from a family member or romantic partner. Therapists say they're seeing more spouses casually tracking each other as well as more clashes over online spying, and lawyers are starting to recommend digital-privacy clauses for prenup and postnup agreements. Such clauses aim to prevent spouses from using personal texts, e-mails, or photos against each other should they wind up in divorce court.

Tech developers by and large didn't set out looking to get involved. As is so often the case with infidelity, it just sort of happened. Take Find My iPhone. Apple did not create the app with suspicious lovers in mind, but users pretty quickly realized its potential. Dr. Fone is marketed primarily as a way to recover lost data. Likewise, messaging apps such as Snapchat have many more uses than concealing naughty talk or naked photos, but the apps are a hit with cheaters.

The multipurpose nature and off-label use of many tools make it difficult to gauge the size of this vast and varied market. The company mSpy offers one of the top-rated programs for monitoring smartphones and computers; 2 million subscribers pay between $20 and $70 a month for the ability to do everything from review browsing history to listen in on phone calls to track a device's whereabouts. Some 40 percent of customers are parents looking to monitor their kids, according to Andrew Lobanoff, the head of sales at mSpy, who says the company does basic consumer research to see who its customers are and what features they want added. Another 10 to 15 percent are small businesses monitoring employees' use of company devices (another growing trend). The remaining 45 to 50 percent? They could be up to anything.

Apps marketed specifically as tools for cheaters and jealous spouses for the most part aren't seeing the download numbers of a heavy hitter like, say, Grindr, the hookup app for gay men (10 million downloads and more than 5 million monthly users). But plenty have piqued consumer interest: The private-texting-and-calling app CoverMe has more than 2 million users. TigerText, which (among other features) causes messages to self-destruct after a set amount of time, has been downloaded 3.5 million times since its introduction in February 2010. (It hit the market a couple of months after the Tiger Woods sexting scandal, though the company maintains that the app is not named for Woods.)

Once the marketplace identifies a revenue stream, of course, the water has been chummed and everyone rushes in for a taste. By now, new offerings are constantly popping up from purveyors large and small. Ashley Madison, the online-dating giant for married people (company slogan: "Life is short. Have an affair."), has a mobile app that provides some 30 million members "on the go" access to its services. Last year, the company introduced an add-on app called BlackBook, which allows users to purchase disposable phone numbers with which to conduct their illicit business. Calls and texts are placed through the app much as they are through Skype, explains the company's chief operating officer, Rizwan Jiwan. "One of the leading ways people get caught in affairs is by their cellphone bill," he observes. But with the disposable numbers, all calls are routed through a user's Ashley Madison account, which appears on his or her credit-card statements under a series of business aliases. "The phone number isn't tied to you in any way."

Both sides of the arms race have ego invested in not getting outgunned. Stressing Ashley Madison's obsession with customer privacy, Jiwan boasts that the shift from computers to mobile devices makes it harder for members to get busted. "It's much more difficult to get spyware on phones," he told me. But mSpy's Lobanoff pushed back: "All applications can be monitored. Let me make it clear for you. If you provide us what application you would like to track, within two weeks we can develop a feature to do that." It all boils down to demand. For instance, he notes, after receiving some 300 calls from customers looking to monitor Snapchat, the company rolled out just such a feature.

Lobanoff admits that iPhones are tougher to monitor than phones from other brands, because Apple is strict about what runs on its operating system (although many Apple users "jail-break" their devices, removing such limits). Which raises the question: Is an iPhone a good investment for cheaters worried about being monitored—or would it too tightly restrict their access to cheating apps? Such are the complexities of modern infidelity.

Of course, no app can remove all risk of getting caught. Technology can, in fact, generate a false sense of security that leads people to push limits or get sloppy. Justin has had several close calls, using CATE to conceal indiscreet texts and voicemails but forgetting to hide explicit photos. When a girlfriend found a naked picture of him that he'd failed to delete after sexting another woman, Justin had to think fast. "The way I talk my way out of it is that I say I was going to send it to her." Then, of course, there is the peril of creeping obsolescence: after several months, regular upgrades to the operating system on Justin's phone outpaced CATE's, and more and more private messages began to slip through the cracks. (A scan of user reviews suggests this is a common problem.)

Virtual surveillance has its risks as well. Stumbling across an incriminating e-mail your partner left open is one thing; premeditated spying can land you in court—or worse. Sometime in 2008 or 2009, a Minnesota man named Danny Lee Hormann, suspecting his wife of infidelity, installed a GPS tracker on her car and allegedly downloaded spyware onto her phone and the family computer. His now-ex-wife, Michele Mathias (who denied having an affair), began wondering how her husband always knew what she was up to. In March 2010, Mathias had a mechanic search her car. The tracker was found. Mathias called the police, and Hormann spent a month in jail on stalking charges. (It's worth noting that a second conviction, specifically for illegally tracking her car, was overturned on appeal when the judge ruled that joint ownership gave Hormann the right to install the GPS tracker.)

Staying on the right side of the law is trickier than one might imagine. There are a few absolute no-nos. At the top of the list: never install software on a device that you do not own without first obtaining the user's consent. Software sellers are careful to shift the legal burden onto consumers. On its site, mSpy warns that misuse of the software "may result in severe monetary and criminal penalties." Similarly, SpyBubble, which offers cellphone-tracking software, reminds its customers of their duty to "notify users of the device that they are being monitored." Even so, questions of ownership and privacy get messy between married partners, and the landscape remains in flux as courts struggle to apply old laws to new technology.

In 2010, a Texas man named Larry Bagley was acquitted of charges that he violated federal wiretapping laws by installing audio-recording devices around his house and keystroke-monitoring software on his then-wife's computer. In his ruling, the district judge pointed to a split opinion among U.S. circuit courts as to whether the federal law applies to "interspousal wiretaps." (The Fourth, Sixth, Eighth, Tenth, and Eleventh Circuit Courts said it does, he noted; the Second and Fifth said it doesn't.) Similarly, in California, Virginia, Texas, Minnesota, and as of this summer New York, it is a misdemeanor to install a GPS tracker on someone's vehicle without their consent. But when a vehicle is jointly owned, things get fuzzy.

"I always tell people two things: (1) do it legally, and (2) do it right," says John Paul Lucich, a computer-forensics expert and the author of *Cyber Lies,* a do-it-yourself guide for spouses looking to become virtual sleuths. Lucich has worked his share of ugly divorces, and he stresses that even the most damning digital evidence of infidelity will prove worthless in court—and potentially land you in trouble—if improperly gathered. His blanket advice: Get a really good lawyer. Stat.

Such apps clearly have the potential to blow up relationships, but the question now may be whether they can be used to salvage them as well. Many of the betrayed partners I spoke with believe they can.

A couple of years ago, Ginger discovered that her husband, Tim, was having an affair with a woman he'd met through a nonprofit on whose board he sat. (As Ginger tells it, this was a classic case of a middle-aged man having his head turned by a much younger woman.) The affair lasted less than a year, but it took another eight months before Tim's lover stopped sending him gifts and showing up in awkward places (even church!).

Ginger and Tim decided to tough it out—they've been married for 35 years and have two adult children—but that took some doing. For the first year and a half, certain things Tim did or said would trigger Ginger's anxiety. He would announce that he was going to the store; Ginger would fire up her tracking software to ensure he did just that. Business travel called for even more elaborate reassurances. "When he was away, I would be like, 'I want you to FaceTime the whole room—the bathroom, the closet; open the hallway door.'"

Ginger's anxiety has dimmed, but not vanished. She still occasionally uses Find My iPhone to make sure Tim is, in fact, staying late at the office. "And we use FaceTime all the time. He knows that if I try to FaceTime him, he'd better answer right then or have a very, very good reason why he didn't."

Jay and Ann, of the boudoir photo shoot, also decided to try to repair their marriage. When he first confronted her with a record of her texts, Ann denied that the sex talk was ever more than fantasy. But when Jay scheduled a polygraph, she confessed to a full-blown, physical affair.

As hard as it has been for Jay, one year later he reports that tech tools are helping. Ann's affair grew out of her sense of neglect, Jay told me: "She wasn't getting the attention she wanted from me, so she found someone else to give it to her." To strengthen their bond, Jay and Ann have started using Couple, a relationship app geared toward promoting intimacy by setting up a private line of communication for texts, pics, video clips, and, of course, updates on each person's whereabouts. Every now and again, Jay sneaks a peek at Find My iPhone. He also has set his iPad to receive copies of Ann's texts. "I don't know if she realizes I'm doing that," he told me. But in general, she understands his desire for extra oversight. "She's like, 'Whatever you want.'"

In fact, post-affair surveillance seems to be an increasingly popular counseling prescription. Even as marriage and family therapists take a dim view of unprovoked snooping, once the scent of infidelity is in the air, many become enthusiastically pro-snooping—initially to help uncover the truth about a partner's behavior but then to help couples reconcile by reestablishing accountability and trust. The psychotherapist and syndicated columnist Barton Goldsmith says he often advocates virtual monitoring in the aftermath of an affair. Even if a spouse never exercises the option of checking up, having it makes him or her feel more secure. "It's like a digital leash."

And that can be a powerful deterrent, says Frank, whose wife of 37 years learned of his fondness for hookers last February, after he forgot to close an e-mail exchange with an escort. "He had set up a Gmail account I had no idea he had," Carol, his wife, told me. Frank tried to convince her that the e-mails were just spam, even after she pointed out that the exchange included his cell number and photos of him.

Frank agreed to marriage counseling and enrolled in a 12-step program for sexual addiction. Carol now tracks his phone and regularly checks messages on both his phone and his computer. Still, she told me sadly, "I don't think that I'm ever going to get the whole story. I believe he thinks that if I know everything, the marriage will come to an end."

For his part, Frank—who comes across as a gruff, traditional sort of guy, uneasy sharing his feelings even with his wife—calls Carol's discovery of his betrayal "excruciating," but he mostly seems angry at the oversexed culture that he feels landed him in this mess. He grumbles about how "the ease and the accessibility and the anonymity of the Internet" made it "entirely too easy" for him to feed his addiction.

Frank has clearly absorbed some of the language and lessons of therapy. "As well as it is a learned behavior to act out, it is a learned behavior not to," he told me. He doesn't much like his wife's having total access to his phone, but he claims that his sole concern is for the privacy of others in his 12-step group, who text one another for support. Frank himself clearly feels the tug of his digital leash. "Now that she checks my phone and computer, I have a deterrent."

Even as he calls virtual surveillance "a powerful tool," though, Frank also declares it a limited one. No matter how clever the technology becomes, there will always be workarounds. For someone looking to stray, "absolutely nothing is going to stop it," says Frank, emphatically. "Nothing."

Critical Thinking

1. Have you ever spied on the cell phone or Internet activities of a romantic partner or loved one? How did you do it and why? What did you learn and how did it make you feel?

2. How has technology and virtual surveillance changed the nature of intimate relationships and cheating? What are ethical, legal, and emotional issues surrounding spying on partners which need to be considered?

3. How can technological surveillance and our digital trail be used to help restore trust between partners who have experienced infidelity?

Internet References

American Association for Marriage and Family Therapy: Infidelity
www.aamft.org/imis15/content/Consumer_Updates/Infidelity.aspx
Beyond Affairs Network
http://beyondaffairs.com/
Dear Peggy: Extramarital Affairs Resource Center
http://www.dearpeggy.com/

MICHELLE COTTLE is a senior writer for National Journal.

Article

Prepared by: Patricia Hrusa Williams,
University of Maine at Farmington

International Perspectives on Work-Family Policies: Lessons from the World's Most Competitive Economies

ALISON EARLE, ZITHA MOKOMANE, AND JODY HEYMANN

Learning Outcomes

After reading this article, you will be able to:

- Identify family-friendly work policies.

- Understand the differences between the United States' and other nations' work-family policies.

- Discuss the challenges parents have in dividing time between work and family.

In the majority of American families with children today, all parents are employed. In 67 percent of families with school-age children, 64 percent of families with preschool-age children, and 60 percent of families with children age three and younger, the parents are working for pay.[1] As a result, the workplace policies that parents face—such as how many hours they need to be away from home, the leave they can take to care for a sick child, and the work schedules that determine whether and when they are able to visit a son's or daughter's school—shape not only their income but also the time they have available for childrearing.

U.S. policies on parental leave, sick leave, vacation days, and days of rest are often in sharp contrast to other developed and developing countries, but those who want to make these policies more supportive of parents and their children face stiff opposition from those who say such policies will harm the United States' ability to compete economically with other countries. This article takes an international perspective to evaluate whether having workplace policies that support parents' ability to be available to meet their children's needs is compatible with economic competitiveness and low unemployment. We analyze a unique global database of labor legislation, focusing specifically on those measures dealing with parental availability in the first year of life, when caregiving needs are particularly intensive; parental availability to meet children's health needs; and their availability to meet their children's developmental needs.

We first review the evidence on the relationship of parental working conditions to children's outcomes. Second, we discuss the claims made in the public debates regarding the potential costs and benefits of family-supportive labor policies to individual employers and national economies, and review the academic literature on this topic. We then use new cross-national data to examine the extent to which highly competitive countries and countries with low unemployment rates do or do not provide these policies. Finally, we summarize the implications of our findings for U.S. policy.

Relationship of Parental Working Conditions to Children's Outcomes

Research in the United States and in other developed as well as developing countries suggests that workplace policies that support parents' ability to be available for their children at crucial periods of their lives have measurable effects on children's outcomes.

Paid Parental Leave

Research shows that the availability of paid leave following childbirth has the potential to improve infant and child health by making it affordable and feasible for parents to stay home and provide the intensive care newborns and infants need, including breast-feeding and a high caregiver-to-infant ratio that most child-care centers are unable to match.[2] Parental leave can have substantial benefits for child health. Christopher Ruhm's examination of more than two decades of data from sixteen European countries found that paid parental leave policies were associated with lower rates of infant and child mortality after taking into account per capita income, the availability of health services and technology, and other factors linked with child health. Ruhm found that a ten-week paid maternity leave was associated with a reduction in infant mortality rates of 1–2 percent; a twenty-week leave, with a 2–4 percent reduction; and a thirty-week leave, with a 7–9 percent reduction.[3]

Sasiko Tanaka reaffirmed these findings in a study that analyzed data from Ruhm's sixteen European countries plus the United States and Japan. The data covered the thirty years between 1969 and 2000 including the period between 1995 and 2000 when several significant changes were made in parental leave policies.[4] Tanaka found that a ten-week extension in paid leave was associated with a 2.6 percent decrease in infant mortality rates and a 3.0 percent decrease in child mortality rates. Maternity leave without pay or a guarantee of a job at the end of the leave had no significant effect on infant or child mortality rates in either study.

One of the most important mechanisms through which paid parental leave can benefit infants is by increasing a mother's ability to initiate and sustain breast-feeding, which a wealth of research has shown to be associated with a markedly lower risk of gastrointestinal, respiratory tract, skin, ear, and other infections; sudden infant death syndrome; and overall mortality.[5] Health benefits of breast-feeding have also been reported for mothers, including reduced risk of premenopausal breast cancer and potentially reduced risks of ovarian cancer and osteoporosis.[6]

Generous maternity leave benefits available across European countries make it possible for mothers to breast-feed their infants for a lengthy period of time without having to supplement feedings with formula. In some cases the leave is long enough that mothers can exclusively breast-feed for at least six months, as recommended by the World Health Organization; and in countries with more than half a year of leave, mothers can continue breast-feeding (while also adding appropriate solid foods).[7] In contrast, in countries with less generous maternity leave, such as the United States, working women are less likely to start breast-feeding their babies, and those who do breast-feed stop sooner, on average, than mothers in countries with these supportive policies.[8] Lacking paid maternity leave, American mothers also return to work earlier than mothers in most other advanced countries, and research has found that early return to work is associated with lower rates of breast-feeding and immunizations.[9]

While far less research has been conducted on the impact of paternity leave policies, there is ample reason to believe that paternal leave can support children's healthy development in ways parallel to maternal leave, with the obvious exception of breast-feeding. Although fathers can take time off under parental leave policies that can be used by one or both parents, they are more likely to stay at home to care for a new child when paternity leave is available.[10]

The longer the period of leave allowed, the more involved with their infants and families fathers are.[11] Moreover, longer leaves increase the probability that fathers will continue their involvement and share in child care even after the leave ends.[12] The benefits of fathers' engagement for children's social, psychological, behavioral, emotional, and cognitive functioning are significant.[13] In short, paternity leave policies are associated with greater gender equity at home and, through fathers' increased involvement with their infants, with positive cognitive and social development of young children.

Leave for Children's Health Needs

Four decades of research have documented that children's health outcomes improve when parents participate in their children's health care, whether it is a treatment for an acute illness or injury or management of a chronic condition.[14] As Mark Schuster, Paul Chung, and Katherine Vestal discuss in this volume, children heal faster and have shorter hospital stays when parents are present and involved during inpatient surgeries and treatments as well as during outpatient medical procedures.[15] Parents' assistance is especially important for children with chronic conditions such as diabetes and asthma, among others.[16] Parents can help improve children's health outcomes in many ways including by maintaining daily medical routines, administering medication, and providing emotional support as children adjust to having a chronic physical or mental health problem.[17]

If children are sick and parents do not have any schedule flexibility or paid leave that can be used to address a family member's health issue, children may be left home alone, unable to get themselves to a doctor or pharmacy for medication or to a hospital if a crisis occurs. Alternatively, parents may have no choice but to send a sick child to school or day care. The contact with other children and teachers contributes to the rapid spread and thus high incidence of infectious diseases in day-care centers, including respiratory infections, otitis media, and gastrointestinal infections.[18]

Research has also documented how significantly parental availability influences the level of preventive care children receive. Getting a child to a clinic or doctor's office for a physical exam or immunizations usually requires parents or other caregivers to take time off work. Working parents in a range of countries have cited schedule conflicts and workplace inflexibility as important obstacles to getting their children immunized against preventable childhood diseases.[19] One study of a large company in the United States found that employees who faced difficulties taking time off from work were far more likely to report that their children were not fully immunized.[20]

In contrast to the vast majority of countries around the globe, the United States has no federal policy requiring employers to provide paid leave for personal illness, let alone to address family members' health issues. (The Family and Medical Leave Act covers only serious health issues of immediate family members and is unpaid.) Only 30 percent of Americans report that their employer voluntarily offers paid sick leave that can be used for family members' care.[21] As a result, many parents are unable to be present to attend to their children's health needs. Parents whose employers provide paid sick days are more than five times as likely to be able to personally provide care to their sick children as parents whose employers do not offer paid sick days.[22] Working adults with no paid leave who take time off to care for ill family members are at risk of losing wages or even their job.[23] The risk of job loss is even greater for parents whose child has a chronic health problem, which typically involves more visits to the doctor or the hospital and more days of illness. In a longitudinal study of working poor families in the United States, we found that having a child with health problems was associated with a 36 percent increase in job loss.[24]

Leave and Availability for Children's Educational and Developmental Needs

When parents are involved in their children's education, whether at the preschool, elementary, or secondary level, children perform better in school.[25] Parental involvement has been linked with children's improved test scores in language and math, fewer emotional and behavioral problems, lower dropout rates, and better planning for and transitions into adulthood.[26] Greater parental involvement in schools appears to improve the quality of the education received by all students in the school.[27] Research has found that fathers' involvement, like that of mothers, is associated with significantly better exam scores, higher educational expectations, and higher grades.[28]

Parental participation and assistance can improve school outcomes for at-risk children.[29] Educational outcomes for children with learning disabilities improve when parents are involved in their education both at school and helping at home with homework in math as well as reading.[30] Low-income children can also benefit markedly when their parents are involved in their classrooms and with their teachers at school.[31] Studies suggest that low-income children benefit as much or more when their parents also spend time assisting their children in learning skills and material outside the classroom; training or instructing parents in providing this assistance further boosts the gains of time spent together.[32]

Parents' working conditions can markedly affect their ability to play an active role in their children's education. Active parental involvement often requires the flexibility to meet with teachers or consult with specialists during the workday. To be able to help with homework, parents need to have a work schedule that allows them time with their children after school and before children go to sleep. Our national research on the availability of paid leave and schedule flexibility among parents of school-age children in the United States shows that parents whose children were struggling academically and most needed parental support were at a significant disadvantage. More than half of parents who had a child scoring in the bottom quartile on math assessments did not have consistent access to any kind of paid leave, and nearly three-fourths could not count on schedule flexibility. One in six of these parents worked during evening hours, and more than one in ten worked nights, making it impossible to help their children routinely. Families in which a child scored in the bottom quartile in reading had equally challenging working conditions.[33]

Economic Feasibility of Workplace Policies Supporting Parents

Despite substantial evidence that children gain when parents have adequate paid leave and work flexibility, the economic costs and benefits of providing this leave and flexibility are still the subject of great contention in the United States. Each time legislation to guarantee parental leave, family medical leave, and related policies has been brought to Congress, the debate has revolved around questions of financial feasibility. In particular, legislators and others have questioned whether the United States can provide these benefits and still remain economically competitive.

For example, the proposed Healthy Families Act would guarantee a minimum of seven paid sick days—a small number by international standards—to American workers so they could stay home when they or family members fall ill. At a hearing in 2007 on the legislation, G. Roger King, a partner at the Jones Day corporate law firm, summarized the general argument raised against the legislation, saying that the Healthy Families Act, or any similar "regulations" to protect employees, would diminish U.S. competitiveness in the global economy. "Employers in this country are already burdened by numerous federal, state and local regulations which result in millions of dollars in compliance costs," King stated in his written testimony. "These mandated and largely unfunded 'cost of doing business' requirements in certain instances not only hinder and impede the creation of new jobs, but also inhibit our nation's employers from competing globally."[34]

We report findings from our recent research that examines the relationship between work-family legislation and national competitiveness and unemployment rates. First, however, we briefly summarize some of the evidence on costs and benefits to employers from policies that support families.

A series of studies including data from the United States, Japan, and the United Kingdom show that women who receive paid maternity leave are significantly more likely to return to the same employer after giving birth.[35] Increased employee retention reduces hiring and training costs, which can be significant (and include the costs of publicizing the job opening, conducting job interviews, training new employees, and suboptimal productivity among newly hired workers during the period just after they start).

There is no research known to us about the costs or benefits to individual American employers related to paid leave for children's health issues, most likely because this type of leave is uncommon in the United States. To the extent that the leave allows parents to ensure their children have time to rest and recuperate and avoid exacerbating health problems that could result in additional lost workdays in the future, parents' productivity could increase and absenteeism be reduced.

Similarly, while we are not aware of any studies that examine the costs and benefits to employers of legislation guaranteeing time off for employees to be with children, recent studies showing that long hours are associated with lower productivity suggest that similar productivity losses may exist for employees who work for long periods of time without a substantial block of time away from work or, in the shorter term, for those who work without a weekly day of rest. A study of eighteen manufacturing industries in the United States over a thirty-five-year period found that for every 10 percent increase in overtime hours, productivity declined 2–4 percent.[36] Although small in absolute size, in the context of a forty-hour workweek, these productivity losses suggest that employers may be able to increase productivity by guaranteeing regular time off.

A study of highly "effective" employers by the Families and Work Institute found that many report a series of economic benefits resulting from their flexibility policies that include paid leave for new mothers and time off for caregiving among other scheduling and training policies.[37] Benefits cited by employers include "increasing employee engagement and retention; reducing turnover; reducing absenteeism and sick days; increasing customer satisfaction; reducing business costs; increasing productivity and profitability; improving staffing coverage to meet business demands; [and] enhancing innovation and creativity."[38]

The centrality of the economic arguments in policy debates calls for further examination of the empirical evidence on workplace policies important to parents and their children. We examine two important indicators of economic performance. The first is a measure of global economic competitiveness, a concept encompassing productivity, a country's capacity for growth, and the level of prosperity or income that can be attained. This indicator is of particular salience to businesses and is used by international organizations such as the World Economic Forum (WEF). The second is the national unemployment rate, the indicator more often cited as being of high concern in the public's mind.

To evaluate the claim that nationally mandating paid leave would cause a reduction in jobs or loss of competitiveness, one ideally would have evidence from a randomized or natural experiment where the policy in place is not associated with other country or state characteristics that could influence the outcome. That approach is not possible, because there have been no such experiments. However, to test whether policies supporting working families inevitably lead countries to be uncompetitive or to have high unemployment, it is sufficient to find counterexamples. To that end, we ask a straightforward question: Are paid leave and other work-family policies that support children's development economically feasible?

To answer this question, we developed a global database of national labor policies and global economic data on competitiveness and unemployment in all countries that belong to the United Nations. The database includes information from original legislation, labor codes, and relevant amendments in 175 countries, as well as summaries of legislation for these and additional countries. The vast majority of the legislation was gathered from NATLEX, the International Labour Organization's (ILO) global database of legislation pertaining to labor, social security, and human rights from 189 countries. Additional sources included global databases that compile and summarize national legislation.[39]

Public Policies Supporting Working Families in Highly Competitive Countries

Using our global labor policy database, we set out to assess whether the countries that have consistently been at the top of the rankings in economic competitiveness provide working conditions that give employed parents the ability to support their children's healthy development. To identify these "highly competitive" countries, we use data from the business-led WEF.[40] Its annual Global Competitiveness Report includes

country "competitiveness" rankings based on dozens of indicators of institutions, policies, and other factors that WEF members judge to be the key drivers of economic competitiveness. These factors include, among others, the efficiency of the goods market, efficiency of the labor market, financial market development, technological readiness, market size, business sophistication, innovation, infrastructure, and the macroeconomic environment.[41] We define "highly competitive" countries to be those that were ranked among the top twenty countries in competitiveness in at least eight of the ten years between 1999 and 2008. Fifteen countries meet this definition: Australia, Austria, Canada, Denmark, Finland, Germany, Iceland, Japan, the Netherlands, Norway, Singapore, Sweden, Switzerland, the United Kingdom, and the United States. Although India and China are not among the fifteen, we also present data on their family-supportive policies for two reasons. First, the press and laypersons often single out China and India as U.S. "competitors," and second, they have the two largest labor forces in the world.[42]

Paid Parental Leave

Paid leave for new mothers is guaranteed in all but one of the fifteen most competitive countries (Table 1). The exception is the United States, which has no federal policy providing paid leave for new parents. (As noted, leave provided under the federal Family and Medical Leave Act is unpaid.) Australia's paid leave policy took effect starting in January 2011; under the Paid Parental Leave Act, all workers—full time, part time, or casual—who are primary caregivers and earn $150,000 or less a year are guaranteed eighteen weeks of leave paid at the federal minimum wage. All of the most competitive countries with paid leave for new mothers provide at least fourteen weeks of leave, counting both maternity and parental leave, as recommended by the ILO. The norm of six months or more far exceeds the recommended minimum. China offers eighteen weeks (ninety working days) of leave for new mothers at full pay; India offers twelve weeks.

Table 1 also shows that although the duration of paid leave for new fathers is far less than for mothers, almost all highly competitive countries provide this type of leave. Switzerland is the lone top-ranked nation that provides paid leave to new mothers but not to new fathers. Neither India nor China has paid leave for new fathers.[43]

Breast-Feeding Breaks

Guaranteeing new mothers a breast-feeding break during the workday is the law in about half of the highly competitive countries, including Austria, Germany, Japan, the Netherlands, Norway, Sweden, Switzerland, and the United States (Table 2). India mandates two breaks a day in the child's first fifteen months. China guarantees new mothers breast-feeding breaks totaling an hour a day for the baby's first year.

Leave for Children's Health Needs

Unpaid leave from work to address children's health needs is ensured in every highly competitive nation (see Table 2). All but four of the fifteen most competitive countries provide paid leave for this purpose; the exceptions are Finland, Switzerland, the United Kingdom, and the United States.

Table 1 Parental Leave Policies in Highly Competitive Countries

Country	Paid Leave for Mothers			Paid Leave for Fathers		
	Availability	Duration (Weeks)	Wage Replacement Rate (%)	Availability	Duration (Weeks)	Wage Replacement Rate (%)
Australia	Yes	18	flat rate	Yes	18	flat rate
Austria	Yes	81–146	100, flat rate	Yes	65–130	flat rate
Canada	Yes	50	55	Yes	35	55
Denmark	Yes	50–58	80–100	Yes	34–42	80–100
Finland	Yes	164	25–90	Yes	154	25–70
Germany	Yes	66–118	33–100	Yes	52–104	33–67
Iceland	Yes	26	80	Yes	26	80
Japan	Yes	58	30–60	Yes	44	30–40
Netherlands	Yes	16	100	Yes	0.4	100
Norway	Yes	90–100	80–100, flat rate	Yes	87–97	80–100, flat rate
Singapore	Yes	14	100	Yes	2	100
Sweden	Yes	69*	80, flat rate	Yes	67*	80, flat rate
Switzerland	Yes	14	80	No	n.a.	n.a.
United Kingdom	Yes	39	90	Yes	2	90
United States	No	n.a.	n.a.	No	n.a.	n.a.

Notes: In the database and all tables, data reflect national policy. Coverage conditions such as firm size, sector, and duration of employment vary by country. Paid leave for mothers includes paid leave for women only (maternity leave) and parental leave that is available to women. Paid leave for fathers includes paid leave for men only (paternity leave) and parental leave that is available to men. The table presents data on the maximum amount of leave available to the mother if she takes all of the maternity leave available to mothers and all of the parental leave available to either parent. Parallel data are presented for fathers. The minimum and maximum (as a range) are presented to reflect that country's policy of providing parents with a choice between a shorter leave at a higher benefit level (percentage of wages or flat rate) and a longer leave at a lower benefit.

Source: Based on updated data from Jody Heymann and Alison Earle, *Raising the Global Floor: Dismantling the Myth That We Can't Afford Good Working Conditions for Everyone* (Stanford University Press, 2010).

n.a. = Not applicable.

*Sweden's parental leave policy also allows parents to take part-time leave with partial benefits for a longer duration.

Table 2 Leave Policies to Attend to Children's Health Care in Highly Competitive Countries

Country	Breast-Feeding Breaks	Age of Child When Breast-Feeding Breaks End	Break Time of At Least One Hour a Day	Leave to Care for Children's Health Needs	Leave Is Paid
Australia	No	n.a.	n.a.	Yes	Yes
Austria	Yes	For duration	Yes	Yes	Yes
Canada	No	n.a.	n.a.	Yes	Yes
Denmark	No	n.a.	n.a.	Yes	Yes
Finland	No	n.a.	n.a.	Yes	No
Germany	Yes	For duration	Yes	Yes	Yes
Iceland	No	n.a.	n.a.	Yes	Yes
Japan	Yes	1 year	Yes	Yes	Yes
Netherlands	Yes	9 months	Yes	Yes	Yes
Norway	Yes	For duration	Yes	Yes	Yes
Singapore	No	n.a.	n.a.	Yes	Yes
Sweden	Yes	For duration	Yes	Yes	Yes
Switzerland	Yes	1 year	Yes	Yes	No
United Kingdom	No	n.a.	n.a.	Yes	No
United States	Yes	1 year	Yes	Yes	No

n.a. = Not applicable.
Source: See Table 1.

Leave and Availability for Children's Developmental and Educational Needs

Neither paid vacation leave nor a day off each week is designed specifically for parents; these rest periods benefit all working adults. Yet weekly time off and vacations do provide an important assurance that working parents can spend time with their children and be available to support their educational, social, and emotional development. All of the most highly competitive countries except the United States guarantee paid annual or vacation leave (Table 3). The vast majority of these countries provide generous amounts of leave at full pay. Half provide more than four weeks a year: Austria, Denmark, Finland, Germany, Iceland, Norway, Sweden, and the United Kingdom. China's labor laws guarantee five days of paid leave after one year of service, ten days after ten years on the job, and fifteen days after twenty years. In India workers are provided one day of paid leave for every twenty days worked during the previous year.

Virtually all highly competitive nations also guarantee at least one day of rest a week. The exceptions are the United States and Australia (see Table 3). Both China and India guarantee workers a day of rest a week.

Labor legislation is relatively less common around a small number of issues that are receiving attention as a result of recent economic and technological developments. Countries are still adjusting their labor policies in response to the rise of the "24/7" schedule that has come about as global trade, communications, and sourcing of products have increased. Policies either to restrict or compensate for work at times when school-age children in particular benefit from a parent's presence—evenings and nights—exist in many highly competitive countries. Guaranteeing a wage premium increases the likelihood that a wide range of workers will volunteer for night work and decreases the likelihood that parents will need to work at night merely because of limited seniority. Finland, Norway, and Sweden have passed laws placing broad restrictions on night work for all workers. Germany, Japan, and Switzerland instead guarantee a wage premium for those who are required to work at night. Over half of the highly competitive nations allow night work but restrict or ban it for workers who might be harmed by it: children, pregnant or nursing women, or employees with medical conditions that make them unable to work at night (see Table 3). China bans night work for pregnant women. Although India bans night work for all women, some states have lifted it for women working in information technology and telecommunications.

Not new to parents but to some policy makers is the need for adults to occasionally take time off during the day to address a child's academic, social, or behavioral issue, or to attend a school event. Although leave during the day to meet with a teacher or attend an event typically does not involve a great deal of the employee's time in any given period, only four of the fifteen countries provide leave explicitly for such purposes. Labor laws in Denmark and Sweden require employers to provide leave to attend to "children's needs" including educational issues. Switzerland takes a different approach, requiring

Table 3   Policies on Paid Annual Leave, a Day of Rest, and Night Work in Highly Competitive Countries

Country	Availability of Paid Annual Leave	Duration of Paid Annual Leave (Weeks)	Weekly Day of Rest	Premium for Night Work	Ban or Broad Restrictions on Night Work	Ban or Restriction for Children, Pregnant or Nursing Women, or Medical Reasons
Australia	Yes	4.0	No	No	No	No
Austria	Yes	5.0	Yes	No	No	Yes
Canada	Yes	2.0	Yes	No	No	Yes
Denmark	Yes	5.5	Yes	No	No	Yes
Finland	Yes	4.4	Yes	No	Yes	No
Germany	Yes	4.4	Yes	After 11 P.M.	No	Yes
Iceland	Yes	4.4	Yes	No	No	No
Japan	Yes	1.8	Yes	After 10 P.M.	No	Yes
Netherlands	Yes	4.0	Yes	No	No	Yes
Norway	Yes	4.2	Yes	No	Yes	Yes
Singapore	Yes	1.3	Yes	No	No	No
Sweden	Yes	5.0	Yes	No	Yes	No
Switzerland	Yes	4.0	Yes	After 11 P.M.	No	Yes
United Kingdom	Yes	5.1	Yes	No	No	Yes
United States	No	n.a.	No	No	No	No

n.a. = Not applicable.
Source: See Table 1.

employers to structure work schedules and rest periods keeping in mind employees' family responsibilities including attending to the educational needs of children up to age fifteen. In addition, Switzerland also requires employers to provide a lunch break of at least an hour and a half to parents if requested. Parents in Singapore can take leave for their children's educational needs under the country's family leave law. Neither India nor China provides paid leave for general family needs and issues or for children's education.

Public Policies Supporting Working Families in Low Unemployment Countries

As an additional check, we also examined whether it was possible to have relatively low unemployment rates while guaranteeing a floor of working conditions that help parents care for children. We looked specifically at members of the Organization for Economic Cooperation and Development (OECD). The OECD definition of unemployment is comprehensive, including employment in formal and informal jobs.[44] We defined low unemployment countries as those OECD members ranked in the better half of countries in terms of unemployment at least 80 percent of the time in the decade between 1998 and 2007. Thirteen countries fit these criteria: Austria, Denmark, Iceland, Ireland, Japan, Republic of Korea (South Korea), Luxembourg, Mexico, the Netherlands, Norway, Switzerland, the United Kingdom, and the United States. Overall, do these countries provide working conditions that can help parents support children's healthy development? In short, yes.

Paid Parental Leave

Every low unemployment country but one, the United States, has national legislation guaranteeing paid leave for new mothers. The length of the leaves ranges from twelve weeks in Mexico to more than a year in Austria, Japan, Norway, and South Korea. In the middle are Iceland and Ireland, where new mothers receive six months, and Luxembourg and the United Kingdom, with nine months. All but one of those with paid leave replace 80 percent or more of wages, and seven guarantee 100 percent.

Paid leave for new fathers, whether in the form of leave for fathers only or leave that can be used by either parent, is not universally available but is provided in nine of the thirteen low unemployment countries. Ireland, Mexico, Switzerland, and the United States do not provide this type of leave. New fathers are entitled to take between six months and a year in Denmark, Iceland, Japan, and Luxembourg, and more than a year in Austria, Norway, and South Korea.

Breast-Feeding Breaks

Ten of the thirteen countries ensure that new mothers can continue breast-feeding for at least six months after they return to work, and eight of those ten ensure this right for a year or until the mother chooses to stop.

Leave for Children's Health Needs

Guaranteed leave to address children's health needs is the norm; all but two low unemployment countries—Mexico and South Korea—provide either paid or unpaid leave of this type. The leave is paid in Austria, Denmark, Iceland, Ireland, Japan, Luxembourg, the Netherlands, and Norway and unpaid in Switzerland, the United Kingdom, and the United States.

Leave and Availability for Children's Developmental and Educational Needs

Every low unemployment country except the United States guarantees workers a weekly day of rest and a period of paid vacation leave once a year. Mexico and Japan guarantee from one to two weeks while nine of the thirteen guarantee four weeks or more. As noted earlier, labor laws in Denmark and Switzerland also require employers to provide leave to address "children's needs," which in the Swiss legislation explicitly include educational issues.

These findings show that mandating workplace policies that support parents' ability to ensure their children's healthy development does not inevitably lead to high job loss or high unemployment rates. As this discussion shows, many OECD countries kept unemployment rates relatively low while passing and enforcing legislation that supports parents. In fact, the majority of consistently low unemployment countries have adopted nearly all the policies shown to be important for children's health and well-being. Whether these nations would have had somewhat lower or higher unemployment in the absence of family support policies is not known. But our research clearly shows that it is possible for a nation to guarantee paid leave and other policies that provide parents with time to address their children's needs and at the same time maintain relatively low unemployment.

Summary of Findings

Longitudinal data are not available that would enable researchers to determine conclusively the immediate and long-term impact on national economic outcomes of changing guarantees of parental leave and other family-support policies. However, an examination of the most competitive economies as well as the economies with low unemployment rates makes clear that ensuring that all parents are available to care for their children's healthy development does not preclude a country from being highly competitive economically. Moreover, as noted, evidence from decades of research on parents' roles during children's infancy and in caring for children's health and education makes clear that policies enabling working fathers and mothers to provide that care are likely to have substantial positive effects on the health and developmental outcomes of American children.

Few of the policies that would help working parents raise healthy children are guaranteed in the United States. As noted, the federal Family and Medical Leave Act allows new parents to take unpaid time off without fear of job loss when they adopt or give birth, or to attend to a parent or child suffering from a serious illness. Half of Americans are not covered by the act because of the size of the firms in which they work, the number of hours they have worked, or a recent job change, and many of those who are covered cannot afford to take all the leave they are entitled to because it is unpaid. Only in 2010 did the United States pass federal legislation requiring employers to provide breast-feeding breaks and facilities for breast-feeding (as part of the health care reform bill and without much public awareness). Paid parental leave and child health care leave policies are the norm in the countries that have been highly competitive and those that have maintained low unemployment for a decade. The analysis of global data presented here suggests that guaranteeing paid parental leave as well as paid leave when a child is sick would be feasible for the United States without jeopardizing its highly competitive economy or low unemployment rates in the future.

The overwhelming majority of countries guarantee paid parental leave through a social insurance system. While many countries provide some kind of tax credit or stipend at the birth of a child, next to none rely only on this for paid parental leave. A critical step that European countries have increasingly followed is to guarantee that a percentage of the leave is dedicated to fathers as well as some dedicated solely to mothers. This approach ensures that men have in practice, and not just on paper, an equal chance of using the leave.

The countries that guarantee paid sick leave finance it through a variety of means ranging from requiring employers to pay employees benefits (that is, continue to pay salary or wages during the leave) to establishing a social security system whereby some combination of employees, employers, and government pay into a fund out of which payments are made to individuals while they are unable to work. One two-stage model requires employers to pay wages for short periods of illness but provides benefits from the social insurance system for longer leaves associated with major illnesses. Reasonably short employer liability periods—seven to ten days a year—make it feasible for the employer to reimburse wages at a high rate and keeps administrative costs low, while ensuring that paid leave covers most common illnessess that adults and children suffer. Covering longer illnesses through social insurance ensures that employers will not be overburdened with long-term payments.

The overwhelming majority of countries around the world guarantee all working women and men some paid annual leave and a weekly day of rest. In these nations the right to reasonable work hours is built into employers' labor costs and is often seen as a sensible, basic human right that also enhances productivity.

Considering policy change is always difficult, and recommending programs with public and private sector budgetary implications is particularly difficult when the United States is only now recovering from the Great Recession. That said, many of the country's most important social and labor policies date from the Great Depression. While periods of economic duress raise understandable questions about the feasibility of change, they also naturally focus attention on how critical safety nets are to American of all ages. As articles throughout this issue of the *Future of Children* demonstrate, guaranteeing a floor of decent working conditions and social supports is essential not only to working parents but also to the healthy development of their children. We believe that evidence is equally compelling that such guarantees are economically feasible for the United States.

Notes

1. U.S. Bureau of Labor Statistics, "Employment Characteristics of Families, Table 4: Families with Own Children: Employment Status of Parents by Age of Youngest Child and Family Type, 2008–09 Annual Averages" (www.bls.gov/news.release/archives/famee_05272010.htm); U.S. Bureau of the Census, "Women in the Labor Force: A Databook" (2009 ed.), Table 7, "Employment Status of Women by Presence and Age of Youngest Child" (March) (www.bls.gov/cps/wlftable7.htm).

2. Lawrence Berger, Jennifer Hill, and Jane Waldfogel, "Maternity Leave, Early Maternal Employment and Child Health and Development in the U.S.," *Economic Journal* 115, no. 501 (2005): F29–F47; Sheila B. Kamerman, "Maternity, Paternity, and Parental Leave Policies: The Potential Impacts on Children and Their Families (rev. ed.)," in *Encyclopedia on Early Childhood Development (online),* edited by R. E. Tremlay, R. G. Barr, and R. D. Peters (Montreal: Centre of Excellence for Early Childhood Development, 2005) (www.child-encyclopedia.com/documents/KamermanANGxp_rev-Parental.pdf).

3. Christopher J. Ruhm, "Parental Leave and Child Health," *Journal of Health Economics* 19, no. 6 (2000): 931–60.

4. Sasiko Tanaka, "Parental Leave and Child Health across OECD Countries," *Economic Journal* 115, no. 501 (2005): F7–F28.

5. Richard G. Feachem and Marge A. Koblinsky, "Interventions for the Control of Diarrhoeal Diseases among Young Children: Promotion of Breast-feeding," *Bulletin of World Health Organization* 62, no. 2 (1984): 271–91; Kathryn G. Dewey, M. Jane Heinig, and Laurie A. Nommsen-Rivers, "Differences in Morbidity between Breastfed and Formula-Fed Infants. Part 1," *Journal of Pediatrics* 126, no. 5 (1995): 696–702; Peter W. Howie, and others, "Protective Effect of Breast-feeding against Infection," *British Medical Journal* 300, no. 6716 (1990): 11–16; Philippe Lepage, Christophe Munyakazi, and Philippe Hennart, "Breastfeeding and Hospital Mortality in Children in Rwanda," *Lancet* 319, no. 8268 (1982): 403; M. Cristina Cerqueriro and others, "Epidemiologic Risk Factors for Children with Acute Lower Respiratory Tract Infection in Buenos Aires, Argentina: A Matched Case-Control Study," *Reviews of Infectious Diseases,* suppl. 8, no. 12 (1990): S1021–28; Christopher J. Watkins, Stephen R. Leeder, and Richard T. Corkhill, "The Relationship between Breast and Bottle Feeding and Respiratory Illness in the First Year of Life," *Journal of Epidemiology and Community Health* 33, no. 3 (1979): 180–82; Anne L. Wright and others, "Breast-feeding and Lower Respiratory Tract Illness in the First Year of Life," *British Medical Journal* 299, no. 6705 (1989): 946–49; Michael Gdalevich and others, "Breast-Feeding and the Onset of Atopic Dermatitis in Childhood: A Systematic Review and Meta-Analysis of Prospective Studies," *Journal of American Academy of Dermatology* 45, no. 4 (2001): 487–647; Jennifer Baxter, "Breastfeeding, Employment and Leave: An Analysis of Mothers Growing Up in Australia," *Family Matters* no. 80 (2008): 17–26; Amanda R. Cooklin, Susan M. Donath, and Lisa H. Amir, "Maternal Employment and Breastfeeding:

Results from the Longitudinal Study of Australian Children," *Acta Paediatrica* 97, no. 5 (2008): 620–23; Gustaf Aniansson and others, "A Prospective Cohort Study on Breast-Feeding and Otitis Media in Swedish Infants," *Pediatric Infectious Disease Journal* 13, no. 3 (1994): 183–88; Burris Duncan and others, "Exclusive Breast-Feeding for at Least 4 Months Protects against Otitis Media," *Pediatrics* 91, no. 5 (1993): 867–72; Cody Arnold, Susan Makintube, and Gregory Istre, "Daycare Attendance and Other Risk Factors for Invasive Haemophilus Influenzae Type B Disease," *American Journal of Epidemiology* 138, no. 5 (1993): 333–40; Stanley Ip and others, "Breastfeeding and Maternal and Infant Health Outcomes in Developed Countries," Agency for Healthcare Research and Quality, AHRQ Publication 07-E007 (April 2007).

6. Ip and others. "Breastfeeding and Maternal and Infant Health Outcomes in Developed Countries" (see note 5).

7. Adriano Cattaneo and others, "Protection, Promotion and Support of Breast-Feeding in Europe: Current Situation," *Public Health Nutrition* 8, no. 1 (2005): 39–46.

8. Sylvia Guendelman and others, "Juggling Work and Breastfeeding: Effects of Maternity Leave and Occupational Characteristics," *Pediatrics* 123, no. 1 (2010): e38–46; Baxter, "Breastfeeding, Employment and Leave" (see note 5); Cooklin, Donath, and Amir, "Maternal Employment and Breastfeeding" (see note 5).

9. Berger, Hill, and Waldfogel, "Maternity Leave, Early Maternal Employment and Child Health and Development in the U.S." (see note 2).

10. Berit Brandth and Elin Kvande, "Flexible Work and Flexible Fathers," *Work, Employment and Society* 15 no. 2 (2001): 251–67.

11. Ruth Feldman, Amy L. Sussman, and Edward Zigler, "Parental Leave and Work Adaptation at the Transition to Parenthood: Individual, Marital and Social Correlates," *Applied Developmental Psychology* 25, no. 4 (2004): 459–79; Rudy Ray Seward, Dale E. Yeatts, and Lisa K. Zottarelli, "Parental Leave and Father Involvement in Child Care: Sweden and the United States," *Journal of Comparative Family Studies* 33, no. 3 (2002): 387–99.

12. Linda Haas and Phillip Hwang, "The Impact of Taking Parental Leave on Fathers' Participation in Childcare and Relationships with Children: Lessons from Sweden," *Community, Work and Family* 11, no. 1 (2008): 85–104; Lindy Fursman and Paul Callister, *Men's Participation in Unpaid Care: A Review of the Literature* (Wellington: New Zealand Department of Labour 2009) (www.dol.govt.nz/publication-view.asp?ID=289).

13. According to Catherine S. Tamis-LeMonda and others, "Fathers and Mothers at Play with Their 2- and 3-Year-Olds: Contributions to Language and Cognitive Development," *Child Development* 75, no. 6 (2004): 1806–20, one example is resident fathers who engage their children in more cognitive stimulation have children with higher mental development (that is, memory skills, problem-solving skills, vocalization, language skills) at twenty-four months (as measured by the Bayley Scales of Infant Development, Second Edition Mental Development Index). For a brief summary of this research, see Andrew Kang and Julie Weber, "Opportunities for Policy Leadership on Fathers," Policy Briefing Series 20 (Sloan Work and Family Research Network, Chestnut Hill, Mass., 2009) (www.wfnetwork.bc.edu). See also Ann M. Taubenheim,

"Paternal-Infant Bonding in the First-Time Father," *Journal of Obstetric, Gynecologic, and Neonatal Nursing* 10, no. 4 (1981): 261–64; Per Nettelbladt, "Father/Son Relationship during the Preschool Years: An Integrative Review with Special Reference to Recent Swedish Findings," *Acta Psychiatrica Scandinavica* 68, no. 6 (1983): 399–407. Although the bulk of the literature has focused on the bonds between mothers and infants, no evidence exists to suggest that bonding with fathers is any less significant to children.

14. Inger Kristensson-Hallstrom, Gunnel Elander, and Gerhard Malmfors, "Increased Parental Participation in a Pediatric Surgical Daycare Unit," *Journal of Clinical Nursing* 6, no. 4 (1997): 297–302; Mervyn R. H. Taylor and Peter O'Connor, "Resident Parents and Shorter Hospital Stay," *Archives of Disease in Childhood* 64, no. 2 (1989): 274–76; Patricia A. LaRosa-Nash and Jane M. Murphy, "An Approach to Pediatric Perioperative Care: Parent-Present Induction," *Nursing Clinics of North America* 32, no. 1 (1997): 183–99; Alan George and Janice Hancock, "Reducing Pediatric Burn Pain with Parent Participation," *Journal of Burn Care and Rehabilitation* 14, no. 1 (1993): 104–07; Sarah J. Palmer, "Care of Sick Children by Parents: A Meaningful Role," *Journal of Advanced Nursing* 18, no. 2 (1993): 185; Perry Mahaffy, "The Effects of Hospitalization on Children Admitted for Tonsillectomy and Adenoidectomy," *Nursing Review* 14 (1965): 12–19; John Bowlby, *Child Care and the Growth of Love* (London: Pelican, 1964); James Robertson, *Young Children in Hospital* (London: Tavistock, 1970).

15. See also Taylor and O'Connor, "Resident Parents and Shorter Hospital Stay" (see note 14); Kristensson-Hallstrom, Elander, and Malmfors, "Increased Parental Participation in a Pediatric Surgical Daycare Unit" (see note 14).

16. Annete M. LaGreca and others, "I Get By with a Little Help from My Family and Friends: Adolescents' Support for Diabetes Care," *Journal of Pediatric Psychology* 20, no. 4 (1995): 449–76; Barbara J. Anderson and others, "Family Characteristics of Diabetic Adolescents: Relationship to Metabolic Control," *Diabetes Care* 4, no. 6 (1981): 586–94; Kim W. Hamlett, David S. Pellegrini, and Kathy S. Katz, "Childhood Chronic Illness as a Family Stressor," *Journal of Pediatric Psychology* 17, no. 1 (1992): 33–47; Clara Wolman and others, "Emotional Well-Being among Adolescents with and without Chronic Conditions," *Adolescent Medicine* 15, no. 3 (1994): 199–204; Cindy L. Hanson and others, "Comparing Social Learning and Family Systems Correlates of Adaptation in Youths with IDDM," *Journal of Pediatric Psychology* 17, no. 5 (1992): 555–72.

17. LaGreca and others, "I Get By with a Little Help from My Family and Friends" (see note 16); Wolman and others, "Emotional Well-Being among Adolescents with and without Chronic Conditions" (see note 16); Hamlett, Pellegrini, and Katz, "Childhood Chronic Illness as a Family Stressor" (see note 16); Stuart T. Hauser and others, "Adherence among Children and Adolescents with Insulin-Dependent Diabetes Mellitus over a Four-Year Longitudinal Follow-Up: II. Immediate and Long-Term Linkages with the Family Milieu," *Journal of Pediatric Psychology* 15, no. 4 (1990): 527–42; E. Wayne Holden and others, "Controlling for General and Disease-Specific Effects in Child and Family Adjustment to Chronic Childhood Illness," *Journal of Pediatric Psychology* 22, no. 1 (1997): 15–27; Katrina Johnson, "Children with Special

Health Needs: Ensuring Appropriate Coverage and Care under Health Care Reform," *Health Policy and Child Health* 1, no. 3 (1994): 1–5; Timothy A. Waugh and Diane L. Kjos, "Parental Involvement and the Effectiveness of an Adolescent Day Treatment Program," *Journal of Youth and Adolescence* 21 (1992): 487–97; J. Cleary and others, "Parental Involvement in the Lives of Children in Hospital," *Archives of Disease in Childhood* 61 (1986): 779–87; C. P. Sainsbury and others, "Care by Parents of Their Children in Hospital," *Archives of Disease in Childhood* 61, no. 6 (1986): 612–15; Michael W. L. Gauderer, June L. Lorig, and Douglas W. Eastwood, "Is There a Place for Parents in the Operating Room?" *Journal of Pediatric Surgery* 24, no. 7 (1989): 705–06.

18. Isabelle Diehl, "The Prevalence of Colds in Nursery School Children and Non-Nursery School Children," *Journal of Pediatrics* 34, no. 1 (1949): 52–61; Peggy Sullivan and others, "Longitudinal Study of Occurrence of Diarrheal Disease in Day Care Centers," *American Journal of Public Health* 74, no. 9 (1984): 987–91; Merja Möttönen and Matti Uhari, "Absences for Sickness among Children in Day Care," *Acta Paediatrica* 81, no. 11 (1992): 929. Frank A. Loda, W. Paul Glezen, and Wallace A. Clyde Jr., "Respiratory Disease in Group Day Care," *Pediatrics* 49, no. 3 (1972): 428–37; K. Strangert, "Respiratory Illness in Preschool Children with Different Forms of Day Care," *Pediatrics* 57, no. 2 (1976): 191; Anna-Beth Doyle, "Incidence of Illness in Early Group and Family Day-Care," *Pediatrics* 58, no. 4 (1976): 607; Ron Haskins and Jonathan Kotch, "Day Care and Illness: Evidence, Costs, and Public Policy," *Pediatrics* 77, no. 6, (1986): 951–80; Muriel Oyediran and Anne Bamisaiye, "A Study of the Child-Care Arrangements and the Health Status of Pre-School Children of Employed Women in Lagos," *Public Health* 97, no. 5 (1983): 267; Susan D. Hillis and others, "Day Care Center Attendance and Diarrheal Morbidity in Colombia," *Pediatrics* 90, no. 4 (1992): 582; Centers for Disease Control and Prevention, "National Immunization Program: "Estimated Vaccination Coverage with Individual Vaccines and Selected Vaccination Series among Children Nineteen to Thirty-Five Months-of-Age by State" (Atlanta: 2001); World Health Organization (WHO), *WHO Vaccine Preventable Diseases: Monitoring System* (Geneva: WHO Department of Vaccines and Biologicals, 2000); Kim Streatfield and Masri Singarimbun, "Social Factors Affecting the Use of Immunization in Indonesia," *Social Science and Medicine* 27, no. 11 (1988): 1237–45.

19. Centers for Disease Control and Prevention, "National Immunization Program" (see note 18); World Health Organization, *WHO Vaccine Preventable Diseases* (see note 18).

20. J. E. Fielding, W. G. Cumberland, and L. Pettitt, "Immunization Status of Children of Employees in a Large Corporation," *Journal of the American Medical Association* 271, no. 7 (1994): 525–30.

21. Vicky Lovell. *No Time to Be Sick: Why Everyone Suffers When Workers Don't Have Paid Sick Leave* (Washington: Institute for Women's Policy Research, 2004) (www.iwpr.org/pdf/B242.pdf).

22. S. Jody Heymann, Sara Toomey, and Frank Furstenberg, "Working Parents: What Factors Are Involved in Their Ability to Take Time Off from Work When Their Children Are Sick?" *Archives of Pediatrics and Adolescent Medicine* 153, no. 8 (1999): 870–74; Jody Heymann, *The Widening Gap: Why America's Working Families Are in Jeopardy and What Can Be Done about It* (New York: Basic Books, 2000).

23. National Alliance for Caregiving and American Association of Retired People, "Caregiving in the U.S." (Bethesda: 2004); Heymann, *The Widening Gap* (see note 22).

24. Alison Earle and S. Jody Heymann, "What Causes Job Loss among Former Welfare Recipients? The Role of Family Health Problems," *Journal of the American Medical Women's Association* 57 (2002): 5–10.

25. Charles Desforges and Alberto Abouchaar, "The Impact of Parental Involvement, Parental Support, and Family Education on Pupil Achievement and Adjustment: A Literature Review," *DfES Research Report* 433 (Chelsea: Department for Education and Skills, 2003) (http://publications.dcsf.gov.uk/eOrderingDownload/RR433.pdf); Arthur Reynolds, "Early Schooling of Children at Risk," *American Educational Research Journal* 28, no. 2 (1991): 392–422; Kevin Callahan, Joyce A. Rademacher, and Bertina A. Hildreth, "The Effect of Parent Participation in Strategies to Improve the Homework Performance of Students Who Are at Risk," *Remedial and Special Education* 19, no. 3 (1998): 131–41; Timothy Z. Keith and others, "Does Parental Involvement Affect Eighth-Grade Student Achievement? Structural Analysis of National Data," *School Psychology Review* 22, no. 3 (1993): 474–76; Paul G. Fehrmann, Timothy Z. Keith, and Thomas M. Reimers, "Home Influences on School Learning: Direct and Indirect Effects of Parental Involvement on High School Grades," *Journal of Educational Research* 80, no. 6 (1987): 330–37.

26. Leon Feinstein and James Symons, "Attainment in Secondary School," *Oxford Economics Papers* 51, no. 2 (1999): 300–21. This study found that parental interest had a much stronger effect than either in-school factors such as teacher-student ratios or social factors such as the family's socioeconomic status and parental educational attainment. See also Arthur J. Reynolds, "Comparing Measures of Parental Involvement and Their Effects on Academic Achievement," *Early Childhood Research Quarterly* 7, no. 3 (1992): 441–62; James Griffith, "Relation of Parental Involvement, Empowerment, and School Traits to Student Academic Performance," *Journal of Educational Research* 90, no. 1 (1996): 33–41; Sandra L. Christenson, Theresa Rounds, and Deborah Gorney, "Family Factors and Student Achievement: An Avenue to Increase Students' Success," *School Psychology Quarterly* 7, no. 3 (1992): 178–206; Deborah L. Miller and Mary L. Kelley, "Interventions for Improving Homework Performance: A Critical Review," *School Psychology Quarterly* 6, no. 3 (1991): 174–85; James P. Comer, "Home-School Relationships as They Affect the Academic Success of Children," *Education and Urban Society* 16, no. 3 (1984): 323–37; John W. Fantuzzo, Gwendolyn Y. Davis, and Marika D. Ginsburg, "Effects of Parental Involvement in Isolation or in Combination with Peer Tutoring on Student Self-Concept and Mathematics Achievement," *Journal of Educational Psychology* 87, no. 2 (1995): 272–81; Tracey Frigo and others, "Australian Young People, Their Families, and Post-School Plans" (Melbourne: Australian Council for Educational Research, 2007).

27. James P. Comer and Norris M. Haynes. "Parent Involvement in Schools: An Ecological Approach," *Elementary School Journal* 91, no. 3 (1991): 271–77; Griffith, "Relation of Parental Involvement, Empowerment, and School Traits to Student Academic Performance" (see note 26); Arthur J. Reynolds and others, "Cognitive and Family-Support Mediators of Preschool Effectiveness: A Confirmatory Analysis," *Child Development* 67, no. 3 (1996): 1119–40.

28. National Center for Education Statistics, "Father's Involvement in the Children's Schools," NCES 98-091 (U.S. Department of Education, 1997); Christine Winquist Nord, DeeAnn Brimhall, and Jerry West, "Dads' Involvement in Their Kids' Schools," *Education Digest* 63, no. 7 (March 1998): 29–35; Michael E. Lamb, "The Emergent American Father," in *The Father's Role: Cross-Cultural Perspectives,* edited by Michael E. Lamb (Hillsdale, NY: Lawrence Erlbaum Associates Publishers, 1987); Rebecca Goldman, *Fathers' Involvement in Their Children's Education* (London: National Family and Parenting Institute, 2005).

29. Desforges and Abouchaar, "The Impact of Parental Involvement, Parental Support, and Family Education on Pupil Achievement and Adjustment" (see note 25); Reynolds, "Early Schooling of Children at Risk" (see note 25); Callahan, Rademacher, and Hildreth, "The Effect of Parent Participation in Strategies to Improve the Homework Performance of Students Who Are at Risk" (see note 25).

30. F. Davis, "Understanding Underachievers," *American Education* 20, no. 10 (1984): 12–14; M. Gajria and S. Salend, "Homework Practices of Students with and without Learning Disabilities: A Comparison," *Journal of Learning Disabilities* 28 (1995): 291–96; S. Salend and J. Schliff, "An Examination of the Homework Practices of Teachers of Students with Learning Disabilities," *Journal of Learning Disabilities* 22, no. 10 (1989): 621–23; H. Cooper and B. Nye, "Homework for Students with Learning Disabilities: The Implications of Research for Policy and Practice," *Journal of Learning Disabilities* 27, no. 8 (1994): 470–79; S. Salend and M. Gajria, "Increasing the Homework Completion Rates of Students with Mild Disabilities," *Remedial and Special Education* 16, no. 5 (1995): 271–78.

31. Arthur J. Reynolds, "A Structural Model of First Grade Outcomes for an Urban, Low Socioeconomic Status, Minority Population," *Journal of Educational Psychology* 81, no. 4 (1989): 594–603; C. S. Benson, E. A. Medrich, and S. Buckley, "The New View of School Efficiency: Household Time Contributions to School Achievement," in *School Finance Policies and Practices: 1980's Decade of Conflict,* edited by James W. Guthrie (Cambridge, Mass.: Ballinger Publishers, 2005); Reginald M. Clark, "Why Disadvantaged Students Succeed: What Happens Outside Schools' Critical Period," *Public Welfare* (Spring 1990): 17–23.

32. Joyce L. Epstein, "Parent Involvement: What Research Says to Administrators," *Education in Urban Society* 19, no. 2 (1987): 119–36; Ray T. J. Wilks and Valerie A. Clarke, "Training versus Non-Training of Mothers as Home Reading Tutors," *Perceptual and Motor Skills* 67 (1988): 135–42; United Nations Children's Fund (UNICEF), *The State of the World's Children 2001* (New York: 2001); R. Myers, *The Twelve Who Survive: Strengthening Programmes of Early Childhood Development in the Third World* (London and New York: Routledge in cooperation with UNESCO for the Consultative Group on Early Childhood Care and Development, 1992); Linda P. Thurston and Kathy Dasta, "An Analysis of In-Home Parent Tutoring Procedures: Effects on Children's Academic Behavior at Home and in School and on Parents' Tutoring Behaviors," *Remedial and Special Education* 11, no. 4 (1990): 41–52.

33. Heymann, Toomey, and Furstenberg, "Working Parents" (see note 22); Heymann, *The Widening Gap* (see note 22).

34. G. Roger King, "The Healthy Families Act: Safeguarding Americans' Livelihood, Families and Health with Paid Sick Days," Testimony before the U.S. Senate Committee on Health, Education, Labor, and Pensions, February 13, 2007.

35. Berger, Hill, and Waldfogel, "Maternity Leave, Early Maternal Employment and Child Health and Development in the U.S." (see note 2); Susan Macran, Heather Joshi, and Shirley Dex, "Employment after Childbearing: A Survival Analysis," *Work, Employment, and Society* 10, no. 2 (1996): 273–96.

36. Edward Shepard and Thomas Clifton, "Are Longer Hours Reducing Productivity in Manufacturing?" *International Journal of Manpower* 21, no. 7 (2000): 540–52.

37. Defined as meeting six criteria: job autonomy, learning opportunities, decision making, involvement, coworker/supervisor support, and flexibility.

38. Ellen Galinsky, Sheila Eby, and Shanny Peer, "2008 Guide to Bold New Ideas for Making Work Work from the 2007 Winners of the Alfred P. Sloan Awards for Business Excellence in Workplace Flexibility" (New York: Families and Work Institute, 2008) (http://familiesandwork.org/3w/boldideas.pdf).

39. For a full description of the adult labor database, see Jody Heymann and Alison Earle, *Raising the Global Floor: Dismantling the Myth That We Can't Afford Good Working Conditions for Everyone* (Stanford: Stanford University Press, 2010).

40. The World Economic Forum (WEF) is an international organization made up primarily of business leaders, as well as government officials and academic researchers. Its aims are to be "the foremost organization which builds and energizes leading global communities; the creative force shaping global, regional and industry strategies; [and] the catalyst of choice for its communities when undertaking global initiatives to improve the state the world." WEF primarily gathers together business leaders at summits, conferences, and meetings to discuss and develop solutions to global issues (www.weforum.org).

41. From 1987 to 2005 the WEF published the Growth Competitiveness Index, which ranked each nation according to its score on thirty-five variables that represent three conceptual areas: the macroeconomic environment, the quality of public institutions, and technology. Beginning with the 2006 report, this report was renamed the Global Competitiveness Index. The WEF reported rankings based on each nation's scores on more than ninety competitiveness indicators organized into nine areas: institutions; infrastructure; macroeconomy; health and primary education; higher education and training; market efficiency; technological readiness; business sophistication; and innovation. Many of the data used in the competitiveness reports are obtained through a global network of 104 research institutions and academics that partner and collaborate with WEF, as well as from a survey of 11,000 business leaders in 131 nations. The categories are weighted to account more accurately for levels of development in measuring each indicator's impact on competitiveness.

42. World Bank, World Development Indicators, "Labor Force, Total, 2009" (http://data.worldbank.org/indicator/SL.TLF.TOTL.IN?order=wbapi_data_value_2009+wbapi_data_value+wbapi_data_ value-last&sort=asc).

43. China has no national standard, but leave is available in certain circumstances in some provinces.

44. The agreed definition of "unemployed" is working-age individuals who are not working and are available for and actively seeking work. The unemployment rate is then equal to the number of unemployed persons as a percentage of civilian employees, the self-employed, unpaid family workers, and the unemployed. For further information on the selection and development of this unemployment definition, see Eurostat Internet site (http://europa.eu.int/comm/eurostat). The original data from each individual country that are merged to create the OECD unemployment database are either "registered" unemployment from administrative data sources or are from national household surveys (for example, the U.S. Census Bureau's Current Population Survey). In the early 1990s almost all OECD nations agreed to use a common set of criteria for classifying individuals as "unemployed" based on common household survey information. The only variations that still exist are the age group included in the calculation of the unemployment rate and the definition of an "active" job search. Over the past two decades (the time period from which our data come), the consistency, quality, and comparability of the OECD data have increased. In addition to consensus on the definitions, data collection and processing methods have converged.

Critical Thinking

1. Is it incompatible for a country to be economically competitive and family friendly in its workplace and leave policies?

2. How do work-family policies in the United States compare with those in 15 economically competitive nations?

3. What are the two work-family policies that you feel are most important to family well-being? Why are these policies important and needed?

Create Central

www.mhhe.com/createcentral

Internet References

Families and Work Institute
www.familiesandwork.org

Modern Family or Modernized Family Traditionalism?: Master Status and the Gender Order in Switzerland
www.sociology.org/content/vol006.004/lwk.html

Sociological Perspectives of Work and Family
www.scribd.com/doc/24528839

ALISON EARLE is a principal research scientist at Northeastern University. ZITHA MOKOMANE is a senior research specialist at the Human Sciences Research Council of South Africa. JODY HEYMANN is the founding director of the Institute for Health and Social Policy at McGill University.

From *The Future of Children*, Fall 2011, pp. 191–200, a publication of the David and Lucile Packard Foundation from 1991 to 2004. Copyright © Princeton University, all rights reserved.

Article

Prepared by: Patricia Hrusa Williams,
University of Maine at Farmington

Behind Every Great Woman

Carol Hymowitz

Learning Outcomes

After reading this article, you will be able to:

- Explain why women are becoming primary breadwinners in families.

- Describe the challenges faced by families where mothers are employed outside of the home and fathers assume primary responsibility for childrearing.

- Identify how parents can balance their time spent with their family and their career.

A mong the 80 or so customers crammed into Bare Escentuals, it's easy to spot Leslie Blodgett. It's not merely her six-inch platform heels and bright magenta-and-blue dress that set her apart in the Thousand Oaks (Calif.) mall boutique, but her confidence. To the woman concerned she's too old for shimmery eye shadow, Blodgett swoops in and encourages her to wear whatever she wants. With a deft sweep of a brush, she demonstrates a new shade of blush on another customer's cheek. And when she isn't helping anyone, she pivots on her heels for admirers gushing about her dress, made by the breakout designer Erdem.

Blodgett, 49, has spent the past 18 years nurturing Bare Escentuals from a startup into a global cosmetics empire. She sold the company for $1.7 billion to Shiseido in March 2010 but still pitches products in stores around the world and chats incessantly with customers online. Scores of fans post daily messages on Blodgett's Facebook page, confessing details about their personal lives and offering opinions on her additive-free makeup. She only wishes her 19-year-old son, Trent, were in touch with her as frequently as he is with her husband, Keith. In 1995, at 38, Keith quit making television commercials to raise Trent, freeing up Leslie to build her business. She'd do it all again, but she's jealous of her husband's relationship with her son. Trent, a college sophomore, texts his father almost every day; he often goes a week without texting her.

"Once I knew my role was providing for the family, I took that very seriously. But there was envy knowing I wasn't there for our son during the day," says Blodgett. "Keith does everything at home—the cooking, repairs, finances, vacation planning—and I could work long hours and travel a lot, knowing he took such good care of Trent. I love my work, but I would have liked to have a little more balance or even understand what that means."

Blodgett's lament is becoming more familiar as a generation of female breadwinners look back on the sacrifices—some little, some profound—required to have the careers they wanted. Like hundreds of thousands of women who have advanced into management roles in the past two decades—and, in particular, the hundreds who've become senior corporate officers—she figured out early what every man with a corner office has long known: To make it to the top, you need a wife. If that wife happens to be a husband, and increasingly it is, so be it.

When Carly Fiorina became Hewlett-Packard's first female chief executive officer, the existence of her househusband, Frank Fiorina, who had retired early from AT&T to support her career, was a mini-sensation; nine years later, this arrangement isn't at all unusual. Seven of the 18 women who are currently CEOs of Fortune 500 companies—including Xerox's Ursula Burns, PepsiCo's Indra Nooyi, and WellPoint's Angela Braly—have, or at some point have had, a stay-at-home husband. So do scores of female CEOs of smaller companies and women in other senior executive jobs. Others, like IBM's new CEO, Ginni Rometty, have spouses who dialed back their careers to become their powerful wives' chief domestic officers.

This role reversal is occurring more and more as women edge past men at work. Women now fill a majority of jobs in the U.S., including 51.4 percent of managerial and professional positions, according to U.S. Census Bureau data. Some 23 percent of wives now out-earn their husbands, according to a 2010 study by the Pew Research Center. And this earnings trend is more dramatic among younger people. Women 30 and under make more money, on average, than their male counterparts in all but three of the largest cities in the U.S.

During the recent recession, three men lost their jobs for every woman. Many unemployed fathers, casualties of layoffs in manufacturing and finance, have ended up caring for their children full-time while their wives are the primary wage earners. The number of men in the U.S. who regularly care for children under age five increased to 32 percent in 2010 from 19 percent in 1988, according to Census figures. Among those fathers with preschool-age children, one in five served as the main caregiver.

Even as the trend becomes more widespread, stigmas persist. At-home dads are sometimes perceived as freeloaders, even if they've lost jobs. Or they're considered frivolous kept men—gentlemen who golf. The househusbands of highly successful women, after all, live in luxurious homes, take nice vacations, and can afford nannies and housekeepers, which many employ at least part-time. In reaction, at-home dads have launched a spate of support groups and daddy blogs to defend themselves.

"Men are suddenly seeing what it's been like for women throughout history," says Linda R. Hirshman, a lawyer and the author of *Get to Work,* a book that challenges at-home moms to secure paying jobs and insist that their husbands do at least half the housework. Caring for children all day and doing housework is tiring, unappreciated work that few are cut out for—and it leaves men and women alike feeling isolated and diminished.

There's some good news about the at-home dads trend. "By going against the grain, men get to stretch their parenting abilities and women can advance," notes Stephanie Coontz, a family studies professor at Evergreen State College in Olympia, Wash., and author of *Marriage: a History.* And yet the trend underscores something else: When jobs are scarce or one partner is aiming high, a two-career partnership is next to impossible. "Top power jobs are so time-consuming and difficult, you can't have two spouses doing them and maintain a marriage and family," says Coontz. This explains why, even as women make up more of the workforce, they're still a small minority (14 percent, according to New York-based Catalyst) in senior executive jobs. When they reach the always-on, all-consuming executive level, "it's still women who more often put family ahead of their careers," says Ken Matos, a senior director at Families and Work Institute in New York. It may explain, too, why bookstore shelves and e-book catalogs are jammed with self-help books for ambitious women, of which *I'd Rather Be in Charge,* by former Ogilvy-Mather Worldwide CEO Charlotte Beers, is merely the latest. Some, such as Hirshman's top-selling *Get to Work,* recommend that women "marry down"—find husbands who won't mind staying at home—or wed older men who are ready to retire as their careers take off. What's indisputable is that couples increasingly are negotiating whose career will take precedence before they start a family.

"Your wife's career is about to soar, and you need to get out of her way." That's what Ken Gladden says his boss told him shortly before his wife, Dawn Lepore, was named the first female CIO at Charles Schwab in 1994. He was a vice-president at Schwab in computer systems. Lepore's promotion meant she'd become his top boss. "I married above my station," Gladden jokes.

Gladden moved to a job at Visa. When their son, Andrew, was born four years later in 1998, Gladden quit working altogether. He and Lepore had tried for years to have a child and didn't want him raised by a nanny. Being a full-time dad wasn't the biggest adjustment Gladden made for Lepore's career. That came later, when Seattle-based drugstore.com recruited Lepore to become its CEO in 2004.

Gladden had lived in the San Francisco Bay Area for 25 years and wasn't keen to move to a city where it rains a lot and he didn't know anyone. He rejected Lepore's suggestion that she commute between Seattle and San Francisco, and after some long discussions he agreed to relocate—on the condition that they kept their Bay Area home. They still return for holidays and some vacations. "To do what I'm doing, you've got to be able to say 'my wife's the breadwinner, the more powerful one,' and be O.K. with that. But you also need your own interests," says Gladden, who has used his computing skills to launch a home-based business developing software for schools.

The couple's five-bedroom Seattle home overlooks Lake Washington. Gladden, 63, is chief administrator of it and their children, who now are 9 and 13. While they're in school, he works on his software. From 3 P.M. until bedtime, he car-pools to and from sports and music lessons, warms up dinners prepared by a part-time housekeeper, and supervises homework. Lepore, 57, is often out of town. She oversaw the sale of drugstore.com to Walgreens last year, for $429 million. As CEO, she was rarely home before 8 or 9 P.M. and traveled several days a week. Now, as a consultant to several startups and a director at eBay, she still travels frequently. If Gladden envies anything, it's the ease with which his wife can walk into a room filled with well-known executives like Bill Gates and "go right up to them and start talking. I don't feel like I can participate," he says.

Lepore wishes her "biggest supporter" would get more recognition for everything he does at home. When an executive recently told her "having an at-home husband makes it easy for you to be a CEO," she responded, "No, not easy. He makes it possible." Lepore advises younger women to "choose your spouse carefully. If you want a top job, you need a husband who isn't self-involved and will support your success," even if you go further than him. There are tradeoffs, she warns: "I've missed so much with my kids—school plays, recitals, just seeing them every day."

For Lepore and Gladden, the role reversal paid off, and, as one of the few couples willing to go public about their domestic arrangement, they're a rare source of inspiration for those who are still figuring it out. Like Gladden, Matt Schneider, 36, is an

A Changing Landscape

	1970	Now
Percentage of employees who are women	35%	49%
Percentage of college graduates who are women	36%	54%
Share of husbands whose wives' income tops theirs	4%	23%
Contribution of wives' earnings to family income	27%	36%
The number of Fortune 500 CEOs who are women	0	18

at-home dad. A former technology company manager and then a sixth grade teacher, he cares for his sons Max and Sam, 6 and 3, while his wife, Priyanka, also 36, puts in 10-hour days as chief operating officer at a Manhattan real estate management startup. He feels "privileged," he says, to be with his sons full-time "and see them change every day," while allowing that child care and housework can be mind-numbing. He uses every minute of the 2½ hours each weekday when Sam is in preschool to expand the NYC DADS Group he co-founded, 450 members strong. Members meet for play dates with their kids, discuss parenting, and stand up for at-home dads. "We're still portrayed as bumbling idiots," Schneider says. He rails against a prejudice that moms would do a better job—if only they were there. "Everyone is learning from scratch how to change diapers and toilet-train," he says, "and there's no reason to think this is woman's work."

Schneider and his wife, who met as undergraduates at University of Pennsylvania's Wharton School of Business, decided before they wed that she'd have the big career and he'd be the primary parent. "It's her name on the paycheck, and sure, we've thought about the precariousness of having just one breadwinner. But she wouldn't earn what she does if I wasn't doing what I do," he says. Which is not to say that he doesn't wonder "whether I can get back to a career when I want to and build on what I've done before."

At-home moms have snubbed him at arts and crafts classes and on playgrounds. "Men, even those of us pushing strollers, are perceived as dangerous," Schneider says. He was rejected when he wanted to join an at-home neighborhood moms' group, which prompted him to blog more about the similarities among moms and dads. "I've met moms *and* dads who are happy to give a screaming kid a candy bar to get him to settle down, and moms *and* dads who show up at play dates with containers filled with organic fruit," he says. "The differences aren't gender-specific."

It's no different for gay couples. Brad Kleinerman and Flint Gehre have taken turns being at-home dads for their three sons, now 19, 18, and 10. When their sons—biological siblings they adopted through the Los Angeles County foster care system— were young, Kleinerman and Gehre relied first on a weekday nanny and then a live-in one while both worked full-time. Kleinerman, 50, was an executive in human resources at Walt Disney and NASA. Gehre, 46, was a teacher and then director of global learning and communications at Disney. Five years ago, they decided they no longer wanted to outsource parenting. "We always wanted to have dinner together as a family, but by the time we got home, the nanny had fed our kids," says Gehre. "Our kids were at pivotal ages—the two oldest about to go to high school and the youngest to first grade. We wanted to be the ones instilling our values and be there when they needed help with homework or had to get to a doctor."

In 2007 the couple moved from Los Angeles to Avon, Conn., where they were able to get married legally and find better schools for their kids. Kleinerman became the full-time dad and Gehre kept his Disney job, working partly from home and traveling frequently to Los Angeles. A year later they switched: Gehre quit Disney to parent full-time and Kleinerman found a new job as a human resources director at Cigna Healthcare.

Gehre says he's never felt discriminated against as a gay dad or a stay-at-home dad. "No one has ever said to me, 'Why would you stay home with the kids?' Where we're discriminated is when we pay taxes. We don't qualify for the marriage deduction, we have to file as single people," he says. If he has one regret about being at home, it's the lack of adult conversation and stimulation: "I worked in a very high-intensity atmosphere with very intelligent and hard-driving people, and that keeps you sharp." Any dullness doesn't make Gehre doubt his decision. Having consciously chosen to have a family, he and Kleinerman felt they had not only to provide the essentials, but also to be present.

Is there an alternate universe where both parents can pursue careers without outsourcing child care? The five Nordic countries—Iceland, Norway, Sweden, Finland, and Denmark— are noted leaders in keeping moms, in particular, on the job. "These countries have made it possible to have a better division of labor both at work and at home through policies that both encourage the participation of women in the labor force and men in their families," says Saadia Zahidi, co-author of the World Economic Forum's *Global Gender Gap Report.* The policies Zahidi refers to include mandatory paternal leave in combination with maternity leave; generous, federally mandated parental leave benefits; gender-neutral tax incentives; and post-maternity reentry programs.

There were no such programs or precedents for Jennifer Granholm and Dan Mulhern. When the two met at Harvard Law School, she grilled him about what he expected from a wife. Mulhern accepted that Granholm would never be a homemaker like his mother, but he never expected her to run for political office. "When I was young," he says, "I thought *I'd* be the governor"— not married to the governor. Granholm was governor of Michigan from 2003 through 2010, and her election forced Mulhern to walk away from the Detroit-based consulting business he founded, which had numerous contracts with state-licensed health insurance companies, municipalities, and school districts. Once that happened, he felt "in a backroom somewhere" and in a marriage that was "a lot more give than take."

Mulhern understood that his wife faced "extraordinary pressure" during her two terms, including a $1.7 billion budget deficit and the bankruptcies of General Motors and Chrysler. She had limited time for their three children, who were 6, 11, and 14 when she was elected, and even less for him. "I didn't want to say, 'hey, you missed my birthday' or 'you haven't even noticed what happened with the kids,' but I sometimes felt resentful," he says.

Mulhern says he complained to his wife that they spent 95 percent of the little time they had together talking about her work. He missed the attention she used to give him but felt humiliated asking for it. He gradually changed his expectations. He stopped waiting for Granholm to call him in the middle of the day to share what had happened at meetings they'd spent time talking about the prior evening. And he realized he couldn't re-create for her all the memorable or awkward moments he had with their children—like the time he found his daughter and her high school friends in the outdoor shower, "ostensibly with their clothes on. I had to call all the parents and tell them, as a courtesy, 'I want you to know this happened at the Governor's mansion,'" he says. "While my wife was battling the Republican head of the State Senate, I had a teenage daughter who was a more formidable opponent."

When Granholm left office and was asked "what's next?", she said, "it's Dan's turn." As a former governor, though, she's the one with more obvious opportunities. Later this month, Granholm launches a daily political commentary show on Current TV. She's also teaching at the University of California at Berkeley, where Dan has a part-time gig thanks to his wife.

"The employment opportunities that come my way—and my salary potential—aren't what my wife's are now," says Mulhern. He plans to continue to teach, write, and do some consulting, while also taking care of their 14-year-old son. "Someone has to be focused on him every day," he says.

The experiences and reflections of powerful women and their at-home husbands could lead to changes at work so that neither women nor men have to sacrifice their careers or families. "There's no reason women should feel guilty about achieving great success, but there should be a way for success to include professional and personal happiness for everyone," says *Get to Work* author Hirshman. "If you have to kill yourself at work, that's bad for everyone."

Kathleen Christensen agrees. As program director at the Alfred P. Sloan Foundation, she has focused on work and family issues and says we're back to the 1950s, only "instead of Jane at home, it's John. But it's still one person doing 100 percent of work outside the home and the other doing 100 percent at home." Just as we saw the Feminine Mystique in the 1960s among frustrated housewives, Christensen predicts, "we may see the Masculine Mystique in 2020."

The children of couples who have reversed roles know the stakes better than anyone. One morning last year, when Dawn Lepore was packing for a business trip to New York, her nine-year-old daughter burst into tears. "I don't want you to travel so much," Elizabeth told her mother. Lepore hugged her, called

her school, and said her daughter would be staying home that morning. Then she rescheduled her flight until much later that day. "There have been times when what Elizabeth wants most is a mom who stays home and bakes cookies," she says.

Lepore is sometimes concerned that her children won't be ambitious because they've often heard her complain about how exhausted she is after work. But they're much closer to their father than kids whose dads work full-time, and they have a different perspective about men's and women's potential. When a friend of her daughter's said that fathers go to offices every day, Lepore recalls, "Elizabeth replied, 'Don't be silly, dads are at home.'"

Critical Thinking

1. Why are more women becoming the primary breadwinners in their families?
2. What strategies do families use to create work-family balance?
3. When husbands leave their careers to man the home front, what effect does this role reversal have on children, marriages, and families?
4. What types of supports are needed for families where dads serve as primary caregivers?

Create Central

www.mhhe.com/createcentral

Internet References

Families and Work Institute
www.familiesandwork.org
Modern Family or Modernized Family Traditionalism?: Master Status and the Gender Order in Switzerland
www.sociology.org/content/vol006.004/lwk.html
Sociological Perspectives of Work and Family
www.scribd.com/doc/24528839

Article   Prepared by: Patricia Hrusa Williams, *University of Maine at Farmington*

Exploring the Lived Experiences of Homeless Families with Young Children

STEPHANIE HINTON AND DARLINDA CASSEL

Learning Outcomes

After reading this article, you will be able to:

- Explain the reasons families are homeless.

- Describe how homelessness affects parenting and young children.

- Understand supports needed to assist homeless families and prevent homelessness.

Homelessness is a reality in the United States for many families with young children. Though accurate and thorough accounts of the homeless population are difficult to assemble there are several telling statistics on homeless families with young children. The U.S. Conference of Mayors reported in 2008, "At least 3.5 million people are likely to experience homelessness during a year . . . more than half of this group is women and children," and 42 % of this population is reported to be under the age of 5 by the National Law Center on Homelessness and Poverty (2012, p. 1). Only a year later, U.S. cities saw "the sharpest increase in the demand for hunger assistance since 1991 and an increase in homeless families" (The U.S. Conference of Mayors 2009, p. 1). In 2011 U.S. cities saw, on average, a 6 % increase in homelessness and a 16 % increase among families with children experiencing homelessness (The U.S. Conference of Mayors 2011, p. 3). Young children subjected to experiencing homelessness are "twice as likely to experience learning disabilities and three times as likely to experience an emotional disturbance" compared to housed children (Shaw and Goode 2008, p. 6). The injustice of this life situation on our youngest, most vulnerable citizens was addressed by President Obama in his First Presidential Press Conference. President Obama stated: "It is not acceptable for children and families to be without a roof over their heads in a country as wealthy as ours" (Obama 2009).

In a review of the current literature on the issue of homeless families with young children, much of the research compiled sought to understand homelessness through the parents' perspectives and attempted to provide ideas for resources and solutions to assist families of homelessness. "Housing only addresses the structural needs . . . which does not completely alleviate the often complex stresses associated" with being homeless (Karim et al. 2006, p. 455). Families living homeless are under overwhelming amounts of stress. Homelessness, by itself, is considered a powerful source of stress on parents with young children; however, two common themes throughout current research suggest that the major causes of stress within families of homelessness are chemical dependency and family violence (Swick and Williams 2006). These two factors were not only noted as a cause of homelessness but also a reason for chronic homelessness (Vostains et al. 2001). Swick (2008) reported that homeless children and families experience a great deal of violence; while witnessing a violent act still produces negative effects on young children, creating an atmosphere of "high anxiety, distrust, and chaos within family dynamics" (p. 81).

Homeless families reported not feeling as "safe and secure" in their environment as compared to housed families (Swick 2005, p. 195). Living in shelters can cause families with young children to feel insecure and vulnerable. Shelter conditions can also hinder parents' feelings of control and independence over one's own life. Parents also reported a lack of enabling resources within shelters. Many resources that were supposed to help parents often prevented their ability to gain independence (Swick 2005). Other peripheral themes that emerged from the research included unstable relationships within the family and an abdication of parental responsibility (Morris and Butt 2003). Torquati (2002) also suggested that during "periods of stress, parents may be able to maintain some warmth and support in their relationships with their children, but they may be at higher risk for irritable parenting" (p. 481).

Early childhood educators hold a position in which they can encourage and support homeless parents and young children; however, schools are often "ill equipped to combat the multifaceted problems associated with homelessness" (Gargiulo 2006, p. 360). Through authentic communication, early childhood educators can gather information about "families' perceptions of needs, resources, and strengths," build trusting relationships with homeless families, and connect parents to key supports for food and clothing (Swick and Bailey 2004, p. 212). It is important that homeless parents with young children are heard; homeless mothers "experience the needs of their children every minute of the day" (Swick 2010, p. 299). Swick found many parents wanted "to do a good job in parenting and family life . . . because of their problems, they often want to compensate by increasing their focus on their children" (2010, p. 301). In the same study, the clear and essential needs of most homeless mothers and fathers were listed by parents as supportive help, adequate and affordable housing, high quality child care so they can work or receive training, and education opportunities especially in parenting (Swick 2010). Early childhood educators can begin by "developing an awareness of the challenges and situations experienced by homeless children and families" (Powers-Costello and Swick 2008, p. 243). Educators can also engage "in service-learning roles with shelters and other groups that serve" homeless children and families, through mentoring and tutoring opportunities educators can use their "liaison roles to weave together more supportive school and community settings," and involve "community experts on various issues connected to homelessness" (Powers-Costello and Swick 2008, p. 244). Swick and Williams listed key strategies on how early childhood educators can build relationships and effectively support homeless families. These strategies include: (1) encouraging the family to access education and counseling to address the challenges of their situation; (2) support the family with resources and help that empowers them; and (3) involve family in learning ways to promote healthy life styles (2006). In a later study, Swick and Williams (2010) also pointed out that; since "single parent homeless mothers develop adaptive parenting strategies to accommodate the various contexts they experience . . . early childhood professionals need to better understand the problems faced by single parent homeless mothers" (p. 53). Their research concluded that early childhood educators and shelters serving homeless families needed to: (a) involve "faith-based groups more effectively in supporting and empowering homeless families, (b) seek to dispel the many negative and incorrect stereotypes about homeless mothers and

their children, and (c) interact more with homeless mothers in supportive ways such as mentoring and one-on-one counseling" (Swick and Williams 2010, p. 54).

The research available on homeless families with young children lacks information on how young children experience homelessness and the importance of early childhood educators understanding the homeless experience and effectively providing care to families with young children through that experience. If early childhood educators are going to effectively serve homeless families with young children, research is needed that brings understanding to their life situation through their perspectives. The purpose of this qualitative phenomenological research study is to explore the lived experiences of young children, ages four to eight, and their families who have experienced or are currently experiencing living in [a] fixed, non-transient, homeless situation. Research will seek to understand common themes of the family dynamics and the development of young children who are homeless to help early childhood educators relate to these families and to support their children's learning. The basis for conducting this research study is: (1) to understand reasons families with young children become homeless; (2) become aware of beneficial resources available to families and their perceptions of the resources; (3) and [understand] the developmental effects that homeless living situations can have on young children.

Methodology

Context for the Study

Participants in this study were homeless parents with young children living in a fixed, non-transient, urban downtown shelter in the southwestern United States. This shelter was selected for this study because the mission of the shelter complied with the research of Swick and Williams (2010) on meeting the needs of homeless families. The shelter is a faith-based program that seeks to dispel the many negative and incorrect stereotypes about homeless mothers and their children while interacting with homeless families in supportive ways. All the participants in this study were involved in a faith-based program provided by the shelter. On entering the shelter, any homeless individuals or families are limited to a 30 days stay. Within that 30 days time frame, the individual or family has the option of entering the program the shelter provides. The program offers a variety of classes for individuals and families and is specific to the needs of each individual or family. The classes offered to the residents include Bible study, parenting, marriage, job or skill related education, and GED test preparation. If a resident is married upon entering the shelter he or she is required to attend marriage classes. Likewise, if a resident is a parent, she or he is required to attend parenting classes. Family units lived together in apartment-like housing, fathers were permitted to live in family units if the father was a single parent or was married to the mother. With this exception to fathers, all other women and men were kept separate inside the shelter.

The program has four steps: anger management, spirituality, addiction control, and transition to life outside the shelter. The program's main goal is to educate and equip homeless individuals to be successful after leaving the shelter. Residents can move to a new step after receiving a counselor's approval. The majority of residents completed the entire program within 10 months to 1 year, yet some residents stayed in the program for multiple years. The residents of the shelter agreed to adhere to a specific schedule on entrance into the program. The schedule consisted of a morning wake-up call, periods of free time, three meals, devotions and church services, and work shifts. The shelter consists of common areas and private living areas for the families and individuals. The common areas include the lobby, gym, and dining hall. The living areas are separated according to families with children, individual men, and individual women.

The role of the researcher was that of a participant-observer. The researcher had participated in volunteer work with the children of the families living at the shelter before the research began. The researcher voluntarily participated with children in their activities. These activities were educational and engaging for the children. As a volunteer in the program, the researcher had built relationships with the children and their parents through these interactions prior to the research.

Participants

Eight families who reside at the homeless shelter participated in the study. All parents and children involved in the study volunteered to participate. Each family participating had at least one child between the ages of four and eight. The average age of child participants was 5.4 years. The average number of children living with these families at the shelter was 2.8. All the participants in this study were jobless; four participants were working on completing their GED, three had received their GED, one had a few years of college work completed, and one was seeking a degree in higher education at the time of the study. At the time of the interview, the families had spent an average of 5.5 months at the shelter. The parents' ages ranged from 22 to 38 years old with the average age being 30.3 years old. The families were 25 % white, 50 % African American, and 25 % Hispanic. Only the mother was interviewed due to the fact that only three were married.

Procedures

The research study was a qualitative phenomenological study that was carried out from October 2011 until March 2012.

Weekly interviews occurred in an office at the shelter on Friday after dinner, and observations occurred throughout the week at the shelter in the common areas of the foyer and the dining hall. Interviews lasted approximately 1 h for each family and observations occurred weekly until the completion of the study. After each interview, field notes were written on the details of the interviews.

The interviewer asked parents about their own childhood and what brought their family to living in the shelter, their child(ren)'s strengths and interests, their support system as a homeless family, the impact homelessness has had on their family, and their views on parenting. The children's interview questions focused on the children's favorite activity for fun and play, who they like to play with, their favorite thing about school, and what makes them happy and scared. An audiotape was used to help accurately record interviews; without the use of the audiotape important details of the participants' responses might have been missed. Families were observed interacting twice per week.

While conducting observations, the researcher focused on parent and child interactions and types of communication between the child(ren) and parent. During the observations the researcher observed from the common areas during the residents' dinner time and their 2 h of free time in the evening. During free time the families were observed in the foyer, the dining hall, and the apartments. The researcher interacted with the participants while observing only when participants initiated an interaction with the researcher.

Data Collection

Reasons for Homelessness

Data were gathered into three themes: (1) reasons families with young children become homeless, (2) beneficial resources available to families and their perceptions of those resources, and (3) effects of homeless living situations on young children's development. The first category indicates reasons for homelessness. Table 1 details the reasons participants cited for being homeless.

During the interview, each participant explained multiple reasons for homelessness. An unhappy childhood was a common theme. They described growing up in poverty, stating that their basic needs were met, even though their childhood felt unstable. One of the participants talked about alcohol usage of caretakers, another participant described the early death of her parents, and seven participants discussed parental fights or the abandonment of parents. While an unhappy childhood was considered by seven participants as a reason for homelessness, these seven mothers further described their unhappy childhoods

Table 1   Reasons for homelessness as stated by homeless parents

Participant in study	Reason for homelessness						
	Unhappy childhood	Teenage pregnancy	Multiple children	High school drop out	Drug use	Spouse (father) abandonment	Jobless
1	X	X	X	X			X
2	X	X	X	X		X	X
3	X	X	X	X		X	X
4	X	X	X	X	X		X
5	X		X	X	X	X	X
6			X	X	X	X	X
7	X		X	X	X	X	X
8	X	X	X		X	X	X

as being the source of their lack of resources and support system as an adult.

Teenage pregnancies were common with five participants. All of the participants in the study had at least two children. Teenage pregnancies and multiple children were cited as reasons for homelessness because it led many of the participants to dropping out of high school. The participants who became pregnant as teenagers felt they could not juggle the responsibilities of a baby with the demands of high school. These parents also found it difficult to find affordable housing with minimum wage jobs. Five of the families who participated in the study also cited a lack of paternal involvement as a source of their homelessness, stating the difficulties of being a single mother. Multiple children increased the chances of a homeless lifestyle because of the increased financial responsibility.

All but two of the participants in the study dropped out of high school. At the time of the interviews three of the participants had obtained their GED and the other three were working to obtain their GED through courses the shelter provided. All participants were jobless before coming to the shelter. Thus a cycle formed; dropping out of high school causes a lack of job opportunities which in turn caused financial problems leading to homelessness.

Four of the participants cited that joblessness and the stress of having multiple children led to their drug usage. One participant explained that she had started using drugs at the age of 17 which led to her [to] (1) drop out, (2) multiple children, and (3) [a] jobless condition. Drugs were explained as being a reason for homelessness by participants because they could not leave their addiction without support. The shelter is a drug rehabilitation center; therefore, participants were able to receive the interventions needed to quit using drugs without the concern that their children might be taken from them.

Individuals participating in the shelter's rehabilitation process are encouraged to take responsibility for life decisions that led to their current situation. The interviews with homeless parents revealed similar themes among each family's reasons for being homeless. These factors included unhappy childhoods, young pregnancies, multiple children, failure to complete schooling, drug or substance abuse, paternal abandonment, and unemployment.

Resources and Perceptions of Resources

The second category analyzed participants' comments about available resources. The shelter provides clients with a four-step process to recovery from homelessness; these steps are anger management, spirituality, addiction control, and transition to life outside of the shelter. At each step a variety of resources are provided to the families. Resources that were used by the participating families include: mentoring, family and marriage counseling, drug rehabilitation, parenting classes, GED preparation courses, Bible study classes, and classes on finding and maintaining a job. Counselors at the shelter are responsible for evaluating clients and, together with the client, deciding what resources to use. Participants interviewed discussed which resources they used, which ones were most effective for their families, and ideas for resources that would potentially benefit them and their family.

Support from others; including counselors, mentors, or other homeless families, was viewed by seven of the participants as an important resource. Having these supports in place led participants to feel successful in the program. Seven of the participants were positive about life at the shelter. Some of the participants with a positive view of life at the shelter cited that other families living in the shelter were part of the needed support system. Participants also explained their positive experience came from the staff and the program itself. These parents explained the positive effect that the mandatory regular and predictable schedule had on their young children, as well as how this aspect of shelter life taught them how to maintain a normalcy in their family that they did not have before.

As a part of the shelter's program, clients are encouraged to plan for the future when they leave the shelter. Two of the participants discussed job plans. One participant wanted to be a nurse and was enrolled in college courses. Many participants explained how they would like to give back to the homeless community by becoming a resource to other homeless families. All of the participants expressed a desire to be stable and independent. The goal of the resources was to ensure their success in this area. Because of the shelter's decision to constantly discuss life beyond the shelter, participants were able to look ahead and plan for their next step; the resources that the shelter provides gave participants the opportunity to make their goals a reality.

The shelter provided tutoring and after school activities for school aged children. However, children up to age five, who were not in an outside program such as a child care facility, were required to stay with their parents. Children in prekindergarten, kindergarten, or Head Start were not engaged in any tutoring or after school activities. One parent described a need for more opportunities for the younger children, she stated the shelter needs to get ". . . . a class together for the kids" with more opportunities to learn. This resource could have the potential to use developmentally appropriate practices, such as engaging children in play with materials like water, sand, while also giving children early literacy opportunities. There is also a need for parenting classes to include what parents should expect at different developmental stages as well as ways that parents can promote learning in the home for their young child.

The interviews revealed that the parents felt positively about the resources provided by the shelter. The shelter provides individualized, specific resources matched to each client's needs and goals. However, there is a need to develop more engaging resources for the young children, resources that engage and promote learning.

Effects on Young Children

Data placed into the third category revealed information about the effects on young children. Parents were asked to describe how their child(ren)'s behavior had changed since moving to the shelter. Many parents who had described a positive experience also described their young child(ren) as being angry and emotional since arriving at the shelter. One parent described her 6-year-old as "getting more emotional and he has more issues

going on with him cause he's able to see and know what's going on around him." Another parent stated "they like that there's a lot of other kids," while still another parent explained that; "sometimes it's rough on my kids" having other people around all the time. One parent felt that due to the stability and constant routine her children were "a lot happier" since moving into the shelter than when they were living on the streets. Each child reacted to the experience of moving to the shelter differently, but each of the participants stated that they saw a change in their child(ren).

In observations of parent and child interactions, behaviors of educational support, such as reading and completing homework, were not observed at any time. One parent did discuss listening to her child read. Four parents were active in their young child's play or engaged in play with the child; four parents were not observed playing with their child(ren) nor was there parental supervision of the child when playing was observed. At times when parents were required to be supervising their children, children were observed to be running around the common area, going in and out, and climbing on tables and chairs. During these observations children were seen interacting freely with others in the shelter. Lack of supervision had effects on the young child(ren)'s behavior; which led to negative behaviors displayed by the children throughout the shelter.

Families were required to eat meals together while the children were not in school. Regular observations were made of seven of the families eating dinner together. Observations included family communication and affection, especially between parent and child. Three of the parents spent time having conversations with their child(ren); while five of the parents communicated through short verbal directions or did not communicate with their child(ren). Parents were also observed yelling and making negative comments towards the young child(ren). Affection, such as hugs and kisses, was observed frequently in three of the families. Restrictions, harsh tones, and general disapproval were observed with five of the families. Verbal and nonverbal communication affected the young children living in the shelter. When interviewing the young children, single word responses to questions were common with all but two of the children. During observations, single word responses were also common from child to parent. In interviews with the young children, all the children stated an interest in learning. Nine children were interviewed. Three of the nine attended school, another three participated in an early childhood program, and the last three children stayed at the shelter. All of the children exhibited an inability to engage in conversation during the interview questions and they all were easily distracted.

Through interviews and observations, research verified that moving into the homeless shelter affected the young children participating in this study. Parents interviewed described behavioral changes that occurred with their children; issues of anger and anxiety were raised as a result of being homeless. A behavior change was noticed by all participating parents. Observations and interviews on parent–child interactions and communication revealed effects on homeless children's behavior and vocabulary.

Conclusion

The basis for conducting this study was: (1) to understand reasons families with young children become homeless; (2) become aware of beneficial resources available to families and their perceptions of the resources; (3) and the developmental effects that homeless living situations can have on young children. Conclusions were assembled based on themes that emerged from the observations and the interviews conducted for the research study. Reasons for homelessness that emerged from the parent interviews; themes included: unhappy childhoods, young pregnancies, multiple children, failure to complete schooling, drug or substance abuse, paternal abandonment, and unemployment. These factors were considered to be the cause of homelessness and reasons for continual homelessness resulting in an inability to leave a homeless lifestyle. These factors are consistent with research conducted by Swick (2008).

By interviewing the parents and observing the family interactions it became apparent that particular resources were beneficial to the families with young children. Overall the interviews revealed that the parents felt positively about the resources the shelter provided. The shelter provided very individual and specific resources to the clients thus ensuring their clients' needs and goals were met. However, there were some resources lacking. There is a need to develop more resources that engage young children in learning. Another needed resource is educational support for parents with young children.

Interviews with the parents and children as well as observations of family interactions and their ways of communicating revealed that moving into the homeless shelter affected the young children. Parents described behavioral changes in their children; such as anger and anxiety. Observations and interviews also revealed that homeless children's vocabulary is underdeveloped. Living in the shelter affected the development of the young children.

In conclusion, common themes emerged from the families that participated in this study, participants shared similarities in understanding the circumstances that led to homelessness and to the shelter as well as expressing responsibility for the actions that led them to homelessness. Other similarities involved setting goals and reporting a strong support system. However, observations proved that families still struggled in understanding the basic needs of their children. It also seemed that parents

did not fully understand the importance of early education and intervention. The study validates the importance of educating families of young children who are homeless as well as the importance of early childhood educators developing an awareness of ways to support children in a homeless situation (Powers-Costello and Swick 2008).

Implications

Research suggested that parents and young children were affected by homelessness and found common themes which occurred throughout the parents' reasons for being homeless, their perception of resources, and their perceptions of themselves and their children. Early childhood educators know the value of understanding the young child's background story and know the importance of providing care and support to the entire family. By knowing why families with young children become homeless, the early childhood educator becomes aware of the families circumstances. This information can only help the early childhood educator in supporting the family as well as educating the whole child while meeting his or her needs.

Not all homeless families are part of a working program. Many homeless families with young children are unaccounted for and available resources are limited. Swick and Williams suggested three key strategies for early childhood educators to remember when working with homeless families, no matter their current location: (1) encourage the family to access education and counseling to address the challenges of their situation; (2) support the family with resources and help empower them; and (3) involve the family in learning ways to promote healthy lifestyles (2006). Any early childhood educator who is aware of the family with young children's situation can be essential in ensuring that the family feels supported and empowered.

It is vital that early childhood educators are aware that homelessness affects young children and their development. Developmental delays, such as below average vocabulary, an inability to focus, or issues of anger and resentment towards life may be present. Early childhood educators can play a crucial role in providing support to these young children as they transition into a public school environment. Therefore, it is important for early childhood educators to be unbiasedly aware of the reasons families with young children become homeless, the resources that are available to these families as well as ways that an educator can be a liaison to resources, and understand the effects that homelessness can have on young children.

Further research should consider looking into the family structures of homelessness and the benefits of engaging activities for young children who are homeless. Research should look into the differences between families with young children who are transient and ones who are not and are living [in] a fixed location, such as a shelter. Early childhood educators also need to be informed on the dynamics of life that lead homeless families into their current predicament, as well as the developmental needs of young children. This information is valuable to help families navigate their own way back out of their homelessness.

References

Gargiulo, R. M. (2006). Homeless and disabled: Rights, responsibilities, and recommendations for serving young children with special needs. *Early Childhood Education Journal, 33* (5), 357–362. doi:10.1007/s10643-006-0067-1.

Karim, K., Tishcler, V., Gregory, P., & Vostanis, P. (2006). Homeless children and parents: Short-term mental health outcome. *International Journal of Social Psychiatry, 52* (5), 447–458. doi: 10.1177/0020764006066830.

Morris, R. I., & Butt, R. A. (2003). Parents' perspectives on homelessness and its effects on the educational development of their children. *The Journal of School Nursing, 19* (1), 43–50. doi: 10.1177/10598405030190010701.

National Law Center on Homelessness and Poverty. (2012). *Some facts on homelessness, housing, and violence against women.* Retrieved from www.nlchp.org.

Obama, B. (2009). *First Presidential press conference.* The East Room: The White House Washington D.C.

Powers-Costello, E., & Swick, K. J. (2008). Exploring the dynamics of teacher perceptions of homeless children and families during the early years. *Early Childhood Education Journal, 36,* 241–245. doi:10.1007/s10643-008-0249-0.

Shaw, E., & Goode, S. (2008). Fact sheet: Vulnerable young children. *The National Early Childhood Technical Assistance Center.* Retrieved from http://www.nectac.org/~pdfs/pubs/nectacfact sheet_vulnerableyoungchildren.pdf.

Swick, K. J. (2005). Helping homeless families overcome barriers to successful functioning. *Early Childhood Education Journal, 33* (3), 195–199. doi:10:1007/s10643-005-0044-0.

Swick, K. J. (2008). The dynamics of violence and homelessness among young families. *Early Childhood Education Journal, 36,* 81–85. doi:10.1007/s10643-007-0220-5.

Swick, K. J. (2010). Responding to the voices of homeless preschool children and their families. *Early Childhood Education Journal, 38,* 299–304. doi:10.1007/s10643-010-0404-2.

Swick, K. J., & Bailey, L. B. (2004). Working with families: Communicating effectively with parents and families who are homeless. *Early Childhood Education Journal, 32* (3), 211–214.

Swick, K. J., & Williams, R. D. (2006). An analysis of Bronfenbrenner's bio-ecological perspective for early childhood educators: Implications for working with families experiencing stress. *Early Childhood Education Journal, 33* (5), 371–378. doi:10.1007/s10643-006-0078-y.

Swick, K. J., & Williams, R. (2010). The voices of single parent mothers who are homeless: Implications for early childhood professionals. *Early Childhood Education Journal, 38,* 49–55. doi:10.1007/s10643-010-0378-0.

The United States Conference of Mayors. (2008). *Hunger and homelessness survey: A status report on hunger and homelessness in America's cities.* Retrieved from http://www.usmayors.org/pressreleases/ documentshungerhomelessnessreport_121208.pdf.

The United States Conference of Mayors. (2009). *U.S. cities see sharp increases in the need for food assistance; decreases in individual homelessness: Mayors issue annual report on hunger, homelessness in cities.* Retrieved from: http://www.usmayors.org/ pressreleases/uploads/RELEASEHUNGERHOMELESSNESS 2009FINALRevised.pdf.

The United States Conference of Mayors. (2011). *Hunger and homelessness survey: A status report of hunger and homelessness in America's cities.* Retrieved from: http:// usmayors.org/pressreleases/uploads/2011-hhreport.pdf.

Torquati, J. C. (2002). Personal and social resources as predictors of parenting in homeless families. *Journal of Family Issues, 23* (4), 463–485. doi:10.177/0192513X02023004001.

Vostains, P., Tischler, V., Cumella, S., & Bellerby, T. (2001). Mental health problems and social supports among homeless mothers and children victims of domestic and community violence. *International Journal of Social Psychiatry, 47* (4), 30–40. doi:10.1177/002076400104700403.

Critical Thinking

1. What factors are contributing to an increase in homeless families in the United States?
2. What are challenges for children, parents, and families in adapting in the face of residential instability and homelessness?
3. What supports are needed by families to prevent homelessness?
4. What supports are needed to ensure child and family wellbeing while homeless?

Create Central

www.mhhe.com/createcentral

Internet References

National Alliance to End Homelessness
www.endhomelessness.org/pages/families
The National Center on Family Homelessness
www.familyhomelessness.org

Article   Prepared by: Patricia Hrusa Williams, *University of Maine at Farmington*

Caregiving Support and Help

Tips for Making Family Caregiving Easier

MELINDA SMITH AND JEANNE SEGAL

Learning Outcomes

After reading this article, you will be able to:

- Understand the term family caregiver.

- Recognize the positive aspects and challenges faced by family caregivers.

- Identify supports needed by family caregivers.

As a family caregiver, you may find yourself facing a host of new responsibilities, many of which are unfamiliar or intimidating. At times, you may feel overwhelmed and alone. But despite its challenges, caregiving can also be rewarding. And there are a lot of things you can do to make the caregiving process easier for both you and your loved one. These tips can help you get the support you need while caring for someone you love.

A Look at Family Caregiving

Providing care for a family member in need is an age-old act of kindness, love, and loyalty. And as life expectancies increase, medical treatments advance, and increasing numbers of people live with chronic illness and disabilities, more and more of us will participate in the caregiving process.

There are many different types of family caregiver situations. You may be taking care of an aging parent or a handicapped spouse. Or perhaps you're caring for a child with a physical or mental illness. But regardless of your particular circumstances, you're facing a challenging new role.

If you're like most family caregivers, you aren't trained for the responsibilities you now face. And you probably never anticipated you'd be in this situation. You may not even live very close to your loved one. At the same time, you love your family member and want to provide the best care you can.

The good news is that you don't have to be a nursing expert, a superhero, or a saint in order to be a good caregiver. With the right help and support, you can be a good caregiver without having to sacrifice yourself in the process.

New to Family Caregiving?

- **Learn as much as you can** about your family member's illness and about how to be a caregiver. The more you know, the less anxiety you'll feel about your new role and the more effective you'll be.

- **Seek out other caregivers.** It helps to know you're not alone. It's comforting to give and receive support from others who understand what you're going through.

- **Trust your instincts.** Remember, you know your family member best. Don't ignore what doctors and specialists tell you, but listen to your gut, too.

- **Encourage your loved one's independence.** Caregiving does not mean doing everything for your loved one. Be open to technologies and strategies that allow your family member to be as independent as possible.

- **Know your limits.** Be realistic about how much of your time and yourself you can give. Set clear limits, and communicate those limits to doctors, family members, and other people involved.

Family Caregiving Tip 1: Accept Your Feelings

Caregiving can trigger a host of difficult emotions, including anger, fear, resentment, guilt, helplessness, and grief. It's important to acknowledge and accept what you're feeling, both good and bad. Don't beat yourself up over your doubts and misgivings. These feelings don't mean that you don't love your family member—they simply mean you're human.

What You May Feel about Being a Family Caregiver

- **Anxiety and worry**—You may worry about how you will handle the additional responsibilities of caregiving and what will happen to your family member if something happens to you. You may also fear what will happen in the future as your loved one's illness progresses.
- **Anger or resentment**—You may feel angry or resentful toward the person you're caring for, even though you know it's irrational. Or you might be angry at the world in general, or resentful of other friends or family members who don't have your responsibilities.
- **Guilt**—You may feel guilty for not doing more, being a "better" caregiver, having more patience, accepting your situation with more equanimity, or in the case of long distance caregiving, not being available more often.
- **Grief**—There are many losses that can come with caregiving (the healthy future you envisioned with your spouse or child; the goals and dreams you've had to set aside). If the person you're caring for is terminally ill, you're also dealing with that grief.

Even when you understand why you're feeling the way you do, it can still be upsetting. In order to deal with your feelings, it's important to talk about them. Don't keep your emotions bottled up, but find at least one person you trust to confide in.

Places You Can Turn for Caregiver Support Include

- Family members or friends who will listen without judgment
- Your church, temple, or other place of worship
- Caregiver support groups at a local hospital or online
- A therapist, social worker, or counselor
- National caregiver organizations
- Organizations specific to your family member's illness or disability

Family Caregiving Tip 2: Don't Try to Do It All

Even if you're the primary family caregiver, you can't do everything on your own, especially if you're caregiving from a distance (more than an hour's drive from your family member). You'll need help from friends, siblings, and other family members, as well as health professionals. If you don't get the support you need, you'll quickly burn out—which will compromise your ability to provide care.

But before you can ask for help, you need to have a clear understanding of your family member's needs. Take some time to list all the caregiving tasks required, being as specific as possible. Then determine which activities you are able to meet (be realistic about your capabilities and time). The remaining tasks on the list are ones you'll need to ask others to help you with.

Asking Family and Friends for Help

It's not always easy to ask for help, even when you desperately need it. Perhaps you're afraid to impose on others or worried that your request will be resented or rejected. But if you simply make your needs known, you may be pleasantly surprised by the willingness of others to pitch in. Many times, friends and family members want to help, but don't know how. Make it easier for them:

- Set aside one-on-one time to talk to the person
- Go over the list of caregiving needs you previously drew up
- Point out areas in which they might be of service (maybe your brother is good at Internet research, or your friend is a financial whiz)
- Ask the person if they'd like to help, and if so, in what way
- Make sure the person understands what would be most helpful to both you and the caregiving recipient

Family Caregiving Tip 3: Attend to Your Own Needs

Pablo Casals, the world-renowned cellist, said, "The capacity to care is the thing that gives life its deepest significance and meaning." It's essential that you receive the support you need, so you don't lose that capacity. While you're caring for your loved one, don't forget about your own needs. Caregivers need care, too.

Emotional Needs of Family Caregivers

- **Take time to relax daily** and learn how to regulate yourself and de-stress when you start to feel overwhelmed.
- **Keep a journal.** Write down your thoughts and feelings. This will give you perspective and serve as a way to release strong feelings.
- **Talk with someone** to make sense of your situation and your feelings.

- **Feed your spirit.** Pray, meditate, or do another activity that makes you feel part of something greater. Try to find meaning in your life and in your role as a caregiver.
- **Watch out for signs of depression and anxiety,** and get professional help if needed.

Social & Recreational Needs of Family Caregivers

- **Stay social.** Make it a priority to visit regularly with other people. Nurture your close relationships. Don't let yourself become isolated.
- **Do things you enjoy.** Laughter and joy can help keep you [keep] going when you face trials, stress, and pain.
- **Maintain balance in your life.** Don't give up activities that are important to you, such as your work or your hobbies.
- **Give yourself a break.** Take regular breaks from caregiving, and give yourself an extended break at least once a week.
- **Find a community.** Join or reestablish your connection to a religious group, social club, or civic organization. The broader your support network, the better.

Physical Needs of Family Caregivers

- **Exercise regularly.** Try to get in at least 30 minutes of exercise, three times per week. Exercise is one of the best ways to relieve stress and boost your energy. So get moving, even if you're tired.
- **Eat right.** Well-nourished bodies are better prepared to cope with stress and get through busy days. Keep your energy up and your mind clear by eating nutritious meals at regular times throughout the day.
- **Avoid alcohol and drugs.** It can be tempting to turn to substances for escape when life feels overwhelming, but they can easily compromise the quality of your caregiving. Instead, try dealing with problems head on and with a clear mind.
- **Get enough sleep.** Aim for an average of eight hours of solid, uninterrupted sleep every night. Otherwise, your energy level, productivity, and ability to handle stress will suffer.
- **Keep up with your own health care.** Go to the doctor and dentist on schedule, and keep up with your own prescriptions or medical therapy. As a caregiver, you need to stay as strong and healthy as possible.

Family Caregiving Tip 4: Take Advantage of Community Services

There are services to help caregivers in most communities, and the cost is often based on ability to pay or covered by the care receiver's insurance. Services that may be available in your community include adult day care centers, home health aides, home-delivered meals, respite care, transportation services, and skilled nursing.

- **Caregiver services in your community**—Call your local senior center, senior services organization, county information and referral service, university gerontology department, family service, or hospital social work unit for contact suggestions. In the U.S. call your local Area Agency on Aging.
- **Caregiver support for veterans**—If your care recipient is a veteran in the U.S., home health care coverage, financial support, nursing home care, and adult day care benefits may be available. Some Veterans Administration programs are free, while others require co-payments, depending upon the veteran's status, income, and other criteria.
- **Your family member's affiliations**—Fraternal organizations such as the Elks, Eagles, or Moose lodges may offer some assistance if your family member is a longtime dues-paying member. This help may take the form of phone check-ins, home visits, or transportation.
- **Community transportation services**—Many community transportation services are free for your care recipient, while others may have a nominal fee or ask for a donation. In the U.S., your local Area Agency on Aging can help you locate transportation to and from adult day care, senior centers, shopping malls, and doctor's appointments.
- **Telephone check-ins**—Telephone reassurance provides prescheduled calls to homebound older adults to reduce their isolation and monitor their well-being. Check with local religious groups, senior centers, and other public or nonprofit organizations.
- **Adult day care**—If your loved one is well enough, consider the possibility of adult day care. An adult day care center can provide you with needed breaks during the day or week, and your loved one with some valuable diversions and activities.

Family Caregiving Tip 5: Provide Long Distance Care

Many people take on the role of designated caregiver for a family member—often an older relative or sibling—while living more than an hour's travel away. Trying to manage a loved one's care from a distance can add to feelings of guilt and anxiety and present many other obstacles. But there are steps you can take to prepare for caregiving emergencies and ease the burden of responsibility.

- **Set up an alarm system for your loved one.** Because of the distance between you, you won't be able to respond in time to a life-threatening emergency, so subscribe to an electronic alert system. Your loved one wears the small device and can use it to summon immediate help.
- **Manage doctor and medical appointments.** Try to schedule all medical appointments together, at a time when you'll be in the area. Make the time to get to know your loved one's doctors and arrange to be kept up-to-date on all medical issues via the phone when you're not in the area. Your relative may need to sign a privacy release to enable their doctors to do this.
- **Investigate local services.** When you're not there, try to find local services that can offer home help services, deliver meals, or provide local transportation for your loved one. A geriatric care manager can offer a variety of services to long-distance caregivers, including providing and monitoring in-home help for your relative.
- **Schedule regular communication with your loved one.** A daily e-mail, text message, or quick phone call can let your relative know that they're not forgotten and give you peace of mind.

More Help for Caregiving
Next Step . . .
Manage caregiver stress and avoid burnout. There's no getting around it, caregiving is stressful. But you don't have to be overwhelmed by your responsibilities. Learning to manage stress is part of being a good caregiver. And it's not as impossible as you may think. Read Caregiver Stress and Burnout.

Support for Caregivers
Respite Care: Finding and Choosing Respite Services
Stress Management: How to Reduce, Prevent, and Cope with Stress
Home Care Services for Seniors: Services to Help You Stay at Home

Dementia and Alzheimer's Care: Planning and Preparing for the Road Ahead
Preventing Burnout: Signs, Symptoms, Causes, and Coping Strategies
Easy Ways to Start Exercising: Making Exercise a Fun Part of Your Everyday Life
Adult Day Care Services: Finding the Best Center for Your Needs
Support for Alzheimer's and Dementia Caregivers: How to Get the Caregiving Help You Need

Resources and References

Family Caregiving
AARP—Tools, work sheets and tips on how to plan, prepare and succeed as a caregiver.
Eldercare Locator—Connects families to community-based resources for senior care.
Family Caregiver Alliance—Covers a wide range of issues, from how to talk to an attorney to federal and state legislation related to caregiving.
Next Step in Care—Helps family caregivers of chronically or seriously ill patients navigate the health care system as they transition between care settings.
A Place for Mom—Free referral service that directs families to housing and assisted living facilities.
National Family Caregivers Association—Tips to help caregivers care for themselves.
National Association of Area Agencies on Aging—Portal for options that allow people to choose home and community-based services and living arrangements that suit them best.

Family Caregiving Services—Internationally
Looking for Local Carers' Services?—NHS services available to UK carers of disabled children and adults, including respite care. (NHS)
Commonwealth Respite and Carelink Centres—For Australian residents, provides information and support services for older people, people with disabilities and those who provide care and services. (Australian Government)
Carers New Zealand—Offers help and advice for New Zealand carers, including guidance on respite care services. (Carers NZ)
Programs and Services—Information on services for seniors in Canada, including in-home support. (Government of Canada)

Long Distance Caregiving
Caring From a Distance—An organization for long-distance caregivers in the U.S., providing service directories and helplines. (CFAD.org)
National Association of Professional Geriatric Care Managers—Offers information about care management and how to find and hire a geriatric care manager. (NAPGCM)

Critical Thinking

1. We tend to think about family caregiving as a task we undertake with aging family members. What are some of the other circumstances and situations where family members serve as caregivers?

2. What do you think would be the greatest challenge of being a family caregiver?

3. If you needed to assume the role of a family caregiver, what would be two supports you think you'd need in order to manage the challenges of your new role? How or why might these supports be beneficial to you?

Internet References

Caregiver Action Network
http://www.caregiveraction.org/

Family Caregiver Alliance, National Center on Caregiving
http://caregiver.org

National Council on Aging
http://www.ncoa.org/

Article

Prepared by: Patricia Hrusa Williams,
University of Maine at Farmington

Family Members' Informal Roles in End-of-Life Decision Making in Adult Intensive Care Units

Jill R. Quinn, RN, PhD, CS-ANP et al.

Learning Outcomes

After reading this article, you will be able to:

- Understand the types of decisions that need to be made when a family member is critically ill.

- Identify the different formal and informal roles family members take in the decision making process.

- Explain how family dynamics are influenced when someone is critically ill.

Background To support the process of effective family decision making, it is important to recognize and understand informal roles that various family members may play in the end-of-life decision making process.

Objective To describe some informal roles consistently enacted by family members involved in the process of end-of-life decision making in intensive care units.

Methods Ethnographic study. Data were collected via participant observation with field notes and semistructured interviews on 4 intensive care units in an academic health center in the mid-Atlantic United States from 2001 to 2004. The units studied were a medical, a surgical, a burn and trauma, and a cardiovascular intensive care unit.

Participants Health care clinicians, patients, and family members.

Results Informal roles for family members consistently observed were primary caregiver, primary decision maker, family spokesperson, out-of-towner, patient's wishes expert, protector, vulnerable member, and health care expert. The identified informal roles were part of families' decision making processes, and each role was part of a potentially complicated family dynamic for end-of-life decision making within the family system and between the family and health care domains.

Conclusions These informal roles reflect the diverse responses to demands for family decision making in what is usually a novel and stressful situation. Identification and description of these informal roles of family members can help clinicians recognize and understand the functions of these roles in families' decision making at the end of life and guide development of strategies to support and facilitate increased effectiveness of family discussions and decision making processes.

Health care clinicians in settings such as intensive care units (ICUs) are part of an institutional social system and are linked through a variety of relationships. They fill formal roles (eg, nurse, physician), exercise rights and privileges, and are expected to discharge obligations and responsibilities in conformity with established values, norms, and rules for behavior.[1] Similarly, persons in a family comprise a small social system; they function in a different sociocultural domain. They occupy formal roles (eg, mother, son), exercise rights and privileges, and discharge obligations and responsibilities in conformity with established family values, norms, and rules for behavior. When a member of a family becomes a patient in the ICU, members of these 2 domains come into dynamic interaction with each other. Family members are often involved in decision making for withdrawal of life-sustaining treatment.[2]

Sometimes a family member has been named the legally designated surrogate end-of-life decision maker (health care proxy or agent) for an ICU patient who has lost capacity; this formal role has been studied extensively.[3–8] Although 1 family member is asked or expected to be the "voice" for the patient by clinicians involved with the patient's care, often several family members become involved in the process of end-of-life decision making. Under these circumstances, the complexity of the end-of-life decision making process can escalate. This increased complexity not only affects the level of tension associated with end-of-life decision making, but also the satisfaction of family members involved.[9,10] To understand and support the process of effective family decision making, it is important to understand the informal roles that various family members may play in the end-of-life decision making process.

The findings reported here are part of a larger study of the sociocultural contexts for end-of-life decision making in ICUs.[11] In an earlier article,[11] we focused on variation in cultures of different ICUs related to end-of-life decision making; the focus of this article, that emerged from the data, is on the various informal family roles that are expected of and engaged in by family members during end-of-life decision making in an ICU.

Formal family roles are not culturally defined to address every circumstance, or to accommodate the personal characteristics of families and their individual members. Families functioning in an ICU context are not in a usual setting for family life. Informal roles emerge in the context of situational demands and describe how people actually behave in particular situations, rather than how they are expected to behave.[12] Informal roles can reflect responses to the common situational demands of any small system, including families, and a number of these roles have been previously identified. They include the scapegoat, who may be seen as the problem when negative emotions threaten the system, and the deviant, whose behavior helps clarify system boundaries by challenging norms.[13] The emergence of informal roles of clinicians specific to the developing small system of the health care team also has been studied.[14]

Study of informal role behavior is particularly useful in the situation of family members in the ICU because family members have no agreed-upon normative "script" for their behavior. Informal roles emerge in this context to help fill the gaps in how family members respond to the novel challenge of end-of-life decision making.[15–18] Recognizing and understanding the informal roles that family members may play in this setting can help guide clinicians in their strategies for working with family members in end-of-life decision making.

Design and Methods

This ethnographic study was prospective. Data were collected on 4 ICUs in an academic health center in the mid-Atlantic United States from 2001 to 2004. The units studied were a medical ICU, a surgical ICU, a burn and trauma ICU, and a cardiovascular ICU.

The university institutional review board for human subjects protection approved the study. All interviewed participants signed informed consent forms. A full description of the study design has already been published.[11]

Participants

Participants included health care clinicians, patients, and patients' family members interviewed in relation to specific cases or in general on end-of-life decision making. When possible, we interviewed clinicians and patients or family members involved in the same situation. If decision making continued for several days, participants were approached for another interview to assess changes and explore questions raised by field observations and earlier interviews. The total number of interviews conducted was 157, with 130 participants. The interviews were with the following categories of participants: 46 interviews with 30 physicians; 60 interviews with 48 nurses; 13 interviews with 10 other providers such as clergy, social worker, ethicist, and pharmacist; 4 interviews with 4 patients; and 34 interviews with 38 family members. Field notes were included in the analysis, along with recordings from 22 family meetings.[11]

Methods

A 6-member research team used participant observation, field notes, and semistructured interviews to examine the end-of-life decision making process from different participants' perspectives. The semistructured interviews were audiotaped and lasted from 15 to 60 minutes. For this analysis, we focused on interview questions specific to the participation of family members, including questions related to their relationships with the patient, with other family members, and with health care clinicians; their involvement in the decision making; and problems or disagreements related to the decision making process. Information from the medical record was used to identify some circumstances of decision making, for example, the patient's condition and availability of advance directives.

Procedure

Data were collected for approximately 5 hours a day, 5 to 7 days a week for 7 months on each unit sequentially (>700 hours per unit). Once a potential end-of-life decision making situation was identified, the attending physician was asked for permission for a research team member to contact the patient and/or the patient's family. Data collection began as soon as possible. Patients were followed up by the research team until the patient's death or discharge from the ICU.

Data Analysis

All the tapes were transcribed verbatim and reviewed for accuracy. Transcribed corrected interviews, family meetings, field notes, and chart data were dated and entered into the ATLAS.ti program.[19] Analysis, using an ethnographic approach,[20,21] began at the time of the first observation and continued throughout the study.

Small group and family dynamics theories[12,13,14] informed the understanding of family members' informal roles in end-of-life decision making in ICUs that were identified in data analysis. In the analysis for this article, we used data coded as "Roles-Family," which was defined as various key roles that family members played in end-of-life decision making. This general code was generated in our early analysis and subsequently was divided into subcodes for the specific informal roles of family members in end-of-life decision making that consistently emerged as data analysis progressed.

Results

Eight informal roles that family members engaged in during the end-of-life decision making process in these ICU settings were identified: primary caregiver, primary decision maker, family spokesperson, out-of-towner, patient's wishes expert, protector, vulnerable member, and health care expert.

The Primary Caregiver

If family caregiving was involved before ICU admission, the primary caregiver was a role of the family member who had spent the most time caring for the patient before hospitalization. One spouse said:

> *After she had the stroke I took care of her naturally. I'm her husband. I did everything for her or whatever. I made sure that she's had therapy . . . I mean, I've looked out for her best care the best I could. I don't know . . .*

When a loved one was admitted to the ICU, the primary caregiver was confronted with the reality that it was no longer possible for him or her to care for the ill family member. This previously important role was relinquished in the hospital setting. The same spouse explained:

> *"I'm using his [doctor's] judgment [now]. That's why I brought her. I can't take care of her. I can't— I've gotta use their judgment . . ."*

The primary caregiver often experienced great angst over relinquishing this role to hospital personnel. Often clinicians expected a quick shift of the primary caregiver into the role of primary decision maker for treatment decisions in the ICU. A family member of another patient stated:

> *He [doctor] did say go with the way you feel but he also said if that was my wife or my daughter, I would remove life support, and I said but I can't do that. Something in my heart is saying we've got to give her more time.*

The Primary Decision Maker

As others[3,7,22] have described, the role of the primary decision maker emerges in families as a response to the demands for surrogate end-of-life decision making. Sometimes a family member fulfilling this role was formally designated (eg, in the patient's advance directive). Whether this had occurred or not, ICU clinicians sought 1 individual to become the primary decision maker, a family role viewed by clinicians as central to the end-of-life decision making task when the patient was incapacitated. As 1 social worker described this role:

> *Probably the people I work with the most in these situations are the decision makers, you know, the primary people in the family that are there the most and taking the lead and initiative to make the decisions that provide the care. Often families had multiple decision makers rather than 1 primary decision maker as preferred by the clinicians.*

The primary decision maker frequently conversed with other family members in the decision making process, and the burden of decision making could be shared informally among family members. Family language around decision making often contained "we" as the referent, reflecting this shared decision making process. A striking example from the field notes illustrates this process of sharing in the decision making and in the decision itself. The family acted in concert to support the primary decision maker.

> *[The physician] gets the DNR [do not resuscitate] order sheet out and goes over the entire form with the family. He then asks which one is the proxy. [A daughter] says she is; he asks her to sign. [Another daughter] says, "We all want to sign, we don't want only [named proxy] to feel like she's the one who did this." [Two sons] immediately agree; and [one daughter] hugs [the other daughter] who is teary. [The physician] says there is room for everyone to sign. They all sign the form.*

If multiple decision makers were not acceptable to clinicians or family members, either 1 clear primary decision maker emerged or the primary decision maker's role was contested.

On the other hand, discussion could become too inclusive, as shown in the following example from a family meeting, where family friends exerted their own opinion in the decision making process.

> *[Friend of family]: Maybe he [patient] won't do it [recover] as quickly as a 20-year-old. But they want their father, and she wants her husband. And that's what we should be focusing on, rehabilitation, getting him up and getting him going.*

> *Physician: Well, I think it's always important and the thing I was asking [his wife] about. I think there's nobody in the whole world better able to speak to the desire of her husband than she. And I think sometimes families forget that what they really want is what's best for their loved one.*

Family Spokesperson

One informal family role, family spokesperson, was encouraged by clinicians because of the clinician's wish to address families' needs for information efficiently and to facilitate the decision making processes. Despite the complexity of many families' internal decision making processes, many clinicians preferred to deal with 1 family spokesperson, as reflected in the following staff quotation: "The problem often is that we do not have a family spokesperson but a spokesgroup." The nurse manager of 1 ICU spoke of the formal process expected on their unit to be followed to identify the family spokesperson.

> *What we ask is . . . there be a family spokesperson that we can give information to, and we ask that that family spokesperson disseminate the information to the other family members . . . if somebody calls in, it needs to be the spokesperson. . . .*

At least 3 ICUs had this role formally identified in the visitor brochure they provided, which included visitation policy and asked for an individual name with contact information to be placed in the medical record and care plan. Some units were inconsistent with identifying and documenting an individual family member for this role. Further, although this was constructed on several units as a formal role for 1 family member, we found that some families would informally evolve this role to include other members. Although the tendency was for the hospital staff to combine the roles of spokesperson and primary decision maker, it was observed that a family member who acted as a spokesperson with hospital staff was not necessarily the primary decision maker (eg, an adult child as spokesperson for a parent who was making final decisions).

Families, especially when there was disagreement among members, often were reluctant to identify just 1 member as the sole spokesperson. Regardless of whether the unit had a formal process of identifying the spokesperson, clinicians and staff tried to seek one out when a problem arose. However, at times, we observed that any family member who was convenient, at the bedside or in a visitor waiting area, was approached by a clinician and offered information or asked questions about the patient. This clinician's behavior conveyed a message that any family member present could be a spokesperson, but this was also seen as contrary to the formal rule regarding identification of 1 family spokesperson. One nurse expressed this situation well:

> Some nurses will talk to all—a lot of different family members about what's going on. That makes it very, very difficult. I think . . . that it's very important to have it be [the] family spokesperson. Just 1 person should be the proxy to whom that information is going. . . .

The Out-of-Towner

Complex family dynamics of decision making were apparent through other informal roles of family members that were identified. One such role was the out-of-towner, a family member who had not been involved in the daily care giving and may not have been engaged during the early ICU stay and, therefore, often brought a different perspective to the in-town family's end-of-life decision making discussions. End-of-life decisions often were put on hold until in-town family members could communicate with out-of-town relatives and they could be part of the discussion about the patient's condition and the status of decision making thus far. Because they were from out of town, they often also had time limits on their ability to be physically present in the situation and, if present, might be eager to have a firm decision made before their departure. Consequently, their involvement added complexity to the decision making process and could create conflict within the patient's family and with clinicians. An example of this is a brother who described his perspective on his out-of-town sister's role in decision making about their father:

> My sister was—you have to take a lot of things into consideration. She is the child from out of town. She is the one that feels that she has to have this whole thing fixed before she can go home. She is the one that doesn't have the time to wait it out. This illness is a wait out. . . . She is trying to get this whole thing fixed before she goes home. She has to go home and I understand that. She just has to leave and trust that it's gonna happen correctly. . . .

> Especially where family members may not all be in the same city. So, they have not seen mom or dad, [and] you will be in a family meeting and, the one [local] daughter will say, "Look, I'm with Mom all the time; I know what she wants. You see her twice a year. How do you know what she wants?"

This example illustrates another emergent family informal role related to decision making, when the family had not achieved consensus about what the dying family member's wishes might have been as a guide to that decision making.

The Patient's Wishes Expert

Being primary decision maker was difficult, but family members were much more likely to come together in support of a primary decision maker and collectively to feel confident they were following the patient's wishes in the context of known preferences of the patient. In the context of unknown preferences, decision making was often much more difficult for the primary decision maker, and other family members were much more open to differing interpretations of what the patient would have wanted. The patient's wishes experts were family members who claimed that their interpretations of the patients' wishes were the correct interpretations.

> [Son]: You have to listen to everything my father says . . . it's like his living will. I read it, and I know what my mother and sister said, and I said wait a minute, my father doesn't want to be intubated, I understand that. Okay, if he is brain dead, he doesn't want to be intubated; but he is alive, he can get better. My father wants to live; he is afraid to die. This is something that has been on his mind for 10 years.

When this role was enacted by several family members with different interpretations of the patient's wishes, end-of-life decision making was often prolonged and inconclusive.

The Protector and the Vulnerable Family Member

In this situation, a family member who might typically be expected to be the primary decision maker was viewed as vulnerable for some reason, and another family member asserted family decision making authority to protect the vulnerable family member. Commonly, these paired roles emerged when adult children believed they needed to protect an older parent (eg, spouse of the ill family member) from the stress of end-of-life decision making. An example was a daughter who was concerned about her mother being expected to decide about withdrawal of mechanical ventilation from her husband, resulting in end of life too quickly for the mother to handle emotionally. The daughter stated, "Taking him off the respirator is only going to change things by hours, and I think that that would be way too painful for my mom given the rapidity of this event." If the vulnerable member did not accept that role, it caused family conflict that made the decision making process more difficult and delayed the decision making process.

Occasionally, patients had at least some capacity for decision making. However, in such circumstances they could be identified by family members as the vulnerable member. The quotation below is about a dying woman who was intubated but aware. Her husband had been very involved in the decision making and wanted her included in any decision about reintubation if extubation failed. However, some negative information about her condition, known to her husband, had been withheld from her at the husband's request. He questioned whether she would be able to make a decision about reintubation, especially when she did not have all of the relevant clinical information.

> [Husband]: I'm trying to—I'm trying to think if her choice would be a real choice, to her. Because I would be okay with whatever her choice was, so I'm trying to think, would it be a real choice? Would she know that that's a real choice and her deciding, and it might be . . . because she doesn't like that and maybe she had enough of it and she doesn't want it. Or maybe she'd say, "Yup, if I start to lose it, put it back in."

Even though in this rare ICU situation, the patient had the capacity to participate, her protector family member saw her as vulnerable, remained in charge of the family end-of-life decision making process, and asked clinicians to withhold some information about her condition from her.

Another field note observation illustrates the patient's wishes expert and the paired set of family informal roles of protector and vulnerable member roles occurring in the context of a clinician looking for consent to perform a procedure. He said:

> They [mother and father, father is the patient] have been married for 52 years. He [father] never let her [mother] make a decision in 52 years. You are gonna let her [mother] cut her teeth on this one? No, she is not cutting her teeth on life or death. I'll do that. I will give mom my feelings on that and I'm not gonna subject her [mother] to making that decision. I think I know what he [father] wants, so that's what I told her [mother].

In this example, the son claims his own expertise in knowing his father's preferences (or wishes). He also was prepared to protect his mother from having to make a life and death decision about her husband. He saw his mother as vulnerable because, in his view, she had never made decisions during 52 years of marriage.

The Health Care Expert

The health care expert was a family member who could influence decision making in the family system through a claim of clinical expertise by virtue of some connection to the health care domain (eg, nurses, physicians). Family members and sometimes clinicians viewed this role as one that had the potential to facilitate the decision making process. The health care expert might use resources to bridge the gap between the 2 domains, whereas family members who lacked this expertise struggled more with the

situation and with end-of-life decision making. Family members often relied heavily on the family health care expert for direction in the end-of-life decision making process. The quotation that follows illustrates the role of the health care expert, in this case a daughter who was a licensed practical nurse:

> [Daughter]: My brothers and sisters never thought of the antibiotics and you know, I think sometimes you have a little more knowledge. Whether you understand things better, which is why they [my family members] put me down as the spokesperson. Which is why she put me down as her [proxy]. . . .

Clinicians' reactions to family health care experts could be mixed: on the one hand, sometimes they were viewed as able to understand medical situations and expected to be "reasonable" about the treatment decisions or more in line with the clinicians' way of thinking. An example of this is expressed by a registered nurse:

> I think her mother deferred to her [daughter] the physician. . . . It is definitely nice when the family is so knowledgeable about what is going on that, you know, they realize as you realize, at almost the same time, that this is . . . that CPR would be futile.

Other family health care experts challenged the thinking and recommendations of the ICU clinicians, as well as the quality of care that their family members were receiving, stimulating conflict between the family and clinicians. A good example of this from the field notes is when a group of nurses talked one day about a patient's son-in-law, who was a physician. On the phone he had yelled at one of the nurses and then had hung up. From the nurse's perspective, he had conveyed that the nurses were all incompetent. When family health care experts did not agree with the clinicians, there was an element of surprise and frustration expressed, as this resident physician viewed it: "Granted that her son-in-law is a physician, but we are still not getting through."

The situation got even more complicated when more than 1 family member could claim a role as health care expert, and the different "experts" were not in agreement. Family members could also "call in" friends who were health care clinicians to play the role of health care expert for the family or some subgroup of the family; again, calling in multiple experts could complicate the decision making process.

Discussion

As illustrated in these results, the identified informal roles were intricately tied to the family's decision making process, and each helped to create a potentially complicated family dynamic for end-of-life decision making within the family system, and between the family and health care domains. In their expectations for end-of-life decision making, clinicians, on the other hand, often pushed for 1 family member to be both primary decision maker and family spokesperson to facilitate communication and decision making. However, our findings suggest that this often did not happen and made the process more complicated than desired by clinicians.

These 8 informal roles did not all emerge in every family. More than 1 role might be assumed by a single family member (eg, the out-of-towner could also be the health care expert) or the informal roles might be shared among multiple family members. Whether these informal roles facilitated decision making or escalated family conflict or family/clinician conflict depended on the family context (ie, family history and culture around difficult decision making).

In situations where other family members interacted to support a single member both as primary decision maker and family spokesperson, consensus within families was more easily achieved. In other families where there was less cohesion, as more family members became involved there was a greater proliferation of informal roles in the decision making process, potentially more conflict and disagreement, and a more difficult time with making end-of-life decisions. When no consensus was reached among family members around end-of-life decision making, informal roles might be used to leverage a decision in a way that advanced the role of the person in the family system, for example by claiming to be a protector or health care expert.

Jockeying for position in the family system can be viewed as a consequence of the removal, by life-threatening illness, of a member of the system and a scramble for a new status in that altered system. Thus, for example, with the removal of an ill parent, adult children might move to claim status and authority in the system previously held by that parent.

In either circumstance of cohesive or conflict-prone family decision making processes, ICU clinicians who attempted direct communication through identification of a family spokesperson often found that there was a "spokesgroup" of family members playing differing informal roles but all wanting input into the decision making process either directly or indirectly. As others who have studied family involvement with end-of-life decision making have found, the decision to withdraw or withhold treatment generally includes multiple family members,[23] and communication needs for families often go unmet.[9,24,25]

Recognizing and understanding the roles that family members play within the family unit during critical decision making is important in facilitating more effective interaction and consensus among family members and reducing conflict among family and clinicians. Interventions limiting conflict and strengthening family supports should be a major goal, but the manner in which this is done needs to incorporate the cultural differences of families and the expertise of clinicians. Family meetings with clinicians, when held, can make these complex roles involved in family end-of-life decision making visible.

Family meetings can also reduce conflict between clinicians and family members regarding frustration with not having 1 person as family spokesperson and/or primary decision maker.[25] More recently, emphasis has increased on conducting effective family meetings within critical care as well as use of other services, such as palliative care services, that may be called to consult if the process of decision making becomes problematic.[26] Awareness of the potentially complicated dynamics associated with some of these family informal role processes may assist clinicians to seek earlier consultation.

Limitations

Although the purpose of qualitative research is not to make broad generalizations but to examine the depth of individual experience in a phenomenon such as end-of-life decision making, this study had some limitations. First the study was conducted in 1 setting, a university medical center, although different types of ICUs were included to capture cultural differences regarding end-of-life decision making among the units.[11] The data were collected some time ago; however, the nature of the data and analyses reported here, as well as the results, concerning informal roles in family decision making processes in critical care situations, are not likely to "age" quickly, as family systems processes such as the decision making processes identified are fundamental to family life. The approach taken to analysis is theoretically informed, drawing on a rich body of theoretical literature related to informal roles in family systems, family crisis responses, and small group functioning, which became relevant as we explored the data.

The presence of the researchers and the process of audiotaping during family meetings and interviews could have influenced the responses. We describe the results only of participants who agreed to participate, although few potential participants who were approached refused to participate. Finally, we do not claim to have exhausted potentially identifiable informal family roles. There may be other informal roles that did not emerge in these data either because we missed them in our analyses, they are infrequent, or they do not play as prominent a role in the end-of-life decision making process.

Conclusions

End-of-life decision making for patients in ICUs involves an intersection of both the health care domain and the family domain. Promoting family responses to end-of-life questions that honor the wishes of the patient requires an understanding of informal family roles such as those observed and described, as well as an awareness of how these roles may be enacted. Strategies should be developed to facilitate smooth resolution of conflicting views and decisions among family members and between clinicians and family members that foster effective decision making processes. Potentially fruitful areas for further exploration include the identification of other important informal family roles that may be less prominent or less frequently portrayed but may be equally important in some end-of-life decision making, and the role of advance directives in family end-of-life decision making processes. A closer examination of family meetings as a way to foster effective family end-of-life decision making and the role of hospital-based palliative care services in supporting effective family end-of-life decision making processes are vital areas for further study.[27]

Notes

Financial Disclosures

1. This study was supported by grants from the National Institutes of Health/National Institute of Nursing Research (RO1NR04940 and 1R15NR012147).

eLetters

1. Now that you've read the article, create or contribute to an online discussion on this topic. Visit **www.ajcconline.org** and click "Submit a response" in either the full-text or PDF view of the article.

2. To purchase electronic or print reprints, contact The InnoVision Group, 101 Columbia, Aliso Viejo, CA 92656. Phone: (800) 899-1712 or (949) 362-2050 (ext 532); fax: (949) 362-2049; e-mail: reprints@aacn.org.

3. ©2012 American Association of Critical-Care Nurses

References

1. Breitborde LB. *Rebuttal Essay. Int J Soc Lang. 1983;39: 161–177.*

2. Search Google Scholar Kirchhoff KT, Kowalkowski JA *Current practices for withdrawal of life support in intensive care units. Am J Crit Care. 2010;19:532–541.*

3. Abstract/FREE Full Text Tilden VP, Tolle SW, Nelson CA, et al. *Family decision making to withdraw life-sustaining treatments from hospitalized patients. Nurs Res. 2001;50:105–115.*

4. CrossRefMedline Arnold RM, Kellum J. *Moral justifications for surrogate decision making in the intensive care unit: implications and limitations. Crit Care Med. 2003;31:S347–S353.*

5. CrossRefMedline Berger JT, DeRenzo EG, and Schwartz J. *Surrogate decision making: reconciling ethical theory and clinical practice. Ann Intern Med. 2008;149:48–53.*

6. Medline Evans LR, Boyd EA, Malvar G, et al. *Surrogate decision makers' perspectives on discussing prognosis in the face of uncertainty. Am J Respir Crit Care Med. 2009;179:48–53.*

7. Abstract/FREE Full Text Heyland DK, Cook DJ, Rocker GM, et al. *Decision making in the ICU: perspectives of the substitute decision-maker. Intensive Care Med. 2003;29:75–82.*

8. Medline Luce JM *End-of-life decision making in the intensive care unit. Am J Respir Crit Care Med. 2010;182:6–11.*

9. Abstract/FREE Full Text Radwany S, Albanese T, Clough L, et al. *End-of-life decision making and emotional burden: placing family meetings in context. Am J Hosp Palliat Care. 2009;26:376–383.*

10. Abstract/FREE Full Text Westphal DM, McKee SA. *End-of-life decision making in the intensive care unit: physician and nurse perspectives. Am J Med Qual. 2009;24:222–228.*

11. Abstract/FREE Full Text Baggs JG, Norton SA, Schmitt MH, et al. *Intensive care unit cultures and end-of-life decision making. J Crit Care. 2007;22:159–168.*

12. CrossRefMedline Dunphey DC. *The Primary Group: A Handbook for Analysis and Field Research. New York, NY: Appleton-Century-Crofts; 1972.*

13. Search Google Scholar Mills TM. *The Sociology of Small Groups. Englewood Cliffs, NJ: Prentice-Hall; 1984.*

14. Search Google Scholar Farrell MP, Schmitt MH, and Heinemann GD. *Informal roles and the stages of interdisciplinary team development. J Interprof Care. 2001;15:281–295.*

15. CrossRefMedline Abbott KH, Sago JG, Breen CM, et al. *Families looking back: one year after discussion of withdrawal or withholding of life-sustaining support. Crit Care Med. 2001;29:197–201.*

16. CrossRefMedline Bartels DM, Faber-Langendoen K. *Caring in crisis: family perspectives on ventilator withdrawal at the end of life. Fam Syst Health. 2001;19:169–176.*

17. CrossRef Johnson N, Cook D, Giacomini M, et al. *Towards a "good" death: end-of-life narratives constructed in an intensive care unit. Cult Med Psychiatry. 2000;24:275–295.*

18. CrossRefMedline Norton SA, Tilden VP, Tolle SW, et al. *Life support withdrawal: communication and conflict. Am J Crit Care. 2003; 12:548–555.*

19. Abstract/FREE Full Text *ATLAS.ti: The Knowledge Workbench [computer program]. Version 5.0. Berlin, Germany: Atlas.ti; 2004.*

20. Munhall PL, Boyd CP, and Germain CP. *Ethnography: the method. In: Munhall PL, Boyd CP, eds. Nursing Research: A Qualitative Perspective. New York, NY: National League for Nursing; 1993:237–268.*

21. Search Google Scholar Morse JM, Field PA. *Qualitative Research Methods for Health Professionals. Thousand Oaks, CA: Sage; 1995.*

22. Search Google Scholar White DB, Malvar G, Karr J, et al. *Expanding the paradigm of the physician's role in surrogate decision making: an empirically derived framework. Crit Care Med. 2010;38:743–750.*

23. CrossRefMedline Wiegand D. *In their own time: the family experience during the process of withdrawal of life-sustaining therapy. J Palliat Med. 2008;11:1115–1121.*

24. CrossRefMedline Hsieh HF, Shannon SE, Curtis JR. *Contradictions and communication strategies during end-of-life decision making in the intensive care unit. J Crit Care. 2006;21: 294–304.*

25. CrossRefMedline Norton SA, Bowers BJ. *Working toward consensus: providers' strategies to shift patients from curative to palliative treatment choices. Res Nurs Health. 2001;24:258–269.*

26. CrossRefMedline Norton SA, Hogan LA, Holloway RG, et al. *Proactive palliative care in the medical intensive care unit: effects on length of stay for selected high-risk patients. Crit Care Med. 2007; 35:1530–1535.*

27. CrossRefMedline Daly BJ, Douglas SL, O'Toole E, et al. *Effectiveness trial of an intensive communication structure for families of longstay ICU patients. Chest. 2010;138:1340–1348.*

Critical Thinking

1. What are some formal roles that family members take when making decisions about someone who is critically ill? How do you think the decision is made regarding who will formally represent the family?

2. Do you agree with the statement made in the article that health care providers often feel that they "do not have a spokesperson but a spokesgroup?"

3. The study identified a variety of different, informal roles that family members may take on when someone is critically ill. Have you witnessed anyone in your family take on these types of roles or responsibilities?

4. What can be done to support families as they are making important decisions about a critically ill family member?

Create Central

www.mhhe.com/createcentral

Internet References

Family Caregiver Alliance National Center on Caregiving
   http://caregiver.org
Hospice Foundation of America
   www.hospicefoundation.org

JILL R. QUINN is an associate professor, MADELINE SCHMITT is a professor emerita, SALLY A. NORTON is an associate professor, MARY T. DOMBECK is a professor, and CRAIG R. SELLERS is an associate professor of clinical nursing at the University of Rochester School of Nursing in Rochester, New York. JUDITH GEDNEY BAGGS is a distinguished professor at Oregon Health & Science University School of Nursing in Portland.

Corresponding author: Jill R. Quinn, RN, PhD, CS-ANP, University of Rochester School of Nursing, 601 Elmwood Avenue, Box SON, Rochester, NY 14642 (e-mail: jill_quinn@urmc.rochester.edu).

Acknowledgments—We thank the patients, families, and clinicians who made this study possible. We also thank Dr. Nancy Press for her review of this manuscript.

Article

Prepared by: Patricia Hrusa Williams,
University of Maine at Farmington

Why Do Marriages Fail?

JOSEPH N. DUCANTO

Learning Outcomes

After reading this article, you will be able to:

- Identify some common reasons why couples divorce.

- Consider strategies to decrease the frequency of divorce in the United States.

After 56 years as a divorce lawyer, people may assume that I know a lot about marriage and, therefore, can easily answer the inevitable question "why do marriages fail?" Indeed, a divorce lawyer can relate much about his/her personal observation respecting this issue, anticipating that many will take exception to at least one or more of the following views.

Increased Life Span

I blame medical science for a significantly large percentage of failed marriages! During the past 100 years, the average life span of humans in the Western world has increased nearly 60 percent from the start of the 20th century (average 49 years) to 2010 (average 78 years). This increase alone has had an overpowering impact upon marriage, which is a static institution remaining unchanged from the dawn of time. It remains to be seen what civil union marriage will do to both the state of marriage (now at an all-time low) and the absolute numbers of divorce (without reference to customary marriages—as opposed to civil unions), which have fallen in recent years because of increasing disinterest by the young to legally engage in such relationships.

In past centuries, the young married very young, paralleling the onset of puberty, produced numerous children (many of whom died during their infancy), and departed life in their 30's and 40's. Perhaps the greatest love story of all time, Romeo and Juliet, exemplifies this phenomenon with Juliet 14, and Romeo 16, yearning for the nuptial couch. They clearly were not unique in their era, and in many places throughout the world, such early teenage marriages continue as acceptable and are endorsed by cultural principals and religious adherence.

Quite clearly, a marriage duly made "until death do us part," that could be reasonably expected to endure 20 to 25 years at most, is a far different commitment made today, where joint lifespan can see marriages endure for 50, 60, and even 70 years! Clearly, then, medical science, which has so effectively increased the lifespan of people, must bear some responsibility for the proven fact that marriages of long duration enlarge inordinately the number of prospective clients who ultimately find their way to a divorce lawyer's office. Divorce among the "Metamucil Generation" is no longer an unusual event.

Individual Changes Over the Years

Accompanying the incredibly long duration of marriages today is the unhappy fact that married people do not always mature and grow at the same rate and quality over the longer period of years people are married today. She is involved in her career and he is consumed by his occupation. Inevitably—particularly as the kids age and leave home—the parties metamorphose in their interest, attitudes, and aspiration in ways that do not necessarily correlate with the essential unity of the original underlying basis of the marriage. For example, her involvement with professional requirements could create conflicts with the lifestyle adopted over time by him and his colleagues as sports become a passion. Conflict here is inevitable and divorce often a certainty, as neither can abandon the pillars of support each has erected in terms of his or her own individual desires and concerns.

Exacerbation of Pre-Existing Strains

Kids are beautiful and, for many, life would not be worth living without them. Little is said, however, of the disruptive problems that the appearance of children may inflict upon a marriage already experiencing some irritation and doubts. Over my years of practice, I have observed that pre-existing strains in a marriage are strongly exacerbated by additional adverse events which, surprisingly, can often be the appearance of a newborn or, worse, the death of a child, the loss of a job or a business, or the purchase of a new home. Any existing cracks in an otherwise placid marriage will often produce significant fractures when such events occur, thus leading to divorce. These customary strains upon a marriage are intensified when one or both of the parents begin to indulge in escape from drudgery by excessive use of alcohol or drugs, or seek out others to escape from marital unhappiness.

Boredom

Boredom in a relationship is often insidious and corrosive of the marriage bonds. Repetitive behavior, even if initially enjoyed, can soon pale and become irritating. Think, I tell my friends, of eating oatmeal every morning for 40 years and tell me what you believe your reaction would be? Indeed, many marriages are destroyed by boredom and the need or necessity by one of the parties to exit the doldrums of their life for some excitement—any excitement—good or bad—known or unknown.

Life Changes

Virtually nothing has been written relating to the role that menopause plays in leading ultimately to a divorce. Much is known and published that describes the onset and symptoms of menopause in women, which appears around the age of 50 in normal development. With menopause there are numerous psychological and emotional symptoms that present themselves, which can include rapid mood shifts, irritability, and loss of libido.

Many men find these newly-emerging symptoms difficult, and their presence in a wife of many years may lead to emotional and physical withdrawal by both parties. From the female's point of view, many former "quirks" possessed by her husband or supposed personal strengths and long-held opinions may become intolerable during this period, leading to increasing tension and endless arguments between the parties. The husband, if experiencing his wife's coldness or withdrawal altogether from sex, could find easy excuses for infidelity with younger women who "understand and appreciate me" when his wife has failed to do so.

Any meaningful change in the marital relationship coincidentally occurring with the arrival of menopause, such as becoming "empty nesters," a change of occupation or retirement, unemployment, financial instability, plus the unavoidable onset of old age may tip the marital scales toward separation and, inevitably, a mid-life divorce.

Another Man or Woman

The often-supposed "reason" for divorce attributed to the appearance or presence of the other man or woman in the life of one of the partners is simply a symptom of a pre-existing desire to escape the malaise of a moribund relationship. One may seek solace in the other man/woman relationship with the prime purpose of re-injecting life or purpose in an existence that may seem to have become barren. It is not uncommon in my experience that one of the parties to a meretricious relationship will operate with a certainty of detection by the other party, thus motivating the otherwise "innocent" spouse to move for the courthouse door!

Personality Changes

As life goes on, we all undergo personality changes. None of us by age 50 can truthfully believe we are the same person we were at 25. We learn, educate, grow, and change at uneven rates that are heavily dependent upon many variables—including intelligence, receptivity, and intensity of experiences. Uneven growth between spouses is common, and unless great pain is taken to assure continuing effective communication, the marriage can fail. A mother with a high-school education who is housebound for 20 years talking to three-foot-high people over those years may not be expected to maintain a close communion and relationship with an ever-working husband who has acquired several advanced degrees, travels the world over in his occupation, and consorts with the intellectual opinion makers of the world.

Limited Marriage Contract

I have in the past, partially in jest, suggested that there actually be a "marriage contract"—as opposed to a prenuptial one—in which the marriage has a finite term; say five years. At or near the end of that time, the parties are called upon to renew or rewrite their agreement or proceed to divorce. Such a shocking requirement requires a balancing of what is good in the relationship as opposed to that which is destructive. A "time out" to reconstitute the ongoing basis of the marriage is clearly preferable to an inevitable drift toward ending the relationship. Remember, a "civil union" complete written contract is not limited to homosexual relationships, but can be extended to a man/woman relationship that falls outside of the usual bounds of matrimony.

It is imperative, if the marriage is to continue, that both parties commit themselves to a course of re-bonding and enhancement of communication with each other. With kids, it is often difficult but essential that there be frequent "time outs" where a couple can recommit to one another, compare notes so to speak, and plan for their future as a couple in addition to that as a family. A failure to work on the changing nature of a relationship over time is to be confronted by the inescapable fact that the marriage may be dead and, unfortunately, in need of a decent burial!

Critical Thinking

1. With our increased life spans, is it realistic to think that marriages will last "until death do us part?"

2. Of the factors listed as contributing to divorce, which do you see as more important? Why?

3. Given the list of factors that the author states contribute to divorce, what can be done to help couples sustain marriages?

4. What can be done as couples enter marriage to better prepare them for the challenges ahead?

Create Central

www.mhhe.com/createcentral

Internet References

HelpGuide: Children and Divorce
www.helpguide.org/mental/children_divorce.htm

HelpGuide: Divorce and Remarriage
www.helpguide.org/topics/breakup_divorce.htm

Ducanto, Joseph N. From *American Journal of Family Law,* vol. 26, no. 4, Winter 2013, pp. 237–239. Copyright © 2013 by Wolters Kluwer Law & Business. Reprinted by permission.

Prepared by: Patricia Hrusa Williams,
University of Maine at Farmington

Article

Helping Children Endure Divorce

Marlene Eskind Moses

When in the midst of a divorce, it is understandable for a party to become entrenched in what is felt to be a personal battle and preoccupied with details such as where to live, how to maximize the financial settlement, and how to pay the legal fees. Sometimes, this preoccupation leads to losing sight of what is going on with one's children, who are unquestionably also directly affected by that parent's decision to divorce.

Learning Outcomes

After reading this article, you will be able to:

- Describe the impact of divorce on children.
- Summarize how the parent–child relationship survives divorce.
- Explain how divorce can happen without devastating the children involved.

If the divorce practitioner receives little feedback from a client about the children, it is all too easy to focus exclusively on meeting the client's personal goals with minimal awareness of how doing so will truly affect the client's children. However, it is up to us to actively solicit feedback from our clients about their children and educate our clients about how to help their children navigate the transition. We should remain mindful that our clients' children are "shadow clients,"[1] and we should strive to fine-tune our advice and strategies accordingly.

The Effects of Divorce on Children

There has been an abundance of research concluding that growing up in a single-parent household is less than ideal and can be detrimental to a child's well-being. Even in low-conflict divorces, children can suffer in a myriad of ways. The obvious immediate repercussion is the disruption of life as they have known it. Children not living with both biological parents are more likely to experience psychological struggles and academic problems.[2] Long-term effects of divorce on children can include increased susceptibility to substance abuse. Teenagers with divorced parents are 50 percent more likely to drink alcohol than those with married parents.[3] Children of divorce also are more likely to experience divorces of their own down the road.[4]

Research shows that the effects of divorce on a child depend to some extent on the age of the child at the time of divorce, the child's gender and personality, and the degree of conflict between the parents. Infants may react to changes in parents' energy level and mood by losing their appetite or spitting up more. Preschool-aged children often blame themselves for their parent's divorce, viewing it as the consequence of their own misbehavior. They may regress and exhibit behavior such as bedwetting and may become uncooperative or aggressive. School-aged children are old enough to understand that they are hurting because of their parents' separation. They may feel rejected by the parent who left. It is not uncommon for children in this age group to exhibit psychosomatic symptoms such as headaches or stomachaches. Adolescents may become excessively moody, withdrawn, depressed or anxious. They may favor one parent, blaming the other for the divorce.[5]

Some research even suggests gender differences. Certain studies have found that children raised primarily by a parent of the same sex tend to have greater success adjusting to the divorce than those who are raised primarily by a parent of the opposite sex.[6] Although there is little correlation between the sheer amount of time that divorced fathers spend with their children and those children's overall adjustment, children of divorce whose fathers spend quality time actively engaged in their lives and activities tend to perform better in school and exhibit fewer behavioral problems.[7] Father involvement has been linked to children feeling less at the mercy of the world and more willing to behave responsibly.[8]

The quality of a child's relationship with the primary parent is a particularly strong indicator of the child's successful adjustment following a divorce. It also goes without saying that day-to-day involvement of both parents lets a child know that he or she is loved. This does not mean, however, that an equal or near-equal division of parenting time is necessarily the best option. For instance, preschool-aged children may feel they are being punished when they are moved from one household to another. Older children, too, may dislike this type of arrangement if it intrudes on their daily lives. Some parents with equal or near-equal division of time, or who engage in multiple transfers of the children back and forth in a short period of time, fight more often because they are in constant contact, which in turn causes the children to suffer.[9] A child's well-being is particularly affected by the amount and intensity of conflict between the parents. Marital conflict is associated with increased anxiety and depression, and poorer overall social and academic adjustment in children.[10]

So, how can we use this research to educate our clients with the goal of helping ensure that their children adjust with minimal side-effects to the divorce?

Guidelines for Helping Children

1. *Telling children about the divorce:*
   Ideally, children should be told about the divorce as soon as a definite decision has been made to get divorced. Children need to be told before any changes occur, and they should be informed of the changes to expect, such as moving to a new house or school, or beginning a parenting schedule. If possible, both parents should tell the children together, with the parents agreeing on the details of the explanation ahead of time. It is important to present a united front as much as possible.[11]

   Children are entitled to know why their parents are divorcing, and the reasons given should be simple and honest. Telling children that it is too complicated to explain or that they would never understand the reasons could leave them wondering whether they might be able to change their parents' plans. Blanket reassurances do not always work, and children will likely need an opportunity to talk about why they feel at fault for the divorce, oftentimes on more than one occasion. Parents need to acknowledge the reasons for the child's concerns, such as "Yes, you are right that your father and I do argue about how much time we each feel you should spend on the computer or with friends or watching television, and I can see why this makes you worried that the divorce is your fault." Then, words of reassurance need to follow immediately, such as: ". . . but you didn't cause the breakup . . ." If a child's concerns are not cavalierly dismissed but are instead truly heard and discussed, without the parents becoming defensive or dismissive, the child is more likely to feel assured that indeed he or she was not the cause of the parents' divorce. The child who feels at fault could also feel responsible for fixing the problem. Therefore, children need a clear statement from each parent that they cannot prevent or reverse the divorce.[12] They also need to be reassured that while parents and their children do not always get along, they do not stop loving each other and do not get divorced from each other.[13]

   Finally, it may be tempting to place blame on the other parent for the divorce, but such defensiveness sends a message that the children need to take sides, which only serves to increase their anxiety, guilt and stress.[14]

2. *Encouraging a relationship with the other parent:*
   Because of the inherently adversarial nature of divorce, it may seem counter-intuitive to a litigant not to seek to limit the other parent's time with the children. The "winner" gets the kids, and the "loser" does not. In fact, a better legal strategy may be to encourage and facilitate time and a continuing relationship with the other parent. Tennessee's custody statute requires the court to consider, in making a custody determination, "each parent's past and potential . . . willingness and ability . . . to facilitate and encourage a close and continuing parent–child relationship between the child and both of the child's parents, consistent with the best interest of the child. In determining the willingness of each of the parents . . . to facilitate and encourage a close and continuing parent–child relationship between the child and both of the child's parents, the court shall consider the likelihood of each parent . . . to honor and facilitate court ordered parenting arrangements and rights, and the court shall further consider any history of either parent or any caregiver denying parenting time to either parent in violation of a court order."[15]

   In addition to what the law tells us, social research tells us that children are better off with the influence and presence of both parents in their lives, absent extraordinary circumstances. It is important for both parents to be mindful of this and to strive to create a parenting plan that provides this for their children.

   Hand-in-hand with encouraging and facilitating a meaningful relationship with the other parent is showing respect for the other parent. It is harmful to a child for either parent to make derogatory remarks about the other parent. The child can be made to feel as if he or she is expected to take the side of the parent who is disparaging the other parent. This behavior by a parent violates the statutory standard parenting rights set forth in all Tennessee parenting plans. Such rights include "the right to be free of unwarranted derogatory remarks made about the parent or his or her family by the other parent to the child or in the presence of the child."[16] Acting contrary to this mandate can lead to a finding of contempt and sometimes even a change of custody in extreme circumstances.

3. *The parenting schedule.*
   It is usually best for each parent's time with the children to be scheduled at regular and predictable times.[17] Once the schedule is created, it is important that it be honored. Children may see missed visits, especially without notification, as rejection.[18] Children crave consistency, and routines provide a sense of security and may help ease fears of abandonment. If possible, the parents should work together to ensure that the same routines and rules are followed at each home. It is important to resist the temptation to spoil the children during or following a divorce by not enforcing limits or allowing children to break rules.[19]

   Handovers between the two households can be particularly stressful for children, let alone parents. Children often feel guilty and are reluctant to admit to one parent that they are thinking about or missing the other parent. As a result, children are often anticipating the emotional turmoil of the handover back to the other parent instead of enjoying the time remaining before the transfer.[20] The divorce practitioner can counsel clients to minimize the number of handovers each week. Furthermore, it may help for the handovers to occur at a neutral location such as the child's school, as this is likely to cause less stress than handovers occurring on either parent's home turf. The parents will need to commit to making handovers free of arguments and hostility.

Although the typical parenting plan mentions only in passing that each parent has the statutory "right to unimpeded telephone conversations with the child at least twice a week at reasonable times and for reasonable durations,"[21] it may be worthwhile to be proactive and help clients work through the logistics. For instance, it can be wise to avoid phone calls at emotionally charged and more intrusive times such as meal time or bedtime.[22] It is not uncommon for a parent to feel that the ex-spouse is interfering with the phone calls in a multitude of ways, so a word to the wise: address these potential issues before they arise.

Finally, in crafting the parenting schedule, thinking outside the box can make for much more meaningful periods of parenting time. When children have been asked what they would change about their scheduled times with each parent, some have responded that they do not necessarily care to be shuffled back and forth with their siblings as a group. Children enjoy and benefit from one-on-one time with each parent. However, frequently, for the purposes of organizing the schedule, children are indeed "lumped together as a homogenous group, irrespective of their ages and needs."[23] Tennessee's standard parenting plan form treats the children as a group, so we lawyers need to be more proactive and consider suggesting to our clients that separate parenting times for each child be carved out if feasible for the family.

Conclusion

Given the proof that parents have the power to affect their children's reactions to divorce, it is necessary that parents put their children's welfare ahead of their own conflict with their spouse or former spouse. We as divorce practitioners also have the power to influence our clients' behavior by educating them and helping them craft parenting plans that minimize as much as possible the negative effects of divorce on our clients' children.

Notes

1. Sammons, William A.H., and Lewis, Jennifer M. (1999), *Don't Divorce Your Children.*
2. Pendergrast, Val (1997), "Sheathing Solomon's Sword," http://www.weeklywire.com/ww/08-04-97/knox_feat.html.
3. *Family Matters: Substance Abuse and the American Family,* The National Center on Addiction and Substance Abuse at Columbia University (March 2005), http://www.casacolumbia.org/articlefiles/380-Family percent20Matters.pdf.
4. Nuri, Banister, "Children of Divorced Parents Are More Likely to Themselves Divorce," *Journal of Young Investigators,* vol. 23, issue 3, March 2012, http://www.jyi.org/news/nb.php?id=352.
5. Temke, Mary (1998), "The Effects of Divorce on Children," University of New Hampshire, Cooperative Extension, http://extension.unh.edu/Family/Documents/divorce.pdf.
6. *Id.*
7. Nowinski, Joseph (2011), "The New Grief: Helping Children Survive Divorce: Three Critical Factors," http://www.psychologytoday.com/blog/the-new-grief/201110/helping-children-survive-divorce-three-critical-factors.
8. Biller H., Solomon R.S. (1986), *Child Maltreatment and Paternal Deprivation: A Manifesto for Research, Treatment, and Prevention.*
9. Temke, *supra.*
10. Nowinski, *supra.*
11. Ferrer, Millie and McCrea, Sara (2002), *Talking to Children about Divorce,* University of Florida, IFAS Extension.
12. Sammons, *supra.*
13. Block, Jocelyn; Kemp, Gina; Smith, Melinda; Segal, Jeanne (2012), "Children and Divorce: Helping Kids Cope with Separation and Divorce," http://www.helpguide.org/mental/children_divorce.htm.
14. Sammons, *supra.*
15. *Tenn. Code Ann.* § 36-6-106(a)(10).
16. *Tenn. Code Ann.* § 36-6-101(a)(3)(A).
17. Sammons, *supra.*
18. Gold-Bikin, Lynne Z. and Kolodny, Stephen (2003), *The Divorce Trial Manual: From Initial Interview to Closing Argument.*
19. Block, *supra.*
20. Sammons, *supra.*
21. *Tenn. Code Ann.* § 36-6-101(a)(3)(A).
22. Sammons, *supra.*
23. *Id.*

Critical Thinking

1. Do you think divorce is always something children merely endure? What do you think they are aware of during the process?
2. Can divorce ever be beneficial or helpful to children? Are the results always negative?
3. The author makes several recommendations regarding how parents can help their children through a divorce. Do you agree with them? Why or why not?
4. Using information gained from this article, describe an intervention or support program that could be developed to facilitate the positive development of children from families where parents are divorcing.

Create Central

www.mhhe.com/createcentral

Internet References

HelpGuide: Children and Divorce
www.helpguide.org/mental/children_divorce.htm

HelpGuide: Divorce and Remarriage
www.helpguide.org/topics/breakup_divorce.htm

MARLENE ESKIND MOSES is the principal and manager of MTR Family Law PLLC, a family and divorce law firm in Nashville. She is currently serving as a vice president of the International Academy of Matrimonial Lawyers. She has held prior presidencies with the American Academy of Matrimonial Lawyers, Tennessee Board of Law Examiners, Lawyer's Association for Women, and the Tennessee Supreme Court Historical Society. She has also served as vice president for the United States Chapter of the International Academy of Matrimonial Lawyers and first vice president of the Nashville Bar Association. Selected as a Diplomate in the American College of Family Trial Lawyers, she is the only one in the College from Tennessee. The Tennessee Commission on Continuing Legal & Specialization has designated Moses as a Family Law Specialist; she is board certified as a Family Law Trial Specialist in addition to holding certifications in mediation, arbitration, and collaborative law.

The Effects of Co-Parenting Relationships with Ex-Spouses on Couples in Step-Families by Claire Cartwright and Kerry Gibson

221

Article   Prepared by: Patricia Hrusa Williams, *University of Maine at Farmington*

The Effects of Co-Parenting Relationships with Ex-Spouses on Couples in Step-Families

Claire Cartwright and Kerry Gibson

Learning Outcomes

After reading this article, you will be able to:

- Identify stresses experienced in families when a divorced spouse remarries.

- Evaluate the strengths and weaknesses in a study examining step-families.

- Utilize research findings in developing ideas about needed interventions and supports for step-families.

According to the Australian Bureau of Statistics (ABS, 2007) approximately one in ten couple families contain resident step-children. In Wave 3 of the Household, Income and Labour Dynamics in Australia (HILDA) survey, 13% of households had either residential or non-residential step-children, or both (Qu & Weston, 2005). In the United States, approximately 9% of married couple households, and 12% of cohabiting households contain resident step-children (Teachman & Tedrow, 2008). Step-family data are not collected in the New Zealand Census. However, 19% of the 1,265 child participants in the longitudinal Christchurch Health and Development Study had lived in a step-family between the ages of 6 and 16 years (Nicholson, Fergusson, & Horwood, 1999).

The majority of step-families are formed after divorce through the repartnering or remarriage of a parent (Pryor & Rodgers, 2001). As newly formed step-couples begin to live together, they must manage a complex family transition through which they establish a new household and bring together a number of adults and children, some of whom are unrelated (step-parents, step-children and step-siblings). Unlike first-marriage couples, newly repartnered couples do not have the luxury of getting to know each other before becoming parents and step-parents. Instead, they begin life together facing the challenges associated with developing their new couple's relationship and new step-relationships, at the same time as having to deal with multiple changes in their lives and those of their children.

Step-families are also closely linked to other households because of children's relationships with parents in other residences. When parents repartner, former spouses must continue to deal with each other over issues to do with child care, including parenting arrangements and financial support of children (Braithwaite, McBride, & Schrodt, 2003). How well parents manage these co-parenting issues affects both the step-couple and the children (Braithwaite et al., 2003).

This paper comes from the Couples in Repartnered (Step-) Families study, conducted in New Zealand (Cartwright, 2010). The study consisted of an online questionnaire completed by 99 adults living in step-families; and interviews, both individual and joint, with 16 step-couples. The step-couples reflected back on the processes associated with repartnering and establishing a step-family. The effects of co-parenting issues with former spouses emerged as a source of stress for many step-couples, so the decision was made by the authors to examine this area of step-family life. The results present a thematic analysis of the qualitative data from the interviews that are relevant to ongoing co-parenting relationships and interactions with former spouses and the effects of these on the step-couple.

Co-parenting Relationships Following Separation and the Effect on Step-Couples

In a review of the step-family research conducted in the previous decade, Coleman, and Fine (2000) talked about the importance of extending step-family research beyond the step-family household. However, few researchers have since made this move. As Schrodt (2011) noted, co-parenting has been investigated in first-marriage families and divorced families, but researchers have generally neglected the investigation of co-parenting relationships and their effects in the step-family context.

To do so is important, as the remarriage of one parent brings about another family transition and its associated stressors (Coleman et al., 2000). As Christensen & Rettig (1996) noted, systems theory suggests that co-parenting relationships established between parents following divorce are likely to be disrupted with the addition of a new parental partner, and require adjustments to accommodate the presence of the step-parent. There is evidence that some former spouses struggle to accept the development of new relationships, and the arrival of new parental partners is a common stressor for divorced individuals (Hetherington & Kelly, 2002). This may be particularly difficult, for example, for those who did not want to divorce and have remained single, and those who have settled into a comfortable co-parenting arrangement. American clinicians (e.g., Papernow, 2006) and researchers (e.g., Hetherington & Kelly, 2002) have noted that some former spouses feel threatened by new partners. For example, in an interview study with 35 divorced adults, the men and women talked about feeling that they were being replaced, both as a partner and a parent (Miller, 2009). Hence, having one's former spouse repartner may lead to feelings of insecurity and either disrupt settled arrangements or exacerbate ongoing difficulties.

There is evidence from studies in the United States that co-parenting relationships can deteriorate after the addition of a step-parent to the family, leading to increased stress for all family members (Coleman, Fine, Ganong, Downs, & Pauk, 2001). Christensen & Rettig (1996) examined the effects of remarriage on co-parenting relationships in a sample of 372 women and 277 men contacted three years after their divorce. The researchers found that both the women and men in the study reported having less frequent co-parental interaction, less parenting support from former spouses, and more negative attitudes towards their former spouses. Further, in a study of 327 divorced adults' attitudes to co-parenting, Ganong, Coleman, Markham, and Rothrauff (2011) found that repartnered mothers reported a lower level of intention to co-parent in the future compared to mothers who remained single. The authors suggested that

repartnered women may have seen their new partners as being potential father replacements and that this may have affected their attitudes to co-parenting with their former spouses. Alternatively, the authors posited that the change in attitude could be as a result of increased conflict that occurred following remarriage.

On the other hand, a recent study of the interactions of 22 parenting teams including both of the former spouses and a step-parent, found that the participants expressed moderate satisfaction with their interactions with the other household, and interactions were generally not conflicted (Braithwaite et al., 2003). Interactions were mainly child-focused, were between parents, and were rarely initiated by a step-parent. The researchers concluded that this group of volunteer participants, who had been together on average 6 years, had reached a position of equilibrium. This suggests that given time a number of former spouses and their new partners can develop functional ways of interacting around the children that are satisfactory to them. There is also some evidence that contact with a former spouse who is supportive and engages in cooperative co-parenting can have a positive effect on the repartnered parent in the step-family (Weston & Macklin, 1990).

It is also important to note that some researchers believe that fathers whose children are primarily in the care of mothers can lose further contact with their children when the father remarries. However, Ganong and Coleman (2004) concluded in their review of the step-family literature that the small number of studies on the effects of remarriage on father–child contact have shown mixed results. Some studies have found no change in contact between children and fathers (Stephen, Freedman, & Hess, 1994) while other studies have found a decrease in contact (McKenry, McKelvey, Leigh, & Wark, 1996). Given the evidence of the disruption to co-parenting relationships caused by repartnering, it seems likely, as Smyth (2004) concluded, that some children will have less contact with parents who remarry or repartner, but it [is] also possible that some children will have increased contact, and contact for others will remain unchanged.

Finally, some of the problems that arise between divorced co-parents after remarriage relate to financial issues, including support of the children. Just as men fare better economically after divorce than women, women fare relatively better economically after remarriage than men (Ozawa & Yoon, 2002). Fathers who remarry are potentially placed under greater financial stress due to expectations that they will support children from the previous union, step-children, and children born to the new partnership (Hans & Coleman, 2009). Following remarriage, a father's income may thus be further stretched while a mother's is potentially added to. Further, in Hans' (2009) study of social beliefs around child support modification following remarriage, the majority of their sample of 407 people believed that it was appropriate to modify child support following remarriage to maintain an equitable agreement. It seems likely therefore that in such circumstances disagreements over child care payments may re-emerge or, if disagreements are ongoing, be exacerbated following remarriage as there is potentially more competition for economic resources.

Ganong and Coleman (2004) pointed out that many step-couples come together with "an audience of interested and powerful third parties" (p. 76), some of whom (such as former spouses and, in some instances, children) may have an investment in the relationship not succeeding. As discussed, researchers (e.g., Hetherington & Kelly, 2002) and step-family therapists (e.g., Papernow, 2006) have found that some former spouses engage in behaviours that have a negative effect on step-couples. Papernow observed that resentful or jealous former spouses can make managing child care issues difficult for parents and step-parents. Some former spouses also respond to the repartnering as a competition over the children's affection (Ganong & Coleman, 2004), fearing that they might lose their children. This potentially increases the emotional distress associated with child care arrangements; hence, former spouses who are struggling themselves can have a significant psychological presence in the step-family (Ganong & Coleman, 2004), which in turn is likely to affect the step-couple's relationship.

Method

Participants

Participants were recruited from among 99 participants who had taken part in the study's online survey. At the completion of the online questionnaire, participants could volunteer to take part in a couple's interview. Sixteen couples (32 participants) were recruited in this manner. All couples were living in Auckland. Two participants were in the 30–34 age range; 16 were 35–39; 13 were 40–44; and one was over 50 years.

The couples had been living in a step-family household for between one and nine years, with a mean of 3.9 years. Ten of the couples had remarried, the remainder were cohabiting with new partners. They had between one and four children from previous unions living in their households, with a mean of 2.5 children. All the couples had children with them at least one-third of the time, and the majority had step-children in the household for at least two-thirds of the time. Four couples had children born to their relationship and one was expecting. The children from previous unions ranged in age between 4 and 14 years, with a mean of approximately 10 years.

In the group of participants, there were 12 mothers, 12 fathers, and 9 adults who did not have children from a previous marriage. Between them, they had 25 former spouses. Five of these families were step-father families, five were step-mother families, and six were complex step-families in which both adults had children of their own. However, two of the complex step-families were living mainly as step-father families due to them having irregular contact with the step-fathers' children.

Interviews

The couples were interviewed together and then separately. The joint interviews lasted between an hour and an hour and a half, and the individual interviews each lasted around 20 minutes. In the joint interviews, the couples were asked for the story of their relationship and how it began and developed. They were then asked to talk about their children's experiences and how they had responded to the formation of the new relationship and step-family living. The couples were asked to talk about how they had worked out the care arrangements for the children; what they agreed and disagreed about; how they looked after their own relationship; what worked and what did not. They were asked to talk about the positive aspects of their relationship, and any recommendations they would give to couples considering repartnering.

In the individual interviews, the participants were asked if there was anything else that was important to them that they would like to talk about. They were also asked to talk about the greatest challenges they had experienced in their family situation, and the most positive aspects of their experiences.

Data Analysis

The interviews were transcribed and a number of datasets were created to allow for further analysis. These included the challenges internal to the couple's relationship, the responses of children, influences external to the step-family household, positive experiences, and the parenting of children. This paper presents the analysis of the body of data taken from the interviews in regard to ongoing contact with former spouses that was in the dataset relating to influences from outside the step-family. A thematic analysis was conducted on the data using the methods described by Braun and Clarke (2006). This included the process of re-reading the data, and recording a summary of the comments made by participants in regard to interactions with former spouses and the effects of these. These comments were then examined and grouped into sets of related data. From this process, a number of themes were proposed. These proposed themes were then checked against the data to see if they fit and represented the main ideas that were present. The themes were further examined by the second author for their fit to the data and the final themes were defined. These themes are presented in the next section.

Before presenting the themes, it is important to acknowledge that this analysis is based on the step-couples' interviews. The former spouses' stories of their experiences are not included. It is also important to note that the majority of the data is about negative experiences with former spouses. Eight of the 25 parents in the group did not talk about relationships with former spouses in any significant way and four step-couples' experiences did not include issues with spouses. Hence, 12 couples (17 parents) were negatively affected by the nature of the co-parenting relationship and the data presented in the results come from these participants.

Results of the Thematic Analysis

The results section presents four themes that were established from the data analysis process described above. These include: battles over children's residence and financial matters; not pulling their weight; lack of cooperation; and the other parent's negativity towards the step-parent or the new step-family. The effects that these areas had on the step-couples will be examined throughout each theme.

Battles over Children's Residence and Financial Matters

As has been well documented by previous research (Amato, 2000; Pryor & Rodgers, 2001), separated and divorced parents often continue to engage conflictually as they deal with each other over issues concerning their shared children and shared property. In this group of participants, six step-couples described conflict with former spouses over child care and support and/or joint property, which was associated with high levels of stress or distress. For five of the six couples, the discord was between fathers and their ex-wives. For some participants, the conflict with former spouses had mostly resolved at the time of the interviews, for others it was current and ongoing. Participants described a range of feelings they experienced during periods of conflict with former spouses, including feeling frustrated, anxious and exhausted, and sometimes hopeless or desperate. They also described a range of effects on the couple's own relationship. Some couples had conflict between themselves over how to handle difficulties with former spouses, others became united, and one couple considered separating. As might be expected, some also disagreed some of the time and were supportive and felt united at other times.

Three fathers who repartnered quickly after separating, including one whose new relationship pre-dated the separation from his spouse, experienced severe levels of stress that involved legal "battles" over children's residence and financial arrangements. The couples' stories of the beginning of their relationships were dominated by descriptions of these problems. As one step-mother said about the effects of the conflict

between her partner and his ex-wife over joint property and, to a lesser extent, contact with the children:

> The fact that for the first two years it was a battleground. And just constantly in your face everyday. . . . You never had the courting and the dating type scenario. You just go, bang, and you're straight in and we had two and a half, three years of just absolute battle and grief.

The father talked about his experiences in similar terms, describing "a lot of nasty conflict and a lot of expensive lawyers" and two years of "war". He also talked about his perception that his ex-wife was driven by a desire for revenge, as the quote below suggests:

> I guess some of it was, I know the whole of that thing was she was out to sort of ruin me personally and there was no way that was going to happen. . . . For the first two years she was just irrational. Her actions were just irrational and it was driven by vengeance and anger, and trying to rationalise that with someone just doesn't work.

Another father, who had repartnered within six months of separating, had lost regular contact with his pre-adolescent and adolescent children at the time of the interviews. He moved towns and hoped that his ex-spouse would cooperate with transporting the children, but this had not happened. For this couple, the first half of the interview was dominated by the story of his attempts to see his children, his ex-wife's unwillingness to assist with travel, and their contact through lawyers. They talked about trying to "be united as a couple as you have so many things against you". However, the relationship came under pressure over time, as the father missed his children more. The step-mother talked about her frustration, how she tried to assist by talking to the children's mother, and also her annoyance at times with her partner. She had difficulty understanding why it was so difficult, given that her interactions with her own former spouse were uncomplicated:

> I guess the longer it went on, the harder it became. . . . I'd get wound up or I'd have a knot in my stomach. I think the stress side of things came more from frustration. . . . I have such a simple arrang[e]ment with my son's dad . . . and I couldn't understand why we couldn't have that with their mother, because I knew it could be simple. Then I'd say, you know, they're your kids, you can sort it out because she [mother] is not listening to me.

Another couple, who repartnered shortly after their former relationships had ended, had three ex-partners between them, and they experienced difficulties with all of them when they repartnered. While none of the situations were as difficult as the ones described above, the effect of having three ex-partners

The Effects of Co-Parenting Relationships with Ex-Spouses on Couples in Step-Families by Claire Cartwright and Kerry Gibson

225

made their first two years together stressful. The father talked about the challenges of this over the first year, which illustrates the complexity of the issues that some step-couples face:

> When we first met, the children only went to their mother's on a Saturday night, every fortnight. . . . Then she [ex-wife] split up from her husband and then after that she didn't want to work, so went for custody—shared care of the boys—so she could get the benefit. And we fought it for a year, but in the end it was too stressful, and the kids wanted to go to their mother half the time. . . . Just creating your own family unit to fit in with them [his ex-partners] as well, and then we had to do it with my wife's daughter and iron that side out as well!

Two couples talked about their experiences of mothers who complained that the step-mothers were mistreating their children and how these claims were linked with attempting to have increased time with the children. As an example, one of the fathers told the story of his former spouse, who left to live overseas when the children were preschoolers. As the children grew older, they visited their mother occasionally. After the father and the step-mother married some years later, the mother accused the step-mother of mistreating the children. The step-mother talked about the effects on her at the time and how she coped with it:

> I wanted out. I thought, I am not going to do this. We'd only just got married, and then I was worried because she'd sent us a copy, she'd sent the school a copy, she's sent the courts a copy. . . . I raised above it. I knew it wasn't true. The kids knew it wasn't true and denied it. . . . She was just jealous and she still is jealous because I'm bringing up her biological kids.

Finally, one mother was frightened about the welfare of her infant son. The mother separated from her ex-husband when their child was a baby, because of her concern for their physical safety, but the father attempted to gain shared care of the young child. As she said, talking about her ex-husband:

> He's got a hatred for me, has a total hatred for me. . . . He hates the fact that [step-father] is in [son's] life.

The step-father also talked about the effects of this and his caution about getting involved:

> Yeah, whether I really wanted to get myself tangled up in what was happening, a custody dispute, taking on a toddler. . . . So whether I was willing to adjust to that, whether I wanted to get involved in all of that and the baggage, I suppose you would call it.

This custody dispute continued for four years and was coming to an end at the time of the interviews. The mother

commented, "It's gone on for four years. So now that's dealt with, I am finding it a bit hard to believe that this is it". The step-father also spoke about his approach over the recent years and how he tried to be supportive:

> [Partner] was pretty highly strung there for a while. And I just had to keep telling myself I know what's causing this mess. I couldn't possibly understand how she feels, going through a custody battle, and just had to wait for it all to finish really, so at times it was pretty hard.

Hence, these couples came under what could be considered severe levels of stress, often during the early stages of their relationships, because of conflict with former spouses over children's residence and/or financial arrangements. The parents in this group appeared to feel threatened by the former spouses' attitudes towards them, the potential loss of custody of the children, or issues related to joint property. The conflict between the former spouses, including the ongoing legal "battles", sometimes affected the step-couples' relationships, becoming a source of disagreement for some of them, and making it harder for them to develop their relationship and the step-family while they were feeling under a state of "siege".

Not Pulling Their Weight!

Another experience that some participants talked about were the ongoing feelings of frustration or sense of unfairness that arose when some former spouses' demands or lack of contribution led to a sense of increased pressure for the step-couple. These experiences were less severe than those in the previous theme, but were an ongoing source of stress. A number of participants felt that the other parent was not pulling their weight, whether financially, in provision of child care, or both. One mother talked about her frustration at her child's father and her concern for her child that her father was not meeting his parenting responsibilities:

> There's this person who's never grown up and they're not going to. . . . And it frustrates me, for [daughter's] sake as well. It's just that kind of responsibility thing when somebody just doesn't fundamentally get that as a parent they have a responsibility. He's never organised a holiday. He's never paid me a cent of maintenance. He's never been to any of [daughter's] important dates at school!

Couples also talked about the financial pressures they were under, and perceived that these were exacerbated by the demands of former spouses. One couple talked about the stress associated with each of them having an ex-spouse whom they perceived placed a financial burden on their household. They reported that one of the former spouses, a father, contributed nothing financially for his child; and the other former spouse, a mother, made ongoing requests for financial support for her child over and above the monthly support payment. As the couple said about the woman's former spouse:

> We won't go into character assassination, but his father basically told [son], you know, he was not his responsibility. He was entirely my responsibility and not to expect anything from him. (Step-father)

> He's the type of parent who won't go out and get a job to support his other two children and his [new] partner because it means paying me more child support. (Mother)

This couple also felt that the mother of his child, who was on a benefit, was also demanding. He talked about the pressure he was under and his guilt about his daughter, and appeared to feel torn between his former spouse, daughter and wife:

> It was like I was paying out this money [child support], and she would say, "Our child wants to go on a schoo[l] trip". I can't afford to do it and I'd be like, "What do I do now?", because I don't want any more money going out, but its affecting my child and it would really become difficult. And then I would have my wife saying, "We can't afford to do much" . . . and I would think, "I know, but my daugher is missing out", and I used to feel like I was in the middle of everything.

Another father talked about feeling similarly torn and resentful towards his ex-wife for not working and not contributing more to the financial support of their sons:

> I feel resentful sometimes about forking out, because she treats us like the bank. But I don't want the children to go without. Don't get me wrong, but it does piss me off, excuse my language.

Finally, one couple talked about a mother who had given up much of the responsibility for her children, both in terms of child care and economic support, because of her changed personal circumstances. As a result, the step-mother, who was at home with her young children born to her new marriage, had become, by default, the main caregiver for her step-children, and talked about the difficulties of fulfilling a parenting role for them:

> I'm not saying that [father] doesn't take responsibility, but at the moment because of what's been going on, it's just even more highlighted the fact that I'm actually the primary caregiver and making these decisions [about the step-children] and trying to feel my way through this. . . . I find it hard to actually understand and believe that she's just about dropped them like hot potatoes.

While this step-mother appeared to be managing well with her step-children and the couple reported the children were happy in their home, for her it came as an unexpected shock that she should become the primary caregiver for the step-children, and this was also a source of tension between the couple.

Lack of Cooperation

A number of participants talked about their disappointment or frustration at what they perceived to be an ongoing lack of cooperation from the other parent, usually over care of the children. This lack of cooperation took many forms. It included an unwillingness of some spouses to allow some flexibility in care arrangements to fit in with contingencies, to communicate or negotiate, and/or to cooperate with a step-parent, when this was required. For some participants, this lack of cooperation began or was exacerbated when the parent repartnered.

One father, for example, described how he and his ex-spouse had developed a workable routine for handing over the children from one home to the other and how this had changed since he repartnered:

> It'd gone from being businesslike, where we would occasionally, at hand-over time, meet in a café and have a morning tea together with the children and try to normalise things. The kids would say goodbye to me, kiss and cuddle, and off they'd go. . . . [Now] we'll meet outside Burger King. You park on one side of the place, I'll park on the other, and the kids can walk over the carpark. And, you know, back to deep freeze, sort of frosty. We are back to that.

Another couple talked about problems with former partners on both sides. The father had child care issues with an ex-wife and the couple also perceived a lack of cooperation from her ex-husband (as each is both a parent and step-parent, they are referred to by gender):

> *Female:* But then we had other issues on the other side, just trying to make everything fit, and that person [ex-husband], I don't know why, being difficult!
>
> *Male:* Her dad being difficult!
>
> *Female:* Just over school holidays really.
>
> *Male:* Yeah, and other stuff. When he's got one person to think about, we don't understand why he was difficult.
>
> *Female:* He doesn't care!
>
> *Male:* Doesn't care what we do!
>
> *Female:* As far as he's concerned, our family unit is none of his business.

One couple with parents living overseas had difficulty gaining permission from the children's mother to allow the children to visit their grandparents. As the step-mother said:

> When we wanted to go on a holiday, and she had agreed to it, and then she withdrew her agreement. And we'd already

The Effects of Co-Parenting Relationships with Ex-Spouses on Couples in Step-Families by Claire Cartwright and Kerry Gibson

227

bought the overseas tickets and the kids thought they were going. And then she's saying they th[at] couldn't go, or it had to go through the court for the court to say, "Yes, they could go to see their grandparents". And I just hate that!

Another couple also experienced a lack of cooperation from the children's step-mother. This couple had moved house in the early stages of repartnering, and the oldest child, who normally got on well with his step-father, was objecting to the new living situation. The couple told the story of what happened when the mother rang the children's father to ask for support while they worked through the issues with the teenager:

> *Mother:* I asked for the dad's support, which he gave me, but the woman that he's married used the opportunity to undermine us. . . .
>
> *Step-father:* They went to their dad's that night, so we weren't there to talk about it that evening. Then the following night they came back with these questionnaires that the step-mum had written out, like, what do they feel about living here?
>
> *Mother:* And using the same questionnaire to ask the children about what it was like at their place as well. Yeah, that wasn't useful.

Another mother talked about her frustration and disappointment with her daughter's father and his unwillingness to help out, especially during the school holidays. This couple did not have any extended family support:

> For us as a family, we don't have people that help us with our kids. . . . There's just us, so that really is where it kind of bites. You get six weeks of summer holidays and you're both working and there's this other person who's just gone. They're not there for six weeks every summer.

Hence, some of the participants talked about their disappointment and frustration at the lack of cooperation that they experienced with the other parent, or in one case, step-parent. This added to their stresses and appeared to put pressure on them as a couple. Over time, some also appeared to learn to live with the lack of cooperation and were less frustrated by it. As one mother said, referring to the decrease in the effects of problems with the former spouse, "Once it was an elephant in the room, now it's a little mouse in the field".

The Other Parent's Negativity towards the Step-Parent or the New Step-Family

A number of parents and step-parents talked about their concerns or worries that the former parents' negativity towards the step-parent or step-family situation might adversely affect the children and the children's attitude towards the step-parent or living in a step-family, thereby undermining the efforts they were making to build the step-family and care for the children.

One mother did not allow the children to visit the new step-family household for the first few months. Over time, the step-mother became involved in picking the children up from school, assisting them with homework, helping to make lunches for them, and found the mother's treatment of her difficult to accept. This situation came to a head and improved after the step-mother stood up for herself. Following a call where the mother had spoken rudely to her, she said:

> I'm not the nanny. I'm not the receptionist. I'm bringing your children up whether you like it or not. They're with us nearly 50% of the time. . . . You can't even have the decency to be civil to me when I ring up or to acknowledge that fact that I'm picking them up from school! . . . I said I spend my good earned money on them buying them clothes and food, and you've got the nerve to treat me like this! . . . And I said we have the decency to treat [your new partner] with respect and talk to him directly!!

While this type of response might have been followed by ongoing conflict or difficulty between the mother and the step-mother, in this instance, the mother apologised and the relationship became more civil. It is also important to note that in this instance, the young children did not appear to develop any negative attitutides towards their step-mother and were reported to be moving between houses quite happily.

Another couple talked about their worries about the mother's negative attitude towards the step-mother and their concerns about how this affected the children. This couple had a relatively smooth transition into step-family life, and the greatest challenge was the ex-wife's response to the remarriage. The father talked about his ex-wife's reaction to his new partner and his concerns about this:

> My ex-wife hasn't reacted at all well to [step-mother] being on the scene, and insinuated in the early part of our relationship that the girls completely disliked [step-mother]. . . . She wrote this vitriolic email saying about how insensitive it was for me considering marrying someone who the girls obviously disliked so much. . . . The data didn't match what I was seeing. . . . I'm not paranoid about it, but I still worry to an extent what she will feed the girls about us.

A step-father also spoke about what he perceived as interference from the step-mother in the children's other home. He talked about his perceptions that the step-mother acted as if she was the mother of the children but failed to accept his role as a step-father:

> I've met her a few times and she blanked me completely. . . . There's a couple of things she has done that I've felt have been against me . . . Her interference seems to be a lot, and thinking she's the mother, whereas although I've been around less time, I don't think I'm the dad. That's been difficult.

Finally, a mother's story of her preschool child's experience provides some insight into how loyalty issues affect children. She talked about the effects on her son of the non-residential father's attempts, as she perceived it, to turn the child against his step-father. The mother talked about her concerns for her partner's feelings and for the wellbeing of her son:

> The only time we've really had difficulties with [step-father] and [son] is when he's come back from his father's and, "Me and my dad hate you", this sort of stuff. . . . I said to [step-father] at the time, "You need to remember that this is [my ex-] talking. That is not my son because he absolutely idolises [his step-father]". [Later] I said to [my son], "Why did you say that about [step-dad]? You don't hate him", and he said, "Because my dad said". And he was so young!

Hence, some parents and step-parents experienced the other parent(s) as competing for the children, and attempting to turn the children against them or to win the children over to their side. In only one instance, a step-mother was seen as the main instigator of the difficulties. The other instances concerned former spouses' lack of acceptance and angry responses to the step-parent or the new step-family situation.

Discussion

Previous research suggests that co-parenting relationships can deteriorate when a former spouse repartners (Christensen & Rettig, 1996; Coleman et al., 2001). This study provides insights into how this can occur and the effects it has on step-couples. A number of the parents observed an increase after they repartnered in the conflict they experienced with former spouses over the children's residence, child support and/or joint property. This appeared to be heightened for couples where one of them had repartnered early during the post-separation period, when issues around child contact and joint property were not yet resolved, and feelings on both sides were still running high. On the other hand, disturbance in some co-parenting relationships also occurred after repartnering when the divorce had taken place some years earlier. A small number of parents

perceived that former spouses were being deliberately difficult in response to their repartnering.

For some parents, the conflict over child contact and financial issues was associated with high levels of stress and added a great deal to the pressure that couples were experiencing as part of their adjustment to step-family living. It also placed stress on their relationships with each other, and this was exacerbated if they disagreed over how to manage the issues with the former spouse. It was also difficult at times for the step-parents to accept and deal with the stress associated with the conflict between their partners and former spouses. On the other hand, it is important to note that around a third of the parents who participated in the study did not talk about experiencing problems in their co-parenting relationships with former spouses as part of their adjustment to step-family living.

These results support the notion discussed earlier that remarriage and the entrance of new parental partners can destabilise family systems (Christensen & Rettig, 1996), either by exacerbating difficulties that exist or leading to new problems that need to be resolved. It also provides indirect support for previous evidence that the entrance of a new parental partner into the extended family system can lead to feelings of insecurity and a fear that the parent is not only being replaced as partner but also being replaced as a parent (Miller, 2009). This may be particularly difficult for former spouses who observe step-couple closeness and attractive step-parent qualities. It may also be difficult for individuals who are struggling emotionally. This appeared to be so in a small number of instances discussed in the thematic analysis, in which the participants talked about the attitude of the former spouse to the step-parent and had a sense that their ex-partner was attempting to turn the children against the step-parent and perhaps the remarriage. This supports Papernow's (2006) conclusion that some former spouses engage in jealous behaviour that makes co-parenting difficult and places stress on the step-couple. In a small number of instances, couples perceived that the former spouse's negativity was directed at the step-parent. In some instances, this lead to increased tensions between the step-couple and/or feelings of insecurity for the step-parent.

As found previously (Braithwaite et al., 2003), however, step-parents did not appear to deal with or negotiate with former spouses on anything but an occasional basis. This was left mainly to parents. An exception to this was a wife of a former spouse who was seen as interfering directly with the management of the children, and one step-mother who attempted to assist with resolving disagreements. She stepped back from this, however, when it was unsuccessful.

It is also important to note that some of the stressors associated with former spouses were not severe, but were an ongoing source of stress or irritation that made life more difficult for the couples at times. Some former spouses were experienced as being inflexible or refusing to negotiate special requests or one-off changes to routines to allow for special arrangements or events. Some ex-spouses were experienced as not meeting their responsibilities, either through child care (such as assisting with holidays), or in providing financial support of the children. Some parents thought that the other parent was not pulling his or her weight financially and found this added to the financial stessors they were already experiencing. There was also some evidence to support previous finding[s] that some fathers in step-family situations feel torn between former spouses, their children and current partners, in regard to financial support (Hans & Coleman, 2009).

As researchers, we were surprised to note that five of the six co-parenting relationships that we considered came under severe levels of stress, were between repartnered fathers and their ex-wives. On the other hand, it has been found consistently that men tend to repartner more quickly than women (Cartwright, 2010) and some men in this study repartnered within six months of separating, at a time when issues around child care and finances were still under negotiation and the relationship between the two former spouses was still emotionally fraught. Early repartnering is likely to lead to heightened distress for former spouses, especially when they have not wanted to divorce.

American researchers (e.g., Hetherington & Kelly, 2002) and step-family therapists (e.g., Papernow, 2006) have observed that repartnering parents often have unrealistically positive expectations of step-family life, believing, for example, that step-children will love their new partners as much as they do. Some step-couples in this study also appeared surprised or taken aback by their former spouses' responses to them or their new partner following repartnering, including those who repartnered quickly. It may be that some step-couples are not cognisant of the problems that can arise with former spouses if repartnering occurs quickly after a separation, before the necessary period of adjustment has taken place. The likelihood of step-couples having realistic expectations may also be affected by the lack of research in the area of co-parenting following remarriage, and also the lack of norms to guide parents and step-parents in how to relate to each other (Weston & Macklin, 1990). It might be helpful for those considering repartnering to understand that relating to former spouses can become an obstacle course if the former spouse feels threatened or believes that they have not been treated fairly. It may also be helpful for former spouses to be aware of the strong emotions that are evoked by their exes repartnering, and to have guidance about how to manage themselves during this stressful period.

It is important to acknowledge the limitations of this study and briefly discuss future research directions. First, this sample of participants volunteered to be interviewed and may not be representative of step-couples generally. The sample may have included a greater proportion of people who had experienced considerable difficulty and wanted to talk about this to a researcher. Second, the views of former spouses were not included in this study and hence their experiences and viewpoints are missing. Research that includes all the adults involved is likely to provide greater insights into the dynamics of co-parenting within step-family situations. Third, because of the nature of the interviews, participants who told the story of the development of their relationships tended to talk only about the problems and challenges they experienced with former spouses. Hence, this study is informative about the types of problems that step-couples experience, but not of positive co-parenting relationships following repartnering. Around a third of the participants appeared to have non-problematic relationships with former spouses, but little data were collected about these relationships because of the focus on the step-couples' challenges and the experiences they regarded as important to them.

In terms of future research, it is important that family transition researchers in Australia and New Zealand focus more on the areas of co-parenting following remarriage, and the relationships between former spouses, parents and step-parents. No previous research has been conducted in either country in this area. The lack of research in this area may also exacerbate a lack of norms to guide repartnering parents and former spouses. In line with this, in order to better understand how co-parenting relationships work, it is also important to study well-functioning co-parenting relationships and how these develop or are maintained following the repartnering of at least one former spouse. Finally, given that the majority of separated parents will eventually repartner, and some will do so quickly, it may be desirable for educational programs and literature aimed at separated couples to include information about the stressors associated with the transition into step-family life and their potential effects on co-parenting relationships between former spouses.

References

Amato, P. (2000). The consequences of divorce for adults and children. *Journal of Marriage and the Family, 62* (4), 1269–1287.

Australian Bureau of Statistics. (2007). *2006 Census of Population and Housing* (Cat. No. 2008.0). Canberra: ABS.

Braithwaite, D. O., McBride, M. C., & Schrodt, P. (2003). Parent teams and the everyday interactions of co-parenting in stepfamilies. *Communication Reports, 16* (2), 93–111.

Braun, V., & Clarke, V. (2006). Using thematic analysis in psychology. *Qualitative research in psychology, 3,* 77–101.

Cartwright, C. (2010). Preparing to repartner and live in a stepfamily: An exploratory investigation. *Journal of Family Studies, 16* (3), 237–250.

Christensen, D. H., & Rettig, K. D. (1996). The relationship of remarriage to post-divorce co-parenting. *Journal of Divorce & Remarriage, 24* (1–2), 73–88.

Coleman, M., Fine, M. A., Ganong, L. H., Downs, K. J. M., & Pauk, N. (2001). When you're not the Brady Bunch: Identifying perceived conflicts and resolution strategies in stepfamilies. *Personal Relationships, 8* (1), 55–73.

Coleman, M., Ganong, L., & Fine, M. A. (2000). Reinvestigating remarriage: Another decade of progress. *Journal of Marriage and the Family, 62* (4), 1288–1307.

Ganong, L., & Coleman, M. (2004). *Stepfamily relationships: Development, dynamics and interventions.* New York: Kluwer Academic/Plenum Publishers.

Ganong, L. H., Coleman, M., Markham, M., & Rothrauff, T. (2011). Predicting postdivorce co-parental communication. *Journal of Divorce & Remarriage, 52* (1), 1–18.

Hans, J. D. (2009). Beliefs about child support modification following remarriage and subsequent childbirth. *Family Relations, 58* (1), 65–78.

Hans, J. D., & Coleman, M. (2009). The experiences of remarried stepfathers who pay child support. *Personal Relationships, 16* (4), 597–618.

Hetherington, E. M., & Kelly, J. (2002). *For better or for worse: Divorce reconsidered.* New York: W. W. Norton and Company.

McKenry, P. C., McKelvey, M. W., Leigh, D., & Wark, L. (1996). Nonresidential father involvement. *Journal of Divorce & Remarriage, 25* (3–4), 1–14.

Miller, A. E. (2009). Face concerns and facework strategies in maintaining postdivorce co-parenting and dating relationships. *Southern Communication Journal, 74* (2), 157–173.

Nicholson, J. M., Fergusson, D. M., & Horwood, L. J. (1999). Effects on later adjustment of living in a step-family during childhood and adolescence. *Journal of Child Psychology and Psychiatry, 40,* 405–416.

Ozawa, M. N., & Yoon, H.-S. (2002). The economic benefit of remarriage. *Journal of Divorce & Remarriage, 36* (3–4), 21–39.

Papernow, P. (2006). Blended family relationships: Helping people who live in stepfamilies. *Family Therapy Magazine,* May, 34–42.

Pryor, J., & Rodgers, B. (2001). *Children in changing families: Life after parental separation* (Understanding Children' Worlds). Oxford, UK: Blackwell.

Qu, L., & Weston, R. (2005). Snapshot of couple families with stepparent–child relationships. *Family Matters, 70,* 36–37.

Smyth, B. (2004). Postseparation fathering: What does Australian research tell us? *Journal of Family Studies, 10* (1), 20–49.

Stephen, E. H., Freedman, V. A., & Hess, J. (1994). Near and far. *Journal of Divorce & Remarriage, 20* (3–4), 171–191.

Teachman, J., & Tedrow, L. (2008). The demography of step-families in the United States. In J. Pryor (Ed.), *The international handbook of step-families: Policy and practice in legal, research, and clinical environments* (pp. 3–29). Hoboken, NJ: John Wiley.

Weston, C. A., & Macklin, E. D. (1990). The relationship between former-spousal contact and remarital satisfaction in stepfather families. *Journal of Divorce & Remarriage, 14* (2), 25–48.

Critical Thinking

1. What do you see as the biggest challenges faced when a stepfamily is formed?
2. If this study were conducted in the United States, do you think the findings would be the same and why? Are there things about this study that could be strengthened or which limit the generalizability of its findings about step-families?
3. How could the findings of this study be used in developing interventions and supports designed for step-families?

Create Central

www.mhhe.com/createcentral

Internet References

HelpGuide: Children and Divorce
www.helpguide.org/mental/children_divorce.htm

HelpGuide: Divorce and Remarriage
www.helpguide.org/topics/breakup_divorce.htm

National Stepfamily Resource Center
http://www.stepfamilies.info

Stepfamilies Australia
http:// www.stepfamily.org.au

CLAIRE CARTWRIGHT and KERRY GIBSON are both at the Doctor of Clinical Psychology Programme, School of Psychology, the University of Auckland, New Zealand. This paper is based on a presentation made at the 12th Australian Institute of Family Studies Conference, 25 July 2012, Melbourne.

Unit 5

UNIT

Prepared by: Patricia Hrusa Williams, *University of Maine at Farmington*

Families, Now and into the Future

What is the future of the family? Does the family even have a future? These questions and others like them are being asked. Many people fear for the future of the family. As previous units of this volume have shown, the family is an institution which continues to evolve and change. Still, certain elements of family appear to be constant. The family is and will remain a powerful influence in the lives of its members. This is because we all begin life in some type of family, and this early exposure carries a great deal of weight in forming our social selves—who we are and how we relate to others. From our biological families, we are given our basic genetic makeup. In the context of daily routines and rituals we also learn how to care for ourselves and attend to our health. In families, we are given our first exposure to values, and it is through families that we most actively influence others. Our sense of commitment and obligation begins within the family as well as our sense of what we can expect of others.

Much that has been written about families has been less than hopeful, focusing on ways of avoiding or correcting "maladaptive" behaviors and patterns. The articles in this unit take a positive view of family and how it influences its members. Through its diversity, rituals, traditions, history, and new ways of establishing connections, the family still remains a vital and important structure in which we work, play, love, and adapt.

The articles in this unit explore the different shapes and forms families come in and the rituals and celebrations that link them. Articles also consider how technology and changes in societal norms and values are altering how we procreate, relate, marry, and parent the next generation. A goal is to explore the family now and as it might be as we venture into the future, considering its role as a healthy, supportive place for personal growth.

Article   Prepared by: Patricia Hrusa Williams, *University of Maine at Farmington*

The Changing American Family

Natalie Angier

Learning Outcomes

After reading this article, you will be able to:

- Describe shifts in family characteristics and structure in the United States.

- Explain how demographic, social, political, and economic forces have contributed to changes in the family in the United States.

Kristi and Michael Burns have a lot in common. They love crossword puzzles, football, going to museums and reading five or six books at a time. They describe themselves as mild-mannered introverts who suffer from an array of chronic medical problems. The two share similar marital résumés, too. On their wedding day in 2011, the groom was 43 years old and the bride 39, yet it was marriage No. 3 for both.

Today, their blended family is a sprawling, sometimes uneasy ensemble of two sharp-eyed sons from her two previous husbands, a daughter and son from his second marriage, ex-spouses of varying degrees of involvement, the partners of ex-spouses, the bemused in-laws and a kitten named Agnes that likes to sleep on computer keyboards.

If the Burnses seem atypical as an American nuclear family, how about the Schulte-Waysers, a merry band of two married dads, six kids and two dogs? Or the Indrakrishnans, a successful immigrant couple in Atlanta whose teenage daughter divides her time between prosaic homework and the precision footwork of ancient Hindu dance; the Glusacs of Los Angeles, with their two nearly grown children and their litany of middle-class challenges that seem like minor sagas; Ana Perez and Julian Hill of Harlem, unmarried and just getting by, but with Warren Buffett-size dreams for their three young children; and the alarming number of families with incarcerated parents, a sorry byproduct of America's status as the world's leading jailer.

The typical American family, if it ever lived anywhere but on Norman Rockwell's Thanksgiving canvas, has become as multilayered and full of surprises as a holiday turducken—the all-American seasonal portmanteau of deboned turkey, duck and chicken.

Researchers who study the structure and evolution of the American family express unsullied astonishment at how rapidly the family has changed in recent years, the transformations often exceeding or capsizing those same experts' predictions of just a few journal articles ago.

"This churning, this turnover in our intimate partnerships is creating complex families on a scale we've not seen before," said Andrew J. Cherlin, a professor of public policy at Johns Hopkins University. "It's a mistake to think this is the endpoint of enormous change. We are still very much in the midst of it."

Yet for all the restless shape-shifting of the American family, researchers who comb through census, survey and historical data and conduct field studies of ordinary home life have identified a number of key emerging themes.

Families, they say, are becoming more socially egalitarian over all, even as economic disparities widen. Families are more ethnically, racially, religiously and stylistically diverse than half a generation ago—than even half a year ago.

In increasing numbers, blacks marry whites, atheists marry Baptists, men marry men and women women, Democrats marry Republicans and start talk shows. Good friends join forces as part of the "voluntary kin" movement, sharing medical directives, wills, even adopting one another legally.

Single people live alone and proudly consider themselves families of one—more generous and civic-minded than so-called "greedy marrieds."

"There are really good studies showing that single people are more likely than married couples to be in touch with friends, neighbors, siblings and parents," said Bella DePaulo, author of *Singled Out* and a visiting professor of psychology at the University of California, Santa Barbara.

But that doesn't mean they'll be single forever. "There are not just more types of families and living arrangements than there used to be," said Stephanie Coontz, author of the coming book *Intimate Revolutions,* and a social historian at Evergreen State College in Olympia, Wash. "Most people will move through several different types over the course of their lives."

At the same time, the old-fashioned family plan of stably married parents residing with their children remains a source of considerable power in America—but one that is increasingly seen as out of reach to all but the educated elite.

"We're seeing a class divide not only between the haves and the have-nots, but between the I do's and the I do nots," Dr. Coontz said. Those who are enjoying the perks of a good marriage "wouldn't stand for any other kind," she said, while those who would benefit most from marital stability "are the ones least likely to have the resources to sustain it."

Yet across the divide runs a white picket fence, our unshakable star-spangled belief in the value of marriage and family. We marry, divorce and remarry at rates not seen anywhere else in the developed world. We lavish $70 billion a year on weddings, more than we spend on pets, coffee, toothpaste and toilet paper combined.

We're sappy family romantics. When an informal sample of 52 Americans of different ages, professions and hometowns were asked the first thought that came to mind on hearing the word "family," the answers varied hardly at all. Love! Kids! Mom! Dinner!

"It's the backbone of how we live," said David Anderson, 52, an insurance claims adjuster from Chicago. "It means everything," said Linda McAdam, 28, who is in human resources on Long Island.

Yes, everything, and sometimes too many things. "It's almost like a weight," said Rob Fee, 26, a financial analyst in San Francisco, "a heavy weight." Or as the comedian George Burns said, "Happiness is having a large, loving, caring, close-knit family in another city."

In charting the differences between today's families and those of the past, demographers start with the kids—or rather the lack of them.

The nation's birthrate today is half what it was in 1960, and last year hit its lowest point ever. At the end of the baby boom, in 1964, 36 percent of all Americans were under 18 years old; last year, children accounted for just 23.5 percent of the population, and the proportion is dropping, to a projected 21 percent by 2050. Fewer women are becoming mothers—about 80 percent of those of childbearing age today versus 90 percent in the 1970s—and those who reproduce do so more sparingly, averaging two children apiece now, compared with three in the 1970s.

One big reason is the soaring cost of ushering offspring to functional independence. According to the Department of Agriculture, the average middle-class couple will spend $241,080 to raise a child to age 18. Factor in four years of college and maybe graduate school, or a parentally subsidized internship with the local theater company, and say hello to your million-dollar bundle of oh joy.

As steep as the fertility decline has been, the marriage rate has fallen more sharply, particularly among young women, who do most of the nation's childbearing. As a result, 41 percent of babies are now born out of wedlock, a fourfold increase since 1970.

The trend is not demographically uniform, instead tracking the nation's widening gap in income and opportunity. Among women with a bachelor's degree or higher, 90 percent adhere to the old playground song and put marriage before a baby carriage. For everybody else, maternity is often decoupled from matrimony: 40 percent of women with some college but no degree, and 57 percent of women with high school diplomas or less, are unmarried when they give birth to their first child.

More than one-quarter of these unwed mothers are living with a partner who may or may not be their child's biological father. The rise of the cohabiting couple is another striking feature of the evolving American family: From 1996 to 2012, the number jumped almost 170 percent, to 7.8 million from 2.9 million.

Nor are unmarried mothers typically in their teens; contrary to all the talk of an epidemic of teenage motherhood, the birthrate among adolescent girls has dropped by nearly half since 1991 and last year hit an all-time low, a public health triumph that experts attribute to better sex education and birth-control methods. Most unmarried mothers today, demographers say, are in their 20s and early 30s.

Also démodé is the old debate over whether mothers of dependent children should work outside the home. The facts have voted, the issue is settled, and Paycheck Mommy is now a central organizing principle of the modern American family.

The share of mothers employed full or part time has quadrupled since the 1950s and today accounts for nearly three-quarters of women with children at home. The number of women who are their families' sole or primary breadwinner also has soared, to 40 percent today from 11 percent in 1960.

"Yes, I wear the pants in the family," said Ana Perez, 35, a mother of three and a vice president at a financial services company in New York, who was, indeed, wearing pants. "I can say it brings me joy to know I can take care of my family."

Cultural attitudes are adapting accordingly. Sixty-two percent of the public, and 72 percent of adults under 30, view the ideal marriage as one in which husband and wife both work and share child care and household duties; back when Jimmy Carter was president, less than half of the population approved of the dual-income family, and less than half of 1 percent of husbands knew how to operate a sponge mop.

Mothers are bringing home more of the bacon, and of the mortarboards, too. While most couples are an even match scholastically, 28 percent of married women are better educated than their mates; that is true of just 19 percent of married men. Forty years ago, the asymmetry went the other way.

Some experts argue that the growing legion of mothers with advanced degrees has helped sharpen the already brutal competition for admission to the nation's elite universities, which stress the importance of extracurricular activities. Nothing predicts the breadth and busyness of a child's after-school schedule better, it turns out, than the mother's level of education.

One change that caught many family researchers by surprise was the recent dip in the divorce rate. After many decades of upward march, followed by a long, stubborn stay at the familiar 50 percent mark that made every nuptial feel like a coin flip, the rate began falling in 1996 and is now just above 40 percent for first-time marriages.

The decline has been even more striking among middle- and upper-middle-income couples with college degrees. For them, fewer than one in three marriages is expected to end in divorce, a degree of stability that allows elite couples to merge their resources with confidence, maximally invest in their children and otherwise widen the gap between themselves and the struggling masses.

There are exceptions, of course. Among baby boomers, the rate of marriage failure has surged 50 percent in the past 20 years—perhaps out of an irritable nostalgia, researchers said, for the days of free love, better love, anything but this love. Nor do divorce rates appear to have fallen among those who take the old Samuel Johnson quip as a prescription, allowing hope to triumph over experience, and marrying again and again.

For both Mike and Kristi Burns, now in their 40s, the first marriage came young and left early, and the second stuck around for more than a dozen years.

Kristi was 19, living in South Carolina, and her Marine boyfriend was about to be shipped to Japan. "I wasn't attached to him, really," she said, "but for some reason I felt this might be my only chance at marriage."

In Japan, Kristi gave birth to her son Brandon, realized she was lonely and miserable, and left the marriage seven weeks after their first anniversary. Back in the States, Kristi studied to be a travel agent, moved to Michigan and married her second husband at age 23.

He was an electrician. He adopted Brandon, and the couple had a son, Griffin. The marriage lasted 13 years.

"We were really great friends, but we weren't a great husband and wife," Kristi said. "Our parenting styles were too different."

Besides, she went on, "he didn't verbalize a lot, but he was mad a lot, and I was tired of walking around on eggshells."

After the divorce, friends persuaded her to try the online dating service Match.com, and just as her free trial week was about to expire, she noticed a new profile in the mix.

"Kristi was one of the first people to ping me," said Mike Burns, an engineer for an e-commerce company. "This was at 3 in the morning."

They started chatting. Mike told Kristi how he'd married his first wife while he was still in college—"definitely too young," he said—and divorced her two years later. He met his second wife through mutual friends, they had a big church wedding, started a software publishing company together, sold it and had two children, Brianna and Alec.

When the marriage started going downhill, Mike ignored signs of trouble, like the comments from neighbors who noticed his wife was never around on weekends.

"I was delusional, I was depressed," he said. "I still had the attitude that divorce wasn't something you did."

After 15 years of marriage, his wife did it for him, and kicked him out of the house. His divorce papers hadn't yet been finalized, he told Kristi that first chat night. I'll help you get through it, she replied.

Mike and Kristi admit their own three-year-old marriage isn't perfect. The kids are still adjusting to one another. Sometimes Kristi, a homemaker, feels jealous of how much attention her husband showers on his daughter Brianna, 13.

Sometimes Mike retreats into his computer. Yet they are determined to stay together.

"I know everyone thinks this marriage is a joke and people expect it to fail," said Kristi. "But that just makes me work harder at it."

"I'd say our chances of success are better than average," her husband added.

In America, family is at once about home and the next great frontier.

Critical Thinking

1. Would you say you grew up in a typical American family? What does the typical American family look like today?
2. Consider three ways families are different than they were 50 years ago. Why have these changes occurred? How have they served to change American society in both positive and negative ways?
3. Where do you see the future of the family in America going? What trends and changes in families do you anticipate seeing in the next 50 years?

Create Central

www.mhhe.com/createcentral

Internet References

Kearl's Guide to the Sociology of the Family
www.trinity.edu/MKEARL/family.html

U.S. Census: Families and Living Arrangements
http://www.census.gov/hhes/families

U.S. Department of Health and Human Services: Families
http://www.hhs.gov/children/index.html

World Family Map
http://worldfamilymap.org/2014/about

Article   Prepared by: Patricia Hrusa Williams, *University of Maine at Farmington*

A Million First Dates

How Online Romance Is Threatening Monogamy

DAN SLATER

Learning Outcomes

After reading this article, you will be able to:

- Recognize the positive and negative aspects of online dating.

- Understand how technology and changes in ideas about pre-marital sex, marriage, and commitment are changing dating and relationship formation.

- Describe factors important to relationship commitment.

After going to college on the East Coast and spending a few years bouncing around, Jacob moved back to his native Oregon, settling in Portland. Almost immediately, he was surprised by the difficulty he had meeting women. Having lived in New York and the Boston area, he was accustomed to ready-made social scenes. In Portland, by contrast, most of his friends were in long-term relationships with people they'd met in college, and were contemplating marriage.

Jacob was single for two years and then, at 26, began dating a slightly older woman who soon moved in with him. She seemed independent and low-maintenance, important traits for Jacob. Past girlfriends had complained about his lifestyle, which emphasized watching sports and going to concerts and bars. He'd been called lazy, aimless, and irresponsible with money.

Before long, his new relationship fell into that familiar pattern. "I've never been able to make a girl feel like she was the most important thing in my life," he says. "It's always 'I wish I was as important as the basketball game or the concert.'" An only child, Jacob tended to make plans by negotiation: if his girlfriend would watch the game with him, he'd go hiking with her. He was passive in their arguments, hoping to avoid confrontation. Whatever the flaws in their relationship, he told

himself, being with her was better than being single in Portland again.

After five years, she left.

Now in his early 30s, Jacob felt he had no idea how to make a relationship work. Was compatibility something that could be learned? Would permanence simply happen, or would he have to choose it? Around this time, he signed up for two online dating sites: Match.com, a paid site, because he'd seen the TV ads; and Plenty of Fish, a free site he'd heard about around town.

"It was fairly incredible," Jacob remembers. "I'm an average-looking guy. All of a sudden I was going out with one or two very pretty, ambitious women a week. At first I just thought it was some kind of weird lucky streak."

After six weeks, Jacob met a 22-year-old named Rachel, whose youth and good looks he says reinvigorated him. His friends were jealous. Was this The One? They dated for a few months, and then she moved in. (Both names have been changed for anonymity.)

Rachel didn't mind Jacob's sports addiction, and enjoyed going to concerts with him. But there were other issues. She was from a blue-collar military background; he came from doctors. She placed a high value on things he didn't think much about: a solid credit score, a 40-hour workweek. Jacob also felt pressure from his parents, who were getting anxious to see him paired off for good. Although a younger girlfriend bought him some time, biologically speaking, it also alienated him from his friends, who could understand the physical attraction but couldn't really relate to Rachel.

In the past, Jacob had always been the kind of guy who didn't break up well. His relationships tended to drag on. His desire to be with someone, to not have to go looking again, had always trumped whatever doubts he'd had about the person he was with. But something was different this time. "I feel like I underwent a fairly radical change thanks to online dating,"

Jacob says. "I went from being someone who thought of finding someone as this monumental challenge, to being much more relaxed and confident about it. Rachel was young and beautiful, and I'd found her after signing up on a couple dating sites and dating just a few people." Having met Rachel so easily online, he felt confident that, if he became single again, he could always meet someone else.

After two years, when Rachel informed Jacob that she was moving out, he logged on to Match.com the same day. His old profile was still up. Messages had even come in from people who couldn't tell he was no longer active. The site had improved in the two years he'd been away. It was sleeker, faster, more efficient. And the population of online daters in Portland seemed to have tripled. He'd never imagined that so many single people were out there.

"I'm about 95 percent certain," he says, "that if I'd met Rachel offline, and if I'd never done online dating, I would've married her. At that point in my life, I would've overlooked everything else and done whatever it took to make things work. Did online dating change my perception of permanence? No doubt. When I sensed the breakup coming, I was okay with it. It didn't seem like there was going to be much of a mourning period, where you stare at your wall thinking you're destined to be alone and all that. I was eager to see what else was out there."

The positive aspects of online dating are clear: the Internet makes it easier for single people to meet other single people with whom they might be compatible, raising the bar for what they consider a good relationship. But what if online dating makes it *too* easy to meet someone new? What if it raises the bar for a good relationship *too* high? What if the prospect of finding an ever-more-compatible mate with the click of a mouse means a future of relationship instability, in which we keep chasing the elusive rabbit around the dating track?

Of course, no one knows exactly how many partnerships are undermined by the allure of the Internet dating pool. But most of the online-dating-company executives I interviewed while writing my new book, *Love in the Time of Algorithms,* agreed with what research appears to suggest: the rise of online dating will mean an overall decrease in commitment.

"The future will see better relationships but more divorce," predicts Dan Winchester, the founder of a free dating site based in the U.K. "The older you get as a man, the more experienced you get. You know what to do with women, how to treat them and talk to them. Add to that the effect of online dating." He continued, "I often wonder whether matching you up with great people is getting so efficient, and the process so enjoyable, that marriage will become obsolete."

"Historically," says Greg Blatt, the CEO of Match.com's parent company, "relationships have been billed as 'hard' because, historically, commitment has been the goal. You could say online dating is simply changing people's ideas about whether commitment itself is a life value." Mate scarcity also plays

an important role in people's relationship decisions. "Look, if I lived in Iowa, I'd be married with four children by now," says Blatt, a 40-something bachelor in Manhattan. "That's just how it is."

"As we become more secure in our ability to find someone else . . . the old thinking about commitment will be challenged very harshly."

Another online-dating exec hypothesized an inverse correlation between commitment and the efficiency of technology. "I think divorce rates will increase as life in general becomes more real-time," says Niccolò Formai, the head of social-media marketing at Badoo, a meeting-and-dating app with about 25 million active users worldwide. "Think about the evolution of other kinds of content on the Web—stock quotes, news. The goal has always been to make it faster. The same thing will happen with meeting. It's exhilarating to connect with new people, not to mention beneficial for reasons having nothing to do with romance. You network for a job. You find a flatmate. Over time you'll expect that constant flow. People always said that the need for stability would keep commitment alive. But that thinking was based on a world in which you didn't meet that many people."

"Societal values always lose out," says Noel Biderman, the founder of Ashley Madison, which calls itself "the world's leading married dating service for discreet encounters"— that is, cheating. "Premarital sex used to be taboo," explains Biderman. "So women would become miserable in marriages, because they wouldn't know any better. But today, more people have had failed relationships, recovered, moved on, and found happiness. They realize that that happiness, in many ways, depends on having had the failures. As we become more secure and confident in our ability to find someone else, usually someone better, monogamy and the old thinking about commitment will be challenged very harshly."

Even at eHarmony—one of the most conservative sites, where marriage and commitment seem to be the only acceptable goals of dating—Gian Gonzaga, the site's relationship psychologist, acknowledges that commitment is at odds with technology. "You could say online dating allows people to get into relationships, learn things, and ultimately make a better selection," says Gonzaga. "But you could also easily see a world in which online dating leads to people leaving relationships the moment they're not working—an overall weakening of commitment."

Indeed, the profit models of many online-dating sites are at cross-purposes with clients who are trying to develop long-term commitments. A permanently paired-off dater, after all, means a lost revenue stream. Explaining the mentality of a typical dating-site executive, Justin Parfitt, a dating entrepreneur based in San Francisco, puts the matter bluntly: "They're thinking, *Let's keep this fucker coming back to the site as often as we can.*" For instance, long after their accounts become inactive on Match.com and some other sites, lapsed users receive notifications informing them that wonderful people are browsing their profiles and are eager to chat. "Most of our users are return customers," says Match.com's Blatt.

In 2011, Mark Brooks, a consultant to online-dating companies, published the results of an industry survey titled "How Has Internet Dating Changed Society?" The survey responses, from 39 executives, produced the following conclusions:

"Internet dating has made people more disposable."

"Internet dating may be partly responsible for a rise in the divorce rates."

"Low quality, unhappy and unsatisfying marriages are being destroyed as people drift to Internet dating sites."

"The market is hugely more efficient. . . . People expect to—and this will be increasingly the case over time—access people anywhere, anytime, based on complex search requests. . . . Such a feeling of access affects our pursuit of love . . . the whole world (versus, say, the city we live in) will, increasingly, feel like the market for our partner(s). Our pickiness will probably increase."

"Above all, Internet dating has helped people of all ages realize that there's no need to settle for a mediocre relationship."

Alex Mehr, a co-founder of the dating site Zoosk, is the only executive I interviewed who disagrees with the prevailing view. "Online dating does nothing more than remove a barrier to meeting," says Mehr. "Online dating doesn't change my taste, or how I behave on a first date, or whether I'm going to be a good partner. It only changes the process of discovery. As for whether you're the type of person who wants to commit to a long-term monogamous relationship or the type of person who wants to play the field, online dating has nothing to do with that. That's a personality thing."

Surely personality will play a role in the way anyone behaves in the realm of online dating, particularly when it comes to commitment and promiscuity. (Gender, too, may play a role. Researchers are divided on the question of whether men pursue more "short-term mates" than women do.) At the same time, however, the reality that having too many options makes us less content with whatever option we choose is a well-documented phenomenon. In his 2004 book, *The Paradox of Choice,* the psychologist Barry Schwartz indicts a society that "sanctifies freedom of choice so profoundly that the benefits of infinite options seem self-evident." On the contrary, he argues, "a large array of options may diminish the attractiveness of what people *actually* choose, the reason being that thinking about the attractions of some of the unchosen options detracts from the pleasure derived from the chosen one."

Psychologists who study relationships say that three ingredients generally determine the strength of commitment: overall satisfaction with the relationship; the investment one has put into it (time and effort, shared experiences and emotions, etc.); and the quality of perceived alternatives. Two of the three—satisfaction and quality of alternatives—could be directly affected by the larger mating pool that the Internet offers.

At the selection stage, researchers have seen that as the range of options grows larger, mate-seekers are liable to become "cognitively overwhelmed," and deal with the overload by adopting lazy comparison strategies and examining fewer cues. As a result, they are more likely to make careless decisions than they would be if they had fewer options, and this potentially leads to less compatible matches. Moreover, the mere fact of having chosen someone from such a large set of options can lead to doubts about whether the choice was the "right" one. No studies in the romantic sphere have looked at precisely how the range of choices affects overall satisfaction. But research elsewhere has found that people are less satisfied when choosing from a larger group: in one study, for example, subjects who selected a chocolate from an array of six options believed it tasted better than those who selected the same chocolate from an array of 30.

On that other determinant of commitment, the quality of perceived alternatives, the Internet's potential effect is clearer still. Online dating is, at its core, a litany of alternatives. And evidence shows that the perception that one has appealing alternatives to a current romantic partner is a strong predictor of low commitment to that partner.

"You can say three things," says Eli Finkel, a professor of social psychology at Northwestern University who studies how online dating affects relationships. "First, the best marriages are probably unaffected. Happy couples won't be hanging out on dating sites. Second, people who are in marriages that are either bad or average might be at increased risk of divorce, because of increased access to new partners. Third, it's unknown whether that's good or bad for society. On one hand, it's good if fewer people feel like they're stuck in relationships. On the other, evidence is pretty solid that having a stable romantic partner means all kinds of health and wellness benefits." And that's even before one takes into account the ancillary effects of such a decrease in commitment—on children, for example, or even society more broadly.

Gilbert Feibleman, a divorce attorney and member of the American Academy of Matrimonial Lawyers, argues that the phenomenon extends beyond dating sites to the Internet more generally. "I've seen a dramatic increase in cases where something on the computer triggered the breakup," he says. "People are more likely to leave relationships, because they're emboldened by the knowledge that it's no longer as hard as it was to meet new people. But whether it's dating sites, social media, e-mail—it's all related to the fact that the Internet has made it possible for people to communicate and connect, anywhere in the world, in ways that have never before been seen."

Since Rachel left him, Jacob has met lots of women online. Some like going to basketball games and concerts with him. Others enjoy barhopping. Jacob's favorite football team is the Green Bay Packers, and when I last spoke to him, he told me he'd had success using Packers fandom as a search criterion on OkCupid, another (free) dating site he's been trying out.

Many of Jacob's relationships become physical very early. At one point he's seeing a paralegal and a lawyer who work at the same law firm, a naturopath, a pharmacist, and a chef. He slept with three of them on the first or second date. His relationships with the other two are headed toward physical intimacy.

He likes the pharmacist most. She's a girlfriend prospect. The problem is that she wants to take things slow on the physical side. He worries that, with so many alternatives available, he won't be willing to wait.

One night the paralegal confides in him: her prior relationships haven't gone well, but Jacob gives her hope; all she needs in a relationship is honesty. And he thinks, *Oh my God.* He wants to be a nice guy, but he knows that sooner or later he's going to start coming across as a serious asshole. While out with one woman, he has to silence text messages coming in from others. He needs to start paring down the number of women he's seeing.

People seeking commitment—particularly women—have developed strategies to detect deception and guard against it. A woman might withhold sex so she can assess a man's intentions. Theoretically, her withholding sends a message: *I'm not just going to sleep with any guy that comes along.* Theoretically, his willingness to wait sends a message back: *I'm interested in more than sex.*

But the pace of technology is upending these rules and assumptions. Relationships that begin online, Jacob finds, move quickly. He chalks this up to a few things. First, familiarity is established during the messaging process, which also often involves a phone call. By the time two people meet face-to-face, they already have a level of intimacy. Second, if the woman is on a dating site, there's a good chance she's eager to connect. But for Jacob, the most crucial difference between online dating and meeting people in the "real" world is the sense of urgency. Occasionally, he has an acquaintance in common with a woman he meets online, but by and large she comes from a different social pool. "It's not like we're just going to run into each other again," he says. "So you can't afford to be too casual. It's either 'Let's explore this' or 'See you later.'"

> ## "The Internet has made it possible for people to communicate and connect . . . in ways that have never before been seen."

Social scientists say that all sexual strategies carry costs, whether risk to reputation (promiscuity) or foreclosed alternatives (commitment). As online dating becomes increasingly pervasive, the old costs of a short-term mating strategy will give way to new ones. Jacob, for instance, notices he's seeing his friends less often. Their wives get tired of befriending his

latest girlfriend only to see her go when he moves on to someone else. Also, Jacob has noticed that, over time, he feels less excitement before each new date. "Is that about getting older," he muses, "or about dating online?" How much of the enchantment associated with romantic love has to do with scarcity (*this person is exclusively for me*), and how will that enchantment hold up in a marketplace of abundance (*this person could be exclusively for me, but so could the other two people I'm meeting this week*)?

Using OkCupid's Locals app, Jacob can now advertise his location and desired activity and meet women on the fly. Out alone for a beer one night, he responds to the broadcast of a woman who's at the bar across the street, looking for a karaoke partner. He joins her. They spend the evening together, and never speak again.

"Each relationship is its own little education," Jacob says. "You learn more about what works and what doesn't, what you really need and what you can go without. That feels like a useful process. I'm not jumping into something with the wrong person, or committing to something too early, as I've done in the past." But he does wonder: When does it end? At what point does this learning curve become an excuse for not putting in the effort to make a relationship last? "Maybe I have the confidence now to go after the person I really want," he says. "But I'm worried that I'm making it so I can't fall in love."

Critical Thinking

1. What are some advantages and disadvantages of online dating to relationship formation?

2. This article suggests that online dating is contributing to less commitment among singles and higher divorce rates. Do you agree or disagree? Why?

3. List factors important to relationship commitment. Describe how online dating may serve to strengthen or weaken commitment in relationships.

4. How do you see technology changing dating, mate selection, and relationship formation in the future?

Create Central

www.mhhe.com/createcentral

Internet References

Helpguide: How to Find Lasting Love
http://www.helpguide.org/mental/how_to_dating_find_love.htm

Love Is Respect
www.loveisrespect.org

Relationships Australia
www.relationships.org.au

Article

Prepared by: Patricia Hrusa Williams, *University of Maine at Farmington*

Family Diversity Is the New Normal for America's Children

A Briefing Paper Prepared for the Council on Contemporary Families

PHILIP COHEN

Learning Outcomes

After reading this article, you will be able to:

- Identify demographic changes in families in the past 50 years.

- Analyze how societal, political, technological, and cultural changes are contributing to changes in the demographic characteristics of families in the United States.

People often think of social change in the lives of American children since the 1950s as a movement in one direction—from children being raised in married, male-breadwinner families to a new norm of children being raised by working mothers, many of them unmarried. Instead, we can better understand this transformation as an explosion of diversity, a fanning out from a compact center along many different pathways.

The Dramatic Rearrangement of Children's Living Situations Since the 1950s

At the end of the 1950s, if you chose 100 children under age 15 to represent all children, 65 would have been living in a family with married parents, with the father employed and the mother

out of the labor force. Only 18 would have had married parents who were both employed. As for other types of family arrangements, you would find only one child in every 350 living with a never-married mother!

Today, among 100 representative children, just 22 live in a married male-breadwinner family, compared to 23 living with a single mother (only half of whom have ever been married). Seven out of every 100 live with a parent who cohabits with an unmarried partner (a category too rare for the Census Bureau to consider counting in 1960) and six with either a single father (3) or with grandparents but no parents (3). The single largest group of children—34—live with dual-earner married parents, but that largest group is only a third of the total, so that it is really impossible to point to a "typical" family.

With two-thirds of children being raised in male-breadwinner, married-couple families, it is understandable that people from the early 1960s considered such families to be the norm.[i] Today, by contrast, there is no single family arrangement that encompasses the majority of children.

To represent this diversity simply, we can calculate the chance that two children live in the same work-family structure. In 1960 you would have had an 80 percent chance that two children, selected at random, would share the same situation. By 2012, that chance had fallen to just a little more than 50–50.

The diversity masks an additional layer of differences, which come from the expanding variety of pathways in and

---

[i] Interestingly, the dominance of the male-breadwinner nuclear family was not always as great as it was at mid-century. As historian Stephanie Coontz has shown, up until the 1920s, most households contained more than one wage earner—mothers working on the family farm or business, and/or children working for pay as well.

out of these arrangements, or transitions from one to another. For example, among the children living with cohabiting parents in 2012, the resident parent is divorced or separated in about a third of cases. In those cases, the cohabiting-parent family often is a blended family with complex relationships to adults and children outside the household. Many more parents have (or raise) children with more than one partner over their lives than in the past, and many more children cycle through several *different* family arrangements as they grow up.

The children in America's classrooms today come from so many distinct family arrangements that we can no longer assume they share the same experiences and have the same needs. Likewise, policy-makers can no longer design family programs and regulations for a narrow range of family types and assume that they will pretty much meet the needs of all children.

The Decline of Married Couples as the Dominant Household Arrangement

The diversification of family life over time is also shown in the changing proportions of all household types, including ones without children. I put each household into one of five types, using Census data from 1880 to 2010. The largest category is households composed of married couples living with no one except their own children. If there was any other relative living in a household, I counted it as an extended household. The third category is individuals who live alone. Fourth are single parents (most of them mothers) living with no one besides their own children. In the final category are households made up of people who are not related (including unmarried couples).

The married-couple family peaked between 1950 and 1960, when this arrangement characterized two-thirds of households. This was also the peak of the nuclear family, because up until the 1940s, extended families were much more common than they became in the 1950s and 1960s. After that era, the pattern fans out.

By 2010, the proportion of married-couple households had dropped to less than half (45 percent) of the total. The proportion of individuals living alone rose from 13 to 27 percent between 1960 and 2010, and single-parent households rose from 6 to 12 percent. The result is that households composed of lone individuals and single parents accounted for almost 40 percent of all households by 2010. Extended households are less common than they were a century ago, mostly as a result of the greater independence of older people, but their numbers have increased again in the last several decades. In sum, the dominant married-couple household of the first half of the twentieth century was replaced not by a new standard, but rather by a general increase in family diversity.

How Did We Get Here? Market Forces, Social Welfare Reform, and Family Rearrangements

As the market economy generated new products and services that can supplement or substitute for many of the core functional tasks that families had to perform in the past, people became more able to rearrange their family lives. For example, technological innovations made women's traditional household tasks, such as shopping, preserving food, house-cleaning, and making clothes, far less time-consuming, while better birth control technology allowed them to control the timing or number of their births. After 1960, employment rates for both married and unmarried women rocketed upward in a 30-year burst that would finally move women's work primarily from the home to the market.

The shift to market work reinforced women's independence within their families, but also, in many cases, *from* their families. Women freed from family dependence could live singly, even with children; they could afford to risk divorce; and they could live with a man without the commitment of marriage.

In the aftermath of the Depression and World War II, social reformers increased their efforts to provide a social safety net for the elderly, the poor, and the disabled. The combination of pension and welfare programs that resulted also offered opportunities for more people to structure their lives independently.

For older Americans, Social Security benefits were critical. They helped reduce the effective poverty rates of older people from almost 60 percent in the 1960s to 15 percent by 2010, freeing millions of Americans from the need to live with their children in old age. At the beginning of the twentieth century, the Census counted only 1 in 10 people age 55 or older living with no relative. By the end of the century, the proportion was more than 1 in 4. Most of that change occurred between 1940 and 1980.

For younger adults, the combination of expanding work opportunities for women and greater welfare support for children made marriage less of a necessity. In the 1960s and 1970s, Aid to Families with Dependent Children grew rapidly, eventually supporting millions of never-married mothers and their children. Welfare did not create single-mothers—whose numbers rose partly in response to poverty, economic insecurity, and rising incarceration rates, and have continued to rise even after large cutbacks in public assistance—and it always carried a shameful stigma while providing a minimal level of monetary support. But it nevertheless allowed poor women to more easily leave abusive or dangerous relationships.

Market forces were most important in increasing the ability of middle-class and more highly educated women to delay, forego, or leave marriage. Poor women, especially African-American women, had long been more likely to work for pay, but their lower earnings did not offer the same personal independence that those with better jobs enjoyed, so welfare support was a bigger factor in the growing ability of poor women to live on their own. Nevertheless, the market has contributed to the growth of single mother families in a different way over the past 40 years, as falling real wages and increasing job insecurity for less-educated men have made them more risky as potential marriage partners.

As a result of these and other social trends such as women's increasing educational attainment, diversity of family arrangements increased dramatically after the 1950s.

Changes in Women's Work-Family Situations

The work-family situations of both women and children show the same pattern of increasing diversity replacing the dominant-category system that peaked in the 1950s. For women aged 30–34, the rise in education and employment is most dramatic, while marriage and motherhood have become markedly less universal.

Rather than simply see each of these as separate trends, we can create profiles by combining the four characteristics (educational, employment, marital, and parental status) into 16 different categories—employed college graduates who are married mothers on one extreme; non-employed non-graduates who aren't married or mothers on the other. Data indicates there has been a decline in a single profile—the married, non-college educated, not-employed, mother—and the diversity in statuses that have replaced that single type. In 1960, almost 80 percent of women in their early 30s and had not completed college and were married with children. Now such women comprise less than a third of the total—and no category includes more than 18 percent of women. In terms of diversity, in 1960 the chance that two women picked at random would be from from the same category was 40 percent. Today that chance has fallen to 11 percent.

Diversity and Inequality

Some of the new diversity in work-family arrangements is a result of new options for individuals, especially women and older people, whose lives are less constrained than they once were. But some of the new diversity also results from economic changes that are less positive, especially the job loss and wage declines for younger, less-educated men since the late 1970s.

In and of itself, however, family diversity doesn't have to lead to inequality. In the Nordic countries of Finland, Norway and Denmark, for example, unmarried-mother families have poverty rates that barely differ from those of married-couple families—all have poverty rates less than 10 percent. Similarly, many countries do a better job of minimizing the school achievement gap between children of single mothers versus children of married parents—a study of 11 wealthy countries found the gap is largest in the United States.

Different families have different child-rearing challenges and needs, which means we are no longer well-served by policies that assume most children will be raised by married-couple families, especially ones where the mother stays home throughout the children's early years. As we debate social and economic policy, we need to consider the needs of children in many different family situations, and how they will be affected by policy changes, rather than privileging one particular family structure or arrangement.

Critical Thinking

1. The author states that diversity in families is the new normal. What does he mean by this? Do you agree with him and why?

2. Of the statistics presented on children and families in the article, identify the one that surprised you the most. Why?

3. Why are these changes occurring in the family in our society? What do you see as the biggest change in families which will occur in the next 50 years? Will there be a "typical" family? Why/why not?

Internet References

Administration for Children and Families
www.acf.hhs.gov
Child Trends
www.childtrends.org
U.S. Census Bureau
www.census.gov

For further information, contact Professor Cohen at pnc@umd.edu; (301) 405-6414. Most of data can be found in Professor Cohen's new book, The Family: Diversity, Inequality, and Social Change, available now from W.W. Norton: http://books.wwnorton.com/books/978-0-393-93395-6/.

Article   Prepared by: Patricia Hrusa Williams, *University of Maine at Farmington*

What Kids Learn from Hearing Family Stories

ELAINE REESE

Learning Outcomes

After reading this article, you will be able to:

- Define what a personal narrative is.

- Recognize reasons why some parents may not read to their children.

- Identify the benefits of telling family stories and personal narratives to children.

"Dad, tell me a story from when you were little. Tell me the story about the time you met your best friend Chris at school." Six-year-old Alex, who has just started school himself, snuggles into his pillow and catches his dad's hand in the dark. They have finished the nightly reading of *Tin Tin* and now it's time for "just one more story" before Alex goes to sleep.

Most parents know about the benefits of reading stories from books with their young children. Parents are blasted with this message in pediatricians' offices, at preschool, on TV, even with billboards on the city bus. Reading books with children on a daily basis advances their language skills, extends their learning about the world, and helps their own reading later in school. Reading with your child from a young age can instill a lifelong love of books. A new study published in *Science* even shows that reading literary fiction improves adults' ability to understand other people's emotions.

Reading books with your children is clearly a good idea.

The cozy image of cuddling up with your young child while poring over a book, however, doesn't fit with reality for some parents and children. Parents from some cultures are not as comfortable reading with their children because books were not part of their everyday lives growing up. For other parents,

reading with children is a fraught activity because of their own negative experiences learning to read. And for some highly active children, sitting down with a book is a punishment, not a reward. Fortunately, parents can learn new ways of reading books with their children to engage even the most irascible customer—and to engage themselves.

Yet what most parents don't know is that everyday family stories, like the one that Alex's dad spun out that night, confer many of the same benefits of reading—and even some new ones.

Over the last 25 years, a small canon of research on family storytelling shows that when parents share more family stories with their children—especially when they tell those stories in a detailed and responsive way—their children benefit in a host of ways. For instance, experimental studies show that when parents learn to reminisce about everyday events with their preschool children in more detailed ways, their children tell richer, more complete narratives to other adults one to two years later compared to children whose parents didn't learn the new reminiscing techniques. Children of the parents who learned new ways to reminisce also demonstrate better understanding of other people's thoughts and emotions. These advanced narrative and emotional skills serve children well in the school years when reading complex material and learning to get along with others. In the preteen years, children whose families collaboratively discuss everyday events and family history more often have higher self-esteem and stronger self-concepts. And adolescents with a stronger knowledge of family history have more robust identities, better coping skills, and lower rates of depression and anxiety. Family storytelling can help a child grow into a teen who feels connected to the important people in her life.

Best of all, unlike stories from books, family stories are always free and completely portable. You don't even need to have the lights on to share with your child a story about your day, about their day, about your childhood or their grandma's. In the research on family storytelling, all of these kinds of stories are linked to benefits for your child. Family stories can continue to be part of a parent's daily interactions with their children into adolescence, long past the age of the bedtime story.

All families have stories to tell, regardless of their culture or their circumstances. Of course, not all of these stories are idyllic ones. Research shows that children and adolescents can learn a great deal from stories of life's more difficult moments—as long as those stories are told in a way that is sensitive to the child's level of understanding, and as long as something good is gleaned from the experience.

Telling the story about the time the Christmas tree ignited because of faulty wiring and burned up the presents is fine, as long as you can find a tinsel lining. For example: Luckily you were able to save some favorite ornaments from the blaze, and your family ended up at a soup kitchen for Christmas dinner where you met Marion, who would become a treasured family friend.

Books contain narratives, but only family stories contain your family's *personal* narratives. Fortunate children get both. They hear and read stories from books to become part of other people's worlds, and they hear and tell stories of their family to understand who they are and from whence they came.

As Ursula LeGuin said, "There have been great societies that did not use the wheel, but there have been no societies that did not tell stories." Oral storytelling has been part of human existence for millennia. Toddlers start telling primitive stories from nearly as soon as they can speak, beginning with simple sentences about past experiences such as "Cookie allgone." Adults quickly build on these baby stories, "What happened to your cookie? You ate it!" so that by age three or four, most children can tell a relatively sensible story of a past experience that a naïve listener will (mostly) understand. By the time they are in school, children will regale a sympathetic adult with highly detailed stories about events of great importance to them, such as scoring a goal at a soccer game, but they may fail to mention the bigger picture that their team still lost. In the preteen and early adolescent years, children tell highly proficient stories about events in their lives, but they still need help understanding difficult events, such as the time their best friend dumped

them for someone else. It is not until mid-adolescence that teens can understand the impact of events on their lives and on who they are becoming. Even older adolescents still benefit from their parents' help in understanding life's curveballs.

The holidays are prime time for family storytelling. When you're putting up the tree or having your holiday meal, share a story with your children about past holidays. Leave in the funny bits, the sad bits, the gory and smelly bits—kids can tell when a story has been sanitized for their protection. Then invite everyone else to tell a story too. Don't forget the youngest and the oldest storytellers in the group. Their stories may not be as coherent, but they can be the truest, and the most revealing.

Family stories can be told nearly anywhere. They cost us only our time, our memories, our creativity. They can inspire us, protect us, and bind us to others. So be generous with your stories, and be generous *in* your stories. Remember that your children may have them for a lifetime.

Critical Thinking

1. How is the experience of hearing family stories different from the experience of being read books by parents?

2. What are some of the benefits for children of hearing family stories?

3. What is a favorite family story you remember being told as a child? How and why is the story important to you, even now?

Create Central

www.mhhe.com/createcentral

Internet References

Family Narratives Lab, Emory University
   http://www.psychology.emory.edu/cognition/fivush/lab/
   FivushLabWebsite/index.html

Family History and Genealogy
   http://www.usa.gov/Citizen/Topics/History-Family.shtml

Storytelling for Parents
   http://storytellingforparents.com

Article   Prepared by: Patricia Hrusa Williams, *University of Maine at Farmington*

Family Strengths and Resilience:

Insights from a National Study

The Search Institute conducted a study of family assets by surveying parents and adolescents on family strengths and challenges. Remarkably, family strengths, particularly relational factors, are powerfully related to the ability to surmount adversity.

EUGENE C. ROEHLKEPARTAIN AND AMY K. SYVERTSEN

Learning Outcomes

After reading this article, you will be able to:

- Define resilience.
- Explain the Search Institute's Framework of Family Strengths.
- Identify the major findings from the American Family Assets Study.

We often have opportunities to talk with practitioners in education, youth development, family services, and other fields about today's families. When asked about their own families, they will most often admit their quirks and challenges—but they generally express great appreciation for their families and how they add meaning, purpose, and joy to their lives. In contrast, when asked about the families they serve or the families of the young people they seek to teach or engage, they often share quite a different story. There is general consternation with the perceived state of today's families and a defeatist attitude about the chances that they can effectively engage and work with families in ways that improve the well-being of the family, its children, and the broader community. Emerging research is stimulating new understanding about the strengths of families. These strengths emphasize relationships and practices of family life that are malleable and may represent untapped leverage points for engaging with families.

Study Methodology

The American Family Assets Study (Syvertsen, Roehlkepartain, & Scales, 2012) focused on families with young adolescents (a critical period of transitions in family relationships), surveying one parenting adult and one young person (age 10 to 15) in about 1,500 families nationwide. The survey was developed based on a review of the research on family processes, strengths, resilience, interviews and focus groups with youth and parents, and input from a national advisory board. Data were collected online in collaboration with Harris Interactive. Quotas were set to ensure the socioeconomic and cultural diversity of families and the final dataset was weighted to reflect the U.S. Census.

Search Institute's Framework of Family Strengths

Through the years, qualitative researchers have identified more than 80 different strengths that are valued in families around the world (e.g., DeFrain & Asay, 2007). This new study from Search Institute focused on 21 strengths that are relevant to diverse families, widely valued, and measurable through online quantitative surveys. The family strengths we identified (shown in detail in Table 1) are organized in five categories:

- **Nurturing Relationships**—Healthy relationships begin and grow as we show each other we care about what each has to say, how we feel, and our interests.
- **Establishing Routines**—Shared routines, traditions, and activities give a dependable rhythm to family life and help to imbue it with meaning.

Table 1 Search Institute's Framework of Family Strengths

Search Institute has identified 21 research-based family strengths that directly relate to positive outcomes for parenting adults and youth. The percentages indicate how many families experience each asset, based on a study of 1,511 diverse families including at least one parenting adult and one child between the ages of 10 and 15 from across the United States.

Nurturing Relationships
1. *Positive Communication*—Family members listen attentively and speak in respectful ways. — 56%
2. *Affection*—Family members regularly show warmth to each other. — 71%
3. *Emotional Openness*—Family members can be themselves and are comfortable sharing their feelings. — 54%
4. *Support for Sparks*—Family members encourage each other in pursuing their talents and interests. — 64%

Establishing Routines
5. *Family Meals*—Family members eat meals together most days in a typical week. — 58%
6. *Shared Activities*—Family members regularly spend time doing everyday activities together. — 41%
7. *Meaningful Traditions*—Holidays, rituals, and celebrations are part of family life. — 51%
8. *Dependability*—Family members know what to expect from one another. — 27%

Maintaining Expectations
9. *Openness about Tough Topics*—Family members openly discuss sensitive issues, such as sex and substance use. — 60%
10. *Fair Rules*—Family rules and consequences are reasonable. — 44%
11. *Defined Boundaries*—The family sets limits on what young people can do and how they spend their time. — 28%
12. *Clear Expectations*—The family openly articulates its expectations for young people. — 84%
13. *Contributions to Family*—Family members help meet each other's needs and share in getting things done. — 57%

Adapting to Challenge
14. *Management of Daily Commitments*—Family members effectively navigate competing activities and expectations at home, school, and work. — 41%
15. *Adaptability*—The family adapts well when faced with changes. — 28%
16. *Problem Solving*—Family members work together to solve problems and deal with challenges. — 33%
17. *Democratic Decision Making*—Family members have a say in decisions that affect the family. — 53%

Connecting to Community
18. Neighborhood Cohesion—Neighbors look out for one another. — 33%
19. *Relationships with Others*—Family members feel close to teachers, coaches, and others in the community. — 22%
20. *Enriching Activities*—Family members participate in programs and activities that deepen their lives. — 56%
21. *Supportive Resources*—Family members have people and places in the community they can turn to for help. — 45%

Note. Cut-off criterions were selected to best reflect the ideal we strive for in family well-being. The exact cut-off point for each family strength was determined based on a literature review and previous Search Institute research. In general, individuals scoring 75% or higher on a family strength—measured using a Likert-type scale—were considered to have satisfied the criterion for each strength.

- **Maintaining Expectations**—Each person participates in and contributes to family life. Shared expectations require talking about tough topics.
- **Adapting to Challenge**—Every family faces difficulties, large and small. The ways families adapt to those changes together helps them through adversity.
- **Connecting to Community**—Community connections, relationships, and participation sustain, shape, and enrich how families live their lives together.

A Portrait of Families with Young Adolescents

How are families with young adolescents doing? We created a composite Family Assets Index, ranges from 0 to 100. On average, U.S. families scored 47 out of 100. Dividing families into quartiles produced this distribution:

- Struggling [Index Score: 0 to 25] 17 percent
- Challenged [Index Score: 26 to 50] 39 percent

- Adequate [Index Score: 51 to 75] 34 percent
- Thriving [Index Score: 76 to 100] 11 percent

What is surprising to many who have seen the data is that the overall level of family strengths *does not differ significantly* by parent education, single-parent versus two-parent families, immigration status, parents' sexual orientation, or household income. At the same time, there are slight differences by race-ethnicity and different types of communities. However, the study's major conclusion is that there are *more similarities than differences in overall family strengths across demographic groups.* This reinforces the message that all types of families have strengths to tap and challenges to overcome.

Why Family Strengths Matter

Most of the family strengths identified in this research are common sense. This study, though, begins to show the relationship between these everyday strengths and key aspects of well-being for both youth and families. The more of these strengths youth and parents experience, the better off they are in many areas of life.[I] These general patterns are illustrated with the measures shown in Table 2. We found the following:

- Young people in families with more strengths are more engaged in school, take better care of their health, express positive values, and develop the social competencies they need to thrive.
- When parents experience these strengths in their families, they also take better care of their physical and mental health and they contribute more to their communities.

A key finding is that the levels of family strengths generally have a much stronger relationship to positive outcomes than many "fixed" or demographic factors, such as family structure, socioeconomic status, and race-ethnicity. For example, depending on the measure of well-being in question, family strengths account for between 20 and 30 percent of the variance in youth well-being, compared to less than 10 percent of the variance that can be attributed to 10 different demographic measures for the family and the youth (Roehlkepartain, 2013). That is

Table 2   Percent of Youth and Parenting Adults Who Maintain Good Health and Exhibit Positive Behaviors and Values, by Levels of Family Strengths

a. Youth

	Level of Family Strengths			
	Struggling	**Challenged**	**Adequate**	**Thriving**
Health Behavior Index[a]	39	48	75	79
Depression[b]	83	76	72	54
Regulates Emotions and Behaviors[c]	31	43	60	76
Responsible[c]	37	58	71	85
Civically Engaged[c]	24	38	62	86
Socially Responsible[c]	47	63	81	92

b. Parenting Adults

	Level of Family Strengths			
	Struggling	**Challenged**	**Adequate**	**Thriving**
Health Behavior Index[a]	22	32	52	68
Depression[b]	71	69	55	25
Stressed as a Parent[c]	17	13	12	1
Politically Engaged[c]	5	14	27	35
Family Serves Community[d]	43	54	70	88
Satisfied with Life[c]	72	87	94	99

Notes. [a] Percent who engage in a range of healthy behaviors 4–5 days in the average week.
[b]Percent who reported feeling sad or depressed once in a while or more often in the past month.
[c]Percent who averaged 75% or higher on a measure.
[d]Percent of families who spend time together helping other people 1–2 times in the typical month.

[I] Because this is a cross-sectional and correlational study, we cannot establish causality.

good news, because we have the power to build these strengths, which are malleable even if circumstances do not change.

Family Strengths in the Face of Adversity

Family resilience involves the capacity to withstand adversity and overcome challenges. To examine resilience, we focused our analysis on a subset of 207 families (about 1 percent of the sample) that reported the highest levels of family stress based on a new measure of 13 different challenges such as the death of a parent, a separation or divorce in the family, having an accident, being unemployed, being the victim of crime, dealing with substance abuse in the family, or imprisonment of a family member (Roehlkepartain, 2013). We then calculated the odds that the young people would experience high levels of well-being based on whether they were in families with high or low levels of family strengths. Simply, do family strengths offset the potential negative effects of stresses on family life so youth become more resilient in the face of adversity?

What we found is that the odds of youth from highstressed families achieving the high level of six measures of well-being are significantly greater if they experience high levels of family strengths when compared to their peers in high-risk families that do not experience high levels of family strengths. Thus, for example, youth in high-stressed families who experienced high levels of family strengths were compared with those experiencing low levels of strengths. Those with family strengths were nine times more likely to exhibit personal responsibility, seven times more likely to show self-regulation and school engagement, and five times more likely to show caring behavior.

These findings provide important, if preliminary, evidence of the role of family strengths in young people's resilience in the face of challenges. Family relationships, processes, and practices may contribute to well-being for young people whose families face sustained challenges (Walsh, 2006). One does not have to have a perfect, challenge-free life in order to flourish, and many families facing adversity have the capacities needed to survive, regenerate, and do well.

Strategies for Enhancing Family Strengths

Search Institute is seeking opportunities to explore the impact of this study on families in greater depth with partners in communities and organizations, recognizing that the research only points the way toward innovation, which requires ongoing dialogue, experimentation, and refinement over time to discover what really works. In the meantime, here are some initial thoughts on the opportunities this research presents.

Emphasize relationships more than structure. Research, rhetoric, policy, and practice have often focused on the structure and form of families while deemphasizing the relational, affective dimensions of family life. This evidence emphasizes *relational mechanisms* as foundational, often underdeveloped, pathways for positive growth.

In contrast to the dominant evidence-based programs, Li and Julian (2012) propose designing interventions in which building and strengthening developmental relationships—"the active ingredient upon which the effectiveness of other program elements depend" (p. 163)—is a primary focus. Thus, "in program design, the focal question ought to be 'How does a (practice, program, system, or policy) help to strengthen relationships in the developmental setting?'" (p. 163).

Recognize both strengths and challenges. Too often, research on families has been framed in terms of their risks or vulnerabilities. Without denying the challenges families face, a shift to understanding strengths can increase the self-efficacy in families, highlighting the potential of resilience in the face of adversity. This shift in emphasis has tremendous implications for how programs are designed, how professionals are equipped, and how funding and policies are shaped to strengthen rather than label or shame families because of their risks.

Start with families' priorities, passions, and capacities. Too often work with families focuses on how to transfer expertise and knowledge to them. Whereas parent education and family support have historically been expert-driven (Thomas & Lien, 2009), recent years have seen a shift toward parentcentered, empowerment-oriented strategies that emphasize "the role of parents as members of communities and the larger world" (Doherty, Jacob, & Cutting, 2009, p. 303). The professional task shifts from the expert holder of knowledge to facilitating democracy and shared action. Perhaps it is time to shift our focus from engagement as "family support" toward engagement as "family citizenship." This not only benefits the community, but also strengthens families' self-efficacy, their ties in the community, and, as a result, their resilience.

Tapping the Power of Families

There is agreement on the importance of engaging families but this can be an exasperating process, particularly beyond early childhood. None of the strategies to reach, engage, and support parenting adults and families seem to work. Families just do not show up. Thus, family engagement efforts become trivialized. So we have a lot of work to do and innovation to try to break through. Despite entrenched, sometimes generational challenges and the lack of clear approaches, it is critical to the wellbeing of society to find ways to strengthen families. We also must recognize and celebrate the strengths that are present, the qualities that make us smile about our own families, and those that would make us smile if we knew other families better, too.

References

DeFrain, J., & Asay, S. M. (Eds.). (2007). *Strong families around the world: Strengths-based research and perspectives.* New York, NY: Haworth Press.

Doherty, W. J., Jacob, J., & Cutting, B. (2009). Community engaged parent education: Strengthening civic engagement among parents and parent educators. *Family Relations,* 58(3), 303–315. doi:Io.IIII/j.I74I3729.2009.00554.x

Li, J., & Julian, M. M. (2012). Developmental relationships as the active ingredient: A unifying working hypothesis of "what works" across intervention settings. *American Journal of Orthopsychiatry,* 82(2), 157–166. doi:Io.IIII/j.I939-0025.20I2.0II5I.x

Roehlkepartain, E. C. (2013). *Families and communities together: Strength and resilience during early adolescence* (Doctoral dissertation). University of Minnesota, Minneapolis, MN.

Syvertsen, A. K., Roehlkepartain, E. C., & Scales, P. C. (2012). *The American family assets study.* Minneapolis, MN: Search Institute. Retrieved from www.search-institute.org/research/family-strengths

Thomas, R., &Lien,L. (2009). Family education perspectives: Implications for family educators' professional practice and research. *Family & Consumer Sciences Research Journal,* 38(1), 36–55- doi:Io.IIII/j.I552-3934.2009.00004.x

Walsh, F. (2006). *Strengthening family resilience* (2nd ed.). New York, NY: Guilford.

Critical Thinking

1. Looking at the results of the study, what are the top three family strengths identified in the study? What are the bottom three areas identified?

2. How do the authors define resilience? Do you agree or disagree with their definition and why?

3. For families experiencing high stress, which family assets or strengths were most important in helping youth be successful? How can we work to build these skills or strengths through policies and programs in our own community?

Internet References

National Clearinghouse on Families and Youth, Family and Youth Services Bureau
www.ncfy.acf.hhs.gov

Reclaiming Child and Youth Journal
www.reclaimingjournal.com

Search Institute
www.search-institute.org

EUGENE C. ROEHLKEPARTAIN, PhD is vice president of research and development for Search Institute, Minneapolis, Minnesota, where he served in leadership since 1991. Contact him by e-mail at gener@search-institute.org **AMY K. SYVERTSEN, PhD** is a research scientist at Search Institute and was principal investigator on the American Family Assets Study. She may be reached by e-mail at amys@search-institute.org. Search Institute is a nonprofit organization dedicated to discovering what young people need to succeed in their families, schools, and communities. For more information, visit www.search-institute.org